POP CHINESE

A CHENG & TSUI HANDBOOK OF CONTEMPORARY COLLOQUIAL EXPRESSIONS

话是这么说
中国当代流行语手册

COMPILED BY YU FENG, ZHIJIE JIA, JIE CAI, YAOHUA SHI, AND JUDITH M. AMORY

冯禹　贾志杰　蔡杰　史耀华　梅珠迪

CHENG & TSUI COMPANY
BOSTON

11 10 09 08 07 06 05   8 7 6 5 4 3 2 1

Published by

Cheng & Tsui Company
25 West Street
Boston, MA 02111-1213 USA
Fax (617) 426-3669
www.cheng-tsui.com
"Bringing Asia to the World"™

Printed in the U.S.A.

ISBN 0-88727-424-2

Preface

Recent developments in spoken Chinese present enormous challenges for Chinese language teachers. Whether or not teachers approve of these changes, students will have to face them if they hope to understand Chinese film and television. Moreover, the spoken Chinese portions of the HSK test, China's official test for Chinese proficiency in foreign students, include more and more popular and idiomatic expressions.

New dictionaries that attempt to reflect the language changes in modern China include very few of these expressions. Longer phrases, sentences, and proverbs are even harder to find in dictionaries. Those that are included often lack appropriate examples and accurate translations, making it difficult for students to understand the exact meaning of a given expression.

Pop Chinese reflects the changing reality of spoken Chinese by introducing the most common popular vocabulary, phrases, and proverbs. It is intended to aid intermediate and advanced students in understanding Chinese film and television, reading contemporary Chinese fiction, and communicating with native speakers. It is also a useful reference for teachers, scholars, and readers of modern Chinese literature.

All "Chinese" Isn't the Same

The source of the challenge for students lies with the spoken Mandarin taught in beginning and intermediate courses. These courses emphasize a spoken Chinese that is neither the informal daily usage of native speakers, nor the refined, formal speech based on written Chinese. Rather, what is taught is a special, "neutral" language devised for workplaces and educational settings where people from different areas of the country have to communicate for practical purposes. This is just one of three levels of speech in modern Chinese. The other two are the formal speech close to the written language and used in official, diplomatic, and academic contexts; and of particular importance to this book, the informal, lively, natural speech which characterizes today's Chinese media.

Until recently, the "neutral" language was also the language of choice for film and television productions. Rapid changes in the 1990s toward the use of colloquial language and older influences, including popular stories from the Ming and Qing dynasties and genres such as Pingshu from the oral storytelling tradition, created problems for language students trying to watch and understand these productions. Beijing slang now appears in television series that are set in other regions of China, while expressions indigenous to those regions appear in productions about life in Beijing. Even some hosts of China Central Television have now begun to use words that were previously considered regional. Because of the massive influence of the media, especially popular television series, many younger viewers have adopted the new expressions used on television into their daily speech.

Contemporary Chinese fiction has followed the same path. One outstanding example is the work of author Wang Shuo, who seeks to capture the racy slang of young people in Beijing's alleys. Expressions from Shanghai, Guangdong, Northeastern, and Shaanxi dialects have found their way into novels and short stories by authors from all parts of the country, and these lively and humorous idioms now permeate internet chat rooms and bulletin boards.

How should we evaluate this change in the spoken language of film and television? We think it represents a new development in *Putonghua*, which is more and more enriched by the addition of vocabulary, phrases, and syntactic structures from other Chinese dialects. A great many elements from the natural speech of different regions are becoming part of a common language that can be shared by most Chinese speakers, thus we can call this language "popular."

Popular speech has a stronger emotional flavor than neutral speech. It is characterized by lively, humorous, and hyperbolic expressions that range from monosyllabic words to aphorisms and proverbs in the form of compound sentences. For example, "掉钱眼儿里去了" ("to be stuck in the hole of a gold coin"—old Chinese coins had holes in the center) is both more vivid and more insulting than "只想赚钱" ("to think of nothing but making money"). "死哪儿去了你?" or "Where the hell (where in the name of death) have you been?" conveys much more displeasure in fewer words than "你到什么地方去了，怎么这么晚才回来?" ("Where have you been, and why didn't you come back until now?").

Even the grammar and syntax of popular expressions may not agree with the rules students have learned. For example, the general rule for the "把" sentence construction demands that the verb be followed by a verbal complement or the particle "了." In the following sentence, the rule is broken because the complement is replaced by the particle "的" (把 + Sb + V + 的): "我是说着玩儿的，看把你吓的." ("I was just kidding; who knew you'd be scared stiff?").

About the Entries in This Handbook

Since the boundaries between "neutral" speech and popular speech are not (and can never be) absolute, choosing the entries was a complex process. It is difficult to distinguish between popularly used idioms and those that have remained strictly regional. We have used the source of each expression as a helpful guide. Generally speaking, strictly regional expressions present less difficulty to readers of literary works, who can reread a problem passage. Viewers of film and television do not have this option; dialogue must be immediately comprehensible. Moreover, the commercial nature of mass media demands language that is understood by the broadest possible audience. Therefore, we have selected our entries primarily from film and television with emphasis on the most frequently heard expressions. As a rule, expressions found only in literary works have not been included.

Many entries have their origins in the Beijing dialect, since that dialect provides the expressions most frequently heard in film and television. However, this handbook is not a dictionary of the Beijing dialect; terms that are used to reflect only Beijing life specifically, or that are not used beyond the boundary of Beijing, have been excluded. On the other hand, for the convenience of users, we included a small number of expressions from southern dialects and from Taiwanese film and television.

Coarse and vulgar expressions presented a particular challenge. With a rich vocabulary and high frequency of use, they constitute an intrinsic part of everyday speech. Some novels record such language vividly, and it is heard more and more often in television and film productions. Although mass media only reflects the more widespread and least offensive varieties, students need to learn to recognize such vocabulary. Therefore, we have included a small number of these expressions. Of course, we don't recommend that foreign students include them in their speech, so we have clearly labeled vulgar expressions to prevent mistaken use.

Two examples accompany each entry in order to clarify the meaning of the expression and illustrate its correct usage. At least one example is an authentic sample of dialogue from film, television, or fiction. Such selections may be difficult to understand out of context, and in such cases we supply some brief background in English. Often, dialogue spoken by actors does not exactly match the Chinese subtitles that usually accompany film and television productions released in China. In that case, we have chosen to use the actual dialogue. When pronunciation and tones differ from those given in standard dictionaries, we have elected to present them "as-heard." In most cases, the second example has been created by the authors for the sake of greater clarity.

Of course, many expressions do not have an exact English equivalent. Therefore, we have supplied a literal translation so that students can understand the words comprising the expression, as well as its actual meaning in speech. Whenever possible, we strove to translate the examples into contemporary, idiomatic American English.

Acknowledgments

Work on this handbook has been accomplished by the five authors as follows: Yu Feng collected and selected the entries, which were then translated and annotated by Yaohua Shi, Zhijie Jia, and Judith Amory. Jie Cai supplied the editing, page layout, and proofreading.

Jill Cheng, the president of Cheng & Tsui Company, and Kristen Wanner, our editor, read each draft carefully and offered strong support as well as valuable insights into the selection and translation of entries. We would also like to take this opportunity to thank those individuals who offered their collections of Chinese films, television series, and novels for our research. Our gratitude also goes to our families, friends, and colleagues for their support and suggestions.

A

ā māo ā gǒu 阿猫阿狗 (阿貓阿狗)

"Mr. Cat and Mr. Dog"; anyone and everyone; any Tom, Dick, and Harry; any warm body

◆　这种工作太简单了，找个**阿猫阿狗**都能干.

　　This kind of work isn't rocket science. Anyone could do it.

◆　你别给我唱高调，现在**阿猫阿狗**都当官儿了，我为什么不能？

(From the TV series 孙中山)

Don't get on your high horse with me. These days, any warm body can serve as an official. Why not me? [Sun Yat-sen's older brother is demanding an official position. He's unhappy with Sun Yat-sen's insistence on qualifications.]

āi cīr 挨呲儿 (挨呲兒)

Receive a dressing down; get scolded or criticized; be bawled out

◆　本慧和二子往一块一站，男的精神女的漂亮。我心里可是暗暗替他们担心，二子是**挨呲儿**挨惯了的，本慧可没怎么挨过骂。

(From the short story 二子的故事)

When Benhui and Erzi stood side by side, the boy looked sharp and the girl looked pretty, but I was worried for them. Erzi was used to being bawled out, but Benhui had never been scolded much before. [The two high school students are being disciplined by the school for starting to date at too young an age.]

◆　怎么了你，耷拉着脸？　又**挨**老师**呲儿**了吧？

What's wrong? Why the long face? Did the teacher get on your case again?

ǎi yì jiér 矮一截儿 (矮一截兒)

"Shorter by a length"; greatly inferior

◆　没儿子怎么了？　您不是有五个闺女五个女婿吗？　您不比别人**矮一截** 。

(From the TV series 今生是亲人)

So what if you don't have a son! You've got five daughters and five sons-in-law. You don't have to take second place to anyone. [The mother just found out that there had been a mix-up: her son is not really hers. Her daughter is trying to console her.]

◆　老张看看人家穿的名牌西服，再看看自己穿的打着补丁的衣服，还没开口说话就觉得比人家**矮了一截儿**。

Lao Zhang looked at the designer suits everyone else was wearing, and then at his own patched clothing. He hadn't even opened his mouth to speak yet, and he felt inferior to the others.

ài nǐ shénme shì 碍你什么事 (礙你什麼事)

How does it hinder you? What's it to you? What skin is it off your nose?

◆　说她丑？　她丑又**碍你什么事**？你自己又有多美？说她丑，我不嫌弃她就行 。

(From the short story 祸福无常)

> You think she's ugly? If she's ugly, what's it to you? You're not so gorgeous yourself. If I don't mind her looks, that's all that matters.

◆　"你是不是办了遗体捐赠手续？""干嘛？ 犯法啊？"阿奇头皮发麻。"我的确是瞒着老爹娘亲去办的，**碍你什么事**？"

(From the short story 成魔记)

> "Did you do all the paperwork to donate your body?" "Why, is it against the law?" Ah Qi froze, "I admit, I did it behind my parents' back. What's it to you?" [A complete stranger is questioning Ah Qi's decision to donate his body.]

ài shéi shéi 爱谁谁 (愛誰誰)

Whoever you like; whoever; whatever

◆　当掉工作带着九只玫瑰过来找我时，我想都没想就和他住在了一起。我错了吗？他妈的，不想了，头疼，**爱谁谁**吧！

(From the short story 我不是坏孩子，只是想做点出格的事)

> When he quit his job and came looking for me with a bunch of roses, I didn't even give it a second thought; I just moved in with him. Was it a mistake? The hell with it, I don't want to think about it anymore. It gives me a headache. Whatever!

◆　**爱谁谁**，胡判吧你就。谁坚决，闹得凶 ，你就判给谁，到那天再说吧。

(From the novel 我是你爸爸)

> Whatever! Do what you want. Give the custody to whoever's the most pigheaded, whoever kicks up the most fuss. Let's see what happens when the time comes. [The court has to decide on the son's custody and is seeking the son's opinion. The child doesn't care.]

ài zěnme zěnme zhāo 爱怎么怎么着 (愛怎麼怎麼著)

Do what you want; do as you please

◆　这事儿我管不了，**爱怎么着怎么着**吧！

(From the TV series 今生是亲人)

> I can't get involved in this. Do what you want! [A woman realizes that her child was switched and wants to find her biological son. The speaker, her husband, doesn't believe that there was a mix-up. He thinks that his wife had the child with someone else. He's not interested in finding the child.]

◆　侍卫也没法儿跟这位倒霉皇上叫真儿了，得嘞 ，您**爱怎么怎么着**吧！

(From the novel 王莽)

> The guards can't lock horns with this unfortunate emperor anymore. [Finally they give in, telling him,] "All right, do as you please." [A successful uprising has reached the palace gates. The guards are trying to convince the emperor to hide, but he believes he still has the mandate of heaven and will not agree.]

ān qián mǎ hòu 鞍前马后 (鞍前馬後)

"Before the saddle and behind the horse"; if not before the saddle, then behind the horse; serve as a faithful lackey

◆　这么多年我一直**鞍前马后**地跑，没有功劳也总有苦劳吧？

(From the TV series 欲罢不能)

All these years I've been running around doing your scutwork. Even if I don't get any recognition, at least give me credit for my hard work! [A boss who is being accused of financial improprieties tries to shift the responsibility to a subordinate, who begs his boss not to use him as a scapegoat.]

◆ 虽说成天跟著书记段长**鞍前马后地跑，时不时还挨一顿熊**，可大家都很融洽。

   (From the short story 笔杆儿们)

   Even though they run themselves ragged for the party secretaries and section chiefs all day long and still get told off sometimes, everybody gets along fine. [Describing people who work as secretaries for higher-ups.]

áo chū tóur le 熬出头儿了 (熬出頭兒了)

Tough it out to the end; see light at the end of the tunnel

◆ 吃了这么多年苦，总算**熬出头了**。

   (From the short story 我的初恋就这样幻灭)

   After so many years of hardship, there's light at the end of the tunnel. [The young people sent down to the countryside can finally return to the cities.]

◆ 梅生娘，你才三十几岁的人，可别说这丧气话，**咬咬牙**，把孩子**拉扯**大了，你就**熬出头了**。

   (From the short story 粮食)

   Meisheng's Mom, you're barely past thirty. Stop talking doom and gloom. Bite the bullet, bring the kid up, and you'll see light at the end of the tunnel. [Meisheng's mother doesn't have any food, and thinks it would best to die and put an end to her misery.]

āo zhe chī 熬着吃 (熬著吃)

"Stew it and eat it"; go off one's rocker; crazy

◆ "挣那么多钱干什么啊？**熬着吃**、炒着吃也咬不动。" "我也这么想，可她心气儿太高。"

   (From the TV series 贫嘴张大民的幸福生活)

   "What's the point of making so much money? Stew it, stir fry it—you still can't bite into it." "That's the way I think, too, but she's too driven." [She is determined to open a second store.]

◆ 咱们在这个城市最多住一个星期，你买那么多地图干吗？ **熬着吃啊！**

   We're staying in this city for a week at the most. What did you buy so many maps for? Are you crazy? ["Are you going to cook them and eat them?"]

B

bā bǎo shān 八宝山 (八寶山)

Name of a crematorium in Beijing; go to one's grave

◆ 年轻时候的事儿，咱们也不能带到八宝儿山去啊！

   (From the TV series 今生是亲人)

   We shouldn't carry the problems of our youth all the way to the grave. [The two were rivals when they were young.]

◆ 我快七十了，马上去八宝山也不算少亡！

   (From the novel 寻访画儿韩)

I'm almost seventy; if I die right now it wouldn't be considered dying young!

bā chéngr 八成儿 (八成兒)
Eighty percent (certain); most likely

♦ 我在电视里瞅见的，八成儿就是他。

(From the TV drama 昝见胡同)

The man I saw on TV was most likely him. [The speaker saw someone on TV who looked like her long lost son. Now the person is standing before her. The more she looks at him the more she is convinced that he is her son.]

♦ 姑爷回来说，那女鬼八成是被砍死的洋婆子。

(From the novel 曾国藩)

Uncle came back and said that the female ghost was almost certainly that foreign woman who had been hacked to death. [A tall female ghost was seen in the area.]

bā gān zi dǎ bù zháo 八竿子打不着 (八竿子打不著)
"Couldn't hit or reach even with eight poles"; barely related

♦ 八竿子打不着的事，我给他递什么话？

(From the TV series 大雪无痕)

This matter has nothing to do with me. Why would I pass on a message to him? [The police want a reporter to deliver a message to an important man who is a crime suspect. The reporter doesn't want to do it.]

♦ 韩家在北京没有任何亲戚，都是梁家的，而且是八竿子打不着的，久已不来往的。

(From the novel 穆斯林的葬礼)

The Han family has no relatives in Beijing. All the relatives are from the Liang family, and distant relatives at that. They haven't had anything to do with each other for a long time.

bā jiǔ bù lí shí 八九不离十 (八九不離十)
"Eight, nine out of ten"; almost certain

♦ "我大概得了AIDS了。" "什么？筛检过了？" "没有，不过我想八九不离十了。"

(From the novel 逆女)

"I probably have AIDS." "What? Have you had the test?" "Not yet, but I think it's almost certain."

♦ 只消一看衣着打扮，是暴发户拿钱砸门面，还是穷酸文人打肿脸充胖子，总能猜个八九不离十。

(From the novel 孤星)

One look at his clothes and nine times out of ten you can guess whether he's' a nouveau riche type showing off, or a poor scholar trying to "plump up his cheeks by slapping himself in the face."

bā pí mǎ lā bú zhù/huí lái 八匹马拉不住/回来 (八匹馬拉不住/回來)
"Eight horses can't pull [somebody] back"; can't stop somebody

♦ 这杨颖啊，也真他妈能折腾。疯起来，八匹马都拉不住。

(From the movie 北京的乐与路)

This bitch Yang Ying really knows how to make trouble. When she gets crazy, nothing can stop her. [Yang is a dancer, arrested for getting into a fistfight with audience members.]

♦ 他这个人特倔，他认准的事儿就拼命干，八匹马也拉不回来。

He's really stubborn. If he makes up his mind about something, he'll put all he has into it. He won't change his course for anything.

bā tái dà jiào 八抬大轿 (八擡大轎)

"Grand sedan chair carried by eight men"; with great pomp and circumstance

♦ 你就是八抬大轿来请我，我也不去。

(From the TV series 红色康乃馨)

Even if you sent a stretch limo for me, I wouldn't go. [A lawyer is determined not to be talked into doing something she doesn't want to do.]

♦ 城里喝过几瓶墨汁的小伙子，八抬大轿请不动，刀搁脖子上也不愿娶个柴禾妞子呀！

(From the novel 吃青杏的时节)

Those city boys with a few scraps of education wouldn't get off their asses and marry a peasant girl [a "firewood girl"], even if you sent a stretch limo or held a knife to their necks.

bā zìr hái meí yì piěr ne 八字儿还没一撇儿呢 (八字兒還沒一撇兒呢)

"The character for 'eight' is still missing a stroke"; the 't's haven't been crossed and the 'i's haven't been dotted; premature

♦ 我还早呢。八字还没一撇，更何况我现在也没心思想那些。

(From the novel 一屋双男)

It's not the right time yet. Besides I'm not in the right frame of mind to think about this. [The speaker is being urged to find a girlfriend.]

♦ 花露婵哧哧笑了，她笑男人就是这份德行。八字还没有一撇，就先吃醋。

(From the novel 蛇神)

Hua Luchan started to giggle. She found the boorish ways of men funny. Nothing is even settled yet and he's already jealous. [A man is staking his claim on Hua Luchan's affection. Hua Luchan finds that ridiculous. They are hardly that close.]

bā bù de 巴不得

I wish; if only; can't wait for

♦ 他和小玉恋爱，很好呀，我巴不得他们快点结婚！陈虎要是成了咱们家庭的一员，胳膊肘还能往外拐吗？

(From the novel 都市危情)

It's great that he's dating Xiaoyu. If only they would get married right away! If Chen Hu becomes part of our family, the left hand will surely take care of the right ["elbows can't turn outwards"]. [Chen Hu is a policeman who is investigating the speaker's economic crime. Xiao Yu is his cousin.]

♦ 我就巴不得他早点死，拿毒药毒死了他，陈家的财产不就让我一个人给占了，百万家产呀，我眼红着呢！

(From the novel 红檀板)

I can't wait for him to die. If we poison him, the Chen family fortune will be all mine. We're talking a million dollars worth of property. I'm dying to have it!

bā sb de pí 扒Sb的皮

"Peel somebody's skin off"; skin somebody; punish somebody severely

♦ 你小子要是假公济私，我扒了你的皮！

(From the TV series 黑洞)

Asshole, if you try to use public office for private gain, I'll skin you alive. [The police chief is warning a subordinate not to mix personal grievances with police cases.]

♦ 告儿你们，没事儿是没事儿，要是有事儿我扒你们几个的皮！

(From the TV series 贫嘴张大民的幸福生活)

OK, if there's no problem, there's no problem. But I'm warning you, if something is wrong, I'll skin you people alive.

bǎ sb v de 把SbV的

Colloquial, idiomatic use of the passive voice generally used to show emotion or for emphasis; cause somebody to act in a certain way

♦ 上回小张也是，胃不舒服，乱吃药，结果是怀孕了，**把她后悔的**。

(From the TV series 走过花季)

Last time Xiao Zhang did the same thing. She had a stomachache, so she just took any old medicine. Turned out she was pregnant. She really lived to regret it! [The speaker thinks that the listener is pregnant, too, and is warning her not to harm her unborn baby.]

♦ 牛继红说："这可坏了！这可坏了！"牛大爷说："啥就坏了看**把你急的**！" 牛继红说："军军开始早恋了！"

(From the novel 东北一家人)

Niu Jihong said, "Oh, my God! Oh, my God!" Grandpa Niu asked, "What's the problem? Look at you, what are you getting so worked up about?" Niu Jihong replied, "Junjun is dating!"

bǎ sb zěnme zhāo 把Sb怎么着 (把Sb怎麼著)

What can they/you do to somebody?

♦ 别担心，他们不能**把我怎么着**。

(From the TV series 欲罢不能)

Don't worry. What can they do to me? [They wouldn't dare retaliate.]

♦ 我就不搬，看他们能**把我怎么着**！

(From the TV drama 眷晃胡同)

I'm not moving no matter what they say. We'll see if they can do anything to me! [The speaker refuses to be relocated for urban renewal.]

bǎ wǒ zhè X zì dào guò lái xiě 把我这X字儿倒过来写 (把我這X字兒倒過來寫)

"I'll write my family name upside down"; I'll eat my hat

♦ 要是能从账上查出聂明宇的问题，我把这李字倒过来写。

(From the TV series 黑洞)

If they can find anything wrong with Nie Mingyu's books, I'll eat my hat. [Nie Mingyu is the boss of a big company. He's under suspicion of financial misdeeds. The speaker thinks that even if Nie had committed an economic crime, there wouldn't be any evidence in the books.]

♦ 他只会说大话，一点儿实际经验也没有。要是他能赚到钱你**把我这徐字儿倒过来写**。

All he can do is talk big. He has hardly any practical experience to speak of. If he makes any money, I'll eat my hat.

bāi bù kāi niè zi le 掰不开镊子了(掰不開鑷子了)

"Can't open the pinchers"; feeling the pinch

♦ 我是实在实在的**掰不开镊子了**。

(From the TV series 北京人在纽约)

I'm really feeling the pinch. [Talking about money problems.]

♦ 这五十块钱虽然不多，谁家要是真**掰不开镊子了**，还真是俩救命钱儿。

(From the TV series 贫嘴张大民的幸福生活)

Fifty yuan isn't much, but if a family's feeling the pinch it can be a lifesaver. [The union president is urging people to apply for poverty relief.]

bái dā 白搭

"Thrown in for nothing"; in vain

♦ 在我们见到这批走私车之前，说什么都**白搭**。

(From the TV series 黑洞)

Before we lay eyes on the smuggled cars, talk is cheap. [The police are looking for evidence. Even with a tipoff, there's no case if there's no concrete evidence.]

♦ 美国好是好，就是找不着工作，念多少书也**白搭**。

(From the TV series 贫嘴张大民的幸福生活)

America is fine, but you can't find work there. Doesn't matter how many degrees you have—you'll search in vain. [A working-class man makes a snide remark about a student returning from America for a family visit.]

bái dāo zi jìn qu hóng dāo zi chū lai 白刀子进去红刀子出来 (白刀子進去紅刀子出來)

"The knife goes in white and comes out red"; kill someone

♦ 都听着，把钱掏出来！ 要不，就**白刀子进去，红刀子出来**。

(From the short story 歹徒・警察・小孩)

All of you listen! Your money or your lives! [Criminals try to hijack a bus and rob the passengers.]

♦ 这钱他要是少支一分，我让他**白刀子进去，红刀子出来**。

(From the short story 母子外伤后)

If he pays even one cent less than the full amount, I'll have his life. [His car hit and killedthe speaker's mother. The speakeris demanding a huge sum of money for damages.]

bái dīngr 白丁儿 (白丁兒)

An illiterate man; small potato; average Joe; a nobody

♦   你们都是共产党员，我呢，什么都不是，白丁儿一个。

(From the TV series 大赢家)
You're all party members. What I am? Nothing, just an average Joe.

♦   这个连中学都没上完的白丁儿怎么当上你们杂志的主编了？
This nonentity who barely finished high school, how did he get to be editor-in-chief of your magazine?

bái fěn 白粉

"White powder"; heroin

♦   你琢磨呀，抽"白粉"，可比上牌桌和上酒桌往里"吃"钱。你是当"雷子"的，应该门儿清呀！

(From the novel 百年德性)
Think about it, smoking heroin burns up your money faster than gambling or drinking. You're a cop. You should know better than that!

♦   那家伙贩卖白粉和摇头丸，听说已经被判了死刑。
That man was pushing heroin and Ecstasy. I heard that he was sentenced to death. [Ecstasy is known as "the head shaking pill" in Chinese.]

bái hu 白乎/唬

Talk nonsense

♦   这娘儿们回来，跟我白乎，说她如何如何勇斗歹徒。

(From the movie 洗澡)
That broad came back bragging about taking on some criminal. [The speaker's wife was taking a bath at a public bathhouse when a thief took her necklace. She rushed out naked trying to get it back. Her husband is very angry with her.]

♦   怎么说随你，你这张嘴不是挺能白唬的吗？但有一样儿，别暴露我的身份。

(From the novel 百年德性)
I'll let you do the talking. You're a smooth talker. But just one thing: don't reveal my identity. [A policeman wants to work undercover at a nightclub, so he asks a friend to arrange a job for him there.]

bái yǎnr láng 白眼儿狼 (白眼兒狼)

"White-eyed wolf"; ingrate

♦   刘震这孩子不是没心没肺的白眼儿狼。

(From the TV series 今生是亲人)
This kid Liu Zhen is not a heartless monster. [Liu Zhen just found out that he was adopted. He was so shocked that he left home. The narrator thinks that Liu will come back.]

♦   他省吃俭用送儿子上了大学，没想到儿子是个白眼儿狼，一毕业就跑到海南去了，三年没回过一次家，更别说给家了钱了。

(From the TV series 其实男人最辛苦)

He scrimped and saved to send his son to college. Who knew, his son turned out to be an ungrateful bastard. Right after graduation he set out for Hainan. For three years he didn't come home even once, let alone send money.

bái zhǐ hēi zìr 白纸黑字儿 (白紙黑字兒)

"Black characters on white paper"; in black and white; proof

♦ 反正我们没有白纸黑字，你想毁约我也没辙。

(From the novel 风雪缘)

Anyway there's nothing in writing. If you want to go back on our agreement, there's nothing I can do. [Speaking of an oral business agreement.]

♦ 离婚书上白纸黑字儿，受法律约束，你怎么能胡搅蛮缠呢？

(From the TV series 其实男人最辛苦)

The divorce papers are signed and sealed; it's legal now. Why are you still harassing me with your unreasonable demands?

bǎi píng 摆平 (擺平)

Balance; pacify; appease; placate

♦ 这好办，出几万块钱就把那几个人儿摆平了。

(From the TV series 红色康乃馨)

That's easy. A few thousand yuan should take care of them. [The speaker is confident that a payoff can prevent people from giving damaging testimony in court.]

♦ 现在不是讨论谁是谁非的时候，得赶紧想办法把外面那些人摆平。

(From the TV series 走过花季)

Now is not the time to discuss who's right and who's wrong. We have to think of a way to placate the people outside. [The company's promotional sale has gone awry. The prize winners did not get their prizes and are protesting outside.]

bǎi pǔr 摆谱儿 (擺譜兒)

Put on airs; act arrogantly

♦ 一个九品官儿摆个屁谱儿！

(From the TV series 康熙帝国)

A stinking low-level official putting on airs! [屁: pì, fart] [A eunuch is inviting a low-level official to an audience with the emperor. The official is putting on airs, enraging the eunuch.]

♦ "先租辆好车！" "这笔钱还没到手呢，就摆谱儿了？"

(From the TV series 大赢家)

"First of all, let's rent a good car!" "We haven't seen a cent of that money, and you already want to put on a display?" [The man's loan application was just approved.]

bài jiā zǐr 败家子儿 (敗家子兒)

Destroyer of the family fortune; wastrel; prodigal

♦ "一达最近怎么样？" "不要提他了，这个败家子儿！"

(From the TV series 一年又一年)

"How's Yida?" "Don't ask. That good-for-nothing!" [The father is angry at his son Yida, who got into trouble through illegal business practices and escaped to the south.]

♦   那个**败家子**，当上总经理不到两年就把个好端端的公司弄破产了。

That wastrel. He was the manager for barely two years and ran a perfectly good company into the ground.

bài mǎ tou 拜码头 (拜碼頭)

(Of a ship) make a courtesy call at a port; visit important people to cultivate connections

♦   我今天来呀，就是想先**拜拜**你爸爸这个**码头**。

(From the TV series 汽车城)

I'm here today to pay my respects to your father. [A man visits his girlfriend's father, hoping to make some money through the father's connections.]

♦   现在当领导的新到一地，总有些人要来**拜码头**，这已是规矩了，你想回避也回避不了。

(From the novel 夜郎西)

Nowadays whenever a new official arrives, there are always people lining up to pay their respects. You can count on it. You can't avoid that, even if you want to.

bài tuō 拜托 (拜託)

(Ironic) "trust or rely on someone (not to do something)"; please, I beg you

♦   苟云齐同学，**拜托**，请不要再**嗲声嗲气**的说话了，好不好？

(From the novel 梦幻魔界王)

Please, Gou Yunqi, stop all that sweet talk. I beg you.

♦   老大，**拜托拜托**，这回练练那些咱们自己写的曲子成不成？

(From the short story 十一月的雨)

Please oh please, boss, this time can we play something we wrote ourselves? [The musicians are tired of rehearsing the same piece again and again.]

bǎn shàng dìng dīng 板上钉钉 (板上釘釘)

"Put the nail in the board"; a done deal

♦   你看那姓彭的来头儿，跟小玉已经是**板上钉钉**了，你去找又有什么用呢？

(From the TV series 北京女人)

Xiao Yu and that Peng guy are an item now. What good would it do you to pursue her? [Xiao Yu used to be the listener's girlfriend. She is now going to someone else.]

♦   房子下来了。但第一榜分配方案中，没有陈维高的名字。陈维高迷惑不解，本以为**板上钉钉**，绝对有自己的一间，这一下可把他弄傻眼了。

(From the novel 热狗)

The apartments were assigned, but Chen Weigao's name was not on the first list of recipients. He didn't understand; he thought his getting one was a done deal. He was dumbfounded.

bàn fēngr 半疯儿 (半瘋兒)

"Half-crazy"; crazy

◆ 我看你们这位大人是个半疯儿。

(From the TV series 铁齿铜牙纪晓兰)

I think your master has gone mad. [The official's action goes against convention.]

◆ 早在上高中的时候，她对男人的看法就已基本定型。那个她的另一半应当是善良稳重，有才学有见识，人缘好又能干的。她不需要天才，天才大都是半疯。

(From the novel 纽约丽人)

Even in high school, her opinions about men were firm. Her mate must be kind and dignified, educated and knowledgeable, popular and capable. She 'doesn't need a genius. Geniuses are almost all crazy.

bàn lā 半拉

Half

◆ 臭显派！结个婚把小半拉北京城都惊动了。

(From the TV series 北京女人)

Such rotten showing-off! Arranging a wedding that inconveniences half of Beijing! [Speaking of an ostentatious wedding procession.]

◆ 他哪里是什么计算机专家！只不过半半拉拉地学了几天，水平还不如我呢！

He's a computer expert? Yeah, right! All he had was a few days of half-baked training. He knows even less than I do.

bàn píng cù 半瓶醋

"Half bottle of vinegar;" dilettante; amateur; dabbler

◆ 自以为喝茶老道，其实也不过是半瓶醋。

(From the TV series 田教授的二十八个保姆)

And you imagine you're a tea connoisseur! Turns out you're just an amateur, if anything. [A wife is mocking her husband's failure to identify the variety of tea that he is sampling.]

◆ 你们二位是中国的大家，我是半瓶醋晃荡，何敢称家。

(From the novel 四个秀才一台戏)

You are two of China's great authorities, but I'm just a dabbler messing around. I wouldn't dare call myself an expert.

bàn suàn 拌蒜

"Toss garlic"; shake; tremble

◆ 他嘴里拌蒜似地解释着："你别瞎想啊。我又不是和欧阳兰兰住一个屋。她家有的是地方。"

(From the novel 永不瞑目)

He stammered as he tried to explain, "Don't go imagining things. Ouyang Lanlan and I didn't sleep in the same room. She has plenty of rooms at her house."

◆ "你看啊，小张还真有点儿大将风度，这么大的场面一点儿都不紧张。""还不紧张呢？我看他脚底下直**拌蒜**。"

"Look, Xiao Zhang really looks like he's in command. Such a big occasion and he's not a bit nervous." "Not nervous? Seems to me he's shaking in his boots."

bǎng dà kuǎn 傍大款

Befriend or marry a wealthy older man; have a sugar daddy

◆ 我爸就不管我，那天还对我说呢，我不反对你谈恋爱，可你不能太傻，找个没有经济实力的人你不得苦一辈子？我说那我就**傍大款**，他说有本事你就**傍**。

(From the TV movie script 老宋和他的女儿)

My dad doesn't interfere in my life. Just the other day he said to me, "I don't mind you dating. Just don't be stupid and hook up with someone poor, or you'll have a hard life." I said, "OK, then I'll find a sugar daddy." He said, "go ahead if you can pull it off."

◆ 肖童你是不是**傍**上个女大款呀？

(From the novel 永不瞑目)

Xiao Tong, did you land an heiress or something? [Xiao Tong is a college student. He has been seen driving around in a luxury car.]

bǎng piàor 绑票儿 (綁票兒)

Kidnap

◆ 我老觉着这绑票儿的不是**冲着银子来的**，他是趁咱们之危，**给咱们点儿颜色看看**，就算把银子送去，孩子也未必领得回来。"

(From the TV series 大宅门)

I somehow feel this kidnapper isn't after the money. He just wants to take advantage of our difficulties and give us a taste of his power. Suppose we give him the money, there's still no guarantee we'll get the kid back.

◆ 你们干什么，青天白日就想**绑票儿**啊？

What do you think you're doing? Trying to carry off a kidnapping in broad daylight?

bàng chui dàng zhēn 棒槌当针（真）(棒槌當針（真）)

"Mistake a wooden club for a needle"; misjudge (a pun, because zhēn 针, a needle, sounds exactly like zhēn 真, truth); be conned; be led astray

◆ 他是给了**棒槌就当针（真）**，他那耳朵根子是棉花捏的。

(From the TV series 其实男人最辛苦)

He's very easily misled. Anyone can talk him into anything. [His ex-wife sweet talked him into waiting on her hand and foot. Friends and relatives are being sarcastic.]

◆ 你凭什么这么跟我讲话，哼，你以为你是谁呀？ 给个**棒槌就当针**！告诉你，我爸都不敢这么骂我！

(From the novel 其实不想走)

How dare you talk to me this way? Who do you think you are? Someone gives you an opening, and you take advantage! Let me tell you, not even my dad yells at me like this! [A chat between two Internet acquaintances has turned nasty.]

bāo èr nǎi 包二奶

Keep a mistress (包: have exclusive use of; 二奶: secondary wife, mistress)

◆ 乔芳晓得丈夫章大虎**包二奶**的消息后，一下子就六神无主了。

(From the short story 第三者)

When Qiao Fang found out her husband was keeping a mistress, she was totally disoriented by the news.

◆ 现在的男人个个儿都没有良心，一有点儿钱就想着**包二奶**。

Nowadays men have no conscience. As soon as they have a little bit of money they want to keep a mistress.

bāo yúanr 包圆儿 (包圓兒)

Take the whole lot

◆ 我就喜欢吃胡的，这菜我**包圆儿**了。

(From the movie 爱情麻辣烫)

I like it charred. Give it all to me. [A boy tries to cook for the first time and burns the food. His father wants to encourage him.]

◆ 这本书卖得真不错，两天功夫就卖了三万多本，剩下的一个外地书商全**包圆儿**了。

The book is selling well. Thirty thousand copies were sold in two days. A book dealer from out of town took the rest.

bāo zài sb shēn shang 包在Sb身上

Leave it to somebody

◆ 往后啊，小妹的事儿就**包在**大姨妈**身**上了。

(From the TV series 其实男人最辛苦)

From now on, leave Xiao Mei's love life to me. [An aunt volunteers to find a boyfriend for her niece, Xiao Mei.]

◆ 那个工厂的厂长我认识，这事儿**包在我身上**了，放心吧，三天以后他们就会把机器送过来。

I know the director of that factory. Leave it to me. Don't you worry. They'll deliver the machine in three days.

bǎo bù qí 保不齐 (保不齊)

Can't guarantee completely

◆ 嗨，人哪，谁也**保不齐**有犯胡涂的时候。

(From the novel 找乐)

Hey, we're only human. People can't guarantee they won't make mistakes.

◆ 那歌厅人那么杂，**保不齐**还得出事儿。

(From the TV series 手心手背)

That nightclub attracts all sorts of people. There's no guarantee it won't happen again. [There was a brawl at the club.]

bǎo hàn zi bù zhī è hān zi jī 饱汉子不知饿汉子饥 (飽漢子不知餓漢子饑)

"A man with a full belly can't understand a starving man's hunger"; to not know how lucky one is; be spoiled

◆ 那么多的女孩，你就一个也看不上？真是**饱汉子不知饿汉子饥**呀！你要是不要，我可就要动手了啊！

(From the short story 一切重头再来)

So many girls, and you don't like any of them? You don't understand how lucky you are! If you're not interested, I'll make a move.

◆ 我们厂都快关门了，您还来要什么赞助费，真是**饱汉子不知饿汉子饥**。

Our factory is about to be shut down, and you're looking for sponsorship. You don't know how good you have it!

bào dà/cū tuǐ 抱大/粗腿

"Hold on to a big/thick leg"; seek protection from someone powerful; ride on someone's coattails

◆ 只要焦书记不倒，你**抱紧他的大腿**，你也倒不了。

(From the novel 都市危情)

As long as the party secretary doesn't fall, you won't fall. Just hang on to his coattails.

◆ 我看他的官儿还得往上升，你可要**抱住了他的粗腿**！

I think he'll get promoted again. Cling to him for dear life.

bēi hēi guō 背黑锅 (背黑鍋)

"Carry ablack pot on the back"; take the blame

◆ 上回，还不是我替你**背的黑锅**？

(From the TV series 今生是亲人)

Didn't I take the blame for you last time? [Two young people got into a fight after getting drunk. One of them hurt someone. The other took the blame for it.]

◆ 你是经理，现在生意赔了，你让我去跟股东解释，我可不愿意为你**背这个黑锅**。

You're the manager. Now that we lost money on the deal, you want me to talk to the shareholders. I'm not going to take the blame for you.

bèi bú zhǔ 备不住 (備不住)

"You can't be prepared"(for all eventualities); you never know

◆ 孩子毕竟是孩子，懂得什么好歹？平时一天三顿地给他讲道理，他还**备不住**要出点事，这回可好，大撒把没人管了，那他还不上**房揭瓦**？

(From the novel 我是你爸爸)

Kids are kids. What do they know? Even when I try to talk some sense into him three times a day, I still never know when he's going to get in trouble. Now that there isn't anyone to supervise him, he'll probably wreck the house.

♦ 路上多带点钱，**备不住**有用得着的时候。

Take some more money with you on the trip. You never know when you'll need it.

bèi guò qì 背过气 (背過氣)

Lose one's breath; pass out; faint

♦ 哭可以。愿意掉泪就让她掉几滴，但不要让她哭得**背过气**去，在大街上引起围观，这样影响不好。

(From the movie 顽主)

She can have a cry. Let her shed a few tears if she wants, but make sure she doesn't cry so hard that she faints. We don't want to draw a crowd on the street. That wouldn't look good. [A man dumped his girlfriend and is asking a "service company" to console her.]

♦ 我说我要出国留学，这话刚一出口我妈就**背过气**去了。

I said I wanted to go abroad to study. The words had hardly left my mouth when my mother fainted.

bèi hòu tǒng dāo zi 背后捅刀子(背後捅刀子)

Stab in the back

♦ 万钢也算是聪明，知道是我**背后捅了他一刀**，可你心里再明白也没用，你抓不住我半点把柄。

(From the novel 大雪作证)

Wan Gang isn't stupid. He knows I stabbed him in the back. But knowing about it doesn't do you any good if you don't have evidence against me. [The speaker took pictures of Wan Gang fooling around with a young woman at a hotel.]

♦ 老刘这人真够阴的，别看见了面儿笑嘻嘻的，**背后常给你捅刀子**。

Lao Liu is really devious. Don't be fooled by his smile. He'll stab you in the back.

bèir 倍儿 (倍兒)

Double; doubly; extremely

♦ 我挺讨厌街上那批警察的，没什么文化，有点权就**倍儿**横。

(From the novel 永不瞑目)

I can't stand these crude policemen on the streets. Give them a little power, and they'll be twice as obnoxious.

♦ 齐大妈包的饺子，**倍儿**香！

(From the movie 甲方乙方)

Mrs. Qi's dumplings are incredibly good.

bèng dī 蹦的/蹦迪

Dance disco; go to a discotheque

♦ 今儿晚上咱们**蹦的**去！

(From the TV series 蓝色马蹄莲)

Let's disco tonight.

♦ "你怎么这么晚才回来？" "唱歌、跳舞、**蹦迪**去了。"

(From the TV series 失乐园)

"How come you got back so late?" "We went singing, dancing, and discoing."

bí zi bú shì bí zi liǎn bú shì liǎn 鼻子不是鼻子脸不是脸 (鼻子不是鼻子臉不是臉)

"The nose is not the nose; the face is not the face"; the nose is out of joint; look unhappy

◆ 大胖子**鼻子不是鼻子脸不是脸**，摔摔打打，庭内『法庭』空气陡然紧张起来。

(From the novel 一点正经没有)

The fat guy got ticked off and started smashing things around. The atmosphere in the courtroom suddenly became tense.

◆ 这两天老李也不是怎么了，一跟他商量事儿就**鼻子不是鼻子脸不是脸**的。

What's with Lao Li these couple of days? The minute you try to discuss anything with him, his nose is out of joint.

bí zi qì wāi le 鼻子气歪了 (鼻子氣歪了)

So angry that the nose is out of joint; furious

◆ 咱们**收摊儿**吧，都快把我**鼻子气歪了**！

(From the TV series 孙中山)

Let's pack up and leave. I'm furious. [An effort to organize a village election failed.]

◆ 我给我儿子三千块钱交学费，结果他一个晚上就赌个精光，我**鼻子都快气歪了**。

I gave my son three thousand dollars for his tuition. He gambled it away in one night. I was really pissed.

bì shang nǐ de gǒu zuǐ 闭上你的狗嘴 (閉上你的狗嘴)

"Shut your dog mouth"; shut your mouth; shut up

◆ "**闭上你的狗嘴**，你不配叫我的名字。" 婷婷恶狠狠地说。

(From the novel 不婚贵族撞情记)

"Shut your mouth. You're not fit to address me," Tingting said rudely. [Tingting is from an upper-class family. She is insulted when a male model is presumptuous enough to greet her.]

◆ **闭上你的狗嘴**！竖起你的驴耳听清了，我问你，到底谁欺人太甚？你得还我公道！

(From the novel 草莽芳华)

Shutup! Prick up your donkey ears and listen carefully. I'm asking you, just who is doing the bullying here? I demand justice.

biǎn 扁

(Taiwan expression) flatten; beat up; rough up

◆ 要不要**扁**他？

(From the movie 台北爱情故事)

Should we beat the crap out of him? [His bad suggestion caused an accident during the shooting of a film. One of the director's assistants asks the director if they should rough him up.]

♦　要不是看在大哥跟你爸的交情啊，我他妈的早就扁你了！

(From the movie 黑暗之光)

If your father weren't my friend, I'd have beaten the shit out of you a long time ago.

biàn fāngr de/fǎ de 变方儿的/法的 (變方兒的/法的)

"Varying the pattern/method"; try different ways

♦　受了点儿处分，就变了方的跟领导拿搪？

(From the TV series 大雪无痕)

You get a slap on the wrist and you stonewall the boss in every possible way?

♦　王主任这两天变着方儿地整我。

These last few days Director Wang has been trying to punish me in all sorts of ways.

biàn guà 变卦 (變卦)

"Change the divinatory symbols"; flip-flop; change one's mind

♦　"我不答应你就走不成。" "弟弟，说好了的事怎么又变卦了？"
　　"我没有答应，我从来没有答应，我永远也不会答应。"

(From the novel 地主的女儿)

"If I don't agree, you can't leave." "But brother, this matter was already settled. How come you changed your mind again?" "I didn't agree. I never agreed, and I never will."

♦　宋大哥，咱们不是都说好了吗，你怎么又变卦了？

(From the novel 狗不理传奇)

"Brother Song, didn't we already agree to it? How come you changed your mind again?"[The two are discussing opening a shop.]

biāo chē 飚车 (飚車)

Drive at an extremely high speed for the thrill of it; drive like a speed demon; burn rubber (飚: whirlwind)

♦　"刚才飚车的时候，你挺那个的。" "哪个的？" "挺男子气的。"

(From the TV series 汽车城)

"You were really something when you were burning rubber just now." "What do you mean, really something?" "Really macho."

♦　不少人向我反映了，说他老婆天天泡舞厅，飚车，玩儿狗。

(From the TV series 红色康乃馨)

I heard from lots of people that his wife hangs out in dance halls, drives fast cars, and keeps pet dogs to play with.

biē qu 憋屈

Put up with (shabby, unfair treatment, poor conditions, etc.)

◆ 咱们到什么时候也是条汉子，还能**憋屈**死？

No matter what happens I'll take it like a man. [So I've been screwed], but it won't kill me. [The speaker, a policeman, has been unfairly treated and sent to work in the boondocks. The pronoun 咱们 has a singular meaning here.]

◆ 说句心里话，这儿的条件太差，**憋屈**你了。

To be honest with you, the conditions here are really bad. Sorry you have to put up with them. [A rural villager is afraid a city dweller will not be able to stand the difficult conditions of rural life.]

biē zhe 憋着（憋著）

Hold in; suppress

◆ 和着你昨天什么都知道，**楞憋着**让我现眼是吗？

(From the TV series 其实男人最辛苦)

So you knew it all yesterday, but you deliberately sat on it so that I'd make a fool of myself? [和着你: so you... could it be that you?]

◆ "得嘞嘿，谢哥，我的那点旧账您就别翻了，您说我不是为了混口饭吃吗？也没给您找大麻烦。""合着你还**憋着**去抢银行是怎么着？"

(From the novel 百年德性)

"OK, OK, Brother Xie. Why bring up my old history again? You know I was just trying to put food in my stomach. [您说我不是: surely you know I was just...] I didn't give you too much trouble, did I?" "You mean, you were dying to rob a bank or something?"

bié dòu le 别逗了

Don't kid around; stop joking around

◆ "我给你介绍介绍当专业模特吧？""**别逗了**，就我这个儿啊，没戏。"

(From the TV drama 旮旯胡同)

"Want me to introduce you to some contacts who can help you get professional modeling jobs?" "Are you kidding me? Short as I am? I don't stand a chance." [She is an amateur fashion model. She knows that she's not tall enough to turn pro.]

◆ "听说你是局里内定的保留人员，还有新的重用呢！""**别逗了**，拿我开心啊？"

(From the TV series 问问你的心)

"I hear you're definitely one of those the department is going to keep. Not only that, but you're getting a big promotion." "Stop kidding around. Are you jerking my chain?"

biē jie 别介/别价 (別介/別價)

Don't

◆ 别，**别介**，您把这银子用到该用的地方去，我和朱顺一家是三代人的交情，有朱叔一句话，我就不敢不尽力。

(From the TV series 大宅门)

Don't. Please don't. You can find a better use for the money. We've been friends with the Zhu family for three generations. All Uncle Zhu has to do is say the word, and I'll do my best. [Uncle Zhu has offered money to a prison guard to take care of a friend who is in jail. The guard won't accept the money but will comply out of friendship.]

♦　别介，世上你什么东西都能恨，唯独这个东西恨不得。

(From the TV series 笑傲江湖)

Don't. You can despise anything else in the world, but you can't despise this. [One of the speakers thinks that the money being offered isn't clean and doesn't want it.]

bié miǎo tóu 别苗头 (別苗頭)

(Shanghai dialect) have a showdown or show of force; see who is on top (苗头: sign of a trend)

♦　这些家伙是来找我的，因为前天刚刚被我赶跑过，他们现在找来这个号称左宰府第一剑士的西罗非哈，一定是来和我别别苗头的。

(From the novel 风月大陆)

These fellows are looking for me. I kicked them out the other day. Now they've found this self-proclaimed Number One Swordsman in the Office of the Prime Minister of the Left Xiluofeiha to have a showdown with me.

♦　最近这段时间，霞光和大华这两个公司别上苗头了，这可是咱们的好机会。

Lately these two companies, Xiaguang and Dahua, have been battling each other. Here's our chance.

bié wàng xīn lǐ qù 别往心里去 (別往心裏去)

Don't let it get to you; don't mind; don't take it to heart

♦　刚才的事儿，你别往心里去啊！可能我哥在外面遇到了什么不顺心的事儿。

(From the TV series 手心手背)

Don't take what just happened to heart. Probably my brother had something unpleasant happen to him outside.

♦　他那个人说话就是这么没心没肺的，你可千万别往心里去。

He's like that, shooting off his mouth whenever he talks. Don't let it get to you.

bīng xióng xióng yí gè, jiàng xióng xióng yì wō 兵熊熊一个，将熊熊一窝 (兵熊熊一個，將熊熊一窩)

"If a soldier is incompetent, that's one incompetent soldier; if a general is incompetent, you have an incompetent army" (熊: *dialect*, stupid, incompetent, weak)

♦　要我说，兵熊熊一个，将熊熊一窝，咱独立团老捞不着肉吃，就是他娘的政委在上级面前太熊。

(From the novel 亮剑)

If you ask me, when the general's a loser, the whole army pays the price. Our independent regiment never gets any important assignments because our fucking party secretary is so clueless dealing with the higher-ups.

♦　咱们路头儿太废物了！ 兵熊熊一个，将熊熊一窝，全车间的人都跟着他挨板子。

(From the novel 基础)

That Chief Lu of ours is totally useless! When the leader is a loser, the whole group suffers. All the people in the workshop took a beating along with him.

bō lang gǔ 拨浪鼓 (撥浪鼓)

Rattle-drum (a toy drum that sways back and forth to hit fixed mallets)

◆ 假如我告诉他，我找的对象是个歌厅的小姐，他的脑袋准成**拨浪鼓**，一百个不相信：你，会找个歌厅小姐？想不想当警察啦？是不是**吃错了药**，看花了眼？

(From the novel 百年德性)

If I told him my girlfriend works at a nightclub, he'd shake his head like a rattle-drum. He just wouldn't believe it. "You, going with a nightclub girl? Don't you want to be a policeman anymore? Did you take the wrong medicine, and it gave you hallucinations?"

◆ 我刚一提借钱的事儿，那小子的脑袋就摇得跟**拨浪鼓**似的。

As soon as I mentioned borrowing money, that bastard began to shake his head like a rattle-drum.

bú dà lír 不大离儿 (不大離兒)

Almost completely; just about

◆ 我看你也折腾得**不大离**儿了，就请你到后台歇会儿，把郭长达换上来，我揍的就是他，打别人我**不过瘾**呀。

(From the novel 白眉大侠)

I think you're about done. Go backstage and take a break. Get Guo Changda up here. He's the one I want to beat; it's not much fun fighting with [you] others. [Spoken at a martial arts contest.]

◆ 我看你们俩**不大离**儿的也该把事儿办了吧？总这样人家会**说闲话**的。

I think it's about that time; you two should make it official. Otherwise people will begin to talk. [An unmarried couple are living together.]

bú duì jìngr 不对劲儿 (不對勁兒)

Not quite right; do not feel right

◆ 这事儿怎么琢磨怎么**不对劲儿**啊！

(From the TV series 今生是亲人)

No matter how you look at it, this doesn't feel quite right. [A couple visiting from the city shows unusual interest in the speaker's child. Turns out the couple suspects their children were switched at birth.]

◆ 我觉得冰冰这几天有点儿**不对劲儿**，训练的时候总是魂不守舍的。

(From the TV series 失乐园)

Bingbing doesn't seem quite right these last few days. Her mind keeps wandering during practice sessions [魂不守舍: hú bù shǒu shè, the soul is not holding court]. [Bingbing is a professional marksperson.]

bú guò huà 不过话 (不過話)

Do not speak to each other; not on speaking terms

◆ 他跟我哥**不过话**。

(From the TV series 今生是亲人)

He and my brother don't talk. [Although the two were schoolmates, they don't hang out together.]

♦ 自从他在老师那儿告了我的状以后，我跟他再也不过话了。

    After he ratted on me to the teacher, I stopped talking to him.

bú jiàn guān cai bú luò lèi 不见棺材不落泪 (不見棺材不落淚)

"Will not shed tears until the coffin is in sight"; will not acknowledge defeat till the last minute

♦ 贺清明这小子是不见棺材不落泪啊！

(From the TV series 黑洞)

    That bastard Qingming won't give up until his feet are in the grave. [He Qingming is a customs agent in charge of anti-smuggling operations. He is unfazed by the speaker's intimidation and insists on reporting his findings to his superiors.]

♦ "这股票一个劲儿的往下掉，老张怎么还往里投钱啊？" "他这个人就是这样，不见棺材不落泪。"

    "The stocks just keep plunging. Why is Lao Zhang still throwing money into them?" "He's like that. For him, it's not over till the fat lady sings."

bú jiàn tù zi bù sā yīng 不见兔子不撒鹰 (不見兔子不撒鷹)

(Proverb) "Will not release the hawk until the hare is sighted"; will not commit financially until there is adequate guarantee

♦ 抱歉，我是不见兔子不撒鹰的，尤其跟巴大爷打交道，得特别当心，钱拿来！

(From the novel 黄金美人)

    Sorry, I have to see the color of your money first. I have to be extra careful dealing with you, Ba Daye. Give me the money!

♦ 我这个人是不见兔子不撒鹰，让你们老板亲自来，要不然我绝对不会在合同上签字。

    I'm the sort who doesn't leap without looking. Get your boss to come in person. Otherwise there's no way I'm going to put my signature on the agreement.

bú jiàn zhēn fó bù shāo xiāng 不见真佛不烧香 (不見真佛不燒香)

(Proverb) "Will not burn any incense until the genuine Buddha is in sight"; will not make any investment unless one can expect a good return (only the genuine Buddha can answer one's prayers)

♦ 可是现在的年轻人都精得象兔子，不象我们年轻的时侯，党叫干啥就干啥，他们是不见真佛不烧香啊。

(From the short story 迷途的羔羊)

Young people are as sharp as knives now, not like us. If the party asked us to do something, we jumped. But they want to see the color of the money first.

♦ "我是公司的代表，你有事儿就跟我说吧。" "你啊，太嫩了点儿。我可是**不见真佛不烧香**。要是你们董事长没有时间我就改日再来。"

   "I represent the company. Whatever you have to say, you can say it to me." "You're just a kid. I only deal with decision-makers. If your director doesn't have time, I'll come another day."

bú jiù jié le ma不就结了吗 (不就結了嗎)
And be done with it; that'll be the end of it; that's all

♦ "你相信你哥哥吗？" "当然相信。" "这不就结了吗？"

   (From the TV series 黑洞)

   "Do you believe your brother?" "Of course I do." "Then that settles it." [The brother has been suspended from his position. His sister is worried.]

♦ 写错了？没事儿！再要张表儿来重填一遍不就结了吗？

   You wrote it wrong? No big deal. Get another form and fill it out again, that's all.

bú kàn sēng miàn kàn fó miàn 不看僧面看佛面
"If not for the sake of the monk, then for the sake of the Buddha"; for mercy's sake, for God's sake

♦ 你不看僧面看佛面，我们可都弹尽粮绝了！

   (From the TV series 其实男人最辛苦)

   Have mercy on us! We don't have a scrap of food left ["out of all ammunition and food"]. [They are begging for help.]

♦ 你看，小王也不是故意的，您就原谅他吧。再说了，他舅舅就是李局长，您**不看僧面也得看佛面**啊！

   You see, Xiao Wang didn't do it on purpose. Let him off the hook. Besides, his uncle is Li, the bureau chief. If you can't do it for Xiao Wang's sake, do it for his uncle's sake.

bú lào rěn 不落忍
Can't bear to do it; can't bring oneself to do it

♦ 要是让他们伤心，我这儿不落忍。

   (From the TV series 今生是亲人)

   If it would hurt them, I couldn't bear to do it. [The speaker realizes that he is not the biological child of his parents, but he can't bring himself to tell them the truth.]

♦ 他的能力是差点儿，但真是个大好人，**炒他的鱿鱼我真有点儿不落忍**。

   He is not that capable, but he's a genuinely good person. I really can't bring myself to fire him.

bú lìn 不论 (不論)
(Beijing Dialect) don't pay attention to anyone; don't care; not afraid of anyone

♦ 你又不是不知道我的脾气，**不论**！

   (From the TV series 今生是亲人)

It's not as if you didn't know what I'm like. I don't give a shit!

♦ 他这个人什么都**不论**，连经理都**敬他三分**。

He doesn't care about anything. Even the manager walks on eggs around him.

bú shì dōng xi 不是东西 (不是東西)

"Not a thing"; not an honorable man; jerk

♦ 算我胡说，我**不是东西**，行了吧？

(From the TV series 一年又一年)

All right, I was talking nonsense. I'm a jerk, OK? [The husband wants to quit his job and strike out on his own. His wife is unhappy, so he apologizes to appease her.]

♦ 彭东东啊彭东东，我今儿才发现，你真**不是个东西**！

(From the TV series 北京女人)

Peng Dongdong, I just realized what a scumbag you are! [The speaker thinks Peng Dongdong treats his wife badly.]

bú shì ge shìr 不是个事儿 (不是個事兒)

"Not a thing"; not proper; not a solution; not an answer

♦ 让他住在家里，时间长了，**不是个事儿**。

(From the TV series 今生是亲人)

Letting him keep living at home is not a solution in the long run. [Keeping a family secret from their son while letting him live at home is difficult.]

♦ 大妈对客人说："这是我们老赵的侄女，高中毕业了，在家呆着。"
客人又问："安排个工作么，老在家呆着也**不是个事儿**。"

(From the novel 越轨诉讼)

My aunt said to the guest, "This is my husband's niece. She graduated from high school, and she's been hanging around home." The guest replied, "Better get her a job. Hanging around home isn't a good idea."

bú shì wǒ shuō nǐ 不是我说你 (不是我說你)

It's not that I want to criticize you

♦ **不是我说你**，你在家庭问题上太优柔寡断了。

(From the TV series 都市情感)

I'm not criticizing you, but when it comes to family problems you're not decisive enough. [The listener should get a divorce, but can't make up his mind.]

♦ 瞧你，这么大人了，**不是妈说你**，你说，这进门儿也没有进门儿的样儿，这包儿就随便一放，回头这大哥大压坏了怎么办？

(From the TV series 北京女人)

Look at you. You're an adult. It's not that I enjoy nagging you. You just walked in the door without paying any attention and dumped your handbag any old way. Suppose you broke your cell phone, then what would you do?

bú shì yú sǐ, jiù shì wǎng pò 不是鱼死，就是网破 (不是魚死，就是網破)

See 鱼死网破 yú sǐ wǎng pò

...bù chéng …不成

Will not do unless; have to; insist on

◆   "这是开展业务的需要。" "开展业务就非得唱唱跳跳、吃吃喝喝不成？"
(From the TV series 红色康乃馨)
"We need to do this to develop the business." "Are singing and dancing, wining and dining, all indispensable for developing the business?" [The honchos at the company headquarters are not happy that executives of a subsidiary company have spent big sums of money on entertainment.]

◆   你是我爸，就算什么事做过了点儿头，难道我还和你计较不成？
(From the novel 我是你爸爸)
You're my dad. Even if you went overboard on something, do you think I'll insist on counting the pennies? [A father apologizes to his son for having been unreasonably demanding in the past. His son tries to reassure him that there are no hard feelings.]

bù chī mán tou zhēng kǒu qì 不吃馒头蒸（争）口气 (不吃饅頭蒸（争）口氣)

"Not really interested in eating the steamed buns but interested in the steam" (蒸: zhēng, to steam, but 争: zhēng, to fight for; 争口气: zhēng kǒu qì, fight for public vindication after being wronged or slighted)

◆   我争的是这个理，不吃馒头蒸［争］口气。
(From the novel 空洞)
I'm fighting for the principle of it. I want public vindication. [A hospital has been ordered to suspend operations and the director seeks to appeal.]

◆   你得不蒸馒头蒸口气，别叫人骂你是狗肉上不了正席。
(From the novel 村风)
You have to have some dignity, if nothing else. Don't let people say you're dogmeat, not fit to sit at the table with them. [A father is lecturing his loafer of a son.]

bù dā gā 不搭界

(Shanghai dialect) have nothing to do with; irrelevant

◆   我有麻烦，但是和犯罪不搭界。
(From the TV series 花非花)

I'm in trouble, but it's nothing to do with the law. [The company is in financial trouble.]

♦ 你说这老张啊，总在**节骨眼儿**上说些**不搭界**的话。

That Lao Zhang! When things are really tense you can count on him to say something straight out of left field.

bù dāng jiā bù zhī chái mǐ yóu yán guì 不当家不知柴米油盐贵 (不當家不知柴米油鹽貴)

(Proverb) "If you don't manage a household, you don't know how much firewood, rice, cooking oil, and salt cost"; if you don't pay the bills, you don't know the price of bread

♦ 您**不当家不知柴米油盐贵**，我实在是捉襟见肘呀！不过是给太后修园子，我回去再想想办法，但估摸不会太多，也就二三十万两吧。

(From the novel 李莲英)

If you don't pay the bills, you don't know the price of bread. As it is, I'm really stretched ["pull down the jacket to cover raggedness, only to expose the elbows"] But we're talking about building a garden for the Empress Dowager. I'll go back and see if I can come up with something, but it probably won't be much...maybe two, three hundred thousand taels of silver. [A minister responds to a eunuch seeking donations to build a garden for the Empress Dowager.]

♦ "头儿，咱们这货卖得不错啊，怎么还不发奖金啊？" "**不当家不知柴米油盐贵**。别看咱们卖了不少，把方方面面的钱一扣，就剩不下几个钱了。"

"Boss, this product is really selling well. How come we're not getting a bonus?" "You're not the accountant; you haven't seen the books. It's not just a matter of sales. Deduct the expenses, and we're not left with much."

bù dé jìngr 不得劲儿 (不得劲兒)

Feel listless

♦ 我啊，看电影看惯了，要是一天不看就**不得劲儿**。

(From the TV series 一年又一年)

I got hooked on movies. If I let a day go by without seeing one, I don't feel well.

♦ 我的老病可能又犯了，这两天特别**不得劲儿**。

Maybe my old illness is coming back. I've been feeling really listless the last couple of days.

bù dé liǎo (le) 不得了(了)

1. as an exclamation: Oh no! Oh God! It's a disaster! 2. as a complement after a verb or adjective: extremely; as much as possible

♦ **不得了了**！你哥出事儿了！安子又把你哥抓走了！

(From the TV series 其实男人最辛苦)

Bad news! Your brother is in trouble. The policeman Anzi detained him again.

♦ 现在喜欢运动的人越来越多，大大小小健身房的生意都火得**不得了**。

(From the TV series 黑冰)

More and more people are into exercise these days. Gyms, small ones as well as big ones, do a roaring business.

bù gǎn dāng 不敢当 (不敢當)

Do not dare; would not presume to be

♦ 继往嘛，朕还担得起，开来嘛，朕可**不敢当**。

(From the TV series 康熙帝国)
Carrying on the tradition, yes, we accept that. But "opening a path to the future"–I wouldn't dare accept that compliment [朕: zhèn, imperial self-reference]. [An emperor reacts to flattery that he is carrying on the tradition and opening a path to the future: 继往开来.]

♦ "您就是那位神医张先生吧？" "神医可**不敢当**。"

"Are you the legendary Doctor Zhang?" "Legendary doctor? I wouldn't presume."

bù guǎn sān qī èr shí yī 不管三七二十一

"Do not care if three times seven equals twenty-one"; act first without thinking about the consequences; with no rhyme or reason

♦ 几个人扑了上去，**不管三七二十一**就把那女的绑了起来，还剥光了她的衣服，弄到院子里展览。

(From the short story 第三者)
Several people pounced on her and without hesitation tied her up, stripped her naked, dragged her to the courtyard, and put her on display. [A mob caught a woman having illicit sex.]

♦ 他们觉得是我坏了他们的事儿，抓住我，**不管三七二十一**就一通儿毒打。

They thought I had ruined their deal. They grabbed me and, just like that, beat the living daylights out of me.

bù hēng bù hā 不哼不哈

Without making any sound; without saying anything

♦ 这件事不能这么**不哼不哈**地就完了，他彭东东起码得赔你个青春损失费。

(From the TV series 北京女人)
You shouldn't let this thing go without speaking up. At a minimum, Peng Dongdong should recompense you for your lost youth. [Peng Dongdong is demanding a divorce from the speaker's daughter.]

♦ 你们暧昧，**不哼不哈**，我可是观点明确，旗帜鲜明，而且**白纸黑字**，写成材料，怎么样？

(From the novel 城无雪)
You're all hemming and hawing and not saying anything. My viewpoint is clear, and my stand unambiguous. Do you want it in black and white? Shall I put it in writing?

bù kāi qiào 不开窍 (不開竅)

"The aperture won't open"; the light bulb won't go on; too stupid to understand

♦ 你的中文说得不错，不像前两天我见的一老外，在中国待了五年，就是**不开窍**！

(From the TV series 大赢家)

You speak Chinese well, not like the foreign guy I saw the other day. He'd lived in China for five years but he didn't have a clue.

◆ "我觉得给领导送红包不太好。" "你怎么这么**不开窍**儿？ 现在没有红包什么事情都办不成。"

> "I don't think it's such a good idea to give money to the leader." "How can you be so clueless? You won't get anywhere without a bribe these days."

...bù liǎo nǎr qù/bù dào nǎr qù ···不了哪儿去/不到哪儿去 (不了哪兒去/不到哪兒去)

Not any more than; not any better than

◆ 你不就比我多个好媳妇，可少那么一截腿，也**强不到哪儿去**。

(From the novel 浮出海面)

> The only thing you have that I don't is a good wife. But you've got a bad leg, so I think we're about even.

◆ "你考上的这个学校虽然比不上北大、清华，但是也**差不了哪儿去**。" "你别安慰我了。"

> "OK, you didn't get into Beijing or Tsinghua University, but the school you got into is almost as good." "You're just saying that to make me feel better."

bù mán nín/nǐ shuō 不瞒您/你说 (不瞞您/你說)

I won't deceive you; I'll be straight with you

◆ **不瞒您说**，我是真心实意来钓鱼的，在家跟老婆打过赌。

(From the novel 打鱼的和钓鱼的)

> I'll be honest with you. I really did come here to fish. I made a bet with my wife. [His wife doesn't believe he can catch anything.]

◆ **不瞒你说**，我们家老孙和孩子都是属猫的，穷命偏偏长个富贵胃，不吃蔬菜，吃鱼，只要是腥的，什么鱼都吃。

(From the short story 人民的鱼)

> To tell you the truth, my husband and children are like cats; they only want to eat fish. Too bad they have champagne tastes but a beer pocketbook ["paupers with an aristocratic stomach"]. They won't eat vegetables, just fish. As long as it smells fishy, they'll eat it.

bù qí yǎnr 不起眼儿 (不起眼兒)

Not eye-catching; inconspicuous; nondescript

◆ 当很**不起眼**的一座厂房终于在市郊很**不起眼**的一条小街的街口落成之后，韩德宝的体重减轻了十四斤半，被送入医院打过三次"点滴"。

(From the short story 激杀)

> A nondescript factory finally got built on a small, nondescript street corner on the outskirts of the city. By then Han Debao had lost over fourteen kilos and been in the hospital three times with an IV in his arm.

◆ 你们把饭馆开在这么个**不起眼儿**的地方，能赚得了钱吗？

> You opened a restaurant in such a godforsaken place! How can you make any money?

bù v bái bù v 不V白不V

Your loss if you don't

◆ "抽烟！" "我不抽！" "不抽可白不抽啊！"

(From the TV series 大雪无痕)

"Have a smoke." "I don't smoke!" "Well, that's your loss!"

◆   他们钱闲着也是闲着，咱**不挣白不挣**啊！

(From the TV series 黑洞)

Their money is just sitting there. If we don't make something off it, it's our loss.

bù zǎ dì 不咋的

Not so great; not so hot

◆   我看你这个书记**不咋的**，怎么总从门缝里看人？

(From the TV series 大赢家)

If you ask me, you're not such a great party secretary. How come you always underestimate people ["look at people through the crevice of a door"]?

◆   这种新产品吹得挺神，但是用起来实在**不咋的**。

There's so much hype about this new product, but once you try to use it, it's not really so great.

bù zháo jiā 不着家 (不著家)

"Do not come into contact with home"; never home

◆   我怀凤霞的时候，你爹天天都**不着家**。

(From the movie 活着)

When I was pregnant with Fengxia, your dad was never home.

◆   我丈夫整天**不着家**，孩子都三岁了，只跟他爹见过两三次。

My husband is never home. The kid is almost three. He's only seen his dad two or three times.

bù zhī něi tóur kàng rè 不知哪头儿炕热 (不知哪頭兒炕熱)

"Do not know which side of the *kang* bed is warm"; do not know what really counts or where one's interests lie

◆   太皇太后王政君本来就没准主意，听四个人慷慨激昂痛陈了一通利害，一时间也**不知哪头炕热**了。

(From the novel 王莽)

The Empress Dowager was indecisive to begin with. After hearing the four mens' passionate speeches about the consequences [of firing Wang Meng], she didn't know which way to turn. [Her grandson the emperor wants to fire Wang Meng, but four high-ranking ministers come to Wang Meng's defense. 太皇太后 is the title of the grandmother of the emperor.]

◆   我看你是**不知哪儿头儿炕热**了。我警告你啊，总这么**脚踩两条船**可不行。

I think you're forgetting which side your bread is buttered on. I'm warning you, you can't stay on the fence ["have a foot on each boat"] like this.

bù zhī zì jǐ xìng shén me 不知自己姓什么 (不知自己姓什麼)

"Do not know what one's family name is"; get carried away; forget who you really are, lose your' bearings

◆   美得你**不知自己姓什么**了吧？

(From the TV series 蓝色马蹄莲)

You were so psyched that you got carried away, didn't you? [The other person made a large sum of money.]

♦ 嘿！ 刚当上个小小的经理就**不知自己姓什么**了？
   Huh! A few days as a low-level manager and you forget who you are?

C

cā biān qíu 擦边球 (擦邊球)
"Edge or touch ball" (table tennis or tennis term for a ball that brushes the boundary); gray area

♦ 他说，这种打**擦边球**的事他是不能签字的。
   (From the TV series 汽车城)
   He said he couldn't put his signature to this sort of questionable undertaking. [The general manager of a company refuses to approve a possibly illegal proposition.]

♦ 明显的违法乱纪的事儿咱们不能做，但是打打**擦边球**儿我看没有什么关系。
   We can't do anything that's obviously illegal, but I think it's all right to take advantage of a gray area.

cā hēir 擦黑儿 (擦黑兒)
"Brush darkness"; get dark

♦ 天**擦黑儿**的时候，安国和最红回来，当然是先得去看奶奶。
   (From the novel 空洞)
   Anguo and Zuihong returned just as it was getting dark. Of course, they had to go see grandma first.

♦ 他现在可忙了，天不亮就走，**擦黑儿**了还回不来呢！
   He's really busy these days. He leaves before sunrise and isn't home before dark.

cā pì gu 擦屁股
(Vulgar) wipe ass; clean up the mess

♦ 干了一个活儿，还不是**擦屁股**的事儿？
   (From the TV series 今生是亲人)
   We did manage one job, but it was just cleaning after someone. [Two carpenters are having trouble finding lucrative work.]

♦ 公司的领导把钱拿去乱花，听说上面要来查，就让我们这些会计给他们**擦屁股**，这叫什么事儿啊？
   The company big shots spent the money recklessly. Now they hear the higher-ups want to check the books, so they're asking us accountants to wipe their asses for them. Is that outrageous or what?

cái bù ne 才不呢
No way; not at all

♦ 她熟练地在大车小车间穿梭着，我笑称她是"恐怖份子"。"**才不呢**！这是在台北生存的法则。"
   (From the short story 星期日的野餐)

She skillfully weaved in and out through the cars, large and small. Laughing, I said,
"You're a demon driver ['a terrorist']!" "No way! This is how you survive in Taipei."

♦　"他那个人特**抠门儿**，一分钱也不会借给别人。" "**才不呢**！　我昨天
刚从他那儿借了二十万。"

He's really tightfisted. He won't lend a cent to anyone." "Where do you get that idea
from? I just borrowed two hundred grand from him yesterday."

cǎi dào diǎnr shàng 踩到点儿上 (踩到點兒上)

"Step on the (right) spot"; hit the nail on the head

♦　我发现我这个人命不好，干什么都**踩**不到点儿上。这不，刚刚买了一
套房，我们单位又分房了。

(From the TV series 天堂鸟)

Turns out I'm really unlucky. I never get it right. I just bought an apartment, and then my
work unit starts handing them out.

♦　高考制度恢复后，整顿学校的管理又被提到日程上来。蒋子禾算**踩到
点儿上**了，很快就被提到处长的位置上，又凭学历和资历，不久就当
上了学校行政副校长。

After college entrance exams were reinstated, reforming school administration was back
on the agenda. Jiang Zihe was in the right place at the right time and was quickly
promoted to section chief. Based on his education and seniority, he soon became
executive vice president of the college.

cǎi hu 踩乎

"Step on"; denigrate; badmouth

♦　你姐一见面儿就**踩乎**人。

(From the TV series 空镜子)

Your sister starts badmouthing people the moment she sees them.

♦　你别老是**踩乎**别人，有本事你自己干出个样儿来，也让大家服气

Stop putting everyone else down. If you've got the stuff, go ahead and show us. Then
we'll believe you.

cāng ying yě shì ròu 苍蝇也是肉 (蒼蠅也是肉)

(Facetious) "even a fly has some meat on it"; No matter how poor a client or situation is, there
may be profit to be made

♦　**苍蝇也是肉**呀，好歹还算个客人，徐老板换了张和气的脸，**屁颠屁颠**
地迎了上去。

(From the novel 浴佛楼)

Even a fly has some meat on it. A customer is a customer. The owner beamed and rushed forward obsequiously. [The restaurant is not doing much business. When a customer does show up, he turns out to be an abstemious monk.]

♦ "你看这笔生意赚不了几个钱，还做不做了？" "做，**苍蝇脑袋也是肉**。"

 "We're not going to make much off this deal. Shall we go ahead anyway?" "Of course. Profit is profit, no matter how small."

cāo xián xīn 操闲心 (操閒心)

Worry about other people's business (闲: idle)

♦ "得了，妈妈不**操**你们这份**闲心**了！"

 (From the TV series 北京女人)

 "All right. I'll keep out of your affairs." [After asking a lot of questions, a concerned mother is getting the silent treatment from her daughter.]

♦ "咱们公司的办公楼不小了，为什么还要盖新楼呢？" "你又不是领导，**操**那么多**闲心**干什么？"

 "Our company office building is big enough; why do we need to build a new one?" "You're not running the company. Why are you poking your nose in where it doesn't belong?"

cào dàn 操蛋

 (Vulgar) Fuck! (操: *crude, fuck*)

♦ 真他妈**操蛋**！那小子把我给涮了。

 (From the TV series 黑冰)

 Fuck! That son of a bitch took me for a ride.

♦ 真是我干的？那我可是有点**操蛋**了。

 (From the novel 我是你爸爸)

 Did I really do that? I must have been totally fucked up. [A father behaved badly when he was drunk; after he's sober he can't believe he acted that way.]

cào xing 操行

 See 造性 zào xing

cèng fàn 蹭饭 (蹭飯)

 Sponge a meal (蹭: rub)

♦ 老**蹭**你们家的**饭**嫂子不会有意见吧？

 (From the TV series 黑洞)

 I'm always sponging meals at your house. Will your wife mind? [The two are colleagues.]

♦ 我知道她来就是想**蹭**一顿**饭**吃。

 (From the TV series 贫嘴张大民的幸福生活)

I knew she just wanted to sponge a meal. [The first time his girlfriend was invited to eat at his family's home, she finished her meal and then broke up with him.]

chā yí gàng zi/héng chā yí gàng zi 插一杠子/横插一杠子

"Slide a block in"; interject; interfere; horn in

♦ 不等王老师说完，旁边一个人横插一杠子："胡说，这里你经常来的，最近我就看见你来过不少次！"

(From the novel 第五个是丈夫)

Before the teacher could finish, a bystander cut in, "That's a lie. You come here all the time. I've seen you here many times just recently." [The teacher insists that he doesn't' go there often.]

♦ 蓉蓉从周小凡那里知道了孔飞不理睬自己的原因原来是爸爸插了一杠子，非常生气。

(From the TV drama script 老宋和他的女儿)

Rongrong was really upset when Zhou Xiaofan told her the reason Kong Fei didn't want anything to do with her was because her father had horned in. [Rongrong wants to be friends with Kong Fei.]

chān he 掺和 (掺和)

"Mix and incorporate"; get involved

♦ 你小孩子家别掺和大人的事儿！

(From the TV series 今生是亲人)

You're a kid. Stay out of grown-ups' business! [The parents are getting a divorce.]

♦ 这件事本来与你无关，你犯不上往里边掺和。

(From the novel 神灯前传)

This really had nothing to do with you. It wasn't worth it for you to get involved. [Spoken to a martial arts master whose disciple had killed a man.]

chǎng kāir 敞开儿 (敞開兒)

Go all out; do not hold back

♦ 敞开儿吃啊！面条儿有的是！

(From the TV series 一年又一年)

Go ahead, eat as much as you want! We've got plenty of noodles. [A poor relative from the country sees noodles and wolfs down five or six bowls.]

♦ "你们这儿的鱼真不错，我能给我老婆带两条回去吗？" "我们这儿鱼有的是，你敞开儿拿。"

"Your fish is really good. Can I take a couple home for my wife?" "We have tons of fish. Take as many as you want."

cháng tòng bù rú duǎn tòng 长痛不如短痛 (長痛不如短痛)

(Proverb) "long-term pain is worse than short-term pain"; better now than later; the sooner you get it over with, the better

♦ 自行车厂亏损就赶紧卖掉，长痛不如短痛。下不了狠心也许会把整个公司拖垮了。

(From the TV series 蓝色马蹄莲)

If the bicycle factory is losing money, shut it down. Better now than later. If you can't bite the bullet now, it'll drag the whole company down.

♦ 我看长痛不如短痛，一厂的拆迁必须马上开始。

(From the TV series 大赢家)

I think the sooner we get it over with the better. We have to start the factory relocation immediately. [The relocation will temporarily disrupt the company's business.]

cháng zài hé biān zǒu, nǎ néng bù shī xié 常在河边走，哪能不湿鞋 (常在河邊走，哪能不濕鞋)

(Proverb) "If you often walk along a river, you can't help getting your shoes wet"; you can't touch pitch without being defiled; it's inevitable; it's to be expected

♦ 有道是常在河边走，哪能不湿鞋！漕运衙门本身就是一个大染缸，谁进来都得染得一身黑。

(From the novel 铁面钦差刘罗锅)

You can't touch pitch without being defiled, that's for sure. The Canal Administration is a cesspool of corruption ["a big dye vat"]. Anyone who goes in there gets corrupted ["dyed black all over"].

♦ 他从厂里拿了点儿东西也不是什么大不了的事。俗话说，常在河边走，哪能不湿鞋？以后注意点儿就行了。

So he took some stuff from the factory—big deal! As the saying goes, if you often walk by the river, you can't help getting your shoes wet. He just needs to be careful after this.

chàng gāo diào 唱高调 (唱高調)

"Sing a high-pitched tune"; be highfalutin

♦ 爸爸："穷不怕，只要有志气就行。"女儿："现在什么年代了，不流行唱高调儿了，你们别委屈自己了，还不够吗？"

(From the TV series 走过花季)

Father: "I'm not afraid of poverty. As long as I have my pride, that's enough." Daughter: "What year do you think we're living in? That high-flown rhetoric isn't in fashion anymore. Give yourself a break. Haven't you had enough?"

♦ 你别给我唱高调，现在阿猫阿狗都当官儿了，我为什么不能？

(From the TV series 孙中山)

Don't get on your high horse with me. These days, any warm body can serve as an official. Why not me?

chàng hóng liǎn, chàng bái/hēi liǎn 唱红脸，唱白/黑脸 (唱紅臉，唱白/黑臉)

"One sings the red face while the other sings the black face (the conventional make-up for hero and villain in Chinese opera)"; one plays the good cop while the other plays the bad cop

♦ 好啊，你再去谈谈也好，咱们一个唱红脸，一个唱白脸，打个战术配合！

(From the novel 永不瞑目)

OK, it's a good idea to have another talk. We can play good cop, bad cop, and work as a team. [Two policemen are trying to make a suspect talk.]

◆ "我觉得王主任真不错，不像李书记，一见面就批评人。" "他们两个其实是一条心，只不过一个唱红脸，一个唱黑脸罢了。"

    "I think Director Wang's all right, not like Secretary Li, always criticizing people." "Actually, they're just the same, but they're playing good cop, bad cop."

chàng kōng chéng jì 唱空城计 (唱空城計)

"Sing *The Vacating-the-Fortress Strategy*"; to be alone; to be deserted (The allusion is to a famous Beijing opera adapted from an episode in the novel, *Romance of the Three Kingdoms*. The master strategist, Zhuge Liang, comes up with a daring plan to avert an inevitable disaster. Besieged and vastly outnumbered by the enemy army, Zhuge Liang orders his troops to vacate the fortress. Fearing an ambush, the enemy turns back.)

◆ 老周，你看看他们这一对老同学、老朋友，一个要辞去组长职务，一个要退出项目组。看起来，就剩下咱们两个老头子了，要唱空城计啦。

    (From the novel 都市危情)

    Lao Zhou, look at those two old school friends. One of them wants to resign as the team leader, and the other wants to quit the special investigation team. Looks like it's just going to be the two of us holding the fort.

◆ 我来了八趟了，你们主任总是不在，跟我唱空城计是不是？

    I've come here eight times and your director is never around. Is he trying to avoid me?

chǎo yóu yú 炒鱿鱼 (炒鱿魚)

(Cantonese) "stir-fry squid"; fire; sack (short form: 炒)

◆ "今儿你别去上班儿了。" "不上班儿等着老板炒鱿鱼啊？"

    (From the TV drama 昔儿胡同)

    "Don't go to work today." "Skip work and wait for the boss to fire me?"

◆ 你为什么当时不举报，到被炒了鱿鱼才去举报？

    (From the TV series 天下第一情)

    Why didn't you report it right away? Why wait until after you got fired? [The employee knew the manager was breaking the law.]

chē gú lu huà 车轱辘话 (車軲轆話)

"Talk like a wheel"; go back and go forth; talk incessantly about something

◆ 这几位老兄车轱辘话来回说，软磨硬泡就是要姚纲把价格一降再降。

    (From the novel 桑拿小姐)

These guys kept at it in order to wear Yao Gang down and get him to lower the price again and again.

♦ 我最怕我们局长，他一作报告就**车轱辘**话来回来去地说，没有两个小时绝对说不完，其实里面没有多少新鲜的东西。

I'm scared of our bureau chief. Whenever he makes a report he goes on and on like a broken record. It's always at least two hours until he's finished, and there's never much that's new or original.

chě dàn 扯淡/扯蛋

(Vulgar) bullshit

♦ 正义？真理？ 那是哄小孩儿的，**扯蛋**！

(From the novel 都市危情)

Justice? Truth? That's for fooling little kids. It's all bullshit!

♦ "你涉嫌对案犯家属暴力性侵犯，检察院将对你提起公诉。" "瞎**扯淡**！"

(From the TV series 红色康乃馨)

"You're accused of sexual offenses against a family member of the suspect. The Prosecutor's Office is bringing a case against you." "Bullshit!"

chě pí 扯皮

"Pull skin"; go back and forth fruitlessly

♦ 柿红问银杏道："妈，长栓媳妇出去一个多小时了，咋还不见回来."银杏："跟王元宝**扯皮**呗！王元宝这人，不把他憋到一定程度，修庙的钱是不会掏出来的。"

(From the novel 山乡情话)

Shihong asked Yinxing, "Mom, Changshuan's wife has been gone for more than an hour. How come she's still not back?" Yinxing answered, "She must be having a war of words with Wang Yuanbao. If you don't wear him down to some extent, he won't give any money to repair the temple."

♦ "咱们建立中医诊所的申请报告批下来没有？" "难啊！卫生局说诊所只能开在河东，城建局说只能盖在河西，他们**扯皮**扯个没完，咱们着急也没有办法。"

"Did our application to open a Chinese medicine clinic get approved?" "It's a problem. The Health Department says we can only open it east of the river. The Urban Construction Department says we can only build west of the river. They've been going back and forth on it endlessly. No matter how impatient we are, there's nothing we can do."

chě píng 扯平

"Pull even"; call it even

♦ 咱们当初说好的，你付钱，我帮忙封他的帐号。现在我们两相**扯平**，谁也不欠谁。

(From the novel 浮沈商海)

We had a deal. You pay and I freeze his account. Now we're even. We don't owe each other anything.

◆   过去你救了我一命，今天我救了你一命，咱们这回**扯平**了，以后谁也不欠谁的了。

(From the TV series 笑傲江湖)

You saved my life once and today I saved yours. Now we're even. From now on we don't owe each other anything.

chén zhī ma làn gǔ zi 陈芝麻烂谷子 (陳芝麻爛穀子)

"Old sesame seeds and rotten grains"; old things; same old stories; clichés

◆   这些**陈芝麻烂谷子**的事儿你还提它干什么啊？

(From the TV series 今生是亲人)

Why bring up ancient history? [The two were rivals twenty years ago.]

◆   他也就那点儿**陈芝麻烂谷子**，请他来做报告大家非得睡着了不可。

All he knows are a few old platitudes. If you ask him to give a speech, everyone will fall asleep for sure.

chèn 趁

Have loads of

◆   "带这么多鞋干吗？" "咱们不是不**趁**别的吗？"

(From the TV series 贫嘴张大民的幸福生活)

"Why did you bring so many shoes?" "We've got nothing but shoes." [The speaker owns a shoe store. He is visiting his mother and brothers and has brought them lots of shoes.]

◆   人家都以为我们家出了大款，指不定多**趁**钱呢！

(From the TV series 一年又一年)

Everybody thinks we now have a millionaire in our family. They probably think we're loaded. [Actually, they are a very poor family.]

chēng sǐ dǎnr dà de, è sǐ dǎnr xiǎo de 撑死胆儿大的，饿死胆儿小的 (撐死膽兒大的，餓死膽兒小的)

(Proverb) "The daring die of overeating; the timid die of hunger"; nothing ventured, nothing gained

◆   我姐夫可赚钱了！这就叫**撑死胆儿大的，饿死胆儿小的**。

(From the TV series 一年又一年)

My brother-in-law made a killing! You've got to have some guts, or you'll die hungry. [In the early days of economic reform, many people were afraid that if they went into business, they would be accused of being speculators.]

◆   这年头儿是**撑死胆儿大的，饿死胆儿小的**，你要想规规矩矩地赚钱门儿也没有。

Nowadays it's nothing ventured, nothing gained. If you try to earn money by following every rule, you haven't got a prayer.

chēng sǐ le (yě jìu) 撑死了（也就）(撐死了（也就）)

"Stretched to death... no more than"; at most; at the outside; tops

◆   "那女的多大岁数？" "也就十八九，**撑死了**二十。"

(From the TV series 黑洞)

"How old is that woman?" "Eighteen, nineteen, twenty at the outside."

♦ 有好几家杂志要给我写传记，嗨，要钱呗。其实要价也不算太高，**撑死了也就**十万块钱。

(From the TV series 一年又一年)

A lot of magazines want my story. OK, but they've got to pay. Actually, I'm not asking too much—a hundred grand, tops.

chēng yāo 撑腰 (撐腰)

"Hold up the back"; support

♦ 我实在**挺不住**了。你输了有国家**撑腰**，我输了可就倾家荡产了！

(From the TV series 大赢家)

I really can't sustain any further losses. If you lose money, the state backs you up, but if I lose money, I lose everything. [The manager of a private business is talking to the manager of a state-owned enterprise.]

♦ 郑科长，有政府来给我们**撑腰**，我们就不怕了。

(From the TV series 问问你的心)

Section Chief Zheng, we have nothing to worry about if the government is backing us up. [Workers are negotiating with the management of a factory.]

chéng qì hou 成气候 (成氣候)

"Make a climate"; have an impact

♦ 婆婆妈妈像个老娘儿们似的，还能**成什么气候**？

(From the TV series 黑洞)

You go back and forth like an old woman. How can you ever accomplish anything?

♦ 稍有个风吹草动，马上就惶惶不可终日，天上掉下来个树叶子也怕把自己给砸着，像你这样的人还能**成了气候**！

(From the novel 抉择)

The slightest sign of trouble and you're scared shitless all day long! You act as if a leaf falling from a tree could knock you dead. How can a guy like you get anywhere?

chéng quán 成全

"Make complete"; help realize

♦ 他刘统勋想当干隆朝第一个掉脑袋的大臣，好！朕**成全**他！

(From the TV series 天下粮仓)

That Liu Tongxun wants to be the first minister to lose his head. Great! We'll make his dream come true. [Liu Tongxun angered the emperor by dwelling on what the emperor was most unwilling to hear, the hunger of the common people.]

◆ 我知道小文爱上王刚了，可是她又不好意思跟我分手。我这次辞职去海南就是为了**成全**他们。

I know that Xiao Wen fell in love with Wang Gang, but she couldn't bring herself to break up with me. I'm quitting my job and going to Hainan to help them work it out.

chī bái shí 吃白食

See 打秋风 dǎ qiū fēng

chī bǎo le chēng de 吃饱了撑的 (吃飽了撐的)

"Feel full because of overeating"; do something out of sheer boredom

◆ 这么说可不对了，当然关你的事，要不然我给你打电话干什么？**吃饱了撑的**？ 你嫂子够意思吧？ 还想着你这兄弟的终身大事呢。

(From the novel 亮剑)

You're wrong there. Of course this is about you. Otherwise, why would I call you? Out of sheer boredom? My wife is a true friend, right? She was worrying about your marriage. [An older brother expresses his family's concern for his younger brother, who still hasn't gotten married.]

◆ **吃饱了撑的**，打听这打听那的，瞧这点儿素质！

(From the TV series 北京女人)

Haven't you got anything better to do than poke your nose into everything? Have a little class!

chī bǎo le hùn tiān hēi 吃饱了混天黑 (吃飽了混天黑)

"Eat your fill and kill time until dark"; be idle

◆ 他啊，整个一**吃饱了混天黑**的滚刀肉。

(From the TV series 一年又一年)

Him? He's nothing but a lazy bag of bones—just eats and waits around for bedtime.

◆ 我们乡下人比不了你们城里人，整天讲什么理想啊、境界啊，在这儿人人都是**吃饱了混天黑**。

We country folks are not like you city people, always talking about dreams and ideals [境界: realm of awareness]. Around here it's three meals a day and kill time until night.

chī bù liǎo dōu zhe zǒu 吃不了兜着走 (吃不了兜著走)

"If you can't eat it all up, you'll have to carry it away with you"; you have to be prepared to accept the consequences

◆ 这回，该让他这个劳动模范**吃不了兜着走**了。

(From the TV drama 咎见胡同)

This time that "model worker" will have to accept the consequences. [The speaker is gloating after hearing that his enemy was in an accident.]

◆ 我是你们老板请来的客人，你们要是欺负我，回头让你们**吃不了兜着走**！

(From the TV series 天堂鸟)

Your boss invited me as his guest. If you give me a hard time, you'll end up paying for it.

chī bù zhǔn 吃不准

Not sure; can't put a finger on it

♦ "这个月的活能按时完成吗？""看看吧，我也**吃不准**，现在大家都憋着要工资呢，没钱大家不愿干。"

(From the novel 大厂)

"Can we finish this month's work on time?" "We'll see. I'm not sure, either. Right now everyone's holding their breath waiting for pay. Without money no one wants to lift a finger."

♦ 我还是有些**吃不准**。X－1号虽说是个好药，但他们两任总代理都没把市场开拓好。我们行吗？

(From the novel 浮沈商海)

I'm still not sure. Although X-1 is a good drug, two successive distributors failed to find a market for it. Do you think we can?

chī cù 吃醋

"Eat vinegar"; be jealous (of a rival in love)

♦ 女："你**吃醋**了？"男："人家又投资又送花儿，这醋我吃得起吗？"

(From the TV series 手心手背)

Woman: "Are you jealous?" Man: "He's been sending you money and flowers. How can I afford to be jealous?" [The woman opened a hair salon. A businessman from Hong Kong came in for a haircut, was very pleased with her work, and promised to invest in the salon's expansion. Her boyfriend feels uneasy but knows he can't compete.]

♦ "**吃醋**了？""**吃醋**？我哪有那么多醋吃啊！要不我天天还不泡在醋缸里了？""哦，那你的意思是你每天都在**吃醋**？"

(From the TV series 问问你的心)

"Jealous?" "Jealous? Whatever for? I'd be stewing in it, if I let myself be jealous." "So you're jealous all the time?"

chī cuò yào le 吃错药了 (吃錯藥了)

"Took the wrong medicine"; gone crazy

♦ "你是不是**吃错药了**？""你才**吃错药了**！你现在基本上不会说人话了。"

(From the TV series 黑冰)

"Have you lost it?" "You're the one who's lost it! You don't know how to talk like a human being anymore."

♦ "想不到你也来看我的笑话！""你**吃错药了**？人家是来帮你一把的！"

"I never thought you'd come too and watch me make a fool of myself." "Are you crazy? I came to help you!"

chī de kāi 吃得开 (吃得開)

Have currency; be popular or effective

♦ 模范顶个屁！而今有后门比啥都**吃得开**！

(From the movie 人生)

> To call someone a "model worker" is just hot air. Nowadays getting in through the back door is the way to go.

♦ 我真佩服老王，过去跟着李经理没少赚黑心钱，李经理倒台了他照样**吃得开**。

> I have to hand it to Lao Wang. Back then he made a pile of shady money together with Manager Li. Now Manager Li is out of the picture but [Lao Wang's]' as hot as ever.

chī dòu fu 吃豆腐

"Eat tofu"; take liberties with a woman

♦ 这个死老外这几天总是想尽办法跟我搭讪，趁机**吃豆腐**…。

(From the short story 无尽的爱)

> For the last few days that damned foreigner has been trying to find a way to strike up a conversation and get a chance to hit on me.

♦ 老老头贼头贼脑结结巴巴，像一世没看见女人，我一看就晓得他不转好念头，想干**吃豆腐**。

(From the novel 一座坟坑腾出一间房)

> The old man was shifty and stammered as if he had never seen a woman before. The moment I saw him I knew he was up to no good, and just wanted to take advantage of me.

chī gān fàn de 吃干饭的 (吃乾飯的)

"Eat dry rice"; all that one can do is eat; be useless

♦ 三个大老爷们儿还看不住个女的，你们都是**吃干饭的**？

(From the TV series 欲罢不能)

> Three grown men couldn't keep an eye on a woman? Are you all totally useless?

♦ 你们公司的那帮人净是**吃干饭的**，吃苦受累的事儿光耍你一个人儿。我看你不如早点儿**跳槽**。

> The people at your company are all useless. You have to do it all. I think it's time for you to bail out.

chī huáng liáng 吃皇粮 (吃皇糧)

"Eat imperial grain"; enjoy imperial, state, or government support or privileges

♦ "他的父亲是个将军。" "哦，是**吃皇粮**长大的。"

(From the TV series 红色康乃馨)

> "His father is a general." "Oh, so he was born with a silver spoon in his mouth."

♦ 我们这些小个体户怎么能和你们国营大厂比呢？ 你们是**吃皇粮**的，我们什么都得精打细算。

> How can small private businesses like ours compete with you big state factories? The government gives you subsidies, but we have to count every penny.

chī le bào zi dǎn 吃了豹子胆 (吃了豹子膽)

"Ate leopard liver"; foolhardy; reckless

♦ 你小子**吃了豹子胆**了你？

(From the TV series 大雪无痕)

> You bastard, are you trying to be some kind of hero? [Repeating 你 at the end of the rhetorical question here makes it more emphatic. It suggests extreme shock, anger, etc.]

[The police want to look into the misdeeds of municipal officials. The police is being sarcasitc.]

♦ 他不过是个普通的工人，却敢告公司的领导贪污受贿，我看他真是**吃了豹子胆了**！

He's just an ordinary worker, but he had the nerve to accuse the company officials of corruption and bribery. I think he's really foolhardy.

chī lǐ pá wài 吃里爬外 (吃裏爬外)

"Eat food from inside while raking things to the outside"; siphoning to others goods provided by a benefactor; hurting one's benefactor by helping someone else

♦ 黄大夫，你可是矿医院的人，所有的关系都在矿上，我提醒你可别**吃里爬外**，到那时候就别怪我不客气了！

(From the novel 空洞)

Doctor Huang, you're an employee of the miners' hospital. All your connections are at the mine. Let me remind you not to bite the hand that feeds you. If you do, don't expect leniency! [There is a conflict between the miners' hospital and the county hospital. The head of the miners' hospital suspects Dr. Huang of secretly aiding the other party.]

♦ 咱们公司都是毁在你们这些**吃里爬外**的小人的手里了！

You ungrateful traitors, our company was ruined at your hands!

chī mí hún yào 吃迷魂药 (吃迷魂藥)

See 灌迷魂汤 guàn mí hún tāng

chī nǎi de jìngr dōu shǐ chū lái le 吃奶的劲儿都使出来了 (吃奶的勁兒都使出來了)

"Using even the suckling muscles"; with all one's might; summon all one's strength; shoot one's bolt

♦ 这小子把**吃奶的劲儿都使出来**，打得我眼冒金星。

(From the novel 血色黄昏)

That bastard gave me everything he had. He hit me so hard that I started to see stars.

♦ 头儿，这么多文件，我就是把**吃奶的劲儿都使出来**也看不完啊？

Boss, there are so many documents here that even if I give it everything I've got, there's no way I can read them all.

chī qiāng yàor le 吃枪药儿了 (吃槍藥兒了)

"Eat gun powder"; blow one's top; hit the roof

♦ "请你们不要干涉我的工作！" "**吃了枪药了**？ 这么大的火。"

(From the TV series 大赢家)

"Keep out of my business!" "Why are you blasting off like that? What's bugging you?"

♦ 小鸥今儿**吃枪药儿了**，非要杀富济贫。

(From the TV series 一年又一年)

Xiao Ou was really off the wall today. He was absolutely determined to rob the rich and give to the poor. [Xiao' Ou asked his brother-in-law for a big donation rather unceremoniously.]

chī rén bù tǔ gú tou 吃人不吐骨头 (吃人不吐骨頭)
"Eat people without spitting out the bones"; be ruthless

◆　他知道，这黄宛氏是个吃人不吐骨头的主儿。
(From the novel 天桥演义)
He knew that Madam Huang was totally ruthless [主儿: *colloquial*, person]. Madame Huangis a cruel brothel mistress.]

◆　让• 保罗他就是八国联军，吃人都不吐骨头。
(From the TV series 大赢家)
Jean Paul is like the Expeditionary Force in the Boxer Rebellion. He'll chew you up and spit you out. ["He's one of those monsters who devours people without spitting out the bones."] [Jean Paul manages a multinational company whose pricecutting makes it impossible for Chinese rivals to compete.]

chī rén jia de zuǐ ruǎn, nà rén jia de shǒu ruǎn 吃人家的嘴软，拿人家的手软 (吃人家的嘴軟，拿人家的手軟)
(Proverb) "The mouth that feeds from others is soft; the hand that takes from others is soft"; become beholden to the favors or generosity of others

◆　秦大记者在两个月内，三下西南，终点站都是咱们师，可算是对咱们情有独钟。吃人家的嘴软，可不要说人家。
(From the novel 突出重围)
That big shot reporter Qin came down to the southwest three times in two months, and it was always just to visit our army. That's really paying special attention to us. We shouldn't be ungrateful, so don't badmouth him. [The reporter has written many complimentary articles about the army.]

◆　这礼物咱们千万别收，宴会也不能去。你忘了那句话了？ 吃人家的嘴软，拿人家的手软。
No way can we accept this gift. We can't go to the banquet, either. Did you forget the saying, "there's no such thing as a free lunch"?

chī ruǎn fàn 吃软饭 (吃軟飯)
"Eat soft food"; live easily off other people; live off a woman

◆　听你说我怎么好象跟吃软饭的似的？
(From the TV series 一年又一年)
To hear you talk, you'd think I'm a kept man! [The husband has lost his job. He is not pleased to hear his wife tell him to stay at home and take it easy; she will support him on her salary.]

◆　红蝶为了这部电视剧把全部情感全部积蓄都搭上了，你呢，吃完你老婆的软饭，又吃到红蝶这儿了。
(From the TV series 北京女人)

Hongdie put all her heart and all her savings into the TV drama. What did you do? First you sponged off your wife, and now you're trying to sponge off Hongdie. [The speaker is addressing the scriptwriter, who accepted Hongdie's help in getting the series off the ground, then dumped her.]

chī xiàn chéngr de 吃现成儿的 (吃現成兒的)

"Eat ready-made food"; get something without having to work for it; get a free ride

♦ "不过很不好意思，没来帮忙，吃现成的！" "你我还说这些吗？"

(From the novel 情在深时)

"I feel bad about it. I didn't come to help out—just to get a cooked meal." "There's no need for that kind of talk between us."

♦ 我老了，让几个儿子外面去闯吧，我自己呢就吃现成儿的了。

I'm old. Let my sons go out and try to succeed. I'll coast on their earnings.

chī xiāng 吃香

"Eat fragrance"; popular; in great demand

♦ 离开这儿，去哪儿？ 咱们这种学文科的最不吃香，不管是申请学校还是找工作都难如登天。

(From the novel 浮躁)

Leave here? Where would we go? It's not as if humanities students were actually in demand. Getting into a school or finding a job is like trying to get into heaven.

♦ 现在连本科学位都不吃香了，没有个博士学位别想在公司里找到好工作。

These days even a college degree doesn't make you marketable. Without a PhD, don't even dream of finding a good job in business.

chī xiāng de hē là de 吃香的喝辣的

"Eat fragrant food, drink spicy drinks"; eat well; live a sumptuous life

♦ 富人什么活不干，却吃香的喝辣的，是穷人养活富人。

(From the novel 雪白血红)

Rich people don't have to do a thing but eat caviar and drink champagne. It's the poor who support them.

♦ 人家当官儿的整天吃香的喝辣的，让咱们在这儿吃苦受累。

The people in power just live it up all day, and make us suffer.

chī xīn 吃心

Paranoid; suspicious

♦ "我说你了吗？ 谁 '粘' 我说的是谁，你吃什么心啊？"

(From the novel 沉浮)

"Was I talking about you? I was talking about whoever leeches onto a foreigner. Why are you being so paranoid?"

♦   "我最恨那些造谣的人。""我造什么谣了？""我又没说你，你吃什么心啊？"

"There's nothing I hate more than people who spread rumors." "What rumor did I spread?" "I wasn't talking about you; how come you're so paranoid?"

chī zhe wǎn lǐ de, xiǎng zhe guō lǐ de 吃着碗里的，想着锅里的 (吃著碗裏的，想著鍋裏的)

"Eat what's in the bowl while thinking about what's in the pot"; be greedy

♦   你可不能吃着碗里的又想着锅里的哟！脚踩两只船早晚会掉进水里！再说像金荔那样痴情的女孩子哪里找去？

(From the novel 血色—东京狂语)

You shouldn't be so greedy'! If you try to straddle two boats at once, you'll end up in the water sooner or later. Besides, where could you find another girl as devoted as Jinli?

♦   敢情这小子吃着碗里的又喝着锅里的啊，也太损了点。

(From the novel 浮沈商海)

So this bastard is trying to hog everything! That's a bit much. [A man who is not yet divorced from his wife is living with another woman.]

chī zhè wǎn fàn de 吃这碗饭的 (吃這碗飯的)

"Eat this bowl of rice"; in this trade or profession

♦   请你千万放心，我就是吃这碗饭的，要是干不好，不是砸自己的饭碗吗！你就回去等消息吧，最迟两周之内，我会给你打电话的。

(From the novel 我在新西兰当警官)

Don't you worry. This is my profession. If I didn't do it right, I couldn't put food on the table. You go home and wait for the news. I'll call you in two weeks at the most. [The speaker is a lawyer handling an immigration application.]

♦   "不会是说着玩儿的吧？""我们就是吃这碗饭的。"

(From the movie 甲方乙方)

"You're kidding, right?" "No, that's what we do." [The company's business is making people's fantasies come true.]

chī zhè yí tào 吃这一套 (吃這一套)

"Eat this routine"; buy this routine; swallow this line

♦   老子不吃这一套，别拿那破枪吓唬我。

(From the movie 紫日)

Don't give me that. Don't try to scare me with that lousy gun of yours.

♦   你这点小把戏骗骗小孩子还差不多，我才不吃你这一套呢！

That little scam of yours might work for fooling little kids, but I don't buy it!

chì bǎngr yìng le 翅膀儿硬了 (翅膀兒硬了)

"The wings are hard now"; grow up and leave the nest; become confident and independent

♦   你翅膀硬了，连什么叫里什么叫外都不懂。

(From the novel 都市危情)

So you've spread your wings and left the nest. Don't you understand that blood is thicker than water? [The speaker is reproaching his niece for helping the police investigate his financial improprieties.]

♦ 你**翅膀硬了**，用不着我老头子了，是不是？

You're all grown up now, and you don't need an old man like me anymore. Is that it?

chì lǎo 赤佬

(Shanghai dialect) jerk

♦ 小**赤佬**瞎话三千，妈妈啥辰光讲过这种话啦？！

(From the short story 家庭风景二十章)

You little jerk, you're lying. When did Mom ever say such a thing? [This sentence is in the Shanghai dialect. 瞎话: nonsense, lies; 三千: numerous; 啥辰光: at what time, when]

♦ 这个小**赤佬**，骂我是中央情报局的。

That little jerk accused me of being with the CIA of the United States.

chòng..lái de 冲...来的 (沖...來的)

Come towards; directed at; aim at (冲: facing)

♦ 所有的女人都是**冲**我的钱**来的**。

(From the TV series 一年又一年)

All the women are after my money. [The speaker is a company manager who has been divorced for many years and hasn't remarried.]

♦ 今天有什么事，你**冲着我来**！ 别拿我妹妹撒气！

(From the TV series 手心手背)

If there's a problem today, take it up with me. Don't take it out on my sister.

chōu fēng 抽风 (抽風)

"Have a convulsion"; have a fit; act crazy

♦ 这就怪了，老何头**抽什么风**？ 前几天对你还冷若冰霜，这几天对你又象春天般温暖。

(From the novel 越轨诉讼)

That's weird. What's gotten into Lao He? A few days ago he was as cold as ice to you, but the last couple of days he's been as warm as springtime.

♦ 你**抽风**啊？ 这彩电刚买了两天就要换？

Are you crazy? You only bought this color TV a couple of days ago, and now you already want a different one?

chǒu bā guài 丑八怪 (醜八怪)

"Ugly monster"; ugly

♦ 要是〖电影演员〗长得都跟**丑八怪**似的，谁上电影院啊？

(From the TV series 一年又一年)

If movie actors were ugly, who would want to go see them?

♦ 还"黑马王子"呢！ 我看一定是一个见光死的**丑八怪**！

(From the TV series 红色康乃馨)

"A prince on a dark horse" indeed! I bet he's an ugly monster who has to hide from daylight ["who'll die if he sees daylight"]. [Spoken to a friend infatuated with someone she met on the Internet.]

chǒu bù lěng zi 瞅不冷子
Sudden; abrupt; out of the blue

◆ 我这个人心里直，遇到瞅不冷子的事儿就拐不过弯儿来。
(From the TV series 今生是亲人)
I'm a straightforward kind of guy. When something comes out of the blue like this, it's hard for me to make the adjustment. [He has just learned his mother and father are not his biological parents.]

◆ 老张这个人你得防着点儿，平时有说有笑的，瞅不冷子就会在背后捅你一刀。
You have to be careful with Lao Zhang. He's usually all jokes and smiles, but then out of the blue he'll stab you in the back.

chǒu huà shuō zài qián tou/tóu li 丑话说在前头/头里 (醜話說在前頭/頭裏)
"Speak the ugly words first"; spell out the unpleasant truth up front; give the bad news first

◆ 我丑话说在前头，要是出了什么意外，有损我嵩山派的名誉，可别怪我左冷禅不讲情面。
(From the TV series 笑傲江湖)
I'll put it bluntly right off the bat. If anything happens that harms the reputation of the Songshan School, don't blame me [Zuo Lengchan] for ignoring our friendship.

◆ 我把丑话说在头里，每人每月拉一个客户，拉不到就走人。
(From the TV series 其实男人最辛苦)
I'm laying it on the line for you right at the start. Everyone has to land one customer a month. If you can't do that, you'll have to leave. [The manager of an advertising company is lecturing his salesmen.]

chǒu xí fu jiàn gōng pó 丑媳妇见公婆 (醜媳婦見公婆)
"Even an ugly daughter-in-law will have to meet her husband's parents"; one can't hide forever from one's insecurities; one can't hide from the truth

◆ 江有礼就在自己上任的第三天，怀着丑媳妇见公婆的心情来到主管集团的办公大楼朝拜顶头上司。
(From the novel 最后一座工厂)
The third day on the job, feeling like an awkward girl meeting her prospective in-laws, Jiang Youli went to the company headquarters and paid his respects to his supervisors.

◆ "减工资的事儿再等两天跟大家说好不好？" "别挨 (ái) 着了，丑媳妇也得见公婆啊！"
"Let's wait a couple of days before telling everyone about the pay cut." "Don't drag it out. The truth has to come out, even if it's ugly."

chòu měi 臭美
"Stinking happiness"; be smug or complacent without justification

◆ 谁爱你啊？ 臭美劲儿！
(From the TV series 一年又一年)

Who do you think is in love with you? You're pretty damn satisfied with yourself! [A girlfriend teasing her boyfriend.]

♦ " 春节到我们家去见见我爹妈吧？ " 臭美！ 我才不去呢！ "

(From the TV series 空镜子)

"How about coming over on New Year's Day to meet my parents?" "You wish! You're pretty sure of yourself! I'm not going. No way." [The two haven't been dating very long, and meeting the parents on New Year's Day is a serious step.]

chū diǎn zi 出点子 (出點子)

Come up with ideas or suggestions

♦ "欣瑶也参与了这件事？" "与韩方合资的事，就是她出的点子。"

(From the TV series 问问你的心)

"Xinyao is involved in this too?" "The joint venture with a Korean partner was her idea."

♦ 我不是让你辞了大学教授到我们公司来，就是想请你当个顾问给我出出点子。这你应该能接受吧？

(From the TV series 一年又一年)

It's not that I want you to give up your professorship and join our company. I just want to ask you to serve as consultant and offer suggestions. You could agree to that, right?

chū fēng tou 出风头 (出風頭)

Steal the show; be in the limelight

♦ 恭喜你了，你出了大风头了！

(From the movie 大腕)

Congratulations! You stole the show! [An obscure actor found favor with a big shot director. The director's assistant is jealous.]

♦ 他老婆什么都好，就是太爱出风头。

His wife is great, except that she always wants to be the center of attention.

chū gér/quānr 出格/圈儿 (出格/圈兒)

Go out of bounds; break the rules

♦ 我是相信你不会干出什么出格儿的事儿来。

(From the TV series 黑洞)

I don't believe you'd step over the line. [A policeman is speaking to a crime suspect who is his longtime friend.]

♦ 其实你也是不得已，有时也真是我太不懂事，闹得太出圈。

(From the novel 我是你爸爸)

Actually, you didn't have a choice. Sometimes I act too stupid and get out of line. [A son is 'responding to his father's promise not to hit him anymore.]

chū rén mìng 出人命

Cause loss of life; cause death

♦ "哥，要不然把他们给做了？" "不行，已经出了几条人命了，不能再干了。"

(From the TV series 黑洞)

"Brother, maybe we should finish them off?" "No. We've already finished off a few. Can't do it anymore." [An exchange between two criminals.]

♦ 这样干下去会出人命的！

If you keep doing it this way, someone's going to get killed. [The speaker is warning that reckless disregard for work safety could cost lives.]

chū xiě 出血

"Bleed"; cough up money

♦ 这老爷子还真出血啊！可也不能当面儿拍啊！

(From the TV drama 昝兒胡同)

That old man is really going to cough up some money! But even so, don't take it directly from him.

♦ 升官了？ 这回你可得出点儿血，请咱们穷哥儿几个一顿。

(From the TV series 欲罢不能)

You got promoted? This time you'll have to lay out some cash and treat your poor friends to a good meal.

chū yáng xiàng 出洋相

"Make a foreign exhibition of oneself"; make a fool of oneself

♦ 我不练了，我不想在这儿出洋相，让大家笑话。

(From the TV series 北京女人)

I'm not going to exercise any more. I don't want to make a fool of myself and have everyone joke about me. [An overweight person is talking about practicing aerobics.]

♦ 这简直是出我的洋相！

(From the TV series 新七十二家房客)

That's like asking me to make myself look ridiculous. [Superiors persuaded the speaker to run for election. After canvassing many people, he was told to stop campaigning.]

chǔ wō zi 怵窝子(怵窝子)

Shy; timid

♦ 文海知趣儿，便不敢吃菜，也不敢吃馒头，只死啃窝头和咸菜。父亲塞给他半个馒头："吃呀，怎么老怵窝子呀？ 这也是你的家！"

(From the novel 孽缘千里)

Wenhai minded his manners and didn't touch the main dishes or the steamed bread. He just nibbled on the sorghum bread and salted vegetables. His father pushed a piece of steamed bread into his hand and said, "Go ahead and eat. What are you afraid of? This is your home, too." [Wenhai is an adopted son who feels he lacks standing in the family.]

♦ 我那老二心眼儿特好，就是忒怵窝子了，见了生人连句话都说不出来。

My second son is good-hearted, but he's just too timid. When he sees a stranger he can't manage to get a word out.

chù 怵

Afraid; scared

♦ 干吗？ 是不是往歌厅跑发怵呀？ 哈哈，怕歌厅里的小姐给你灌迷魂汤，把你拉下水是不是？

(From the novel 百年德性)

What's up? Are you scared of going to the nightclub? Are you afraid that the girls there will give you a love potion and pull you down [拉下水: "pull you under the water"]? [A police chief is teasing a subordinate who is being sent to a nightclub on official business.]

♦   你说这事儿也真奇怪，老刘这么一个天不怕地不怕的人会**怵**新来的那个黄毛丫头。

This is really weird. Lao Liu is scared of nothing on earth, so how come he's afraid of this new young chick?

chù méi tou 触霉头 (觸霉頭)

(Shanghai dialect) run into bad luck

♦   "你的脚再崴了怎么办？" "你不要**触我的霉头**。"

"What if you sprain your ankle again?" [崴 in Shanghai dialect=Mandarin 扭, sprain.] "Don't jinx me." [The woman sprained her ankle. After resting at home for a couple of days, she ventures out again. Her husband worries that she might hurt her ankle again.]

♦   不要气了，大喜之日还带火气，会**触霉头**的。

(From the novel 共效于飞)

Stop being so angry. Getting upset on a happy day like this will bring bad luck.

chuǎi zhe míng bai zhuāng hú tu 揣着明白装胡涂 (揣著明白裝糊塗)

"Carry understanding while feigning incomprehension"; pretend not to understand

♦   咱都别**揣着明白装胡涂**。

(From the TV series 其实男人最辛苦)

Let's not play games. ["Let's not pretend that we don't understand each other."][The speaker's ex-wife had a son and the speaker thinks he is the father. He is negotiating with his ex-wife's second husband to get custody of the child.]

♦   我为什么来你能不知道吗？ 你别这儿**揣着明白装胡涂**了！ 快点儿把钱还给我咱们什么事儿都没有，不然我敢把你们这公司砸了。

You know very well why I came, so don't play games with me. Hand over the money right now, and we're cool. Otherwise I'll smash this company of yours to pieces.

chuān bāngr 穿帮儿 (穿幫兒)

"Poking through the upper of a shoe"; the secret is out

♦   人家大人孩子两头儿瞒着，你这非得**穿帮**点火啊你这是！

(From the TV series 今生是亲人)

They tried to keep both their parents and the kid from finding out, but you had to let the cat out of the bag and stir up trouble! [The parents knew their son wasn't their biological child, but they kept it from their son and their own parents for a long time. A friend inadvertently revealed the secret and caused family upheaval.]

◆   开始的时候他还装得挺像，说是什么省报的记者来采访，我问了他两句就**穿帮**儿了，其实是张大头派他来咱们这儿打探消息的。
    At first he managed his disguise pretty well, and claimed to be a reporter from some provincial newspaper doing interviews. I asked him a couple of questions and the charade fell apart. Actually, he was sent here by Big Head Zhang to gather information about us.

chuān xiǎo xiér 穿小鞋儿 (穿小鞋兒)
"Give someone tight shoes to wear"; deliberately make life difficult for someone

◆   我这人特正派，从来不给人**穿小鞋**儿。
    (From the TV series 贫嘴张大民的幸福生活)
    I stay on the straight and narrow. I never make life difficult for people.

◆   王经理，你要是不想让我在这儿干就明说一句，别总给我**穿小鞋**儿。
    Manager Wang, if you don't want me to work here, just say so. Don't make my life difficult.

chuān yì tiáo kù zi 穿一条裤子 (穿一條褲子)
"Wear the same pair of pants"; in cahoots; form an unholy alliance

◆   我冒着生命危险告他，可你们俩呢，却为他辩护，我看你们是和他合**穿一条裤子**。
    (From the TV series 红色康乃馨)
    I risked my life to take him to court, but you two are defending him. I think you're in cahoots with him.

◆   我明白了，你们俩早就**穿一条裤子**了！
    (From the TV series 其实男人最辛苦)
    Now I get it. You two were already together back then. [The affair began before the divorce was final.]

chuī hú zi dèng yǎn 吹胡子瞪眼 (吹鬍子瞪眼)
"Blow out one's beard and glower"; throw a fit

◆   我只要想到我爷爷被你说得哑口无言、**吹胡子瞪眼**晴的样子，就觉得好好笑。
    (From the novel 迷恋)
    When I think about how you dumbfounded my grandfather and made him throw a fit, I just have to laugh out loud.

◆   你不就一小科长儿吗？ 干吗**吹胡子瞪眼**的？
    You're just a low-level section chief, right? Where do you get off throwing a tantrum?

chuī niú bú yòng shàng shuì 吹牛不用上税
"There are no taxes on bragging"; it doesn't cost anything to brag; talk is cheap

◆   甲："我一磕就能磕上，信不信？"乙："我不信。"丙："我也不信，反正**吹牛不用上税**。"
    (From the TV series 将爱情进行到底)

A: I can get any girl the moment I try. [磕: kē, to accost, "I can chat up any girl I want."] Believe it or not!" B: "I don't believe it." C. "Me neither, but talk is cheap."

◆ "他第一天上班老板就给他配了一辆大奔！" "听他的呢！ **吹牛不用 上税。**"

"On his first day on the job, his boss gave him a big Mercedes to use." "And you believed him! Talk is cheap."

chuō jí liáng (gǔ) 戳脊梁（骨）(戳脊梁（骨）)

"Be poked in the spine"; be criticized; be accused of wrongdoing

◆ 阿灿的娘，是破鞋，人人见了人人躲，人人见了**戳脊梁**。

(From the short story 阿灿的妈妈)

Ah Chan's mom is a slut. Everyone avoids her and badmouths her.

◆ 要说震宝不是我们的儿子，还让他养我们，这不是让乡亲们**戳脊梁骨** 吗？

(From the TV series 今生是亲人)

When you come right down to it, Zhenbao is not our son. People will talk if we let him support us.

cǐ chù bù liú yé, zì yǒu liú yé chù 此处不留爷，自有留爷处 (此處不 留爺，自有留爺處)

"If I'm not wanted here, there are other places that do want me" (爷: a blustery male self-aggrandizing self-reference)

◆ 我可告诉你们，**此处不留爷，自有留爷处**。不收我，哼，我还不爱去 呢！

(From the novel 从深圳到温哥华)

Let me tell you, if you don't want me, there are plenty others who do. You don't want to hire me? I'm not sure that I'd want to go there anyway. [The job is in Vancouver.]

◆ **此处不留爷，自有留爷处**，天地大着呢，干吗非在一棵树上吊死啊？

(From the TV series 大赢家)

If they don't want you here, go somewhere else. It's a big world out there. Why stick around in the same rut? ["You don't have to hang yourself on the same tree."] [A marketing director was suspended. The owner of another company is persuading him to leave his old job.]

cìr tóu 刺儿头 (刺兒頭)

A prickly person

◆ 嘿，这小子真**刺儿头**！

(From the TV series 大宅门)

Hey, this kid is a tough nut! [A kidnapped child turns out to be anything but a pushover.]

◆ 一个叫黄全宝的中年汉子，是全村有名儿的"**刺儿头**"，嘴尖、舌 快、脸皮厚，哪家娶媳妇闹洞房也少不了他。

(From the novel 新媳妇)

A middle-aged man called Huang Jinbao is famous as the terror of the village. He's a thick-skinned loudmouth with a nasty tongue. People marrying off a son can't do without him for the ritual wedding practical jokes.

còu he 凑合 (湊合)

Make do

◆　没吃早饭吧？　**凑合**吃点。别饿坏了身子。

(From the novel 浮沈商海)
> You didn't have breakfast, right? Grab a bite. Don't go hungry.

◆　那个电影也不是特别有意思，不过还能**凑合**看。

> That film wasn't all that interesting, but if you just want to see something it's OK.

còu rè nao 凑热闹 (湊熱鬧)

Join in the fun; add to the trouble

◆　你说美国日本骗咱俩钱儿也就算了，这比利时也跟着**凑热闹**。

(From the TV series 贫嘴张大民的幸福生活)
> If it were just the Americans and the Japanese ripping us off, we could accept that. Who knew, the Belgians want a piece of the action, too! [The prices of cold medicines made in Belgium turned out to be exorbitant.]

◆　"听说你们家老张也参加英文学习班了？"　"嗨！　跟着**凑热闹**。　他说的英文只有他自己听得懂。"

> "I hear your husband's taking the English class too?" "Oh, he follows the herd. When he speaks English, no one but he himself can understand."

cù tán zi 醋坛子 (醋罎子)

"A vinegar jar"; an excessively jealous person

◆　"你去参加武斗了？"黄鹿野苦笑：　"也算是武斗吧，叫我家里的那个**醋坛子**给抓的。"

(From the novel 空洞)
> [Seeing the scar on Huang Luye's face:] "Were you physically 'struggled' too?" Huang Yuye answered with a bitter smile, "I guess you could call it physically struggled. My jealous bitch of a wife grabbed me. [武斗: Cultural Revolutionary jargon for a physical attack as opposed to a verbal attack, or 文斗, on political undesirables.]

◆　你怎么给老刘他太太打电话？　你不知道老刘是个**醋坛子**吗？

> What made you call Lao Liu's wife? Don't you know how jealous Lao Liu is?

cuō huǒ 搓火

" (Flintstone) to generate fire"; become irritated

◆　你就别跟我提工资的事儿，一提我就**搓火**。

(From the TV series 一年又一年)
> Don't ask me about the raise. As soon as someone brings it up I get mad.

◆　急着结婚啊，没地儿放双人床，你说**搓火**不**搓火**？

(From the TV series 贫嘴张大民的幸福生活)

They're dying to get married, but they haven't got room for a double bed. Infuriating, isn't it? [Neighbors are gossiping about a couple who endure severely cramped living conditions.]

cuō má 搓麻

Play mahjong

♦ 他见天儿地去**搓麻**，一搓就是两三点才回来。

(From the TV drama 夸兄胡同)

He goes out to play mahjong at sunrise and doesn't get back till two or three in the morning.

♦ 你是不是又上老谢他们家**搓麻**去了？

Did you go to Lao Xie's place to play mahjong again?

cuō yí dùn 撮一顿 (撮一頓)

Have a meal

♦ 你先把他们稳住，然后请他们到"明珠海鲜" **撮一顿**。

(From the TV drama 夸兄胡同)

First stall them, and then afterwards invite them to a good meal at Pearl Seafood. [Pearl Seafood is the name of a Cantonese restaurant in Beijing fashionable in the late 1980s.]

♦ 今儿晚上我没事儿，咱们出去**撮一顿**怎么样？

I'm free tonight. How about going out for a good meal?

cuó zi lǐ tou bá jiāng jūn 矬子里头拔将军 (矬子裏頭拔將軍)

"Pull up a general among dwarfs"; pick the tallest person in a crowd of dwarfs; the lesser of two evils; the best of a bad lot

♦ 这年选拔办公室副主任，老张正好超过岁数了。**矬子里拔将军**，小王当上了副主任。老张气得害了一场大病。

(From the short story 蚀杀)

That year they were looking for a deputy director of the office. Lao Zhang had just passed the age limit, so they had to choose the best of a bad lot. That's how Xiao Wang became deputy director. Lao Zhang was so angry that he became seriously ill.

♦ "小张那付样子也能当经理吗？" "没办法啊，这叫**矬子里头拔将军**。"

"Can a guy like Xiao Zhang become a manager?" "What can you do? It's called picking the best of a bad lot."

D

dā bǎ shǒur 搭把手儿 (搭把手兒)

Lend a hand

♦ 明儿我们家刷房，大民要是没事儿就让他过来**搭把手儿**。

(From the TV series 贫嘴张大民的幸福生活)

Tomorrow we're going to paint the house. If Damin isn't busy, ask him to come over and give us a hand.

◆ 他这人一点儿**眼力见儿**都没有，看我这儿忙得**四脚朝天**也不过来**搭把手**。

> That guy doesn't notice anything. Here I am up to my eyeballs in work ["I'm so busy that my four limbs are pointing skywards"], and he won't lift a hand to help.

dā li 搭理

Pay attention to; acknowledge; have anything to do with

◆ 说白了，我懒得**搭理**他们。

(From the TV series 今生是亲人)

> To be frank, I couldn't be bothered with them.

◆ 姓韩的流里流气的，往后你少**搭理**他。

> That Han guy is bad news. Stay away from him from now on.

dā shàng xìng mìng/dā jìn xìng mìng 搭上性命/搭进性命 (搭上性命/搭進性命)

"Throw in one's life"; die

◆ 做这种买卖弄不好要**搭上性命**的。

(From the TV series 永不瞑目)

> If you slip up in this kind of business, it could cost you your life. [Talking about the narcotics business.]

◆ 他太爱钱了，得罪了黑社会的人，结果**把命都搭进去**了。

(From the TV series 手心手背)

> He loved money too much. He got on the wrong side of the mafia and got snuffed.

dǎ bǎo piào/bāo piào 打保票/包票

Guarantee

◆ 我可给我爸**打了包票**说你不会脱军装。你别再三心二意了。

(From the novel 突出重围)

> I promised my dad that you wouldn't quit the army ["take off the army uniform"]. Don't keep going back and forth about it.

◆ 方山说："不管是耗子还是猫，反正你要给我下个公的。"老婆说："那谁敢**打保票**？下出来才知道呢！"

(From the short story 地道)

> Fang Shan said, "I don't care if it's a rat or a cat, so long as there's something between its legs." His wife replied, "Who can guarantee that? We won't find out till it's born."

dǎ chà 打岔

Sidetrack; interrupt; change the subject (岔: detour)

◆ 不管别人再拿什么玩笑**打岔**，我也没兴致了。

(From the novel 萧尔布拉克)

The others tried to change the subject by joking, but it didn't matter. I had lost all interest. [Someone insinuated that the speaker's wife had had an affair.]

♦ 少跟我这儿**打岔**，我只要你一句话，昨晚上跟你一块儿喝酒的那女的到底是谁？

Don't try to change the subject. I just want you to tell me one thing. Who was that woman you had a drink with last night? [A wife confronts her husband.]

dǎ dào huí fǔ 打道回府

Return home with great pomp and circumstance (打道: get underlings to clear a path)

♦ 想到这儿，崔老爷子差点儿叫停车，让司机送自己**打道回府**。

(From the novel 耍叉)

As soon as the idea struck him, Grandpa Cui almost asked the driver to stop and take him home.

♦ 既然如此，大人吃杯茶，就请**打道回府**吧。

(From the TV series 康熙帝国)

If that's the case, may I invite Your Excellency to have a cup of tea and then retire to your residence. [Negotiations have broken down.]

dǎ diǎn 打点 (打點)

Deal with; take care of

♦ 我看办法只有一个，上下**打点**。求上边儿把这事儿压下来，魏大人说得对，能弄个是非不分，不予追究，就算万幸！

(From TV series 大宅门)

I think there's only one way out. We have to take care of everybody. We have to beg our superiors to keep this matter quiet. Master Wei was right. We should count ourselves very lucky indeed if they let it pass and do not investigate who was at fault. [A prescription had been tampered with. As a result, someone in the imperial palace died.]

♦ 现在不比从前了，你要想开个工厂，上上下下、左邻右舍你都得**打点**到了，不然你就等着麻烦吧。

Now it's not as simple as it used to be. If you want to open a factory, you've got to take care of everyone around youotherwise you're just asking for trouble.

dǎ duàn gú tou lián zhe jīn 打断骨头连着筋 (打斷骨頭連著筋)

"Even if you break the bones, the sinews are still attached"; inseparable

♦ 我们这些人跟太后是**打断骨头连着筋**哪！您有什么事就吩咐吧！

(From the TV series 康熙帝国)

We will stand by your Majesty through thick and thin. Just tell us what to do, and we'll obey! [Spoken to the Empress Dowager during an armed rebellion.]

◆ 老刘和大华公司那几个小子的关系**铁**着呢，**打断了骨头都连着筋**，要是您的计划让他知道了，不出十分钟大华公司就得知道。

    Lao Liu and those bastards at the Dahua Company are joined at the hip ["their relationship is like iron"]. If Lao Liu hears about your plan, Dahua will know in ten minutes.

dǎ fa 打发 (打發)

Dismiss; dispatch; get rid of

◆ 你总得想个法子把那个顾三军**打发**走。

    (From the TV series 大雪无痕)

    You've got to think of a way to get rid of that Gu Sanjun. [Gu Sanjun, the son of a high-ranking official, has been extorting money from them.]

◆ 你当是给我三双鞋就把我**打发**了，没门儿！

    (From the TV series 贫嘴张大民的幸福生活)

    You thought you could get rid of me with three pairs of shoes? Think again! [The speaker has come to collect debt from a shoe-store owner.]

dǎ gǒu hái děi kàn zhǔ rén 打狗还得看主人 (打狗還得看主人)

(Proverb) "Before you hit the dog, find out who the owner is"; before you attack, know the other person's connections

◆ 你知道她是谁吗？**打狗还得看主人**吧？

    (From the movie 有话好好说)

    Do you know who she is? Before you attack someone, find out who stands behind her. [The speaker thinks that his niece has been unfairly treated.]

◆ 你们**瞎了狗眼**，这位是令狐大侠，**打狗还得看看主人**呢！

    (From the TV series 笑傲江湖)

    Are you blind? This is the famous hero Linghu ["the Grand Knight Errant Linghu"]. Before attacking someone, think about whose guest he is. [Several ruffians are attacking Linghu Chong, a guest of the speaker.]

dǎ guān qiāng 打官腔

Speak officialese; give the official party line

◆ 莫厂长的习惯，只要一**打官腔**，眼睛就看着别处，省得别人尴尬自己也尴尬。

    (From the novel 魔鬼与天使)

The factory director, Mr. Mo, used to look aside whenever he had to talk like an official, in order to avoid embarrassing his listeners and himself.

♦ 大哥我的事儿你还得"研究研究"，好啊！小子。你刚当了几天的官儿啊，怎么这么快就学会打官腔了？

Brother, you say you'll give my request "due consideration"? You bastard! How long have you been on the job? A couple of days? And you're already fluent in officialese!

dǎ hā ha 打哈哈

Crack jokes or make perfunctory, non-committal comments in a difficult situation; insincere

♦ 愚臣这不是打哈哈，这是一片肺腑之言。

(From the TV series 康熙帝国)

I am not joking. I'm speaking from the bottom of my heart. [愚臣: unwise minister, a humble self-reference; 肺腑: lung] [The speaker is recommending that command of the troops be given to an enemy general.]

♦ 周老大，咱们还得赶路，我可没功夫跟你说笑打哈哈。

(From the novel 血嫁)

Brother Zhou, we have to be on our way. I don't have time to kid around with you. [The speaker is the leader of a bridal procession. Zhou Laoda, head of a band of beggars, wants to detain the bride.]

dǎ jī xiě 打鸡血 (打雞血)

"Inject chicken blood"; become revitalized; get pumped up; receive a shot in the arm

♦ 你怎么跟我们班男同学一样，一提起足球就跟打了鸡血似的？

(From the TV series 一年又一年)

How come you're just like the boys in our class? Whenever the word "soccer" is mentioned, you get all pumped up.

♦ "老板让我们加班儿干，月底以前一定得装好三千台计算机。" "不行不行，我们已经加了一个星期的班了，哪有精神再加班儿？就是打鸡血也提不起精神来了。"

"The boss asked us to work overtime. We have to assemble three thousand computers by the end of the month." "No way. We've already been working overtime for a week. Where are we going to find the energy to do more? Not even a shot in the arm would give us enough juice."

dǎ kāi tiān chuāng shuō liàng huà 打开天窗儿说亮话 (打開天窗兒說亮話)

"Open the skylight and speak the clear truth"; in plain words; cut to the chase

♦ 莫厂长，今天你圆乎脸一抹成了长乎脸，要跟我公事公办，那好，咱们今天打开天窗说亮话：别以为你是什么奉公守法的正人君子，你在厂子里都干了些什么，我肚子里有一本账，写得清清楚楚。

(From the novel 魔鬼与天使)

Director Mo, you've changed your tone today ["today your round face turned long"]. Now you want to be businesslike with me. All right, let's lay the cards on the table. Don't kid yourself into thinking that you're some kind of law-abiding honest gentleman. In my mind I have the full balance sheet of every last thing you did at the factory.

◆ 咱们**打开天窗说亮话**，你要是肯出三十万我就把房子卖给你。

OK, let's spell it out. If you're willing to put up three hundred grand, I'll sell the house to you.

dǎ mā hu yǎn 打马虎眼 (打馬虎眼)

Act dumb to get out of a tricky situation; gloss over something

◆ 钱明明是你出的，你为什么不说，还支了个杨胖子来**打马虎眼**？你是把我**当猴耍**了你！

(From the TV series 都市情感)

Obviously it's you who put up the money. Why didn't you say so? Instead, you send Fatso Yang to fool me. Do you think I'm an idiot?

◆ 你甭在妈这儿**打马虎眼**，没人指使你，你好么当央儿的查起市委书记来了，又是你叔叔。

(From the novel 都市危情)

Don't try to blow me, your own mother, off. Unless someone put you up to it, why would you suddenly start investigating the municipal party secretary, who's your own uncle on top of everything?

dǎ pì 打屁

(Taiwan expression) "beat fart"; have a silly or trivial conversation; shoot the breeze

◆ 空服员在替乘客热排餐，端饮料，递毛巾，应付了一些较噜嗦的阿土之余，总可以到后舱斜倚着休息，聊聊天，**打打屁**。

(From the short story 降生十二星座)

After the flight attendants had helped the passengers to their seats, got them beverages, handed out towels, and dealt with the usual talkative yokels, they could always go to the back cabin, put their feet up, and shoot the breeze.

◆ 他这个朋友很欣赏你的小说，他有一些故事，想告诉你，很轻松的，别当回事，就像朋友之间的哈啦**打屁**。

(From the short story 第一个故事)

This friend of his really admires your novel. He has some stories he'd like to tell you. Very entertaining. No big deal, just think of it as a chat between friends.

dǎ qiū fēng 打秋风 (打秋風)

Extort money or things on various pretexts

◆ "他是不是经常到这儿来**打秋风**啊？""那倒不是，他这个人从来不**吃白食**的，连个优惠都不要，这才叫人害怕呢！"

(From the TV series 红色康乃馨)

"Does he come here often to extort stuff?" "Not really. He never looks for a free lunch. He never even asks for a discount. That's even more scary."

◆ 李小姐还待推辞，少芳把手一推说，拿着，不拿，不定还被哪个**打秋风**的刮了去。

(From the novel 红檀板)

Before Miss Li could refuse, Shaofang pushed her hand away and said, "Take it. If you don't take it, some shakedown guy will."

dǎ rù lěng gōng 打入冷宫

"Be banished to a cold palace (like an imperial concubine in disfavor)"; fall out of favor; be put on the shelf

♦ "就算有一天我真的被**打入冷宫**，那个取代我的人也绝对不是你。" 羽容忍不住咬着牙回敬她一句。

(From the novel 复制灵魂)

Yurong couldn't resist answering through clenched teeth, "Even if I fall out of favor someday, you're not the one who'll replace me." [A rivalry between two models.]

♦ 你的那个设计？嗨！早让头儿**打入冷宫**了。

That design of yours? It was put on the shelf by the boss long ago.

dǎ shuǐ piāor 打水漂儿 (打水漂兒)

"Throw a stone over water to create a ripple"; go down the drain

♦ 林静平说是帮忙，可我真向她借，她就推说钱拿不出来……也难怪，谁不知道那钱可能就是**打水漂儿**。

(From the novel 北京故事)

Lin Jingping said she would help out, but when I asked her for a loan, she backed out and said she didn't have the money....I don't blame her though. Everyone knows that money could easily go down the drain.

♦ 三亿七千万的国有资产在不到一年半的时间内全部**打了水漂**。

(From the TV series 红色康乃馨)

Within a year and a half, 370 million yuan in state assets all went down the drain.

dǎ tuì táng gǔ 打退堂鼓

"Beat the drum to signal the end of a court session and disperse the crowd"; beat a retreat; give up

♦ 别**打退堂鼓**啊！继续努力！

(From the TV series 将爱情进行到底)

Don't give up! Keep at it!

♦ 你怎么老**打退堂鼓**啊？刚参加革命就想退休？

(From the TV series 大赢家)

Why do you always want to back out? You just got started in business ["joined the revolution"] and you already want to retire? [A business partner wants to quit while they are ahead.]

dǎ xià shǒu 打下手

Act as assistant

♦ 我要弄你？我今儿把话搁这儿了，给她**打下手**你都**不配**！那已经是抬举你了！

(From the TV series 北京女人)

You think I'm taking you for a ride? I'm just going to say this: you're not even good enough to be her assistant. Even that would be more than you deserve.

♦   "听说这种新款汽车是您设计的，真了不起！" "哪儿的话，我只不过给总设计师打打下手儿。"

> "I hear you're the one who designed this new car model. 'Great job!'" "I'm not sure I deserve any credit. I just helped out the chief designer."

dǎ xiǎo suàn pán/dǎ xiǎo jiǔ jiǔr 打小算盘/打小九九儿 (打小算盤/打小九九兒)

"Play the small abacus"; do the numbers; be too concerned with one's personal advantage

♦   对付这些人该怎么办？大家团结起来，不要**打小算盘**。

(From the novel 人蚁)

> How should we deal with these people? We've got to stand together. Don't just consider your own interests.

♦   大敌当前，好胜心强的雷战却在心中暗自**打起小九九**。

(From the novel 生死决)

> The enemy was in sight, but the ambitious Lei Zhan was inwardly calculating what he himself stood to gain.

dǎ yǎ mí 打哑谜 (打啞謎)

"Act out riddles"; play charades

♦   哎呀老郭啊，**打什么哑谜**啊？有话快讲出来啊！

(From the TV series 黑洞)

> Come on, Lao Guo. No more charades. If you have something to say, spit it out.

♦   对不起，有话直说，有屁快放，我没功夫听你在这儿**打哑谜**。

> I'm sorry. If you have something to say, just say it. If you want to fart, let it out. I haven't got time to listen to riddles.

dǎ yě shí 打野食

"Hunt for food in the wild"; have affairs

♦   焦起周**嘁嘁牙花子**："昨天晚上趁着乱乎儿，你是不是又跑到外边**打野食**去了？"黄鹿野起誓白咧："老同学，怎么连你也把我当成寻花问柳的淫贼？**天地良心**，我是在玉香的家里打扑克。"

(From the novel 空洞)

Jiao Qizhou picked his teeth as he asked, "Did you take advantage of all the ruckus last night and slip out to have a little fun on the side?" Huang Luye desperately tried to deny it. "How come even you – my old classmate – think I'm some kind of promiscuous ["flower-seeking, willow-visiting"] sex fiend? I swear to God, I was playing poker at Yuxiang's place." [Flowers and willows are traditional metaphors for women, often prostitutes.]

◆ 现在有钱的男人谁不到外面**打野食**？真是应了那句话了：男人有钱就变坏，女人变坏就有钱。

Nowadays every rich man has something on the side. It really proves the old saying, "A rich man turns bad; a bad woman gets rich."

dǎ yì qiāng huàn yí gè dì fang 打一枪换一个地方 (打一槍換一個地方)

"Fire a shot and change to a new position"; keep moving

◆ 如今当厂长凭的全是小聪明。小聪明的特点是**打一枪换一个地方**，从不放空枪。

(From the novel 最后的工厂)

Nowadays all it takes to be a factory director is a little shrewdness. The sign of shrewdness is that you shoot your wad and move on. You don't fire a shot without gaining something.

◆ 现在这人怎么都这么草率呵！不能说结就结，说离就离，**打一枪换一个地方**吧？这不成住旅馆了么？

(From the TV series 编辑部的故事)

How come people are so impulsive these days? You can't just say "marry" and get married, say "divorce" and get divorced, fire a shot and move on. That's like living in hotels [and moving from room to room]!

dǎ zhe dēng long yě nán zhǎo/dǎ zhe dēng long zhǎo bú dào 打着灯笼也难找/打着灯笼找不到 (打著燈籠也難找/打著燈籠找不到)

"Difficult to find even while carrying a lantern"; difficult or impossible to find

◆ 她是天底下**打着灯笼也难找**到的女人，你是瞎了眼，身在福中不知福，今儿你不把她接回来，下半辈子等着你的只有两个字：后悔！

(From the TV series 北京女人)

This woman is one in a million. You're totally blind; you don't recognize your own good fortune. If you don't take her back today, you'll regret it for the rest of your life! [The speaker's friend is seeking a divorce.]

◆ 让我怎么说你好啊？人家上门儿来买咱们的东西，这种**打着灯笼也找不到**的好事儿硬让你给推走了！

I don't even know where to begin. People show up on our doorstep to buy our stuff—an unbelievable piece of luck. And for some reason, you drive them away!

dǎ zhǒng liǎn chōng pàng zi 打肿脸充胖子 (打腫臉充胖子)

"Slap one's face till it's swollen enough to pass for a fat person"; put on a brave or false front

◆ 现在他的真心是恨不得一下子跑出这屋去，但是却又**打肿脸充胖子**，硬要表现出一股血战到底的英雄气概。

(From the novel 夜幕下的哈尔滨)

Now he really wished he could leave the room in a flash of lightning. But he had to put on a brave front and assume the air of a hero who was going to fight to the death.

♦ 行了，别**打肿脸充胖子**了！我知道你们工厂已经三个月没开工资了。

All right. Stop pretending that everything's fine when it's not. I know your factory hasn't paid you in three months.

dǎ zhú yi 打主意

Have ideas or designs; plot to take advantage of somebody

♦ 我看他那眼神儿不对，你等着瞧吧，他一定会**打你的主意**。

(From the TV series 天堂鸟)

I thought he looked suspicious. You just wait. He's got designs on you. [The husband feels that the boss of a large business has designs on his wife.]

♦ 你少**打**小徐**的主意**，人家早就有主儿了，是局长的公子，你呀，死了这条心吧！

Don't get any ideas about Xiao Xu. She's already taken by the son of the bureau chief, so you might as well forget about it!

dǎ zhù 打住

Stop; hold

♦ "那你们那位吴小姐对你的意思…""您**打住**吧，别提她了！"

(From the TV series 手心手背)

"Then what do you make of Miss Wu's interest in you…" "Hold it right there, please. Could you please not mention her?" [Miss Wu is carrying a torch for the second speaker.]

♦ 这件事儿就此**打住**，以后谁也不准再提了。

Let's drop the subject right now. We won't ever mention it again. ["Neither of us will be allowed to mention it again."]

dà bái tiānr shuō mèng huà 大白天儿说梦话 (大白天兒說夢話)

"Speak dream talk in broad daylight"; be engaged in wishful thinking or talk; daydream

♦ 凭这点钱，两口子糊口都成问题，想要得到那些好看的衣裳，好吃的东西，不是**大白天说梦话**么？

(From the novel 兄弟)

With so little money, just finding food for two mouths is a problem. Fancy clothes and fine food are just wishful thinking.

♦ 什么？去马来西亚投资？你别**大白天儿说梦话**了。

What? Invest in Malaysia? Stop daydreaming.

dà bu liǎo 大不了

At most; if worse comes to worst

♦ **大不了**，有什么事情我一个人顶下来。

(From the TV series 黑洞)

If worse comes to worst and there's a problem, I'll take the rap. [The general manager is being investigated. A subordinate shows his loyalty.]

♦ 你救了我儿子的命，现在你有了麻烦，**大不了**用我的命去换。

(From the TV series 黑冰)

You saved my son's life, and now you're in trouble. I'll die in your place if it comes to that.

dà da liē liē 大大咧咧

Careless; without any ceremony; extremely casual

♦ " 你们几位这就盘上道了？ 吃菜呀！" 范惠泽大概看出我的疑惑，大大**咧咧**地往我的布碟里夹了几个花生豆。

(From the novel 百年德性)

"Is this all you're having before you leave? Eat something!" Fan Huize probably noticed my hesitation. She very casually picked up a few peanuts with her chopsticks and put them in my dish.

♦ 你会不会觉得我这个人大大**咧咧**的，没心没肺？

(From the TV series 将爱情进行到底)

Would you think that I'm too casual and heartless?

dà...de 大 ... 的

Right at...; right during...

♦ 大清早儿的，你在这儿瞎吆喝什么！

(From the TV series 今生是亲人)

What are you doing yelling here, so early in the morning?

♦ 你也真是的，大过节的，也不在家里歇会儿。

What's wrong with you? How come you're not home taking it easy on a holiday like this?

dà fa 大发 (大發)

(Beijing dialect) a bundle; a lot

♦ 这是干嘛呢？嗨，您跟我那些朋友讲什么客套！这些家伙这两年玩原始股赚大**发**了，钱烧得都不知道怎么办才好。一套两套红木家具对于他们算个什么嘛！没事儿，拿着！

(From the novel 苍天在上)

What's all this about? You don't need to beat around the bush with my friends. Those guys made a killing in IPOs the last couple of years. They made so much money they don't know what to do with it. One or two suites of rosewood furniture is nothing to them. Don't worry. Take it.

♦ 这一下可真要热闹大**发**了！

(From the TV series 北京女人)

Now you can expect some fireworks! [A man will be working under his ex-wife.]

dà huàn xiě 大换血

"Big change of blood"; a complete change of staff

♦ 刘总准备给大厦来个大**换血**，名单都挑好了。

(From the TV series 黑冰)

General Manager Liu plans to hire all new blood at the hotel. He's already made a list.

◆ 你走以后，公司来了个**大换血**，处级以上的干部全都换成新人了，你恐怕一个都不认识。

> After you left, there was a complete change of personnel in the company. Above the sectional level they're all new. You probably don't know any of them.

dà kuǎn 大款

"Big sum"; rich man; millionaire

◆ 街上**大款**有的是，你干吗找我这个要什么没有的穷光蛋呢？

(From the TV series 手心手背)

> Millionaires are a dime a dozen everywhere you look. Why bother with someone like me, who has no money and nothing to offer? [A man is speaking to a young woman with a romantic interest in him.]

◆ 人家都以为我们家出了**大款**，指不定多**趁**钱呢！

(From the TV series 一年又一年)

> Everybody thinks we now have a millionaire in our family. They probably think we're loaded. [Actually, they are a very poor family.]

dǎ láo yuǎn de 大老远的 (大老遠的)

Very distant; very far

◆ **大老远的**请大家来喝杯茶是为什么呢？咱们大清国遇到麻烦了，我琢磨着还得请你们这些老人儿来帮忙。

(From the TV series 康熙帝国)

> Why did I ask all of you to come so far to drink a cup of tea? Our Great Qing Empire is in trouble. I thought it best to ask you older and experienced men to come help us.

◆ **大老远的**到这儿来，不就是为了我那吃苦的梦吗？

(From the movie 甲方乙方)

> If I came all the way here, wasn't it precisely to realize my dream of experiencing hardship? [The owner of a big company wants to find out what hardship is, so he seeks the help of a company whose business is to fulfill people's dreams and fantasies.]

dà lù cháo tiān, gè zǒu yì biān 大路朝天，各走一边 (大路朝天，各走一邊)

"The highway points skyward; let's each take one side of the road"; part company amicably; each go separate ways

◆ 他认出对手就是电视里通辑的犯人，说："你我无冤无仇，还是**大路朝天各走一边**吧。"

(From the novel 喋血假日)

He recognized his opponent as the criminal wanted on TV, so he said, "There are no scores to settle between you and me. Let's just go our separate ways."

◆ 咱们兄弟的情分到此为止了。往后**大路朝天，各走一边**。要是成心想跟我过不去，就别怪我心狠了。

This is where our friendship ends. From now on you and I go our separate ways. If you insist on making life difficult for me, don't blame me for being harsh.

dà máo 大毛

(Beijing dialect) yuan; buck

◆ 吴叔叔，说起来你也是省政府的一个处长，钱呢，一个月也就挣个一百**大毛**，住的房子像鸽子笼。

(From the novel 金钱世界)

Uncle Wu, it's like this. You're a section chief in the provincial government, but as far as pay goes, you only get a hundred a month, and your room is basically a pigeon coop.

◆ 贫困地区的姑娘能嫁个有北京户口，每月旱涝保收挣五百**大毛**的三级工，就是一步登天了。

(From the short story 小傻子的媳妇)

For a girl from a poor area to marry a level three skilled worker with five hundred bucks in monthly wages and a Beijing city residency permit is like hitting the jackpot on the first try ["climbing to heaven with one leap"].

dà ná 大拿

(Beijing dialect) exclusive or foremost authority; the powers that be

◆ 这是我们主编，**大拿**。

(From the TV series 编辑部的故事)

This is our editor-in-chief, the head honcho.

◆ 你别小看那个年轻人，他是咱们这个城市房地产业的**大拿**，听说还是全国五百首富之一呢！

(From the novel 浮沈商海)

Don't underestimate that young man. He's our city's biggest real estate operator, and I've heard he's one of the five hundred richest men in the country!

dà rén bú jì xiǎo rén guò 大人不记小人过 (大人不記小人過)

(Proverb) "A big man forgives and forgets a small man's mistake"; magnanimously pardon an inferior

◆ 赵总，您是大人不记小人过，我家里上有老下有小，您就饶我这一回吧。

(From the TV series 蓝色马蹄莲)

Mr. Zhao [CEO of the company], you're a forgiving man. I have parents and children to support. Please, let me off the hook this time.

♦   我知道您心善，大人不记小人过，您不会跟我为难的。

I know you're a kindhearted man and won't hold a grudge against a little guy like me. You won't make things difficult for me.

dà shuǐ chōng le lóng wáng miào 大水冲了龙王庙 (大水冲了龍王廟)

"A flood washes away the Temple of the Dragon King"; inflict harm on the wrong person [the Dragon King has jurisdiction over floods]; choose the wrong opponent

♦   你跟这家报纸打官司？你这是大水冲了龙王庙！你不知道发行人的太太是县法院的法官？

You want to sue this newspaper? You're choosing the wrong opponent! The publisher's wife is a judge in the County Court.

♦   对不起，我不知道你是我们局长的儿子，就当是大水冲了龙王庙吧！

I'm sorry. I didn't know you were our bureau director's son. I really shot myself in the foot!

dà wànr 大腕儿 (大腕兒)

"Big wrist"; big shot (short form: 腕儿)

♦   "知道泰勒是谁吗？" "知道，名导演，大腕儿。"

(From the movie 大腕)

"Do you know who Taylor is?" "Yes, I know. He's a famous director, a big shot."

♦   你别以为你丫是腕儿，你丫吹吧你！

(From the movie 北京乐与路)

You son of a bitch, don't think you're a hot shot. Keep bragging, asshole! [A singer is complaining about the lighting in the theater; the manager thinks his demands are unreasonable.]

dà yǎn dèng xiǎo yǎnr 大眼儿瞪小眼儿 (大眼兒瞪小眼兒)

"The big eyes stare at the small eyes"; stare at each other; too stunned to know how to react

♦   "哪个同学先来写出自己的名字？"孩子们互相看了看，一个个大眼瞪小眼，但没有一个人应声上来。

(From the short story 深山空谷读书声)

"Which of you wants to be the first to write his name?" The kids stared bug-eyed at each other, but no one made a sound.

♦   你们这帮蠢货，从来不知道用脑子，出了事儿大眼儿瞪小眼儿，连点主意都没有。

You're a bunch of morons. You don't know how to use your brains. When anything happens, all you can do is stare at each other. You can't come up with a single idea.

dà yǐ (wěi) ba láng/dà yǐ (wěi) ba yīng 大尾巴狼/大尾巴鹰

Tough guy; big shot

♦   我想趁政府正乱的时候跟他们多要点儿人权。好多人都签了，大尾巴狼一个没拉。

(From the novel 一点正经没有)

I think we should take advantage of the upheaval in the government to demand more human rights. People have already signed—at least all the people who count. [The speaker is trying to get signatures on a petition.]

◆　"姓郝的，你欺负人家女的算什么能耐？""行啊，来了充大尾巴鹰的啦。"

(From the novel 空洞)

"Hao, you bastard, picking on a woman, is that all you do?" "OK, we're got a knight in shining armor here."

dài 带

Include; go with; not allowed to. Often used in a negative context, "do not go with (the nature of things)."

◆　走好了，不带翻悔的啊！

(From the novel 东北一家人)

Are you sure about this move? You can't change your mind! [The two are playing chess.]

◆　张经理太不象话了！给人家老李的聘书已经发出去了，还带往回收的。

Manager Zhang is too much. He sent Lao Li an appointment letter. Now he wants to take it back. Can you believe it?

dài dà yánr mào de 戴大沿儿帽儿的 (戴大沿兒帽兒的)

"Someone who wears a big-rimmed hat"; policeman; cop

◆　不出一个月，有些戴大沿帽的人找过小茹，寻问老混的去向，小茹指了指小混说，我儿子也天天找他。

(From the short story 严大混子的花花世界)

In less than a month some cops came looking for Xiao Ru to ask her about Lao Hun's whereabouts. Xiao Ru pointed to Xiao Hun and said, "My son's been looking for him every day, too." [Xiao Ru's husband, Lao Hun, did something illegal and fled the country.]

◆　我觉得这件事儿让她办不合适。听说她丈夫是戴大沿儿帽儿的，到时候给我们捅出去就坏了。

I don't think she's the one for the job. I hear her husband's a cop. We'd be in deep shit if she let it out.

dài gāo mào 戴高帽

"Put on a tall hat"; flatter

◆　"尖子道道多，我看还是让尖子说吧！""你别给我戴高帽，事是吉经理办的，咱啥也不了解，能有啥主意呢？"

(From the novel 剑胆琴心)

"Jianzi [a nickname meaning Sharpie] always has lots of ideas. Let's see what he has to say." "Don't flatter me. Manager Ji was in charge. I don't know anything about it. How would I know what to do?"

◆　"鲁师傅，您是天下第一好人啊！""别给我戴高帽子。"

(From the TV series 水浒传)

"Master Lu, you're the kindest man in the world." "Don't flatter me."

dài jian 待见 (待見)

Look upon with favor; like

◆ 我妈养了六个女儿，我是老疙瘩，没人**待见**，爬在炕上哭一天都没人理。

(From the novel 红尘)

My mother had six daughters. I was the youngest. Nobody cared about me. I could be crawling all over the *kang* crying and nobody would take any notice. [老疙瘩: *dialect*, the youngest child; 疙瘩: lump. In some northern dialects 老 can mean "youngest" rather than "old" as in 老女儿, "youngest daughter."]

◆ 别回家，回什么家呀？回家多没劲，你也没媳妇儿，你爸也不**待见**你。

(From the movie 顽主)

Don't go home. What's the point? You don't have a wife, and your dad doesn't think you're anything special. [In some northern dialects in certain contexts 媳妇儿 means "wife" rather than "daughter-in-law."]

dài lǜ mào zi 戴绿帽子 (戴綠帽子)

"Wear a green hat"; be cuckolded

◆ 一个男人如果不被自己的女人所需要，那也是一种致命的损伤，甚至比单纯地**戴绿帽**子还要难受。

(From the novel 空洞)

For a man to be rejected by his woman is a fatal blow. It's even harder to take than if she just cheats on him.

◆ 我看这次乱子闹大了，要是陈总知道自己**戴了绿帽子**，准得和姓林的拼命。

I think the shit really hit the fan this time. If Manager Chen finds out he's been cheated on, he'll sure want to kill that Lin guy, even if he gets himself killed doing it.

dān dài bù qǐ 担待不起 (擔待不起)

Can't accept the consequences; can't take responsibility

◆ 如果你有三长两短，末将可就**担待不起**了。

(From the TV series 康熙帝国)

If anything should happen to you, I couldn't' take responsibility. I'm just a minor general. [末将: a humble self-reference]

◆ 您给我坐这儿，哪儿都不许去。您要是出点儿事儿我可**担待不起**。

Please do me a favor and sit here. Don't go anywhere. I can't take responsibility if anything happens to you.

dàn chū niǎo lái 淡出鸟来 (淡出鳥來)

"Fucking bland"; take no pleasure in life; find no taste in food

◆ 考了两把托福[TOEFL]，全都是599，这可真是气死活人不偿命。看来新闻系MA的奖学金算没戏了，可这日子不能**淡出鸟来**呀，得折腾。

(From the novel 天涯不归路)

I took the TOEFL twice and both times I got 599. I'm so mad I could die! Seems I have to kiss that scholarship for an M.A. in journalism goodbye, but you can't just roll over and die ["but you can't just let your life become a fucking bore"]. You have to fight.

♦ 省里倒是常常来人，但那有地委书记或专员陪同，他很少能到桌子前。一个月下来，嘴里又**淡出鸟来**。一次实在憋不住，只好到街上饭馆里去喝了一场。

(From the novel 官场)

It's true visitors often come from the province, but the regional party secretary or the commissioner escorts them. He himself seldom gets a chance to sit at the banquet table. As the month goes by his mouth starts feeling dull. One time he just couldn't stand it, and he went to a restaurant on the street and drank to his heart's content.

dàn fán 但凡

As long as; if only

♦ 但凡你还瞧得起我，我就干出个样子来，绝不让他们再**踩乎**咱们。

(From the TV series 黑洞)

As long as you have faith in me, I'll do my best and show them. There's no way I'm going to let them step on us anymore.

♦ 但凡占点儿理，我都可以帮你打这个官司，可这回你们卖的是国家明令禁止的进口旧衣服，我实在没有办法替你们辩护。

(From the novel 耍叉)

If your case had any merit at all, I could help you with it. But this time what you sold was imported second-hand clothes, specifically forbidden by the government. There's really no argument I could make on your behalf.

dāng ér xì 当儿戏 (當兒戲)

Regard as child's play; do not take seriously

♦ 你也不能拿招生当儿戏啊！

(From the TV series 祥符春秋)

You shouldn't treat recruitment like a game, no matter what. [The deputy director of a Henan opera troupe recruited a bunch of pretty girls totally ignorant about the art.]

♦ 你怎么能把这么重要的工作交给一个**黄毛丫头**做？这不是拿公司的生意当儿戏吗？

How could you give such an important job to an inexperienced girl? That's treating the company's business as child's play.

dāng fàn chī 当饭吃 (當飯吃)

"Regard as food"; regard as a livelihood

♦ 劳模管什么用？当饭吃？

(From the TV series 一年又一年)

What good is the title "model worker"? It doesn't put food on the table'! [The speaker's wife works very hard in order to ear the title "model worker."]

◆   你也不琢磨琢磨赚钱的道道儿，就知道看书，书能当饭吃吗？

Why don't you think about how to make some money? All you do is bury your head in books. Can you live off them?

dāng hóu shuǎ 当猴耍 (當猴耍)

"Play with someone as if he were a monkey"; not take someone seriously

◆   钱明明是你出的，你为什么不说，还支了个杨胖子来打马虎眼？你是把我当猴耍了你！

(From the TV series 都市情感)

Obviously it's you who put up the money. Why didn't you say so? Instead, you send Fatso Yang to fool me. Do you think I'm an idiot?

◆   说好了五五分成，赚到钱你又变卦了，你想把我当猴儿耍？

We agreed to split fifty-fifty, but now that we got the money, you change your mind? Who do you think I am?

dāng huí shìr 当回事儿 (當回事兒)

"Regard it as a thing"; regard it as something important

◆   我刚开始没把它当回事儿，当回事儿已经晚了。

(From the TV series 贫嘴张大民的幸福生活)

At first I didn't think it was important. When I realized, it was too late. [Speaking of drug addiction.]

◆   男人是不是有了钱，就把女人不当回事儿了？

(From the TV series 一年又一年)

Once they have some money, do men just stop taking women seriously?

dāng jiā de 当家的 (當家的)

Head of household; husband; master or leader

◆   往后您就是当家的了，你吩咐吧！

(From the movie 红高粱)

From now on you're the head of the household. Just tell us what to do. [The boss died and his wife has taken over.]

◆   您二位千万别让我们当家的知道这件事儿。

(From the TV series 今生是亲人)

I beg you two, don't let my husband find out about this. [Their sons were switched at birth twenty years ago.]

dāng kē cài 当棵菜 (當棵菜)

"Regard as a vegetable"; regard as something important

◆   你拿我当不当棵菜是你的事，我是你闺女的男人这谁也改不了。

(From the novel 空洞)

I don't care if you take me seriously or not, but you can't change the fact that I'm your daughter's husband.

♦ 我劝你少说两句，你以为你是谁啊？在这个公司里，没人把你当棵菜。

I advise you to shut up. Who do you think you are? At this company nobody takes you seriously.

dāng le biǎo zi hái yào lì pái fang 当了婊子还要立牌坊 (當了婊子還要立牌坊)

"Work as a prostitute and still want a monument to one's chastity"; be hypocritical; have it both ways

♦ 要不然怎么说你这人常有理呢，你是既当婊子又立牌坊，造成损失了还落一个大手笔。

(From the novel 永不瞑目)

That's why I say you're never wrong. You always manage to have it both ways. The loss was your fault, and yet you managed to make a bundle for yourself.

♦ 你也真想得出来，大把大把的从公司里搞钱，送人情，还要评什么廉政标兵，这不是当了婊子还要立牌坊吗？

Only you could have thought of this. You passed out bundles of the company's money as gifts, and now you want to be the poster child for integrity? That's like a whore wanting to be honored for chastity. [廉政标兵: lián zhèng biāo bīng, a fine example of a clean government official; an example of an upright politician]

dāng miàn luó duì miàn gǔ 当面锣对面鼓 (當面鑼對面鼓)

"One cymbal faces the other and the drum meets the drumstick"; confront someone face to face

♦ 这事儿没有别的办法，就得叔叔阿姨带着刘震当面锣对面鼓地跟他们说清楚。

(From the TV series 今生是亲人)

There's only one solution: for the uncle and aunt to go in person with Liu Zhen and straighten it out with them once and for all. [The speaker wants to inform Liu Zhen's parents that Liu Zhen is their biological son.]

♦ 最近公司里有不少流言，我今天把大家都请来，就是要当面锣对面鼓地把事情讲清楚。

Lately a lot of rumors are going around the company. I asked everyone to come today so I can clear up the matter face to face.

dāng yǎ ba mài 当哑巴卖 (當啞巴賣)

"Be sold as a dumb man"; be mistaken for someone inarticulate

♦ 你可别没事找事，我告诉你，你别出什么风头，提什么意见，谁也不会把你当哑巴卖了！

(From the novel 春寒夜雨)

Don't stir up trouble. I'm telling you, don't stick your neck out and make waves. No one's going to think you're dumb if you keep quiet.

♦ 说吧，说吧！不说回头有人把你当哑巴卖了。

(From the TV series 贫嘴张大民的幸福生活)

Go ahead, talk. If you don't speak, afterwards people will think you don't know how. [A man is being sarcastic to his big-mouth brother.]

dǎng hèngr 挡横儿 (擋橫兒)
"Slide in and block"; meddle; interfere

◆   人家爸爸教育孩子，你挡什么横儿？

(From the novel 我是你爸爸)
I'm his father. I'm trying to teach him a lesson. Why are you meddling in our affairs? [When a father hits his son, classmates try to put a stop to it.]

◆   我不想知道你是谁，你既敢出手挡横，也别想活着回去。

(From the novel 无名岛)
I don't care who you are. Since you were fool enough to butt in, don't expect to get out with your life. [The speaker, a murderer, is threatening someone who tried to prevent the murder from happening.]

dàng zi 当子/档子 (當子/檔子)
(Measure word) item

◆   咱们俩这当子事儿我想了两天了，还是没想明白

(From the movie 有话好好说)
I've been thinking about what happened to us the last couple of days, but I still haven't figured it out.

◆   那当子事儿都过去两年了，你怎么还挂在嘴边儿上？

It's been two years since it happened. Why are you still talking about it?

dáo chi 捣持 (搗持)
(Beijing dialect) "Grind"; fuss over; obsess over

◆   我这么捣持，就是想赛过那些小妖精。

(From the TV series 手心手背)
I've been dolling myself up just to outdo those bimbos. [The speaker is afraid of losing her husband.]

◆   你都这一把年纪了，还瞎捣持什么？我都不敢跟你一块儿上街了！

You're not a spring chicken anymore. Why all the fuss? I'm even afraid to walk down the street with you.

dào chā ménr 倒插门儿 (倒插門兒)
"Bolt the door backwards or from the other side"; move in with the bride's family after marriage

◆   我想倒插门儿，我妈还不干呢！

(From the TV series 贫嘴张大民的幸福生活)
Even if I wanted to move in with your family after we're married, my mother would never agree. [A bridegroom is speaking to his future mother-in-law.]

◆   只要家里有良田千顷，囤里有粮，桌上有肉，吃香的喝辣的穿金带银的—— 倒插门过去我都干！

(From the TV series 编辑部的故事)

Sure I'd move in with the bride's family. Just as long as they have thousands of acres of good land, barns full of grain, meat on the table, fancy food, and expensive clothes!

dào...fènr shàng 到···份儿上 (到···份兒上)

When or if it comes to this (extent, degree, state, etc.)

♦   都闹**到这份儿上**了，还不肯说实话么？

(From the novel 我是你爸爸)

It's come to this, and you still won't speak the truth? [The speaker thinks the other person's son got into trouble because of his poor upbringing.]

♦   我要是和局长**到了那份儿上**，早就升副局长了。

If the director and I were that close, I'd have been promoted to deputy director long ago.

dào hǎo 倒好

Who'd have thought?

♦   我送你出国，是让你回来帮帮我，你可**倒好**，你倒帮起张大庆来了！

(From the TV series 天堂鸟)

I sent you overseas so you could come back and help me. Who'd have thought you'd help Zhang Daqing instead! [The speaker is upset that his daughter is helping a rival.]

♦   人家**求爷爷告奶奶**去帮你借钱，你**倒好**，一顿饭就吃了三千多！

I have been asking everyone I know to loan you money. And here you go spending over three thousand yuan on a meal!

dào kǔ shuǐr 倒苦水儿 (倒苦水兒)

"Pour out bitter water"; relate one's suffering

♦   代克这次是真的气晕了头, 居然鬼使神差地又去找到已分手快半年的咪咪**倒苦水**, 于是咪咪又找男朋友博士**倒苦水**。那位目光深邃的博士很快就找上门来，声言要和代克认真谈谈。

(From the novel 早安，糜鼠)

This time Daike got so mad he couldn't think straight. God knows how he got the idea of telling his sad tale to Mimi, even though it was already six months since they broke up. Mimi then dumped it all on her PhD boyfriend. That gimlet-eyed PhD quickly turned up on Daike's doorstep and proclaimed that they needed to have a serious talk.

♦   你干脆**把肚子里的苦水都倒出来**吧，别瞒着妈了！

(From the TV series 失乐园)

Why don't you tell me what's making you miserable? Don't keep it from your mother.

dào liǎor 到了儿 (到了兒)

When the time comes; in the end

♦   把我们折腾一六**够**，**到了儿**又说不干了。

(From the TV series 今生是亲人)

They put us through an ordeal, but when push came to shove, they backed out. [At first they said they wanted to exchange their sons who had been switched at birth, but then they suddenly changed their minds.]

♦　我是处处提防，可到了儿还是上了那小子的当。

I was always careful, but in the end I still fell for that bastard's scam.

dāo zi zuǐ dòu fu xīn 刀子嘴豆腐心

"A mouth sharp as a knife and a heart soft as tofu"; having a sharp tongue but a soft heart; a heart of gold under a rough exterior

♦　他这个人是刀子嘴豆腐心，尤其是对下面的干警，那真是没的说。

(From the TV series 大雪无痕)

He's got a heart of gold under a rough exterior. When it comes to how he treats his cops, he's the best there is.

♦　李小姐笑着说，瞧瞧你又说笑了，谁不知你是个豆腐心肠刀子嘴。

(From the novel 红檀板)

Miss Li laughed, "You're kidding again. Everyone knows you talk tough, but you're really a softie.

dào zuǐ de ròu 到嘴的肉

"The meat that reaches one's mouth"; a bird in the hand; a sure thing, benefit, or profit

♦　要不要给你盯着点儿，省得到嘴的肉再飞了？

(From the TV series 北京女人)

Do you want me to keep an eye on her for you so that your bird in the hand doesn't fly away again? [The speaker is offering to help keep an eye on the other man's fiancée. His previous girlfriend left him for someone else.]

♦　老黄这人真不够朋友，咱们辛辛苦苦打开了家用跑步机的市场，他的商店突然也卖起跑步机来了，这不是抢咱们到嘴的肉吗？

Lao Huang's really not much of a friend. We work our butts off to open up a market for treadmills, and suddenly he starts selling treadmills at his store. He's taking the bread out of our mouths.

...de huang …得慌

A colloquial intensifier; very; extremely

♦　大叔，你就让他比一次，免得他心里憋屈得慌。

(From the TV series 大赢家)

Uncle, let him race this once. Otherwise he'll die of frustration. [The nephew wants to race horses against a Mongolian jockey.]

♦　在现今的生活中，他觉得自己简直是个废物！"窝囊废！"他自己骂着自己，这样心里才不堵得慌。

(From the novel 立体交叉桥)

He felt that in his present life he was just a piece of trash. "You loser!" He railed at himself, and only then could he breathe easier.

...de xīn dōu yǒu le …的心都有了

"Even have the heart to do…"; would go so far as

♦　告诉你吧，当时我炸什刹海的心都有了。

(From the TV series 其实男人最辛苦)

I'm telling you, at the time I felt like bombing Shichahai (an old neighborhood in Beijing). [The speaker was cheated out of all his hard-earned money.]

◆ 我看孔良是急得连跳江的**心都有了**！

(From the TV series 大赢家)

I think Kong Liang is so upset he's ready to throw himself in the river. [Kong Liang is facing vicious competition.]

...de yí lèng yí lèng de ...得一楞一楞的

Surprised; frozen or speechless with shock

◆ 那时候你跟苏麻〖人名〗顶**得**朕**一楞一楞的**。

(From the TV series 康熙帝国)

In those days you and Su Ma defied me so bitterly that I was at a loss for words.

◆ 现在的大孩子都这样，小鸥当时不也是这样吗？把她妈气**得一楞一楞的**。

(From the TV series 一年又一年)

Nowadays 'teenagers are all like this. Wasn't it the same with Xiao Ou? She drove her mother to distraction.

dé le ba 得了吧

Forget it; stop; come off it

◆ 技术？**得了吧**！我还不知道她是谁？

(From the TV series 古船、女人和网)

Tech skills? Come off it. You don't think I know who she is? [The speaker thinks she is too young to know anything about technical skills.]

◆ "减肥？**得了吧**你。你以为长点肉那么容易呢。"他**打着哈哈儿**，晃悠着闪亮的光头走了。

(From the novel 百年德性)

"Lose weight? Are you kidding? You think it's easy to put the weight on?" He laughed and walked away shaking his bald pate.

dé lǐ bú ràng rén 得理不让人 (得理不讓人)

"Will not yield to people when in the right"; will not easily forgive others; won't give others a break

◆ 你别**得理不让人**行不行？你看看你自己都干了什么事！

(From the TV series 将爱情进行到底)

Don't you get all high and mighty with me. Look what you yourself did!

♦ "淘气是小孩子的天性嘛，你受不了还来做幼师？""你这女孩子怎么这样**得理不让人**？我是凶了一点也用不着说我做不了幼师吧？"

"Mischief is in the nature of little kids. If you can't take it, why become a kindergarten teacher?" "What's with you, a young girl like you? Give me a break. Maybe I came on a little strong, but did you have to say I shouldn't be a kindergarten teacher?"

dé pián yi mài guāi 得便宜卖乖 (得便宜賣乖)

"Think you're clever when you get a lucky break"; take credit for good luck (short form: 卖乖)

♦ 丈夫："你当是我跟你这儿**显派**呢？我是说这老外他**烧包**。"妻子："别**得了便宜卖乖**了！"

(From the TV series 贫嘴张大民的幸福生活)

Husband: "You think I'm bragging? I'm just telling you what a showoff that foreigner was." Wife: "You should be thanking your lucky stars instead of boasting!" [A husband who works as a janitor at a luxury hotel tells his wife that a foreigner gave him a one-hundred-dollar tip.]

♦ 天天陪客**吃白食**，还**卖乖**。什么吃得太痛苦了，好象让你们去受刑似的。

(From the novel 大厂)

Every day you take customers to restaurants and eat free, and you bitch about it? As if it were some kind of hardship!

dé ráo rén chù qiě ráo rén 得饶人处且饶人 (得饒人處且饒人)

Forgive people whenever you can; forgive and forget

♦ 邵常委，俗话说：**得饶人处且饶人**，我劝你不要故意和我们天宇公司过不去，否则对我们双方都没有好处。

(From the TV series 大江东去)

Representative Shao, as the saying goes, "live and let live." I urge you not to create problems for our Tianyu Company. That's not to the advantage of either of us. [Shao, a local People's Congress representative, is questioning the methods Tianyu Company used to obtain a bid.]

♦ 他们这次是做得不地道，不过倒也没造成什么大的损失，常言道，**得饶人处且饶人**，就**放他们一码**吧！

What they did this time wasn't right, but it didn't lead to any great loss. As they say, "forgive and forget." Let them off the hook.

dé xing 德性/德行

(Sarcastic) "virtuous character or behavior"; a real prize; way; manner

♦ 你这孩子怎么跟你哥一个**德性**？烦不烦啊？

(From the TV series 都市情感)

How come you're a real prize, just like your brother? Think you can annoy me even more? [Both her daughter and her son are too proud to use their connections to help their mother.]

♦   房管局的人真够**德性**的，打了那么多电话也不来修，这要是下起雨来怎么办呢？。

How come you're a real prize, just like your brother? Think you can annoy me even more? [Both her daughter and her son are too proud to use their connections to help their mother.]

The Housing Maintenance people are really something. I've called so many times and they still haven't shown up and fixed it. What are we going to do if it rains?

děi shéi gēn shéi 逮谁跟谁 (逮誰跟誰)

"With whoever one can catch"; with everyone and anyone

♦   老布这人是**逮谁跟谁**送秋波。

(From the movie 一见钟情)

Lao Bu flirts with everything in sight.

♦   这两天老王也不知道怎么了，**逮谁跟谁**急。

I don't know what's with Lao Wang the last couple of days, snarling at everyone he meets.

děng zhe qiáo 等着瞧 (等著瞧)

wait and see

♦   我会让你和冯骁大吃一惊的！你**等着瞧**吧！

(From the TV series 北京女人)

I'm going to make you and Feng Xiao sit up and take notice. Just wait and see. [The speaker is talking to his ex-wife. Feng Xiao is her boss and new lover.]

♦   小凤说，我没找到她，她怎么会不答应呢？她是我姑妈呀！汉明立刻冷笑了一声说，空欢喜一场，你**等着瞧**吧。

(From the short story 过渡)

Xiao Feng said, "I didn't find her. There's no way she would have turned me down. She's my aunt, after all." Hanming gave a quick, sarcastic laugh. "You're fooling yourself," he said. "Just wait and see." [The couple have to find temporary housing. The wife thinks she can move in with her aunt for a while. Her husband disagrees.']

dēng 蹬

Kick; dump; ditch

♦   听说你把我表妹给**蹬**了？

(From the movie 一见钟情)

I hear you dumped my cousin.

♦   你怎么和她吹了？是她**蹬**了你还是你**蹬**了她？

How come you two broke up? Did she dump you, or did you dump her?

dèng bí zi shàng liǎn 蹬鼻子上脸 (蹬鼻子上臉)

"If you give someone your nose, they'll take a ladder to climb your face"; give someone an inch, and they'll take a mile (variation: 给鼻子上脸; short form: 上脸)

♦   忍，得有个限度，到了别人**蹬鼻子上脸**这份儿上，我不能再忍着了。忍，岂不是让人拿我当**软柿子捏**着玩。

(From the novel 百年德性)

Tolerance? Well, there's a limit to tolerance. When someone tries to walk all over you to that extent, I can't put up with it. Tolerance, well, that's just another name for being a punching bag.

◆ 这几天谢跃进真是**给鼻子上脸**，有时半夜也有女人往家里打电话，弄得贺玉梅心里起火。

(From the novel 大厂)

The last couple of days Xie Yuejin has been really rubbing her nose in it. Sometimes women call him at midnight, which just ticks He Yumei off to no end. [The wife, He Yumei, has tried to pretend she doesn't know about her husband's womanizing, but he is becoming less and less discreet.]

◆ 农民都这样，你越对他客气，他就越**上脸**，就敢在你家地毯上大模大样地吐痰。

(From the novel 大厂)

Peasants are all like that. The more polite you are, the more they presume. They get so they'll spit on your carpet right in front of you.

dēng tuǐr 蹬腿儿 (蹬腿兒)

"Kick one's leg"; die; kick the bucket

◆ "我不想做女强人，我就是想做个完整的女人。" "你爸爸一**蹬腿儿**归西，你妈就不完整了？"

(From the TV series 北京女人)

Daughter: "I don't want to be Superwoman; I just want to be a complete woman." Mother: "If your dad died, would that make me an incomplete woman?" [The mother wants her daughter to concentrate on her career rather than rush into a remarriage.]

◆ 你们几个就知道花钱，等老爷子一**蹬腿儿**，你们准得喝西北风。

All any of you know how to do is spend money. When I'm out of the picture you'll starve.

dí gu 嘀咕

"Whisper"; wonder; suspect; worry

◆ 电梯是个很奇怪的地方。封闭的匣子关进两个人，除了互相琢磨互相猜测互相犯**嘀咕**之外，想不出还能做什么。

(From the novel 白领公寓)

An elevator's a strange place. Two people enter a sealed box, and besides trying to figure each other out, size each other up, and wonder about each other, they've got nothing to do.

◆ 我母亲有时在我面前**嘀咕**我老婆的种种不是，我总是诺诺，对母亲说，你老人家别跟她计较，当心气出毛病，让我去批评她。

(From the short story 家庭风景二十章)

My mother sometimes complains to me about my wife [不是: faults, weaknesses]. I always agree with her and say, "Mom, don't quibble with her. Just don't upset yourself. Let me straighten her out."

dí tīng 迪厅 (迪廳)

"Disco parlor"; disco

◆ 说白了，你这是上**迪厅**招事儿去你。

(From the TV series 今生是亲人)

In a word, you're going to the disco looking for trouble.

♦ 你是对的。我不是个好人，以后在也别去迪厅，那儿没什么好人。
(From the television play 老宋和他的女儿)
You're right. I'm not a good man. From now on I won't go to discos. People there are no good.

dǐr diào/chuān 底儿掉/穿 (底兒掉/穿)
"The bottom falls off"; completely; thoroughly

♦ 我一警察找她，容易让她起疑。你不是知道她一个**底儿掉**吗，找她，肯定费不了什么事。
(From the novel 百年德性)
I'm a policeman. If I approach her, she'll likely get suspicious. You know her inside out, don't you? If you make the approach there won't be a problem.

♦ 你是不是觉得你一个人就能把这个案子搞个**底儿穿**？
(From the TV series 大雪无痕)
You think you can get to the bottom of this case all by yourself? [A police chief is criticizing his subordinate's arrogance.]

dǐ zi 底子
"Foundation"; grounding

♦ 凭你的**底子**，准能考上研究生。
(From the TV series 一年又一年)
With your solid foundation, you're sure to get into graduate school.

♦ 他们都是有点**底子**的人家，待人接物很讲究礼仪。
(From the short story 家庭风景二十章)
They're a family with background. When they deal with people they are particular about manners.

diǎ 嗲
(Shanghai dialect) act or sound ultra girlish or feminine

♦ 苟云齐同学，**拜托**，请不要再**嗲**声嗲气的说话了，好不好？
(From the novel 梦幻魔界王)
Please, Gou Yunqi, stop talking in that affected tone of voice. I beg you.

♦ 不就欣欣小姐吗？太**嗲**了，**没把我**恶心死！
(From the TV series 其实男人最辛苦)
You mean Miss Xinxin? She's so syrupy I could die puking. [Miss Xinxin is a radio show host.]

diān liang 掂量
"Weigh and measure"; think; weigh mentally

♦ 我**掂量**了一下，咱哥儿几个谁都有难处。
(From the TV series 贫嘴张大民的幸福生活)

I've given it some thought. In this family we've all got our own problems. [Siblings are trying to decide how to divide the money left by their deceased younger sister.]

◆   我觉得这事儿有点儿**不明不白**，大哥，您可得好好**掂量掂量**，别中了他们的奸计。

There's something fishy about it. Brother, you'd better think it over. Don't fall for their shady schemes.

diàn bèi 垫背 (墊背)

"Cushion to prop up the back"; bring up the rear

◆   你就不想想，你们不让我好活，我能让你们活好吗？我就是死，也要拉上几个**垫背**的，你可想好喽！

(From the novel 空洞)

Has it ever occurred to you that if you make my life difficult I won't make yours easy? If I'm going down, some of you are going with me. Think it over!

◆   你不想活是你的事儿，别拿我当**垫背**的！

If you don't want to live, that's your business. Don't drag me along for company.

diàn dēng pàor/dēng pàor 电灯泡儿/灯泡儿 (電燈泡兒/燈泡兒)

"Electric light bulb/light bulb"; fifth wheel

◆   我可不做你们俩的**灯泡儿**。

(From the TV series 大雪无痕)

There's no way I'm going to be a fifth wheel. [The speaker changes his mind about going to dinner with a friend when he learns the friend actually has a date with his girlfriend.]

◆   甲："过去谈了几个（对象），都吹了，眼前么，有一个。哎！你别走啊！"〖正说着那个人来了〗乙："你的'眼前'都来了，我可不愿意当**电灯泡儿**。"

(From the TV series 将爱情进行到底)

A: "I dated a few in the past, but it never worked out. But right now I've got someone. Hey, where are you going?" B: "Your "someone" just got here. I don't want to be a fifth wheel."

diào liàn zi 掉链子 (掉鏈子)

"Drop the link"; drop the ball

◆   你平常不是**人缘儿**挺好的吗？怎么关键时刻**掉链子**啊？

(From the TV series 今生是亲人)

Ordinarily, you're quite popular, aren't you? How could you drop the ball at the crucial moment?

◆   易军，留点精神气儿，明天你是主练，车、仪式、订桌，可别**掉链子**。

(From the novel 邪性)

Yijun, save some of your energy. Tomorrow you're the crucial player. You have to take care of the cars, the ceremony, and reserving tables at the restaurant. You can't drop the ball. [Yijun is coordinating a wedding.]

diào qián yǎnr lǐ qù le 掉钱眼儿里去了 (掉錢眼兒裏去了)

"Fall into the hole of a coin" (ancient Chinese coins had a square hole in the middle); be obsessed with money

◆ 我看你回国来就像**掉进了钱眼儿里**，张口闭口就是挣钱、挣钱，你小小年纪，没有别的追求了吗？

(From the novel 出国留学的少男少女)

> Seems to me ever since you came back to China you've been obsessed with money. All you talk about is money, money, money. You're so young. Don't you have any other dreams?

◆ 什么？看一眼就要收三百块钱！你**掉钱眼儿里去了**吧。

> What? You charge people three hundred yuan for just taking a look? Don't you care about anything but money? [A landlord charges prospective tenants for checking out the apartment.]

diào sb de wèi kǒu 吊/钓Sb的胃口 (吊/釣Sb的胃口)

Whet somebody's' appetite

◆ 千姿没有见过黄老板，天天收到他送的鲜花，又不见这人到后台纠缠，便对他充满了好奇心。方佩在一旁冷眼看着，提醒女儿："他这是**吊你的胃口**呢。"

(From the short story 一篇看后不会后悔的小说)

> Qianzi has never met the boss, Huang. Every day she gets fresh flowers from him, but he never appears backstage to bother her. So she's full of curiosity about him. Fang Pei casts a cold eye on the matter and reminds her daughter, "He's just leading you on." [Qianzi is a singer.]

◆ 你别听他花言巧语的，这是**钓咱们的胃口**呢，懂不懂？

> Don't listen to his slick talk! He's just trying to get us hooked. Don't you understand?

diē fèn/diū fèn 跌份/丢份

Lose face; be humiliated

◆ 咱北京人事事都不能**跌份**，瞧北京电视台的晚会一晚上就捐了多少钱啊！

(From the TV series 北京女人)

> We Beijingers don't want to look bad. Didn't you see how much money was raised in one evening on that BTV show? [The speaker is talking about donations to a disaster relief fund.]

◆ 你别说外头了，我自个儿都觉着**丢份**。

(From the TV drama 耷晃胡同)

Forget about everyone else. I'm embarrassed for myself. [The service manager of a building management agency has repeatedly failed to fix a problem.]

diē pò yǎn jìngr 跌破眼镜儿 (跌破眼鏡兒)

"Eyeglasses fall down and are smashed to pieces"; greatly shocked

◆   "怎么，她就是这个神奇豪宅的主人？"她愕然问。"**跌破眼镜**了吧。太年轻了，是不是？"

(From the novel 纽约情殇)

"What? She owns that incredible mansion?" she asked in amazement. "Completely floors you, right? After all, she's so young."

◆   他们出的这种汽车一个月卖了两千多辆，把专家的**眼镜儿**都**跌破**了。

More than two thousand units of this car model of theirs sold in a month. The experts were amazed.

dǐng míngr 顶名儿 (頂名兒)

"Assume the name of"; pretend to be someone else

◆   杨胖子只是**顶**了个赞助的**名儿**，其实钱还是王留根出的。

(From the TV series 都市情感)

Fatso Yang was a sponsor only in name. Actually, the money came from Wang Liugen.

◆   我觉得这位高经理只是**顶名儿**的，这地下赌场一定有后台老板。

I think Manager Gao is just a front. The real owner of this underground casino is behind the scenes.

dǐng shìr 顶事儿 (頂事兒)

Be effective or sufficient; do the trick

◆   两个新人的衣服被褥和零七碎八下来，三五十块钱根本不**顶事**。

(From the novel 平凡的世界)

Thirty to fifty bucks for all the clothing, bedding, and effects of the newlyweds is hardly enough. [下来: in total]

◆   我礼也送了，好话也说了，可是一点儿都不**顶事儿**，人家环保局就是要重罚我们。

I bribed, I begged, but it didn't help. The EPA wants to slap us with a huge fine.

dìng xīn wán 定心丸

"Heart-calming pill"; reassurance

◆   皇上给明相吃了**定心丸**了。

(From the TV series 康熙帝国)

The emperor gave the prime minister his word [not to punish him].

◆   姑娘的意思再明确不过了，等于给焦安国吃了**定心丸**。

(From the novel 空洞)

The girl couldn't have been any clearer about her intentions. She as good as gave Jiao Anguo her word. [The girl accepted Jiao Anguo's proposal.]

diū rén xiàn yǎn 丢人现眼 (丢人現眼)

Humiliate oneself or someone publicly

◆ 你以后别开着那辆旧吉普到处乱跑，给我丢人现眼。

(From the TV series 大雪无痕)

From now on don't embarrass me by driving around in that old jeep. [A police chief is lecturing a subordinate.]

◆ 快回家去，别给我在这儿丢人现眼。

Go home right away. Don't make a spectacle of yourself. [A man rebukes his wife, who is throwing a public tantrum.]

dōng jiā cháng xī jiā duǎnr/zhāng jiā cháng lǐ jiā duǎnr 东家长西家短儿/张家长李家短儿(東家長西家短兒/張家長李家短兒)

"The long and short of the neighbors to the east and west," or "the long and short of the Li and Zhang families"; gossip about others

◆ 母亲话很多，但是，不是**东家长西家短**的琐碎、更不是嫌弃这不满那的啰嗦。

(From the novel 两代情)

My mother talks a lot, but she doesn't gossip, much less go on and on about how nothing satisfies her.

◆ 你们几个真没出息，就会在一块儿议论些**张家长李家短儿**的事儿，说到正事儿你们一点儿主意也没有！

You're all good for nothing. All you know how to do is gossip about others. When it comes to serious discussion you don't have a single idea.

dōng yì láng tou xī yí gàng/bàng zi 东一榔头西一杠/棒子 (東一榔頭西一杠/棒子)

"Hammer to the east, club to the west"; unfocused, ineffective attack or work

◆ 你总是这么**东一榔头西一杠子**的，也不是长久之计啊！

(From the TV series 今生是亲人)

You just take off in all directions. That's hardly a long-term plan! [He doesn't have steady employment; he just does odd jobs.]

◆ 城建资金要集中起来花，在市中心盖几个象样儿的大楼。总是**东一榔头西一棒子**的，钱没少花，效果看不出来。

We've got to use the urban construction fund where it counts, and put up a few impressive buildings in the town center. If we take a scattershot approach, we'll spend a lot of money to little effect.

dòng yì zhǐ tou 动一指头 (動一指頭)

Lift a finger

◆ 谁敢**动我**妹**一指头**，我就跟谁拼了！

(From the TV series 黑洞)

If someone so much as lifts a finger against my sister, I'll really give it to him!

◆   只要你**动**一**指头**，我就要你好看。

(From the movie 顽主)

If you make a move, I'll eat you alive.

dòng zhēn gér de 动真格儿的 (動真格兒的)

For real

◆   这回可是**动真格儿的**了，区里都开大会了！

(From the movie 洗澡)

This time it's for real. The district already held a meeting. [For a long time there had been talk about tearing down the neighborhood for reconstruction.]

◆   我相信焦书记不会难为你，表面上会发一顿脾气，但不会**动真格的**。

(From the novel 都市危情)

I don't think Secretary Jiao will give you any problems. He'll make a public show of anger, but it won't do anything.

dōu quān zi 兜圈子

"Go around in circles"; talk in circles

◆   结婚就结婚吧，**兜**那么大**圈子**干什么啊？

(From the TV series 贫嘴张大民的幸福生活)

If you want to get married, go ahead. Why didn't you come out and say so? [A family is discussing housing arrangements for newlyweds.]

◆   你想干什么？别**兜圈子**了，说吧！

(From the TV series 大赢家)

What do you want? Don't beat around the bush. Spit it out!

dǒu dà de zì rèn bú dào yì kuāng 斗大的字认不到一筐 (鬥大的字認不到一筐)

"Not know enough bucket-size characters to fill up even one container"; be barely literate

◆   他们什么东西？祖上要饭儿孙还要饭，**斗大的字**一家子**认**全了算来**不到一筐**。

(From the novel 一点正经没有)

They are nobodies. They've been beggars for generations. If you put together all the characters the whole family can read, they're still illiterate.

◆   他是个粗人，**斗大的字认不到一筐**，看家护院的事儿还行，但绝对不是当经理的料儿。

He's a simple man, barely literate. He'd be OK as a security guard, but he's definitely not management material.

dǒu la 抖落

"Shake out"; reveal; expose

◆   这事儿我不想给你**抖落**出来，你自己倒说出来了。

(From the TV series 祥符春秋)

I wasn't going to expose you. You did it to yourself. [Speaking of illegal business dealings.]

♦ 你别把他逼急了，他要是急了说不定会把咱们那些违法的事儿都**抖落**出来，那麻烦就大了！

> Don't drive him into a corner. If he feels cornered, he'll probably rat on our illegal activities. Then we're in big trouble.

dòu ké sou 逗咳嗽

"Tease a cough"; act provocatively; argue for the sake of arguing

♦ 轻的，人家截住了你，跟你**逗会儿咳嗽**；重的，推着自行车过来，往车身上来一下子。哪样你受得了？

(From the novel 耍叉)

> In the best case scenario, the bicyclist will block you and give you a lecture. In the worst case, he'll push his bike over and slam it against your car. Which one can you put up with? [Describing to a motorist what will happen if he has a run-in with a bicyclist].

♦ 你别跟我这儿**逗咳嗽**了，有什么要求直说！

> Don't take all day. If you want to ask for something, get to the point!

dòu mèn zi 逗闷子 (逗悶子)

Joke around; do something just for the fun of it

♦ "接你的电话，我直胆儿小。我心说咱是守法公民，没犯事儿呀。怎么分局的人找我呢。""别**逗闷子**了，跟你说点正事儿。"

(From the novel 百年德性)

> "When you called, I was really scared. I said to myself, I'm a law-abiding citizen. I haven't done anything against the law. Why would the police want to talk to me?" "Don't fool around. I have something serious to discuss with you."

♦ 我看这样吧，勇刚。我这儿也挺忙，不能老陪着你**逗闷子**，咱们效率高点，拟个征婚广告，先征着。

(From the TV series 编辑部的故事)

> Why don't we do it this way, Yonggang? I'm rather busy here. I can't play games with you. Let's be more efficient, draw up a personal ad, put it out there [and then see what happens].

dú mēnr 独闷儿 (獨悶兒)

Monopolize something and keep quiet about it

♦ 拐子，有好处别**独闷儿**，你要人家事主一万银子，这里有我多少？

(From the TV series 大宅门)

Gimpy, don't hog it all. You want the client to pay ten thousand, but how much do I get?

◆ 要是没有我们大伙儿帮忙，这笔钱你可根本赚不到，你可别想**独闷儿**！

If we hadn't helped, there's no way you could have made all this money. Don't imagine you can keep it all for yourself.

dú yí fènr 独一份儿 (獨一份兒)

One and only

◆ 解放军一进城，旧警察们都茫然不知所措，有的跑了，有的脱下黑警服干别的营生去了。像周栓宝这样还照常上班抓小偷的，全北平城大概也是**独一份儿**，难怪别人都觉得好笑。

(From the novel 警察世家)

After the People's Liberation Army entered the city, the old policemen didn't know what to do. Some fled. Some took off their black police uniforms and got other jobs. Zhou Shuanbao was probably the only one in the whole city of Beijing [renamed Beiping by the Nationalist Government] who still went to work as usual and nabbed thieves. No wonder other people thought it was funny.

◆ 放心吧，咱们这个店虽然小点儿，货色在这北京城里可是**独一份儿**。

Don't worry. Our shop may be small, but our stock is unique in Beijing.

dù zi lǐ de huí chóng/dù zi lǐ de chóng zi 肚子里的蛔虫/肚子里的虫子 (肚子裏的蛔蟲/肚子裏的蟲子)

"A roundworm in someone's stomach"; be privy to someone's thoughts

◆ 我又不是他**肚子里的虫子**，怎么知道这信里写的什么？

(From the TV series 康熙帝国)

I'm not inside his head. How could I know what's in the letter?

◆ "雅之，你真是我**肚子里的蛔虫**，竟知道我想吃沙茶火锅！"

(From the novel 情在深时)

"Yazhi, you really know me inside out. However did you know I like hotpot with barbecue sauce?"

duì fu 对付 (對付)

1. deal with; make do 2. inappropriate

◆ 我这儿也没有饮料，就**对付**点儿凉水吧。

(From the TV series 大雪无痕)

I don't have any drinks here. Can you make do with cold water?

◆ 我怕问得不**对付**又给问炸了，她倔脾气一上来假的也变成真的了。

(From the TV series 贫嘴张大民的幸福生活)

I'm afraid that if I ask her in the wrong way she'll blow up. Even if it's not true now, she's so stubborn she might decide to make it true. [The speaker suspects that her daughter has been dating someone without a city residency permit, but is too afraid of her daughter's temper to ask her about it.]

dǔn 趸 (躉)

Buy wholesale

◆ 我一哥们儿从南方**趸**来一批货，想找人帮他卖出去。

(From the TV series 今生是亲人)

A buddy of mine got his hands on a bunch of stuff in the South. He's looking for someone to help him sell it.

♦ 她在医学上格外**死心眼**。心里有问题不彻底弄明白就没有完。这逼得焦起周不得不**丁是丁卯是卯**，自己有不懂的地方只好先查书，弄明白了再**现趸现卖**。

    (From the novel 空洞)

    She's very stubborn when it comes to medicine. If there's a question in her mind she won't rest until she understands it perfectly. That forced Jiao Qizhou to be deadly accurate. If there's something he doesn't understand, he has to look it up. Once he's got it, he explains it to her, like buying goods wholesale and selling them retail.

duō ge xīn yǎnr 多个心眼儿 (多個心眼兒)

See 长心眼儿 zhǎng xīn yǎnr

duō nián de xí fu áo chéng pó 多年的媳妇熬成婆(多年的媳婦熬成婆)

"Become a mother-in-law after years of being a daughter-in-law"; finally assume a position of authority after years of suffering

♦ 新兵老兵不一样，讲怪话是老兵的权利，**多年的媳妇熬成婆**。

    (From the novel 看家护院)

    Rookies are not the same as veterans. Only veterans are allowed to bitch. They've earned the right.

♦ 他啊，**多年的媳妇熬成婆**，现在谁都得听他的了。

    Well, his day has come. Now everybody has to listen to him. [He is now in a position of power.]

duǒ de guò chū yī, duǒ bú guò shí wǔ 躲得过初一，躲不过十五 (躲得過初一，躲不過十五)

"You might be able to hide till the first; you will not be able to hide till the fifteenth"; you can't hide forever

♦ 吊脚楼那间宿舍肯定暂时不能去住了，就是门窗都修好了也不能去住了，因为毛杰知道那地方，要杀她的话**躲得过初一躲不过十五**。

    (From the novel 玉观音)

    For the time being, she definitely couldn't stay in the dormitory at the house on stilts, even if the door and windows were all repaired. Mao Jie knew that place. If he wanted to kill her, she might be able to hide for awhile, but not forever.

♦ 根荣，你**躲得过初一，躲得过十五**吗？

    (From the TV series 大赢家)

    Genrong, you can't hide forever. [Genrong was involved in an accident at his factory. He doesn't dare enter the general manager's office.]

duǒ guò fēng tou 躲过风头 (躲過風頭)

"Escape the front of the storm"; ride out the storm; lie low till something blows over

♦ 我估计他们暂时会按兵不动，**躲过风头**后才会行动。

    (From the novel 表姐表妹)

I think they'll sit tight ["mobilize their army"] for the time being. They'll ride out the storm before making a move. [A law enforcement official is speaking about a group of criminals].

◆ 你先去广东那边儿转转，等**躲**过了这阵风头再回来。

You go to Guangdong for a while. Come back when it blows over.

E

é 讹 (訛)

Extort; blackmail

◆ 县医院是那么好进的吗？去一次不把你**讹**死才怪哪！

(From the novel 空洞)

You think being admitted to the county hospital is a picnic? It's a miracle if they don't take you for all you've got on the first try.

◆ 我眼看着前边的人摔倒了，好心好意地把他扶起来，没想到那小子**讹**上我了，说是我把他推倒的，要我给他医药费。

I saw this guy in front of me fall down, so out of the goodness of my heart I helped him up. Never dreamed the asshole would try to extort money from me, saying I was the one who pushed him. He wanted me to pay for his medical bills.

ěr duo dōu tīng chū jiǎn zi lái le 耳朵都听出茧子来了(耳朵都聽出繭子來了)

"Hear something so many times that the ears harden"; hear something over and over again; hear something ad nauseam (茧子: callus, corn)

◆ 就石天明这句话，平时她听得**耳朵都起茧了**，此时却让她有一种想扑到男人怀里哭一场的感觉。

(From the novel 浮沈商海)

This time Shi Tianming's words, which she had heard a million times before, made her feel like resting her head on her husband's chest and weeping. [Her husband told her to rest a bit sooner than usual?]

◆ 爸爸，别给我讲这些"好好学习"的大道理了，我**耳朵都听出茧子来了**。我根本不想上大学，现在多少大学生毕业了找不到工作，你们知道吗？

Dad, don't preach "study hard" at me anymore. I'm sick of hearing it. I don't want to go to college at all. Do you know how many college grads can't find jobs after graduation?

ěr gēn zi ruǎn 耳根子软 (耳根子軟)

"Have soft ears"; be easily swayed

◆ 我爸耳根子软。

(From the TV series 大雪无痕)

My father's easily swayed. [His father didn't want to do anything illegal, but others begged him, so he did anyway.]

♦   我们当交通警察的，**耳根子绝对不能软**。那些违反交通规则的人，好话说得再多也得罚。

> We traffic cops have to be firm. If people break traffic laws we have to fine them no matter how much they try to talk us out of it.

èr bǎ dāo 二把刀

"Second knife"; second-best; second-rate

♦   千不该万不该，有这么多大小伙子，不该让解净开车，她是个**二把刀**，说不定**把命搭**上还得误了大事。

(From the novel 赤橙黄绿青蓝紫)

> You should never, ever, have allowed Xie Jing to drive. There are so many young men available to do it. She's just a beginner. Probably she'll end up killing herself and mess up the whole project.

♦   我们这个小饭馆请不起手艺好的高级厨师，能找来个二**把刀**就不错了。

> A small restaurant such as ours can't afford a skilled chef. We'll be lucky if we find a half-decent cook.

èr bái wǔ 二百五

A silly person; an idiot; someone who acts without thinking

♦   王莽的老大、老二全死了，老三王安脑筋不大好，有点儿**二百五**，皇太子的位置就归了老四。

(From the novel 王莽)

> Wang Meng's first two sons died. The third son, Wang An, was a bit soft in the head, something of an idiot, so the position of heir apparent went to the fourth son.

♦   咱们办公室的老王真有点儿**二百五**，人家老刘辛辛苦苦整理了二十多年的材料都让他当废纸卖了。

> Lao Wang in our office is such an idiot. He sold Lao Liu's notes as waste paper. Lao Liu had been working on those notes for over twenty years.

èr bàn diào zi 二半吊子

A smidgen; a smattering; dilettante (吊: a string of 1,000 cash)

♦   你这**二半吊子**的英文，也能出国留学？

(From the TV series 空镜子)

> Can you really go study abroad with your two words of English?

♦   别看他在外国公司混过几年，在企业管理方面，最多是个**二半吊子**，我们可不能重用这样的人。

> Forget that he worked at a foreign firm for a couple of years. When it comes to business management, he's an amateur. We can't give him an important position.

èr hu 二乎

Unsure; confused; hesitant

♦   赵师傅觉着还是该去报告派出所。不过挪脚之前他又有点**二乎**。

(From the novel 黑墙)

Master Zhao thought he really should inform the police station, but before taking a single step he had second thoughts. [A neighbor has painted the interior wall of the house black, and Master Zhao can't decide whether to report it to the police.]

◆ "是不是要买这种股票，咱们再研究研究吧！" "嘿！刚才你还说要抓住机会呢，这会怎么儿又二乎了？"

"Let's do some more research before deciding whether we should buy this stock." "What! You just said we should grab the opportunity. How come you're having second thoughts now?"

èr huà méi shuō 二话没说 (二話沒說)

"Didn't utter a second sentence"; didn't say another word

◆ 我弄来张病假条，请他签字，他二话没说就签了。

(From the novel 情人啊)

I got a fake sick leave permit and asked him to sign it. He did it without asking any questions.

◆ 十年前他彭东东说可以给小玉一生的幸福，我二话没说就离开了。可是今天，我可以拍着胸脯对您说，我能给小玉一生的幸福。

(From the TV series 北京女人)

Ten years ago, this guy Peng Dongdong promised Xiaoyu a lifetime of happiness, so I backed off without uttering a word. But today, I swear that it is I who will give Xiaoyu a lifetime of happiness. [The speaker is asking Xiaoyu's mother for permission to marry Xiaoyu after her divorce from Peng Dongdong.]

èr jìn gōng 二进宫 (二進宮)

"Enter the palace for the second time"; be thrown into jail for the second time (the name of a famous Beijing opera)

◆ 他们都是所谓的二进宫，即第二次吃官司了。

(From the novel 不堪回首)

They're all so-called old hands, which means it's the second time they're inside ["the second time they've been sued"].

◆ 看你刚才跟警察说话的时候那沉稳的样子，你是二进宫了吧？

You seemed pretty calm talking to that policeman. I guess this isn't your first time inside?

èr pí liǎn 二皮脸 (二皮臉)

"Two-skinned face"; thick-skinned

◆ 是啊是啊，你哪象我似的，豁出去，二皮脸，跑跑颠颠，求爷爷告奶奶的。

(From the novel 立体交叉桥)

That's right, you're not like me. I was willing to be thick-skinned, to give it everything I've got, to run all over and beg from pillar to post. [The speaker managed to exchange his old apartment for a better one.]

◆ 姓张的整个儿一二**皮脸**，你跟他说什么他就是赖着不走。
That Zhang guy is tough as nails. No matter what you say he just won't budge.

èr wǔ yǎn 二五眼

Not up to standard; sloppy

◆ 通过考核评议，不管是干部还是工人，在业务上稀松二五眼的，出工不出力、出力不出汗的，**占着茅杭不厕屎的**，溜奸滑蹭的，全成了编余人员。
(From the novel 乔厂长上任记)
Everyone was evaluated, cadres and workers alike. Anyone who was lazy on the job, anyone who didn't make an effort, anyone who didn't break a sweat, anyone who wouldn't shit or get off the pot, anyone who just hung around, got laid off. [编=编制, the authorized size of a government body]

◆ 你只当找对象，动点脑子，把各方面情况问明白喽，再告我，别稀松二五眼的。
(From the novel 百年德性)
Pretend you're looking for a girlfriend. Think hard. Investigate every aspect of the situation and let me know. Don't blow it off. [A policeman is asking a friend's help to gather some information.]

F

fā héng cái 发横财 (發橫財)

Make a fortune suddenly and unexpectedly

◆ 听说洪先生在房地产方面**发了一笔横财**。
(From the TV series 一年又一年)
Mr. Hong, I hear you made a killing in real estate.

◆ 老婆总爱**东家长西家短的**，谁最近又**发了一笔横财**，谁前几天又升了官，谁家的小孩学习成绩好，将来肯定要考上北大、清华什么的。
(From the short story 死亡约定)
His wife always likes to gossip about the neighbors: who made a pile of money recently, who got promoted a few days ago, whose kids get good grades and will surely get into Beijing University or Qinghua, and so on.

fā huà 发话 (發話)

"Utter the word"; say the word; pronounce

◆ 您这大书记都**发话**了，我还能说什么呢？
(From the TV series 黑洞)

You, the Party Secretary, have spoken. What's left for me to say?

◆   董事长，这些小事儿还用您亲手办么？　您一**发话**谁敢不听啊？

Mr. Chairman, there's no need for you to get involved in these details. You just have to say the word. No one would dare disobey.

fā máo 发毛 (發毛)

"Feel hairy"; be scared; be nervous

◆   要是换成你，你心里不**发毛**？

(From the TV series 黑洞)

Don't tell me you wouldn't be scared if it were you. [Discussing making money by smuggling.]

◆   虽说卖这种水货不是一次两次的了，但我心里还是觉得有点儿**发毛**。

Even though we've sold these kinds of smuggled goods before, somehow I still feel a bit nervous.

fā shāo yǒu 发烧友 (發燒友)

"Feverish friend"; fanatic; fan; fellow fanatic

◆   你一上车就不停地赞美他，简直成了他的**发烧友**。

(From the TV series 天下第一情)

You haven't stopped singing his praises since you got in the car. You've turned into a real groupie.

◆   我们家那口子钱挣不了几个，还整天跟他那些**发烧友**鼓弄照相机，日本的不行还要买德国的，好象我是他的银行似的。

My husband doesn't make much money, but all day long he and his obsessed friends play with their cameras. Japanese cameras won't do; they've got to be German. It's as if I'm his cash machine.

fà xiǎor 发小儿 (髮小兒)

Childhood friends

◆   我们俩是**发小儿**，熟得很。

(From the TV series 手心手背)

We've been friends since we were little kids. We know each other really well.

◆   听说大刘和你是**发小儿**，他不给我面子也得给你面子吧？

I hear Da Liu and you go way back. Even if he doesn't give me face, he'll sure give you face.

fān le ge gēn tou 翻了个跟头 (翻了個跟頭)

"Turn one somersault"; double (Can also be used to indicate triple, quadruple, etc., when a number is placed before 个, as in 翻了 (number) 个跟头, "turn (several) somersaults";)

◆   自由市场上蔬菜的价格已经**翻了个跟头**。

(From the short story 露营者)

Vegetable prices have doubled at the free market.

♦ 我真后悔去年没买那套房子，今年这房价已经**翻了**三个跟头了。

I really regret not buying that apartment last year. This year the price has already tripled.

fān liǎn bú rèn rén 翻脸不认人 (翻臉不認人)

"Turn one's face and refuse to recognize people"; suddenly become hostile

♦ 大军，你回去告诉沙沙，到时候，可别怪姐姐**翻脸不认人**！

(From the TV series 贫嘴张大民的幸福生活)

Dajun, you go back and tell Shasha. When the time comes, don't blame me for turning against her. [The speaker is addressing her brother Dajun, whose wife Shasha has borrowed money from her and refuses to pay it back.]

♦ "何雷，你这人怎么就能红一阵儿白一阵儿，说狠就狠，**翻脸不认人**，什么揍的？" "变色龙揍的。"

(From the novel 永失我爱)

"He Lei, how can you blow hot and cold like that? Suddenly you're a mad dog, turning on people. What kind of creature are you?" "A chameleon, that's the kind of creature I am."

fán bù fán a 烦不烦啊 (煩不煩啊)

Isn't that annoying? Is that annoying or what?

♦ 你这孩子怎么跟你哥一个**德性**？ 烦不烦啊？

(From the TV series 都市情感)

How come you're a real prize, just like your brother? Think you can annoy me even more? [Both her daughter and her son are too proud to use their connections to help their mother.]

♦ 你烦不烦啊，这么芝麻粒儿大的事说个没完。

Why are you such a pest, going on forever about such a little thing?

fǎn le sb le 反了Sb了

"Somebody rebelled"; how dare ...

♦ **反了你了**！ 跟我你也敢说瞎话？

(From the TV series 省委书记)

How dare you! You have the nerve to lie, even to me? [A provincial party secretary is blasting a municipal party secretary.]

♦ 扣工资，**反了他了**！ 工资是国家给的，他凭什么扣？

(From the TV series 一年又一年)

Take it out of our wages? How dare he! The wages come from the state. What right does he have to make deductions?

fàn bù zháo/fàn bú shàng 犯不着/犯不上 (犯不著/犯不上)

No need to; not worth

♦ 其实这事儿**犯不着**这样。

(From the movie 有话好好说)

There's really no need for this. [Spoken as two parties bring out knives, preparing to fight.]

♦ **犯不着**把自己的良心包成包子端上去巴结人家。

(From the TV series 手心手背)

It's not worth handing over your conscience just to butter someone up ["wrap one's conscience in dumplings and present it to someone in order to curry favor"].

fàn gǎ/gě 犯嘎/葛

Make trouble; obstruct

◆ 辛小亮平常对女同志耍横犯嘎，真到了这节骨眼儿上，什么招儿也没啦。

(From the novel 丹凤眼)

Ordinarily, Xin Xiaoliang makes life difficult for women, but when push comes to shove he hasn't a clue how to deal with them. [招儿: trick, strategy, idea]

◆ 老张原来以为老刘退休之后，经理该轮到他做了，谁知道上面调来了个年轻的大学生当经理。大家都担心，他免不了要对新来的领导犯葛。

Lao Zhang always thought it would be his turn to be manager after Lao Liu retired. Who knew? The higher-ups picked a young college graduate for the job. Everyone worried that he [Lao Zhang] would make problems for the new head.

fàn jú 饭局 (飯局)

"A round of dinner"; dinner engagement (局: a round of a game)

◆ 正找你呢，中午别回公司了，有饭局。

(From the movie 顽主)

I was just looking for you. Don't go back to the company at noon. You have a lunch date.

◆ 人家饭局多着呢！ 忙得厉害，好不容易今天才把他请来。

(From the TV series 手心手背)

He has lots of dinner engagements. He's really busy. It wasn't easy to get him here today. [A private business owner managed to persuade a government official to spend time at his nightclub.]

fàn kǒur 饭口儿 (飯口兒)

About to sit down for a meal

◆ 太晚了到人家，要正赶上饭口儿可怪不好意思的。

(From the novel 空洞)

If we're late getting to their place and they're about to sit down for dinner, it'll be really embarrassing.

◆ 你把我们家当食堂了？ 一到饭口儿就来。

(From the TV series 其实男人最辛苦)

You think our home is your canteen, and you can show up whenever it's meal time?

fàng dānr 放单儿 (放單兒)

Become or be single

◆ 她现在是一个人，你也放单儿，你们俩还不是迟早的事儿吗？

(From the TV series 北京女人)

She's alone now, and you're single too. Don't you think you two will be together sooner or later?

♦ 大学毕业这么多年了，你怎么还**放单儿**呢？

It's been years since you finished college. How come you're still single?

fàng gē zi 放鸽子 (放鴿子)

(Taiwan expression) "release pigeons"; fail to show up; stand somebody up

♦ "反正他们都在台北，**放一次鸽子**也没关系。" "你常**放人家鸽子**吗？"

(From the movie 黑暗之光)

"Anyway they're both in Taipei. It doesn't matter if we stand them up once." [There's plenty in Taipei to keep them entertained.] "You stand people up often?"

♦ 我以后不和他交往了，他昨天又**放了我的鸽子**。

I won't have anything more to do with him. He stood me up again yesterday.

fàng huà 放话 (放話)

Put the word out; let it be known

♦ "敲诈"这些有头有脸的知名人物会让他很有成就感，他玩得很爽，根本不怕人家**放话**要他小心点。

(From the novel 正中红心)

Blackmailing those big names gave him a sense of accomplishment. He was having a great time and paid no attention when people warned him to be more careful.

♦ 现在的人只认钱，这，不，人家马校长把**话放**出来了，不交三万的赞助费咱们的儿子就进不了他们学校。

These days people only know money. You see, Principal Ma sent down the word that if we can't come up with thirty thousand in sponsorship money, our son won't get into the school.

fàng mǎ hòu pào 放马后炮 (放馬後炮)

Offer suggestions from a position of hindsight; play Monday morning quarterback

♦ 直到我寻到一条解决之道，他才来**放马后炮**，又算什么英雄呢？

(From the novel 如意合欢)

He didn't say anything until after I came up with the solution. What kind of hero is that?

♦ "我早就知道这么干不行。" "那怎么不早说啊？ 你这纯粹是**放马后炮**。"

"I knew all along this method wouldn't work." "Then why didn't you say so before? Hindsight is always twenty-twenty."

fàng pì 放屁

(Vulgar) fart; talk nonsense; bullshit

♦ "他这是为了国家啊！" "**放屁**！"

(TV Series 康熙帝国)

"He's doing this for the sake of the country!" "Bullshit!" [An emperor lashes out at a minister.]

♦   什么，这次是他的功劳？ 纯粹是**放屁**！ 我们几个辛辛苦苦干了半天，他连指头都没动一下。

  What? He's getting the credit for this? That's pure bullshit! We worked hard for a long, long time. He didn't even lift a finger.

fàng qì qíu 放气球 (放氣球)

  "Release balloons"; talk big

♦   我看她也就是**放放气球**，说说大话，让上面表扬表扬，提拨提拨。

  (From the TV series 大赢家)

  I think she's full of hot air, talking big to get the higher-ups to compliment and promote her. [A manager says she plans to turn the company into a multinational corporation.]

♦   别光**放气球**，做点儿实实在在的事好不好？

  Enough of your empty talk. Do something real for a change, OK?

fàng shuǐ 放水

  "Let out water"; sabotage

♦   四年前要不是沙特**放水**，咱们早就进世界杯了！

  (From the TV series 一年又一年)

  If the Saudis hadn't sabotaged us four years ago, we would have made the World Cup! [If the Saudis had lost by fewer than five goals to the New Zealanders, China would have been able to make the World Cup. The Saudis lost by five goals.]

♦   这次咱们失败的主要原因是有人**放水**。

  The main reason we failed this time was that someone sabotaged us.

fàng xiě 放血

  "Let blood"; offer a steep discount

♦   他把刚买下不久的铃木王摩托车大**放血**大减价大拍卖地去换来了一把人民币向你作无私的奉献。

  (From the novel 兄弟时代)

  He sold the top-of-the-line Suzuki motorbike he just bought, at a steep discount. He knocked down the price and auctioned it off, just to come up with a bunch of *renminbi* he could selflessly offer you.

♦   清仓大拍卖，全部三折，大**放血**了！

  Warehouse clearance sale! Everything 70 percent off. Huge discounts!

fàng yi mǎ 放一马/码 (放一馬/碼)

  "Release a horse/let out a size"; let someone off the hook

♦   算了吧，这次就**放你一马**。

  (From the novel 时空遗梦)

  Forget about it. I'll let you off the hook this time.

♦   我今儿真不是找你来问罪的，我就是求你高抬贵手，**放我们娘儿俩一马**。

  (From the novel 我是你爸爸)

I really didn't come here to accuse you. I'm begging you to be magnanimous and spare us, both me and my daughter. [The speaker is begging the man to stop spreading rumors about her daughter.]

fàng zhe...bù...放着...不... (放着...不...)
"It's lying there, yet one doesn't... "; reject something that's there for the taking; turn down a good thing

◆ 我真不明白你是怎么想的，**放着**好好的国家干部**不作**，非得下海。
(From the TV series 蓝色马蹄莲)
> I just don't understand what you were thinking. You had a great government job, but you had to quit and go into business. [下海 was originally a Beijing Opera term. An amateur singer leaving his daytime job and turning pro was said to 下海, or "go out to sea." In the 1980s the term came to mean resigning from the state sector and going into business.]

◆ 你**放着**你那房地产的钱**不挣**，非要炒股票，我看你将来一定会后悔。
> The real estate money is there for the taking, but you want to play the stock market. I think you'll live to regret it.

féi shuǐ bù liú wài rén tián 肥水不流外人田
(Proverb) "Do not let the fertile water flow into others' fields"; keep it in the family

◆ 让你当会计一是肥水不流外人田，二是对你说来也是一种生意。
(From the TV series 黑洞)
> Making you our accountant is first to keep it in the family, and second to give you a job. [A family hires a friend to be the company accountant.]

◆ 老赵，说真的，你这辈子肥水流没流过外人田？
(From the movie 顽主)
> Tell the truth, Lao Zhao. You've never spread fertilizer over other people's fields? [Meaning extramarital sex.]

fèi 废 (廢)
(Gangster/mafia jargon) "make someone physically handicapped"; maim or kill

◆ 你们俩什么也别干，专门看着这小子，**把家伙**拽出来放他脖子上，倘若他不老实，或者万一有情况，先把他给我**废**了。
(From the novel 白眉大侠)
> You two don't do anything else. Just keep a watch on this bastard. Hold a knife to his neck [家伙: fellow, weapon]. If he doesn't behave himself, or if anything happens, finish him off for me.

◆ 这小子竟敢跟我作对，去，把他给我**废**了。
> That bastard dared to take me on. Go and finish him off for me.

fèi wu diǎn xin 废物点心 (廢物點心)
(Vulgar) "useless thing"; 'loser; good-for-nothing

◆ 我傻，我傻，我大**傻冒儿**，**废物点心**，好不好？
(From the TV series 一年又一年)

I'm stupid, I'm stupid. I'm a fool, a loser. All right? [The speaker doesn't want to argue with his wife anymore.]

◆   老曹那人纯粹**废物点心**一个，什么事儿也办不成。
    Lao Cao is a total loser. He can't do anything right.

fēn 分

(Beijing dialect) "(how you do it) makes all the difference"; depend on

◆   "我捧不起，捧红一个歌星少说得几十万吧？"我笑着问。"**分**怎么捧了。**有钱得花在刀刃上。**"沉小霞似乎对这个话题很感兴趣。
    (From the novel 百年德性)
    "I can't afford to be a backer. It would take several hundred thousand at least to make someone a pop star, right?" I asked, laughing. "That depends on what kind of backing we're talking about. You have to put the money where it counts." Shen Xiaoxia seemed very interested in the subject.

◆   "这事儿能办成吗？""那得**分**谁去。要是你小子去准得砸了。"
    "Can we pull this thing off?" "That depends on who does it. If it's you, you bastard, you'll mess this thing up for sure."

fēng jiàn 封建

"Feudal"; be conservative in one's morals

◆   "咱们外边儿谈吧。""想不到你还挺**封建**的，进屋吧，怕什么啊？"
    (From the TV series 激情年代)
    "Let's talk outside." "I didn't know you were such a prude! Come on in. What are you afraid of?" [A conversation between a conservative man and an aggressive woman.]

◆   你别不好意思，真的老马，别太**封建**，何苦嘴上硬撑着，放任身心备受摧残。
    (From the novel 我是你爸爸)
    Really, Lao Ma, don't be embarrassed. Don't be so old-fashioned. What's the point of keeping a stiff upper lip and suffering in both mind and body? [Lao Ma has been celibate since getting divorced many years ago.]

fēng shuǐ lún liú zhuàn 风水轮流转 (風水輪流轉)

"Good feng shui flows and shifts"; fortunes change; times change; things come full circle

◆   **风水轮流转**，看来电影的好日子又回来了。
    (From the TV series 一年又一年)
    What goes around comes around. Good times are here again for movies. [People are returning to cinemas after having deserted them for TV.]

◆   现在那帮大学里的臭老九又**吃香**了，真是风水轮流转啊！
    Those rotten university intellectuals are in favor again. How times change!

fū qī diànr 夫妻店儿 (夫妻店兒)

"A store owned and operated by a husband and wife"; mom-and-pop store; a family operation

◆   那好，我也辞职下海，咱们开**夫妻店**去。
    (From the novel 都市危情)

Great, I'll resign and go into business too. Let's start a family operation. [A policeman jokes with his female colleague who is thinking of quitting her job.]

◆ 你不是心里还放不下他吗？ 这下好了，两个人一个办公室，开个**夫妻店儿**。

(From the TV series 北京女人)

You can't let go of him, right? Now you're all set, with both of you working in the same office, a real mom-and-pop store. [A divorced couple end up working in the same office.]

fú dà mìng dà zào hua dà 福大命大造化大 (福大命大造化大)

Be extremely fortunate and blessed (福: fortune; 命: fate; 造化: luck)

◆ 快别这样说，你**福大命大造化大**，我只是拣了个顺水人情而已！

(From the novel 八年闯荡金三角)

Don't talk like that. You had good luck; I really didn't have to do anything [顺水人情: a favor that involves little or no effort or cost]. [A school principal is refusing thanks from a former student whom he has rescued from police detention.]

◆ 老板你真是**福大命大造化大**，这一车的人死的死伤的伤，您连毫毛儿都没碰着一根儿。

Boss, you really are one lucky duck. Everyone else in the car was killed or injured; only you got out without a scratch ["not even one little hair of yours was touched"].

fú le 服了

(Sarcastic) "Acknowledge someone's superiority"; acknowledge defeat; give up

◆ 我算**服了**你了。

(From the movie 洗澡)

OK, I give up. [The opponent refuses to follow the rules of a game.]

◆ 我**服了**你了，说瞎话脸一点儿都不带红的。

I have to hand it to you. You can lie without a blush.

G

gā bēngr 嘎崩儿 (嘎崩兒)

(Onomatopoeia) a cracking, collapsing sound

◆ 你瞧你这**德性**，要是**嘎崩儿**死在我眼前我连眼都不带眨的。

(From the movie 有话好好说)

Look at how shamefully you behave. If you collapsed with a thud and died right in front of me, I wouldn't even bat an eyelash.

♦ 这桌子也**忒**不结实了，刚用了两天这桌子腿儿就**嘎崩儿**断了。

This table is really too flimsy. We only used it for a couple of days before the legs clattered to pieces.

gā da 疙瘩

(Northeastern dialect) corner of the world; place

♦ 这不就是个小孩子家戴的长命锁吗？ 俺们那**疙瘩**家家孩子都戴，你能信这个？

(From the novel 军歌嘹亮)

Isn't this just one of those long-life amulets little children wear? In our neck of the woods every kid wears one. You can't put too much stock in that. [The listener thinks that he's found a long-lost family member. The speaker discredits his proof.]

♦ 我们那**疙瘩**冬天特别冷，不带皮帽子能把耳朵冻掉了。

We have wicked cold winters where I come from. If you don't wear a fur hat, you'll freeze your ears off.

gāi zháor 该着儿 (該著兒)

Should; meant or destined to

♦ **该着**我要发财，刚买了这块地政府就说要在那儿修公路，地价立马儿翻了几番。

(From the TV series 一年又一年)

It was my turn to strike it rich. The moment I bought this plot of land, the government said it was going to build a highway there. Land prices shot up right away.

♦ 这回我给你收拾干净你可别再乱摊了啊，好象我**该着**给你当保姆似的。

I picked up after you and everything's clean, so this time don't go dropping your stuff everywhere. It's like I was born to be your maid.

gài màor 盖帽/冒儿 (蓋帽/冒兒)

(Beijing dialect) superb; fantastic; awesome

♦ 晓棋做了八个菜……同学们一尝，**盖了冒儿了**，大声叫好，连晓棋自己都不信有这本事。

(From the novel 东风西风)

Xiaoqi made eight dishes. Her classmates tried them and said they were superb. Everyone talked loudly about how good they were. Even Xiaoqi herself never thought she was that talented.

♦ "你们这次参赛成功吗？" "**盖帽儿了**！ 团体和个人差不多都让我们给包圆儿了！"

"Did you do well at the competition?" "Out of sight. We collected almost all the individual and team prizes."

gān 干 (幹)

"Dry"; just; simply

♦ **干**坐着好没劲儿，开桌吧？

(From the short story 毛狗不是人)

It's boring just sitting around. Shall we start? [Start to play mahjong, that is.]

♦ 敌人躲无处躲，逃无处逃，只能干等挨打，束手就擒。

(From the novel 中原逐鹿)

The enemy had no place to hide, no place to run. All they could do was sit and wait for defeat and capture.

gān dǎ léi bú xià yǔ 干打雷不下雨 (幹打雷不下雨)

"Thunder without rain"; empty noise without action

♦ 你说要给人家出MTV，就是干打雷不下雨。

(From the TV series 都市情感)

You promised to shoot a music video of me. That was just a lot of hot air, wasn't it?

♦ 上边儿嚷嚷半天说要改善职工生活条件，可就是干打雷不下雨，一点儿实事儿都没做。

The higher-ups made a lot of noise about improving the living conditions of the staff, but it was just empty talk. They never did anything real.

gān huò 干货 (乾貨)

"Dry goods"; substance

♦ "是干货吗，陈虎？" "全是干货。您是先看材料，还是先听我汇报？"

(From the novel 都市危情)

"Is everything solid, Chen Hu?" "It's all solid. Do you want to read the evidence first, or do you want to hear my report?" [Police are collecting evidence for a court investigation.]

♦ 你写的发言稿我看了，虚头八脑儿东西太多，干货太少。

I've gone over your speech. There's too much empty rhetoric and not enough substance.

gānr chàn 肝儿颤 (肝兒顫)

"The liver is shaking"; very scared

♦ "别提，别提，好汉不提当年勇，我那时是仗着人多势众，现在我是一个人，还真肝儿颤。"

(From the novel 都市危情)

"Don't bring that up. Real men don't brag about what they did in the past. In those days I could rely on a lot of help. Now that I'm by myself, I'm terrified."

♦ 他审案子时那双犀利的眼睛，让任何站在他面前的犯人都肝儿颤。

(From the novel 百年德性)

When he hears a case, criminals tremble before his piercing eyes.

gān zhe méi yǒu liǎng tóur tián 甘蔗没有两头儿甜 (甘蔗沒有兩頭兒甜)

(Proverb) "Only one end of the sugar cane is sweet"; there is only one desirable choice; you have to choose; you can't have your cake and eat it, too

♦ 钟政："我知道怎么做。俗话说：甘蔗没有两头甜的—我只能吃一头。"

(From the TV series 红豆生南国)

Zhong Zheng: "I know what to do. As they say, 'You can't have your cake and eat it, too.' I have to make a choice." [The speaker has to choose between his wife and mistress.]

♦ 别耍你那大作家的脾气了，**甘蔗没有两头儿甜**。

(From the TV drama 曾见胡同)

Stop acting like a great, temperamental writer. You can't have your cake and eat it, too. [Choosing between an apartment that's close to work and one that's quiet.]

gǎn míngr 赶明儿 (趕明兒)

Tomorrow; sometime soon

♦ 顶好的是毛长、腿短、大耳朵，两只眼睛还不一样，一只蓝的，一只绿的，最可心的就是有这么一只公猫，你妈**赶明儿**要是能找着，跟咱们也言语声儿，这俩猫的问题就都解决了！

(From the novel 沉浮)

Ideally it should have long hair, short legs, big ears, and eyes of two different colors, one blue and one green. Best to get a tomcat like that. If your mom can find one anytime soon, let us know. Then our cat problem would be solved. [The speaker and her friend are looking for a tomcat because they both have female cats.]

♦ 嘿，说了您也不信，**赶明儿**你得空儿傍晚上我们胡同**拿个弯儿**，那花前月下坐着哭的姑娘都是让我儿子刚给撅出来的。**任谁都瞧不上眼儿**，波姬·小丝漂亮吧，瞅着就生气。

(From the TV series 编辑部的故事)

If I told you, you wouldn't believe it. Tomorrow evening when you have time, walk around our neighborhood 'our hutong']. All those lovesick girls have been dumped by my son. No one is good enough for him. Brooke Shields is pretty, right? He gets annoyed just looking at her. [花前月下坐着哭的: sitting there crying "under the moon before the flowers," a cliché meaning a romantic tryst]

gǎn qing 敢情

So it seems (judging from appearances); naturally

♦ **敢情**你们认识？ 这正好，倒不必我介绍了！

(From the novel 大漠风云)

So you know each other. That's even better. No need for me to introduce you.

♦ "这么着吧，大妈，咱就按您儿子喜欢的模样儿登个广告，有的放矢，这回总行了吧？" "那**敢情**好。"

(From the TV series 编辑部的故事)

"How about this, Auntie. We'll put an ad in the paper for someone with just the kind of looks your son likes. We'll aim right for the target. That should work, don't you think?"
"Sure, that' sounds like a good idea." [的: dì, target; 矢: shì, arrow; 有的放矢: shoot your arrow at a target]

gǎn tàngr 赶趟儿 (趕趟兒)

Be in time for

♦ 我原来是想倒腾点儿东西卖卖，可三十大几的人还当**混混儿**也不**赶趟儿**啊！ 再说了，眼下这北京的自由市场都让外地人**包圆儿**了，咱也竞争不过人家啊！

(From the TV series 一年又一年)

I thought about getting some stuff to sell, but I'm in my thirties already. It's too late for me to goof around [as a street peddler]. Besides, out of towners have a lock on all the free markets in Beijing now. There's no way I could compete with them.

♦ 我老了，**赶不上趟儿**了，算了，还是让你们这些年轻人干吧！

I'm old; it's too late for me. Really, it's better just to let you young people take over.

gǎn yā zi shàng jià 赶鸭子上架 (趕鴨子上架)

"Drive a duck to mount a perch"; force someone to undertake a task beyond his or her capabilities

♦ 阿伟咚咚地跑上楼告诉肖平，我已经替你请假了，你就别回家了。肖平说你又把我留在这儿干什么？ 这不是**赶鸭子上架**吗？

(From the novel 情人时代)

Ah Wei pounded up the stairs and said to Xiao Ping, "I already requested leave for you. Don't go home." Xiao Ping said, "Why are you keeping me here? Are you trying to get me to do something I'm not trained for?" [Ah Wei's wife is giving birth, and he wants his friend Xiao Ping to help.]

♦ 老张小学都没念过，经理让他去学计算机，这不是**赶鸭子上架**吗？

Lao Zhang didn't even graduate from grade school. The manager is making him learn computers. That's like asking a pig to fly.

gàn má dì 干吗的 (幹嗎的)

"What job do you do?"; who do you think you are?

♦ 你算干吗的的？ 你是警察啊？

(From the movie 有话好好说)

Who do you think you are? Are you a cop or something? [Spoken to someone who is trying to prevent an act of violence.]

♦ 我们家的事儿用得着你操心吗？ 你算**干吗的**啊？

Do you need to poke your nose into our family's business? Who do you think you are?

gāo bù chéng dī bú jiù 高不成低不就

Unqualified for a higher position but won't accept a lower one; cannot have what one wants but unwilling to compromise

♦ 告诉你，胡总管又新请了一位教馆的先生，这回你可得好好念书了，别弄得将来跟你爸爸似的，**高不成低不就**，一辈子窝窝囊囊。

(From the TV series 大宅门)

I want you to know that Manager Hu hired a new tutor. This time you've got to study hard. Don't end up like your father, unfit for anything and frustrated his whole life.

◆   "小妹也老大不小的了，你不给她找个主儿，也不是个事儿啊！"

"小妹的条件你也不是不知道，**高不成低不就**，不好找啊！"

(From the TV series 其实男人最辛苦)

"Your sister's no spring chicken. If you don't find someone for her, it's going to be a problem." "You know my sister's situation. She can't marry up and she refuses to marry down. It's not easy to find someone!"

gǎo dìng 搞定

Finish something conclusively; secure something

◆   张律师，你给我三天全部**搞定**。

(From the movie 台北爱情故事)

Lawyer Zhang, I'll give you three days to wrap the whole thing up. [The head of the law firm is speaking.]

◆   那个发型设计师，我来把她**搞定**。

(From the movie 一见钟情)

I'll make sure I get that hairdresser. [Four men are each chasing a different woman.]

gǎo shénme míng tang 搞什么名堂 (搞什麽名堂)

What game are you playing? What are you up to?

◆   刘震汉在**搞什么名堂**？

(From the TV series 黑洞)

What is Liu Zhenhan up to? [Liu Zhenhan is a policeman who did some puzzling things during an investigation.]

◆   你**搞的什么名堂**？ 你个堂堂的大学生，居然娶了个食堂的大师傅！你昏了头了你？

(From the TV series 一年又一年)

What was in your head? You're a respectable college graduate, and you marry a canteen cook? Are you crazy?

gē bo (bei) nǐng bú guò dà tuǐ 胳膊拧不过大腿 (胳膊擰不過大腿)

(Proverb) "An arm cannot wrestle with a leg"; in no position to take on a far stronger opponent

◆   她自己不明白，**胳膊还拧得过大腿**吗？

(From the TV series 大雪无痕)

Doesn't she understand that the weak can't take on the strong? [A low-level official is complaining to superiors about her boss.]

♦ "这次事故是领导的责任，你不能白受伤啊，应该到法院去告他
们。""**胳膊拧不过大腿**，我看这事儿就认倒霉吧。即使法院判我赢
了，我在这个工厂还能待下去吗？"

> "The managers were responsible for this accident. You were injured and you should get compensation. Take them to court." "The little guys can't take on the big ones. I'll just have to consider it my bad luck. Even if I won in court, how could I go on working at this factory?"

gē bo (bei) zhǒur wàng wài guǎi 胳膊肘儿往外拐 (胳膊肘兒往外拐)

"Turn your elbow outwards"; help others instead of family or friends

♦ 你得替你婶、替你叔、替你二哥好好想想。**胳膊肘往外拐**的事，你不
能办哪！

(From the novel 都市危情)

> You have to think about your aunt, uncle, and cousin. You can't do anything to harm your own family. [The listener wants to reveal his cousin's economic crimes.]

♦ 咱们公司和大华公司是竞争对手，可你却给他们公司出主意，这不是
胳膊肘儿往外拐吗？

> Dahua is our competition, but you're giving them ideas. How come you help others and notyour own?

gē sān chà wùr 隔三差/岔五儿 (隔三差/岔五兒)

Every three or five days; intermittently; frequently

♦ 来收草药的是几个外地人，**隔三差五**地来。

(From the novel 第三只手)

> People who come to buy medicinal herbs are all from out of town. They come fairly often.

♦ 问问我妈去问问我爸去，对他们，我还**隔三岔五**横眉立目骂几次。可
对你们，我大声说过一句话没有？

(From the TV series 编辑部的故事)

> Ask my mom and dad. I'm always giving them dirty looks and yelling at them. But have I ever raised my voice to you?

gè bǎ/qiān bǎ/wàn bǎ 个把/千把/万把 (個把/千把/萬把)

A few/roughly a thousand/ten, twenty, thirty thousand

♦ 天都市这么大，藏**个把**人到哪儿找去？

(From the TV series 黑洞)

> Tiandu is such a big city. If a few people are hidden someplace, where would you look for them?

♦ 〖敌军〗不过**千把**人，不值得大惊小怪。

(From the TV series 水浒传)

They've only got a thousand soldiers at most. No need to panic.

gè cūn yǒu gè cūn de gāo zhāor 各村有各村的高招儿 (各村有各村的高招兒)

"Each village has its clever trick"; everyone has his own way of dealing with something

◆ 大姐，这叫**各村有各村的高招**。仔细想想，女人挣钱没什么用。男人有权有钱，玩女人**泡妞**是个乐子，这钱也有个去处。女人就难了，有权有钱也**白搭**，这鸭店就是给有权有钱的女人开的。

(From the novel 都市危情)

> Sister, this is called "different strokes for different folks." When you think about it, women have no use for the money they make. A man with money and power can have a good time womanizing, so he's got a use for his money. It's more of a problem for women. What can they do with their money and power? This male brothel was specially established for rich and powerful women. [Streetwalkers are called 鸡 (jī, chicken) — nearly homonymous with 妓 (jì, prostitute)—or 野鸡 (wild chicken), so male prostitutes are known as 鸭 (yā, duck).]

◆ 他原来以为靠有奖销售大家就只买他的东西了，没想到**各村有各村的高招儿**，别的商店搞什么买一赠一啊，无息贷款啊…他的销售额一点儿也没有提高。

> At first he thought that if he held a promotional sale and gave out prizes everyone would buy only his stuff. He never dreamed that other businesses would think up their own strategies. Stores offered "buy one, get one free" deals or "zero interest loans." His sales didn't go up at all.

gè yang/gè yang/gè ying 疙痒/硌痒/咯硬 (疙癢/硌癢/咯硬)

"Itchy"; yucky; feel funny

◆ 你怕是让人虐待惯了，对你好，你倒**咯硬**了。

(From the novel 我是你爸爸)

> You must be used to bad treatment. You're uncomfortable if someone's nice to you.

◆ 你不想想，这儿是农村，不是大上海，还穿得那么俏，就不怕招人**疙痒**？

> Haven't you noticed that we're in the country, not in big Shanghai? If you wear such flashy clothes, don't you worry you might turn people off?

gěi sb diǎnr yán sè kàn 给Sb点儿颜色看 (給Sb點兒顏色看)

"Show somebody some color"; put on a display of power in order to intimidate someone

◆ 我老觉着这绑票儿的不是**冲着银子来的**，他是趁咱们之危，**给咱们点儿颜色看看**，就算把银子送去，孩子也未必领得回来。

(From the TV series 大宅门)

> Somehow I think the kidnappers weren't after money. They just wanted to take advantage of our problems and intimidate us. Even if we sent them the money, there's no guarantee we'd have gotten our kid back.

◆ 不**给他点儿颜色看看**，还以为我是稽查大员的打工仔呢！

(From the TV series 红色康乃馨)

If I don't put up a show of force, he'll think I'm in the pay of the investigators. [A company is being investigated. The party secretary asked the speaker, the company's lawyer, to cooperate, but he refused because he despises the party secretary.]

gěi tái jiē xià 给台阶下 (給臺階下)

"Provide a staircase to descend"; give someone a face-saving way to get out of an awkward situation; provide a path for retreat

♦ 这只不过是**给**吴三桂一个**台阶儿下**。

(From the TV series 康熙帝国)

That was in order to allow Wu Sangui a graceful retreat. [The emperor knew that Wu Sangui wanted to rebel, but did not confront him. Instead, the emperor tried to show his magnanimity by giving Wu a gift.]

♦ 我是真喜欢你，就算你肯陪他过夜我还不干呢，但是你总得**给他个台阶下**，婉转一点，咱们以后还求着人家呢，你把关系弄得这么僵是不是不好？

(From the novel 男欢女爱)

I really like you. Even if you were willing to spend a night with him, I wouldn't let you, but you have to let him down gently. Be more tactful. We'll need his help later on. Straining the relationship isn't a good idea, right?

[The woman turned down another man's advances.]

gēn bānr/gēn bāo 跟班儿/跟包 (跟班兒/跟包)

Lackey; minion; follower

♦ 这不是原来你那**跟班儿**的吗？

(From the TV series 手心手背)

Isn't that your old hanger-on? [The speaker recognizes the man as his friend's former assistant.]

♦ 甭看我现在是什么副总经理，手机有了，汽车也有了，可这是，这是给人家**跟包**换来的啊！

(From the TV series 北京女人)

So what if they call me "deputy manager." So what if I have a cell phone and a car. It's the reward I get for licking someone's boots.

gēn jīn/shén jīng 根筋/神经 (根筋/神经)

Sinew/nerve; pattern of thought

♦ 他这个人啊，就是一**根筋**，总也转不过弯儿来。

(From the TV series 大雪无痕)

He's got a one-track mind.

♦ 我妈妈不知道哪根**神经**短路了，跟我爸爸搅在一块儿，硬要把这个人介绍给我。

(From the TV series 天下第一情)

My mother's brains must have short-circuited, ganging up with my dad to push this guy on me! [The speaker's parents have been long divorced.]

gēn nǐ shuō yě shì bái fèi tù mo (mie) 跟你说也是白费唾沫 (跟你說也是白費唾沫)

"It would be a waste of my saliva to speak, explain, or reason with you."

◆ 我就知道我**跟你说也是白费唾沫**，去！ 跟你妈说去！

(From the TV series 大宅门)

I knew you'd be wasting your time talking to me. Go talk to your mom. [A father is speaking to his child; the mother makes all the decisions in this family.]

◆ 老王，你**跟他们说得再多也是白费唾沫**，吸毒对身体不好大家都懂，但是一旦吸上了瘾就难戒了。

Lao Wang, it'd just be a waste of breath to keep talking to them. Doing drugs is bad for your health. Everyone knows that. But once you're hooked, quitting is hard.

gēn pì chóngr 跟屁虫儿 (跟屁蟲兒)

"A fart-following insect"; someone's shadow; a yes-man

◆ 阿成说，许的车上坐两种人，一是他的哥们，一是漂亮女人。他永远像**跟屁虫**一样，开着一辆桑塔纳尾随其后。

(From the short story 县委书记，你真酷)

Ah Cheng says two kinds of people ride in Xu's car, cronies and bimbos. He's like their shadow, always tailing them in a [Volkswagen] Santana.

◆ 你天天像**跟屁虫儿**一样跟着我，还说不是缠着我？

(From the TV series 其实男人最辛苦)

You're like my shadow, following me every day, and you say you're not stalking me?

gēn sb guò bú qù 跟Sb过不去 (跟Sb過不去)

Be hard on somebody; make life difficult for somebody

◆ 你今天成心**跟我过不去**。

(From the TV series 大雪无痕)

You're being deliberately hard on me today. [He wants to join the special case team, but his boss won't let him.]

◆ 最近厂长总**跟我过不去**，一会儿说我的设计不实际，一会儿说我的进度太慢，看来我在这个工厂很难再呆下去了。

The factory director's been hard on me lately. One minute he says my design isn't practical; the next minute I'm too slow. Looks like it's going to be tough for me to stay at this factory.

gēn sb yì bān jiàn shi 跟Sb一般见识 (跟Sb一般見識)

"(Stoop to) the same (level of) experience and knowledge as somebody else"; stoop to (somebody's') level

◆ 这是我亲戚，您千万别**跟他一般见识**。

(From the movie 有话好好说)

He's a relative of mine. Please don't sink to his level [let him go]. [The "relative" snatched a cell phone from a passerby to make a call.]

♦   "小张说我是老顽固，真把我气坏了！""老王啊，小张只不过是个刚参加工作的毛孩子，说出话来没轻没重，你何必**跟孩子一般见识**呢？"

   "Xiao Zhang called me an old goat. I was really mad!" "Lao Wang, Xiao Zhang just started work; he's still wet behind the ears. He just runs off at the mouth. Don't stoop to his childish level."

gōng mu liǎ 公母俩 (公母倆)

"Male and female couple"; couple

♦   前些日子从城里来了**公母俩**，说震宝〖人名〗是他们的儿子。

   (From the TV series 今生是亲人)

   A few days ago some couple from the city came and said Zhenbao was their son.

♦   瞧人家老**公母俩**多有福气，儿子女儿个个儿都是**大款**。

   Look how lucky that old couple are. Every one of their kids is a millionaire.

gōng shuō gōng yǒu lǐ, pó shuō pó yǒu lǐ 公说公有理，婆说婆有理 (公說公有理，婆說婆有理)

"He says he's right, and she says she's right"; everyone claims to be right

♦   这**公说公有理，婆是婆有理**，这清官还难断家务事呢！

   (From the TV series 古船、女人和网)

   He says he's right. She says she's right. Even a Solomon ["the most uncorrupted judge"] can't settle a family squabble.

♦   没有证人，**公说公有理，婆说婆有理**，这个案子很难判。

   There are no witnesses. It's his word against hers. This case is hard to judge.

gōng yā sǎngr 公鸭嗓儿 (公鴨嗓兒)

"The voice of a drake"; a croaking voice

♦   我天生一副**公鸭嗓儿**，你们要是不怕我就唱。

   (From the TV series 问问你的心)

   My voice is like a frog's. But if you're not afraid, I'll sing for you.

♦   就他那副**公鸭嗓儿**，也想当歌星？ 您饶了我吧。

   With a voice like that, he wants to be a pop star? Give me a break!

gōng zi gēr 公子哥儿 (公子哥兒)

"A young prince"; a spoiled young man

♦   人们说，这家伙一看就是个**油瓶子倒了也不知道扶**的公子哥儿。

   (From the novel 寻找无双)

They say once you meet this guy you know right off he's a coddled rich kid who 'can't do the simplest things on his own.

◆ 你怎么能把公司交给那个公子哥儿来管呢？

How could you let that spoiled brat manage the company?

gōu gōu kǎnr kǎnr 沟沟坎儿坎儿 (溝溝坎兒坎兒)

"Ditches and ridges"; bumps; difficulties

◆ 自从他们一结婚后，他的位置就突突突地往上顶。不管是什么**沟沟坎坎**，总是一越而过、顺顺当当。

(From the novel 抉择)

After they got married, his rise was meteoric. No matter what problems came up, they never slowed him down.

◆ 社会的事儿不像学校那么简单，难免有个**沟沟坎儿坎儿**的。

Out in the real world things aren't as simple as when you're in school. There are bound to be a few bumps in the road.

gōu húnr 勾魂儿 (勾魂兒)

"Snatch someone's soul"; bewitch; seduce

◆ 忙？ 是不是又有**勾魂儿**的了？

(From the TV drama 昝兄胡同)

Busy? Were you with some tramp again? [A husband came home late and told his wife that he was busy at work. His wife doesn't believe him.]

◆ 嘿，你那个**勾魂儿**的今天给你打了十几个电话找你，还不赶快给人家回一个？

Oh, that bimbo of yours called ten times today. Shouldn't you call her right back?

gǒu gǎi bù liǎo chī shǐ 狗改不了吃屎

(Proverb) "Dogs can't keep from eating shit"; a leopard can't change its spots

◆ 畜牲，又是一夜！『去赌博』**狗改不了吃屎**，你这小王八蛋！

(From the movie 活着)

Asshole, gambling all night again! Will you ever change, you little bastard?

◆ 你一次次地保证，可就是**狗改不了吃屎**。

(From the novel 空洞)

You promised again and again, but a leopard can't change its spots, can it? [A man promised to stop drinking and hitting his wife.]

gǒu ná hào zi, duō guǎn xián shì 狗拿耗子，多管闲事 (狗拿耗子，多管閒事)

"A dog catching mice—not minding his own business"; poke one's nose into other people's business (耗子 is a colloquial equivalent of 老鼠)

◆ 去去去，该你啥事 ，**狗拿耗子，多管闲事**！

(From the novel 反贪局在行动)

Get out of here! It's got nothing to do with you. Mind your own business. [A policeman is speaking to someone who wanted to intercede on another person 's behalf.]

♦ 你是二车间的，这是一车间，知道不知道？ 你别**狗拿耗子，多管闲事**！

You're assigned to the second workshop, and this is the first. Don't you know that? Don't poke your nose into our business!

gǒu niáng yǎng de 狗娘养的 (狗娘養的)

See 狗杂种 gǒu zá zhong

gǒu rì de 狗日的

(Vulgar) motherfucker (日: *vulgar*, have sex with a woman; 狗: *a general abusive term*, despicable)

♦ 没错，就他妈这些人，有时候恨得我，真他妈想轧**狗日的**！
(From the novel 耍叉)

You got that right. It's those damn guys. Sometimes I get so fucking mad that I just want to run over those motherfuckers! [A driver is venting his anger at bicyclists who completely ignore traffic rules.]

♦ 姓王的那**狗日的**又到咱们这儿**找茬儿**来了，我看咱们不能再这么忍下去了。

That motherfucker Wang came here looking for trouble again. I don't think we should put up with him anymore.

gǒu xióng bāi bàng zi 狗熊掰棒子

"A bear peeling cornhusks"; have difficulty holding onto something (According to folklore, bears put ears of corn under their arms when they finish husking them. The ears of corn fall out of their armpits.)

♦ 那天余下的时刻方枪枪破涕为笑，如果算不得**狗熊掰棒子**撂爪就忘。
(From the novel 看上去很美)

For the rest of that day Fang Qiangqiang's tears became smiles. He was as forgetful as the bear in the folktale.

♦ 你怎么跟**狗熊掰棒子**似的，学了新的就把旧的忘了？

How come your brain is like a sieve? The moment you learn something new, you forget what you learned before.

gǒu yǎn kàn rén dī 狗眼看人低

"Look at people from the eye level of a dog"; put someone down

♦ 狗眼看人低！
(From the TV series 田教授的二十八个保姆)

What a snob! [When a man finds out that the speaker is a servant, he turns cold toward her.]

♦ 你别**狗眼看人低**，他虽然穿得破烂，可是个大明星啊。

Don't look down on him. His clothes may be shabby, but he's a big star.

gǒu zá zhong 狗杂种 (狗雜種)

"Mixed-breed dog"; mongrel, mutt; bastard; son of a bitch

♦ 我早就想说他是个**狗杂种**。自打他把我从学校喊回来年年在河里扛石头起，我就想说他是个**狗杂种**了。

(From the short story 河边的田)

I've been wanting to tell you for a long time that he's a rotten bastard. Ever since he pulled me out of school to haul rocks from the river, I wanted to say he's a rotten bastard. [The speaker has been assigned to harvest rocks from the riverbed to build retaining walls.]

♦ "洗劫南河镇当铺，杀死杨老万全家，可也是九爷所为？""别人谁敢？**狗娘养的**不乖乖地送银子，老子不抢不杀，吃啥，喝啥，乐啥？"

(From the short story 根)

"Did you, Master Nine, rob the pawnshop in Nanhe and murder Yang Laowan's whole family?" "Who else would have dared? Those bastards didn't send over the money like they were supposed to. How was I going to eat, drink, and have fun if I didn't rob or kill?"

gǒu zuǐ (lǐ) tù bù chū xiàng yá 狗嘴（里）吐不出象牙 (狗嘴（裏）吐不出象牙)

(Proverb) "A dog cannot spit elephant ivory out of its mouth"; can't expect good or decent speech from someone

♦ 翟哥，你跟他浪费唾沫干吗？丫挺的**狗嘴里吐不出象牙**来。

(From the novel 百年德性)

Brother Zhai, why are you wasting your breath on him? That bastard will never say anything worth listening to.

♦ 你说这**象牙从狗嘴里吐出来**，我也得信呀！

If you tell me pearls of wisdom can come from his mouth, I'll have to believe it.

gòu qiàng 够呛 (夠嗆)

Bad enough; really bad

♦ 这病就是在北京城也十分凶险，在漠北大营就更**够呛**了。

(From the TV series 康熙帝国)

This kind of illness would be dangerous even in Beijing. It's really desperate at a military camp in the north of the Gobi Desert. [An emperor fell ill.]

♦ 真**够呛**，守着个财神爷还受这苦！

(From the TV series 一年又一年)

This really sucks! Your husband's filthy rich and you're still killing yourself working! [Spoken to a woman whose husband makes a lot of money, but who still wants to open a restaurant.]

gòu qiáo de 够瞧的 (夠瞧的)

"Enough to look at"; really something; really bad

♦ 那些走镖的镖师也真**够瞧的**。一会要这，一会要那。

(From the novel 巨剑回龙)

Those transport guards are really a pain. They keep asking for one thing or another. [A waiter at a roadside inn is complaining about the demanding guards who accompany transports.]

♦ 老张那人真**够瞧的**，给他分了套三居他还不满意。

Lao Zhang is really something. He got a three-bedroom apartment, and he's still not satisfied.

gòu yì si 够意思 (夠意思)

"Worthy of significance"; a real friend

♦ "八毛一块，怎么样，等于送给你！"马而立把大腿一拍，"**够意思**，来来，再抽支烟。"

(From the short story 围墙)

"Eighty cents each, OK? I'm practically giving it to you for nothing." Ma Erli slapped his thigh and said, "You're a real friend. Come on, have another smoke." [Negotiating the price of decorative tiles.]

♦ 你这人可真不**够意思**，昨儿说好的事儿今天就变卦了。

Some friend you are! Yesterday we reached an agreement and today you're going back on your word.

gū mo 估摸

Estimate; figure

♦ "再过一天我们就能走出这林子了。""我**估摸**着也该到了。"

(From the movie 紫日)

"One more day and we'll be out of the woods." "I reckon we're getting there ."

♦ 他是属于公安保卫系统的行家，伸手一摸，就知道这个坑里有没有鱼，有多大的鱼，能**估摸**个八九不离十。

(From the short story 锅碗瓢盆交响曲)

He's a police expert. He just probes around a little, and he knows whether there are any fish [criminals] in the hole and how big they are. His guess is never far off the mark.

gū nǎi nai 姑奶奶

1. great-aunt 2. (vulgar) a female self-aggrandizing self-reference

♦ 别往前凑，离**姑奶奶**远点儿！

(From the TV series 贫嘴张大民的幸福生活)

Quit pushing to the front. Leave your elders and betters some space.

♦ 不能让她觉得你们家老拿她当**姑奶奶**供着。

(From the TV series 其实男人最辛苦)

Don't let her get the idea your family worships her like some great lady. [Neighbors are advising a mother-in-law to get the upper hand over her new daughter-in-law, who is very capable and earns a great deal of money.]

gù tóu bú gù dìng 顾头不顾腚 (顧頭不顧腚)

(Vulgar) "take care of the head but not the butt"; fail to cover all the bases

◆ 临睡前，程石想，黑头这人干事就是**顾头不顾腚**，半夜三更领回来这么个坐台小姐，男女杂处一室，万一碰上警察查夜，一千张嘴也说不清。

(From the novel 越轨诉讼)

Before he fell asleep, Cheng Shi thought that Black Head didn't know how to cover his tracks. Bringing a bar hostess back with him in the middle of the night, a man and a woman staying in the same room—try to explain that one if the police knock on his door.

◆ 我跟你们说过多少次了，怎么还干这些**顾头不顾腚**的蠢事？

How many times have I told you to cover your ass? Why do you keep doing such stupid things?

guà zai zuǐ biān shàng 挂在嘴边上 (挂在嘴邊上)

"Hang on the lips"; keep talking about something

◆ 吵归吵，不要把"离婚"两个字**挂在嘴边上**。

(From the TV series 田教授的二十八个保姆)

Fight all you want, but none of that divorce talk. [A father is lecturing his daughter, who is quarrelling with her husband.]

◆ 我开了六年的车，只出过一次事故，你为什么总把那次事故**挂在嘴边儿上**？ 你这是成心**跟我过不去**啊！

I've been driving for six years, and I've only had one accident. Why do you keep dwelling on it? You're just being deliberately hard on me!

guài 怪

Rather; very; quite

◆ 看他那样儿，**怪**可怜的。

(From the TV series 今生是亲人)

Look at him, the poor thing. [He is depressed because he has just learned he is not his parents' biological child.]

◆ 他不过是个刚出校门儿的学生，让他来组织这么大的活动，也**怪**难为他的。

He's only just finished school. Asking him to organize such a big event is too much.

guān cai ráng zi 棺材瓤子

(Beijing dialect) "coffin"; very old (瓤子: the flesh of a fruit)

◆ 我啊快变成**棺材瓤子**了。

(From the TV series 今生是亲人)

I haven't got too much longer to live. [The speaker wants her grandson to get married and have children.]

◆ 您也是一把岁数土埋脖梗子按老话儿讲**棺材瓤子**了。

(From the novel 一点儿正经没有)

You're not that young anymore. You've already got one foot in the grave ["half-buried"]. "Coffin material," as they say.

guān qǐ mén lai dǎ gǒu 关起门来打狗 (關起門來打狗)

"Close the door before beating the dog"; cut off the opponent's path of retreat and then destroy him

♦ 万一叶浩明翻下脸来，到时候关起门来打狗，吃亏的不正是学生们么？

(From the novel 文革风云)

If Ye Haoming turns against the students, they'll have no way out. Won't they be the ones to suffer in the end? [In a story set during the Cultural Revolution, the speaker thinks that the Red Guards should not be taking on the military.]

♦ 你的意思是先把他放进来，然后关起门来打狗？ 我看是个好主意。

You mean, let him in first, then surround and destroy him? I think that's a great idea.

guān sb shénme shì 关Sb什么事 (关Sb什么事)

What business is it of yours, his, etc.?

♦ "你怎么有这么多钱啊？""这关你什么事？"

(From the movie 甜蜜蜜)

"How come you have so much money?" "What business is it of yours?"

♦ "你回答我，这钱是从哪儿来的？""这关你什么事？"

(From the TV series 失乐园)

"Answer me. Where did the money come from?" "None of your business."

guàn huáng tāng 灌黄汤 (灌黃湯)

"Pour the yellow soup down one's throat"; drink alcohol

♦ 人家早晨同你讲得满好的，叫你晚饭回到家里来吃，我还为你亲自去买小菜烧了大半天，谁知你倒在外面灌黄汤开心。

(From the novel 结婚十年)

This morning I distinctly told you I wanted you home for dinner. I even went out grocery shopping myself, and slaved over a hot stove all day. And instead you stayed out drinking and partying!

♦ 他们又灌你了多少黄汤？ 你就答应把咱们的产品底低价卖给他们了？

How many drinks did they give you until you agreed to sell them our products at such rock-bottom prices?

guàn mí hún tāng 灌迷魂汤 (灌迷魂湯)

"Make someone drink a potion that bewitches the soul"; sweet-talk or seduce

♦ 别给我灌迷魂汤，甜言蜜语，有奶便是娘，你瞎老范还怕找不着靠山。

(From the novel 丑末寅初)

Don't try to fool me with your smarmy talk. You'll go along with anyone if it's to your advantage ["if it has milk, it's your mother"]. You'll find a backer for sure, Blind Fan.

♦ 干吗？ 是不是往歌厅跑发忕呀？哈哈，怕歌厅里的小姐给你灌迷魂汤，把你拉下水是不是？

(From the novel 百年德性)

What's up? Are you scared of going to the nightclub? Are you afraid the girls will give you a love potion and corrupt your virtue ["pull you under the water"]? [A police chief is teasing a subordinate who is being sent to a nightclub on official business.]

guāng gǎnr sī lìng 光杆儿司令 (光杆兒司令)

"Lone general"; all by oneself

◆ 我能混到今天，就是靠的手底下有一批肯卖命的弟兄，否则就真成光杆司令了！

(From the novel 汉风)

The only reason I'm where I am today is that I have a lot of real friends who were willing to knock themselves out for me. Otherwise I'd just be on my own.

◆ 别说那辆破桑塔娜，就是大奔爸爸也能开上。迟早啊，爸爸这个光杆儿司令手下也会有千军万马。

(From the TV series 北京女人)

Forget about that lousy Santana. I [your dad] could drive a big Mercedes [if I wanted to]. Sooner or later, I won't be fighting my battles alone anymore; I'll have a whole army under my command. [An exchange between a father and a daughter. The father's ' ex-wife is a mid-level executive and drives a Santana. She has several people working under her. The father, on the other hand, has neither a car nor anybody working under him. The daughter wans to know when he might have a car of his own. The Volkswagen Santana is a mid-priced, utilitarian car made in Shanghai by a Sino-German joint venture.]

guāng gùnr yì tiáo 光棍儿一条 (光棍兒一條)

"A bare club"; a bachelor; a single man

◆ 三十的人了，还光棍一条。

(From the TV series 大雪无痕)

I'm in my thirties and still not married.

◆ 我是光棍儿一条，什么都不怕。

(From the TV series 黑洞)

I'm single, so I'm not afraid of anything.

guāng/chì jiǎo de bú pà chuān xié de 光/赤脚的不怕穿鞋的 (光/赤腳的不怕穿鞋的)

(Proverb) "The shoeless don't fear the shod"; if you don't have anything, you have nothing to lose

◆ 我创办大地〖公司〗没拿自己一文钱，破产了还是一文不文，这赤脚的还怕你穿鞋的？

(From the TV series 大赢家)

I didn't use a cent of my own money to start the Mother Earth Company, so if it goes belly up, I don't lose anything. If you don't have anything, you have nothing to lose. [The speaker is engaged in vicious price-cutting with another company. He thinks he can undersell the other company.]

◆ 有"合同"在手，别说那８０万签字费早已到手，真要开了我或处罚我，咱告他们去。谁怕谁呀，也没老婆孩子，光脚的不怕穿鞋的。

(From the novel 足球黑字)

The contract is already in my hands, and I got the 800,000 signing fee long ago. If they really fire or discipline me, I'll sue them. Who's afraid of whom? I don't have a wife or kids. If you don't have anything, you've got nothing to lose.

guī 归 (歸)

Belong to; fall under

♦ 我希望咱们工作归工作，友情归友情。

(From the TV series 都市情感)

I hope we can keep our work and our friendship separate.

♦ 我丑话说在头里，咱们朋友归朋友，生意归生意，不管是谁买我都得赚钱。

I'm being upfront with you. Friendship is one thing and business is another. I don't care who the buyer is; I have to make a profit.

guī le bāo zuī 归了包堆 (歸了包堆)

Lumped all together; in total

♦ 白家门里，上上下下，里里外外，男男女女，大大小小，归了包堆，全他妈混账王八蛋！

(From the TV series 大宅门)

The whole Bai family—masters and servants, indoor and outdoor help, male and female, young and old—are all without exception fucking bastards.

♦ 谁说人多啊，归了包堆也就百十来人。

Who says it's a lot of people? Counting everyone, it's just a bit over a hundred.

guī qí 归齐 (歸齊)

(Beijing dialect) in the final analysis; all told; everything considered

♦ 可世界您放眼望去，冷眼向洋，人是不少，好的也有，可归齐包圆哪个不是人生爹妈养的？

(From the TV series 编辑部的故事)

Look at the world objectively, there are plenty of people and some of them are decent. But when all is said and done, which of them was not born of a woman and raised by a father and mother?

♦ 瞎讨论半天，归齐这经理的位子还是给董事长他小舅子了。

We wasted our breath talking about it forever, but in the end it was still the chairman of the board's brother-in-law who got the manager position.

guì cuō bǎnr 跪搓板儿 (跪搓板兒)

Kneel on a washboard [as a punishment], take one's punishment without protest

♦ "老大怎么没来？" "你让人家跪搓板儿，他不敢来呀！"

(From the TV series 汽车城)

"How come your son still hasn't come back?" "After the way you put him through the mill, he wouldn't dare!"

♦ "这下惨了，晚上没准得跪搓板啦！" "这年头，哪个男人不跪搓板，这还是轻的。"

(From the novel 女性写真)

"Now I'm in deep trouble. Tonight she'll make me crawl!" "What guy doesn't have to crawl these days? If that's all, you're getting off easy."

gǔn dàn 滚蛋

Get out! Get away! Get the hell out!

♦   嚷什么啊，**滚蛋**！

(From the movie 有话好好说)
What are you hollering about? Get the hell out of here!

♦   还愣在这儿干什么？ 还不快**滚蛋**？

(From the TV series 手心手背)
Why are you still standing here like you're paralyzed? Get lost!

gǔn dāo ròu 滚刀肉

"Meat that rolls from under a knife"; a difficult person; neither the carrot nor the stick works

♦   赵明是个**滚刀肉**，厂里没人敢惹他。前年的承包费就没交，说是赔了。前任许厂长**屁**也**没敢放**一个，就算**拉倒**了。

(From the novel 大厂)
'Zhao Ming is a bully. Nobody at the factory dares to provoke him. Two years ago he didn't pay the required fee for his contract, claiming he lost money. The former director let it go without daring to say a word, and that was the end of it.

♦   他啊，整个一吃饱了混天黑的**滚刀肉**。

(From the TV series 一年又一年)
Him? He's nothing but a lazy bag of bones—just eats and waits around for bedtime.

guó jì wán xiào 国际玩笑 (國際玩笑)

"International joke"; a big joke

♦   "你是不是生气了？" "开什么**国际玩笑**？ 你搞不搞对象跟我有什么关系？"

(From the TV series 一年又一年)
"Are you upset?" "Are you kidding? What's it got to do with me whether you're dating or not?"

♦   我这可不是开**国际玩笑**，我说的是正经的。

I'm not joking about this. I'm dead serious.

guò ān shēng rì zi 过安生日子 (過安生日子)

Live life peacefully; live a quiet life

♦   我什么都不**图**，就**图**过个安生日子。

(From the movie 活着)

All I want is a quiet life.

♦ 你别瞎折腾了好不好，咱们也该过两天**安生日子**了。
Will you stop mucking around? It's about time we had some peace in our lives.

guò de qù 过得去 (過得去)
Pass the mark; pass the test; OK

♦ 璀璨自小就是这副**德性**，不愠不火，做任何事都是马虎随便，**过得去**就行了。
(From the novel 情方璀璨)
Cuican has been like this since he was a kid. Nothing could light a fire in his belly. He's careless and laid back about everything. He just wants to get by, that's all.

♦ 人呢，我也没有太高的要求，**过得去**就行了，但是一定得快，明天就能来上班儿，要不然我不要。
I don't ask much of this hire. He just has to be adequate, and that's enough. But I can't wait. He has to be able to start work tomorrow, or I don't want him.

guò jiā jiā 过家家 (過家家)
Play house

♦ 离婚？ 你以为这是小孩儿**过家家**吗？
(From the TV series 今生是亲人)
Getting a divorce? You think it's a game?

♦ 这婚姻大事又不是小孩儿玩儿**过家家**似的。
(From the TV series 手心手背)
Marriage isn't like playing house.

guò jier 过节儿/过结儿 (過節兒/過結兒)
Hold a grudge; have a conflict

♦ 这两家人有**过节儿**。
(From the TV series 今生是亲人)
There's bad blood between the two families.

♦ 好象你和她之间有什么**过节**吧？ 说话狠巴巴的。
(From the novel 突出重围)
Seems like she and you have some issues. Why did you sound so nasty?

guò lai rénr 过来人儿 (過來人兒)
An experienced person

♦ 姐姐是**过来人儿**了，这种事儿可不能由着性子来。
(From the TV series 空镜子)
I'm your older sister and I have some experience with this. Better not jump the gun. [The newlywed younger sister complains that she's getting no pleasure from sex with her husband.]

♦ 这话应该由我来说，我才是**过来人儿**呢。
(From the movie 一见钟情)

I'm the one who should be talking; I've been there. [A divorced man replies to a single man who says marriage is boring.]

guò mìng 过命 (過命)

"Exchange life"; be willing to sacrifice one's life for someone else

◆ 我和他认识得太晚了，要不然我们一定是**过命**的朋友。

(From the TV series 激情燃烧的岁月)

I met him too late. Otherwise we'd have been the sort of friends who were willing to give our lives for each other.

◆ 你爹在世的时候，我跟他是**过命**的交情。

(From the TV series 一年又一年)

When your dad was alive, we were the closest of friends.

guò tóu 过头 (過頭)

Over the limit; excessive; too much

◆ 最好大家都规规矩矩，别说**过头**话，别有任何出乎常规的举动。

(From the novel 有只鸽子叫红唇)

It's best if everyone follows the rules. No one should speak out of turn and no one should step out of line.

◆ 你可别睡**过头**儿了，今天下午省厅要来人。

(From the TV series 失乐园)

Make sure you don't oversleep. This afternoon there'll be people coming from the provincial [police] department.

guò wǔ guān zhǎn liù jiàng 过五关斩六将 (過五關斬六將)

"Pass five fortresses and kill six generals"; overcome numerous obstacles

◆ 他心中有些叫苦，要追一个长得只有一点点不错的女人，居然
还要**过五关斩六将**！ 做生意也没这么累！

(From the novel 女作家的爱情冒险)

He felt petulant. If you want to court any remotely decent-looking woman, you have to overcome so many obstacles and pass so many tests. It's more exhausting than doing business! [The man is being questioned by the woman's mother. It'll be the father's turn next.]

◆ 自然，当着晚辈儿，他会没结没完地跟你抖落肚子里那些"**过五关斩
六将**"的事儿，生怕没人拿他当关云长。可是"**走麦城**"的事儿，他
就跟你打马虎眼了。

(From the novel 百年德性)

In front of the young people, naturally, he would just spin out all the stories of his victories, fearing that people might not recognize him as a Napoleon. But when it came to his Waterloos, he would just hem and haw. [The reference is to the victories and defeats of the general Guan Yunchang, from the *Romance of the Three Kingdoms*. He was famous for his victories, killing six generals at Five Passes (过五关斩六将) and for his humiliating defeat at Maicheng (麦城).]

guò yi bú qù 过意不去 (過意不去)

Feel guilty

◆ 上次说话说重了，我心里挺**过意**不去的。

(From the movie 有话好好说)

I spoke too harshly last time. I feel pretty bad about that.

♦ 您还有什么**过意不去**的吗？ 画儿韩自己就靠造假画起家，这叫现世报。

(From the novel 寻访画儿韩)

> What do you have to feel guilty about? That painter Han made a fortune forging pictures. This amounts to getting your just deserts in this life [现世报: retribution in this as opposed to a future life]. [The painter Han bought a forgery from the listener, who is now feeling guilty.]

guò yǐn 过瘾 (過癮)

Satisfy an addiction or craving; have a fix

♦ 老公，还是这大彩电**过瘾**吧？

(From the TV series 天堂鸟)

> Dear, this big screen color TV set is just what you longed for, isn't it？

♦ 你的感觉怎么样？ 要是不**过瘾**再搓两圈儿？

> "How are you feeling? If you need another fix, we could play a couple more rounds."

guò zhèi cūnr méi zhèi diànr le 过这村儿没这店儿了 (過這村兒沒這店兒了)

"If you go past this village, you'll miss the inn"; you'll lose the opportunity

♦ 俺姐妹俩说句心里话，**过了这村就没这店了**。上秦局长家求亲的人可是排成串儿啊！

(From the novel 锁链，是柔软的)

> I'll tell you honestly, sister to sister. If you miss the bus, you'll be sorry. People who would like to marry into Bureau Director Qin's family are lining up around the block. [Director Qin's son is in love with the listener's daughter.]

♦ 最近卫视特别需要人，要去快去，**过了这村儿可没这店啊**！

(From the TV series 走过花季)

> Satellite TV desperately needs people. If you want to work for them, grab the chance.

H

hái shuō ne 还说呢 (還說呢)

Don't even mention; look who's talking

♦ 嗨！ **还说呢**，〚他〛根本就没回来。

(From the TV series 今生是亲人)

> That one! He didn't come home at all. [A birthday party was prepared for someone, but he didn't come home for supper.]

♦ "家里怎么这么清净？" 〚孩子都没回来〛 "**还说呢**？ 你哪天按时回来的？"

(From the TV series 一年又一年)

"How come the house is so quiet?" [The kids aren't home yet.] "Look who's talking! When did you ever get home on time?"

hái tīng gè xiǎngr ne 还听个响儿呢 (還聽個響兒呢)

"If only to hear the sound"; do something just because it makes a pretty sound, even if it accomplishes nothing

♦ 没门儿！ 我七老爷从来不心疼钱，也不是要钱不要命的主儿！ 可王喜光这种小人，休想拿一个子儿！ 我扔水里**还听个响儿呢**！

(From the TV series 大宅门)

No way! I, Seventh Master, have never been a moneygrubber, and I'm not the type who cares more for my money than my life! But if a bastard like Wang Xiguang thinks he can get a penny from me, he can think again! I'd rather throw the money into the water just to hear the sound it makes.

♦ 我是一个子儿都不会借给那小子的。掉地下**还听个响儿呢**，借给他保准儿回不来。

I wouldn't lend a cent to that bastard. If you throw the money on the ground, you at least get to hear the jingle it makes. But if you lend it to him, don't ever hope to get it back.

hǎi le qù le 海了去了

"An ocean of"; a great number of

♦ 您说北京这几年盖的房子还少吗？ 四层五层的，十层二十层的，**海了去了**！

(From the TV drama 昏晃胡同)

There's been a lot of new construction in Beijing the last few years, don't you think? Four- and five-story buildings, ten- and twenty-story buildings—it's like a flood!

♦ 我岳母上街让汽车给撞了，司机还跑了，上医院接了三回膀子还没接上，这钱就花**海了**！

(From the TV series 贫嘴张大民的幸福生活)

My mother-in-law was knocked over in the street by a car, and then the driver fled. She's been to the hospital three times trying without success to get her shoulder set, and had to spend a ton of money, too.

hān dà 憨大

(Shanghai dialect) pronounced "gaang doo"; idiot; moron

♦ 你当我**憨大**呀，八十多块的料作和三百多块的料作我还分不清呀？

(From the short story 家庭风景二十章)

You think I'm an idiot? You think I can't tell eighty-yuan material from three-hundred-yuan material? [A husband buys his wife an expensive sweater, but tells her the price is less so she wouldn't think he was being too extravagant. The ruse backfires, because she thinks the sweater is even cheaper than he claims.]

♦ 我实在不明白，她那么好的条件，为什么最后跟那个**憨大**结婚了？

I just can't figure it out. She has so much to offer. Why did she marry that moron?

hán chen 寒碜 (寒磣)

Ashamed; embarrassed; shabby

♦ 现在他是我们厂有名的落后分子，（可是他自己）一点儿都不嫌**寒碜**。

(From the TV series 一年又一年)

Now he's a well-known slacker at our factory, but that doesn't embarrass him in the least.

♦ 人家开宝马去接新娘，你开切诺基去，太**寒碜**了。

They picked up their bride in a BMW. You're doing it in a Cherokee. That's too shabby.

háo dǎi 好歹

"Good or bad"; 1. for better or worse; no matter what; after all 2. illness

♦ **好歹**我这儿是铁饭碗，虽说工资不高，日子还过得去。

(From the TV series 今生是亲人)

At least I have a secure job ["an iron rice bowl"] here. Sure the pay isn't much, but I get by.

♦ "祖宗！别这么傻不傻痴不痴的，你这个样儿，弄得我心里直毛咕，别再急出个**好歹**来，快进屋。"

(From the TV series 大宅门)

"I beg you ["ancestor"]. Don't act so crazy! The way you carry on scares me. Don't worry yourself sick. Quick, come in!" [The couple's child has been kidnapped. The husband is so worried he's stopped sleeping and talking.]

hǎo gāng yòng zai dāo rèn shàng 好钢用在刀刃上 (好鋼用在刀刃上)

(Proverb) "Put the good steel on the edge of the knife"; put the resources where they count

♦ 我知道你不同意，要把钱**用在刀刃上**。但是支持一下公益事业，对公司的形象也有好处。

(From the TV series 失乐园)

I know you don't agree. You think we should put the money where it counts, but giving back to the community ["supporting causes that benefit the community"] is good for the company's image. [The general manager of the company would like to sponsor a shooting team, but the deputy manager disagrees.]

♦ 孩子，你要记住，**好钢要用在刀刃上**。你觉得咱们挣了三百万就可以随便乱花了，这怎么行呢？ 咱们的公司还要再投资啊！

> Remember, kid, you've got to make your money work for you. You think that since we've made three million yuan we can just blow it ["spend money wildly, any way we want"]. We can't do that! Our company needs reinvestment.

hǎo guǒ zi chī 好果子吃

"(Give someone) good fruit to eat"; make it easy for someone (usually used negatively)

♦ 咱们这会儿归顺，他康熙也不会给咱们**好果子吃**。

(From the TV series 康熙帝国)

> Even if we return to the fold now, that Kangxi won't let us off easy. [A general who has revolted is talking to his son.]

♦ 唐龙，你可要小心点，得罪了无冕之王，可没你什么**好果子吃**。

(From the novel 突出重围)

> Tang Long, you have to be careful. If you offend the fourth estate ("uncrowned king," i.e., journalists), you'll have to pay later. [A friend is concerned that Tang Long was impatient with a reporter who wanted to interview him for an article.]

hǎo hàn zuò shì hǎo hàn dāng 好汉作事好汉当 (好漢作事好漢當)

A real man takes responsibility for his actions

♦ 老实告诉我，这事是不是你**牵的头**啊？ **好汉作事好汉当**，你就等着处理吧！

(From the TV series 大赢家)

> Tell me honestly, were you the ringleader? A real man accepts the consequences of his actions. You can count on being punished.

♦ 你们都不用害怕，这件事跟大家没有关系，如果上面查下来，我一个人顶着，**好汉作事好汉当**嘛。

> You guys don't have to worry. This has nothing to do with you. If the higher-ups start asking questions, I'll deal with them. I did it and I'll take responsibility for it.

hǎo jiā hu 好家伙 (好傢夥)

Gosh; God

♦ 哎呀，**好家伙**啊！你们来了一个排的人呐。

(From the TV series 大雪无痕)

I don't believe it! You have an army of people here! [A group of policemen arrive at the provincial Party Committee to vent their grievances.]

◆ **好家伙**，商店还没开门儿呢外面就黑压压一大片人。

My God, the store hasn't even opened and there's already a huge crowd of people outside.

hǎo lài 好赖 (好賴)

See 好歹 hǎo dǎi

hǎo ma 好嘛

(Sarcastic) great; isn't that great; that's just great

◆ 前两天电视说了，开公车办私事要处理的。**好嘛**，这不是顶风作案吗？ 有他好看的！

(From the TV series 北京女人)

A couple of days ago it was announced on TV that anyone using public vehicles for private business will be punished. That's just great. He had the nerve to do it anyway. Watch what happens to him now!

◆ 这么一折腾，**好嘛**，得减十年寿。

Great, after this ordeal, you can take ten years off my life.

hǎo mǎ bù chī huí tóu cǎo 好马不吃回头草 (好馬不吃回頭草)

(Proverb) "A good horse will not go back to the old pasture to graze"; a proud person will not return to a position he or she has left

◆ "给你联系好回厂当临时工了。" "呸！ 别**寒碜**我了！ **好马不吃回头草**。"

(From TV series 一年又一年)

"I fixed it so you can go back to the factory as a temp." "Oh no, don't make me eat crow! No way could I go back." [A man who quit his job and went into business for himself has now seen his business fail.]

◆ **好马不吃回头草**，我就是打一辈子**光棍儿**也不会跟那个女人复婚。

There's no going back to the past. Even if I have to stay single the rest of my life, I'm not going to marry that woman again.

hǎo me dāng yāngr de/hǎo me yǐngr de 好么当央儿的/好么影儿的 (好麼當央兒的/好麼影兒的)

Out of the blue; all of the sudden

◆ 你甭在妈这儿**打马虎眼**，没人指使你，你**好么当央儿的**查起市委书记来了，又是你叔叔。

(From the novel 都市危情)

Don't try to fool your own mother. Unless someone put you up to it, how come you suddenly start investigating the municipal party secretary, who's your own uncle on top of everything?

◆ 这两口子也真怪，刚买了新房子、新车，**好么影儿的**就离婚了。

(From the TV series 一年又一年)

This couple is really strange. They just bought a new house and a new car. How come they're getting a divorce out of the blue?

hǎo nǐ gè... 好你个··· (好你個···)

You son of a gun; you bastard

◆ 好你个姚启圣，皇差你也敢打？

(From the TV series 康熙帝国)

Yao Qisheng, you bastard, you dared to beat up an imperial envoy?

◆ 好你个刘阿根，把病死的猪拿到集市上来卖，这是要吃官司的，你懂吗？

Liu Agen, you crazy bastard, you brought a pig that died of disease to sell at the market? You'll get hauled into court, don't you understand?

hǎo shuō 好说 (好說)

No problem; sure thing

◆ 江帆正在和一个中年人说着话："吴厅长，这次招标还要请你多关照。" 对方说："好说，好说。"

(From the novel 红与黑 2000)

Jiang Fan was talking to a middle-aged man, "Director Wu, please help us with the bid." The other man replied, "Sure thing."

◆ "您看这件事您能不能帮我们想想办法？" "好说，好说。我会把这件事儿当成自己的事儿来办的。"

"Do you think you can figure out a way to help us with this situation?" "Sure. I'll treat this matter as if it were my own affair."

hǎo xīn dāng chéng lú gān fèi 好心当成驴肝肺 (好心當成驢肝肺)

"Regard a good heart as if it were the liver and lungs of a donkey"; misunderstand or fail to appreciate someone's kind intention

◆ 我好心好意把她招到公司里来，她可倒好，好心当成驴肝肺了。

(From the TV series 大雪无痕)

I gave her a job in this company out of the goodness of my heart. But she turns around and treats the favor like dirt.

◆ 给你烫烫脚吧，好心当成驴肝肺，伺候你还嫌烫，真是的！

(From the TV series 水浒传)

I brought you some hot water to soak your feet, but do you appreciate it? Here I am waiting on you, and you complain the water's too hot! Unbelievable!

hǎo xīn méi hǎo bào 好心没好报 (好心沒好報)

"A good heart doesn't get a good reward"; no good deed goes unpunished

◆ "你，你，你，我叫你来帮我证婚，你却来捣乱。你，你，你！" "我什么时候捣乱了？ 我是帮你，真是好心没个好报。"

(From the novel 风乱舞)

♦ 我本来是想帮他的忙，没想到被他骂了一顿，真是**好心没好报**。

> I was only trying to help him. I didn't expect him to chew me out. So much for "one good turn deserves another."

hào 号 (號)

> Kind; sort; number

♦ 咱们走，跟这**号**人，咱犯不上生气。

(From the TV series 红色康乃馨)

> Let's go. It's not worth letting someone like this upset us.

♦ 这龙腾公司的背景可不一般，省市级领导干部的子女就有一百来**号**。

> The backing this Longteng Company has is really unusual. They've got more than a hundred [employees] who are children of provincial and city officials.

hē liáng shuǐ dōu sāi yá 喝凉水都塞牙 (喝涼水都塞牙)

> "Get things stuck in the teeth even while drinking water"; be unlucky; troubles never come singly

♦ 人背啊，**喝凉水都塞牙**。

(From the TV series 一年又一年)

> When you're unlucky, whatever can go wrong, will.

♦ 我这两天特别倒霉，生意不顺，老婆闹离婚，汽车还撞了，真是**喝凉水都塞牙**。

> I've been really unlucky the last few days. My business isn't going well. My wife wants a divorce. On top of that, I crashed my car. Troubles never come singly.

hē mò shuǐr/zhīr 喝墨水儿/墨汁儿 (喝墨水兒/墨汁兒)

> "Drink ink"; be educated

♦ 城里**喝过几瓶墨汁**的小伙子，**八抬大轿**请不动，刀搁脖子上也不愿娶个柴禾妞子呀！

(From the novel 吃青杏的时节)

> Those city boys with a few scraps of education wouldn't get off their asses and marry a peasant girl [a "firewood girl"], even if you sent a stretch limo or held a knife to their necks.

♦ 你也是个秀才，是个**喝过几天墨水儿**的人，别给你爹丢脸了。

(From the TV series 天下粮仓)

> You're a scholar, an educated man. Don't embarrass your father. [The son of a high-ranking official is making a spectacle of himself. A servant tries to persuade him to go home.]

hē xī běi fēng 喝西北风 (喝西北風)

> "Drink the northwest wind"; go hungry

♦ 店老板在楼下大喝道："死小二，在那里磨蹭什么？楼下客人你都给我搁这儿，你他妈想**喝西北风**啊？"

(From the novel 戏子多情，婊子重义)

The owner of the restaurant shouted from downstairs, "Hey waiter, what are you doing dragging your feet up there? If you ignore the customers downstairs, you'll [lose this job and] fucking starve." [小二: *obsolete*, waiter]

◆ 你告诉那些乱**嚼舌头**的贱货，趁早给我放规矩点，别猪油蒙了心。没我，她们早**喝西北风**了。

(From the novel 红檀板)

You tell those gossiping bitches to behave and stop kidding themselves. Without me they'd all be starving.

hē yi hú 喝一壶 (喝一壺)

"Drink one kettle"; have more trouble than one can handle

◆ 王元宝这小子太孬了，打着老阴阳的招牌到处骗人，这回可够他**喝一壶**了。

(From the novel 山乡情话)

Wang Yuanbao is such a fucking bastard, pretending to be a *feng shui* master and conning people everywhere. Now he's going to stew in it. [老阴阳: "Old Yin-yang," an experienced *feng shui* master. The new site that he chose for a factory was a disaster.]

◆ 你还想着外地的那笔生意？ 算了吧，公司里边的这些事儿就够你**喝一壶**的了。

Are you still thinking about that out-of-town deal? Forget it. You have your hands full just with company business.

hé zhe 和着/合着··· (和著/合著···)

Guess; could it be; it turns out

◆ "你要是怕输啊，往后就别玩儿！" "**和着**我输不起啊？"

(From the movie 洗澡)

"If you're afraid of losing, stop playing!" "Are you saying I can't afford to lose?"

◆ 你小子还挺鬼，**合着**这得罪人的事完全推给我们了。

(From the novel 我是你爸爸)

You're really underhanded, you little rascal. You made us play the bad cop, didn't you? [A judge teases a child, who refuses to choose which parent should have custody, thus forcing the court to decide.]

hēi 黑

1. embezzle 2. greedy

◆ 你穷？ 你小子**黑**了多少银子别当我不知道！

(From the TV series 大宅门)

You're broke? You bastard, don't think I don't know how much money you embezzled!

◆ 一个摊位三千？ 办事处可够**黑**的。

(From the TV series 贫嘴张大民的幸福生活)

Three thousand for one stall! Those market officials are really greedy!

héng shi 横是

No matter what

◆ 这小偷儿**心说**了，您**横是**不能光着屁股出来追我吧？

(From the movie 洗澡)

The thief thought to herself, "No way you'd go out buck naked to chase me down, would you?" [A thief stole someone's necklace in a public bath. Both the thief and victim are women.]

♦ 你干的那些事儿别人问你你可以不说，你爹问你你横是不能不说吧？

　　If other people ask about the things you did, you don't have to answer. But if your father asks, you can't possibly keep silent, right?

héng tiāo bí zi shù tiāo yǎn 横挑鼻子竖挑眼 (橫挑鼻子豎挑眼)

"Blame the nose for not being horizontal and the eyes for not being vertical"; be hypercritical

♦ 她们对新娘子横挑鼻子竖挑眼。

(From the short story 家庭风景二十章)

　　They tore the bride to pieces with their comments. [Referring to new sisters-in-law.]

♦ 你要是不想让我在这儿干就明说，别横挑鼻子竖挑眼的。

　　If you don't want me to work here, just say so. Stop nitpicking.

héng xià yì tiáo xīn 横下一条心 (橫下一條心)

Stiffen one's resolve; go all out

♦ 既到了吴国，就要横下一条心，死活有天定！

(From the novel 范蠡与西施)

　　Now that we're in the kingdom of Wu, we have to gather our courage. Whether we live or die is up to fate. [An army from the kingdom of Yue has entered the territory of their enemy, the kingdom of Wu.]

♦ 好，咱们干。我反正是横下一条心了。

　　OK, let's do it. I'm going all out, no matter what.

hóng huā hái yào lǜ yè fú 红花还要绿叶扶 (紅花還要綠葉扶)

(Proverb) "Even a red flower needs green leaves to set it off"; success depends on the support of others; you can't do it all by yourself

♦ 红花还要绿叶扶，您自个站在台上难道不寂寞？

(From the movie 顽主)

　　It can't be a one-man show. Wouldn't you feel lonely standing on the stage all by yourself? [The speaker thinks that others deserve to be on the stage as well to receive acknowledgement for their contributions.]

♦ 不错，他姓王的是挺能干，可红花还要绿叶扶啊！

　　You're right. That Wang guy is very capable, but he can't do it alone.

hóng rénr 红人儿 (紅人兒)

Popular guy; pet; darling

♦ 别看你现在是公司上上下下的大红人儿，并且在陈老总那儿也挂了名儿，你要是用了那个戏子，给我捅出漏子来，我照炒你不误。

(From the TV series 北京女人)

Even though you're the company's golden boy at the moment, and you've gotten a reputation with Chen, the general manager, don't think I won't fire you if you hire that two-bit actor and get us into trouble!

♦ 他是老板的**红人**，你可千万别得罪他。
He's the boss' pet. Don't rub him the wrong way.

hóng yǎnr bìng 红眼儿病 (紅眼兒病)
"The red-eye disease"; jealousy

♦ "你咋不早说全了呀？你坑死我了！"顺子说："我说全了不是怕你嫉妒！你看你妈那**红眼病**。"
(From the novel 东北一家人)
"Why didn't you tell me the whole story? You really did a number on me!" Shunzi replied, "The reason I didn't tell the whole story wasn't because I thought you might be jealous. But you know how easily your mom gets jealous." [The owner of a luxury car was able to pay the entire cost of replacing it after a traffic accident. The second speaker hesitated to mention that fact because the mother of the first speaker, a jealous woman, was present.]

♦ 你看人家小许当了局长有点儿**红眼儿病**，是不是？
You're a bit jealous that Xiao Xu got promoted to bureau chief, aren't you?

hōu 齁
So very; extremely

♦ **齁**冷的天儿，快把大衣穿上！
(From the TV series 大雪无痕)
It's so cold. Put your coat on, quick!

♦ "去游乐场？""去过了**没劲**，**齁**贵的。"
(From the novel 我是你爸爸)
"Want to go to the amusement park?" "I've been there. It's boring, and so expensive."

hóu chī má huā, mǎn nǐng 猴吃麻花，满拧 (猴吃麻花，滿擰)
A monkey eating fried dough, it's all wrong; get it backwards

♦ "听说纯棉涨价，化纤降价。""**猴吃麻花，满拧**！"
(From the TV series 一年又一年)
"I heard the price of pure cotton is rising, and the price of artificial fiber is dropping." "You've got it precisely backwards!" [The second speaker thinks the price of artificial fiber will rise.]

♦ 也不知道经理这广告是怎么做的，今天来了一大帮人要到我们这生产摩托车的工厂来买自行车，真是**猴吃麻花，满拧**！
I can't figure out what was in the manager's head when he published this ad. Today a whole bunch of people came to our motorcycle factory wanting to buy bicycles—he really sent the wrong message!

hóur nián mǎ yuè 猴儿年马月 (猴兒年馬月)
"The year of the monkey and the month of the horse"; 1. who knows when 2. a long time ago

♦ "听说你过去常下馆子。""**猴儿年马月**的事儿！现在能吃碗炸酱面就不错了。"
(From the TV series 一年又一年)

"I hear you used to eat out all the time." "That's ancient history. Now I'm lucky if I get noodles with bean paste sauce."

◆ 〖小偷没抓住〗"狗改不了吃屎，早晚能抓住他！""那得等到**猴儿年马月**啊？"

(From the TV series 其实男人最辛苦)

[A thief got away.] "The leopard can't change its spots. We'll nab him sooner or later." "When would that be?"

hòu huǐ yào 后悔药 (後悔藥)

"Regret pill"; regret

◆ 这**后悔药**该吃得吃，可也别吃起来没完啊！

(From the TV series 古船、女人和网)

It's all right to have second thoughts, but don't dwell on it forever!

◆ 孙搏权这两个月一直十分懊悔。但世上是无**后悔药**可吃的。上了**贼船**，只能当强盗。

(From the novel 浮沈商海)

For the past couple of months, Sun Boquan has had second thoughts. But in this world, what's done is done. Once you board a pirate ship, you have to become a pirate.

hòu niáng yǎng de 后娘养的 (後娘養的)

"Born of (or brought up by) a stepmother"; be treated like a stepchild; of inferior status; second-class citizen

◆ 娘的，咱独立团是**后娘养的**？ 人家吃肉咱不眼馋，可**好歹**也得给口汤喝呀，每次都是咱们团当预备队，这不是他娘的欺负人么？

(From the novel 亮剑)

Fuck it!I Is this a detachment of second-class citizens? We don't mind if the others get to have all the meat, but at least give us some broth. Our detachment is held in reserve every single time. Isn't that treating us like dirt?

◆ 这事儿**忒**不公平了！ 脏活累活都让咱们干，就好象咱们是**后娘养的**似的。

This just isn't fair! We have to do all the dirty work; we're treated like stepchildren.

hòu pà 后怕 (後怕)

Be frightened after the fact; frightened in retrospect

◆ 后来知道了〖那个人是艾滋病患者〗，一连洗十几次手还觉得恶心，现在想起来都**后怕**。

(From the TV series 失乐园)

After I found out [that the man had AIDS], I washed my hands at least ten times, but I still felt like puking. Even now I'm scared when I think about it.

◆ 那天我要是晚出来三分钟就赶上那场大爆炸了，现在想起来真后怕！

   If I went out three minutes later that day, I'd have been blown up. Even now it's scary to think about.

hú li jīng 狐狸精

"Fox spirit"; seductress; temptress

◆ "什么，你说我老爸是花痴？""要不是花痴怎么会把房产留给那个小狐狸精？"

   (From the TV series 红色康乃馨)

   "What, did you call my old man a sex-crazed idiot?" "If he's not a sex-crazed idiot, how come he left his house to that temptress?"

◆ 这么晚才回来，你是不是又去找那个狐狸精了？

   You just got back? Did you go to that slut again?

hú li wěi/yǐ ba lù chū lái le 狐狸尾巴露出来了 (狐狸尾巴露出來了)

"The fox revealed its tail"; show one's true colors

◆ 这回张锋他狐狸尾巴不是露出来了吗？

   (From the TV series 黑洞)

   This time Zhang Feng showed his true colors, didn't he?

◆ 看，这下狐狸尾巴露出来了，你哪儿是找我学书法的？ 你是来骗我这古瓶的！

   See, it's all coming out now. You're not here to get me to take up calligraphy. You want to con me out of this antique vase.

hú lu/huá la 胡噜/划拉 (胡噜/劃拉)

(Onomatopoeia) sweep in; rake in; deal with

◆ 我和桂兰都忙得两脚朝天了，还是胡噜不过来。

   (From the novel 空洞)

   Guilan and I are working our butts off, but we still can't keep up.

◆ 你做事情得分个轻重，不能什么都划拉着。

   You have to prioritize. You can't tackle everything indiscriminately.

hú lu li mài de shénme yào 葫芦里卖的什么药 (葫蘆裏賣的什麽藥)

"What medicine is for sale inside the gourd"; what's up one's sleeve

◆ 刘乡长，你这葫芦里卖的什么药，里面到底是什么人？

   (From the short story 黑屋子里的女人)

Chief Liu, what do you have up your sleeve? Who the hell's inside?

◆ 他这两天总在咱们这儿转来转去的，也不知道他**葫芦里卖的什么药**。

> He's been hanging around here the last couple of days. Who knows what he's got up his sleeve?

hú qìn 胡吣 (胡嗆)

Talk irresponsibly

◆ 妈妈：没有震宝，这家门我还进去干什么呢？爸爸：你少**胡吣**，且得好好活着呢！

(From TV series 今生是亲人)

> Mother: "Without Zhenbao, what's the point of going home?" Father: "Don't talk nonsense. Life goes on. [We have to keep on living well.]" [The court has just given custody of their child, Zhenbao, to another family.]

◆ "苏联老大哥、中国小弟弟，见面握握手，要钱买糖吃。" 跳皮筋儿的小孩唱。"**胡吣**什么？要死了你？不知道苏修早 '修' 了？" 一个老太太过来给了她一巴掌，揪着她耳朵回家了。

(From the novel 混沌加哩咯楞)

> A little girl was skipping rope, chanting, "The Soviet Union's our big brother, China's the little brother, when we meet we shake hands, we ask for money to buy candy." An old woman rushed over and slapped her, "What nonsense are you talking? You want to get yourself in trouble? Don't you know that the Soviets became revisionists a long time ago?" She dragged the little girl home by the ear. [The Soviet Union or 苏联 (sū lián) was China's close ally and popularly known as China's big brother. After an ideological rift in the late 50s, the Soviet Union became 苏修 (sū xiū, Soviet Revisionism). The novel is set during the Cultural Revolution when the consequences for being politically incorrect were often dire.]

hú tòngr chuàn zi 胡同儿串子 (胡同兒串子)

"A hutong hopper"; a loafer

◆ 他整个儿一**胡同串子**，不学无术，整天招猫逗狗的。

(From the TV series 今生是亲人)

> He's a complete deadbeat, ignorant and unskilled, and he hangs around with troublemakers all day.

◆ 我为了什么？不就是为了不让你跟咱们那儿那些**胡同串子**似的灰头土脸过一辈子吗？

(From the TV series 手心手背)

> Why am I doing it? Just because I don't want you to muddle through like those bums in our neighborhood. [灰头土脸: "head and face covered in dust;" ignominiously]

hú tu chóng 糊涂虫 (糊塗蟲)

"Confused bug"; space cadet

◆ 这个**糊涂虫**，整天丢东落西，光钱包已经丢了十几个。

(From the short story 寻与等的爱情逻辑)

He's a space cadet, always losing stuff. He's lost at least ten wallets already.

◆ 你叫他来有什么屁用？整个一糊涂虫！

If you get him to come, what fucking use is it? His head's not screwed on right.

hú zi 胡子 (鬍子)

"Beard"; bandit

◆ 掌柜的早就想离开，只不过找不到借口，无法脱身。他一听胖女人说的暗语，知道是**胡子**来了。

(From the novel 悍匪)

The innkeeper was dying to get away, but couldn't think of an excuse. As soon as he heard the fat woman's code word, he knew the bandits had come.

◆ "你他妈还不趁工夫多挺一会尸去，又在这里瞎噗哧些什么？"程喜春一面擦枪一面瞪起了眼睛大叫，"我他妈早睡足了，**胡子**来了一个枪子穿俩，小日本来了一个枪子穿仨！"

(From the novel 科尔沁旗草原)

"You motherfucker, why don't you grab the chance to catch some shuteye? What are you doing messing around here?" Cheng Chunxi shouted back bug-eyed while polishing his gun, "You motherfucker, I already had enough sleep. If the bandits come, I'll gun them down two at a time. If the Japs come, I'll gun them down three at a time."

hù dú zi 护犊子 (護犢子)

"Be protective of the calf"; be protective of one's child

◆ 这个石光荣打起仗来不要命，打完仗特别**护犊子**。

(From the TV series 激情燃烧的岁月)

This Shi Guangrong is reckless in battle, but when the battle's over, he's like a mother hen with his kids.

◆ 焦家的人都是一个德性：**护犊子**，排外。

(From the novel 空洞)

The Jiao family are all the same, protective of their own and suspicious of outsiders.

hù nong 糊弄

Pull wool over someone's eyes; deceive

◆ 你们俩要干什么就直说吧，别拿找孩子**糊弄**我。

(From the TV series 今生是亲人)

If you two want something, say so! Don't try to fool me with this talk of looking for the kid.

◆ 你的这一套**糊弄**别人还行，我可不会上你的当。

You can fool others with this line of yours, but I won't fall for it.

huā hua cháng zi/diǎn zi 花花肠子/点子 (花花腸子/點子)

"Flowery intestines"; fancy business; clever, crooked ideas

◆ 你别跟我来这套，你这点儿**花花肠子**我还不知道？

(From the TV series 黑洞)

Don't give me that. You think I don't know how your crooked mind works?

◆ 有道理，郑经的**花花点子**多着呢！

(From the TV series 康熙帝国)

You're right. Zheng Jing is full of tricks!

huā li hǔ shào 花里唬/胡哨 (花裏唬/胡哨)
"Flowery and fancy"; gaudy; colorful

♦ 打开纸箱，"哗啦"一倒，**花里胡哨**的塑料玩具立马堆了一地。
(From the novel 耍叉)
When the cardboard box was opened, a pile of gaudy plastic toys fell out.

♦ 我就不喜欢这种宣传材料，印得**花里唬哨**的，一点儿真东西都没有。
I, for one, don't care for this kind of publicity material—all showy presentation [printing] and no substance.

huā xīn 花心
"Flowery heart"; roving eye

♦ 除了你现在的女朋友之外，不许再**花心**。
(From the novel 永不瞑目)
Keep your eyes off everyone but your current girlfriend.

♦ 孔良他不像是那种**花心**的男人，你别冤枉他。
(From the TV series 大赢家)
Kong Liang doesn't look to me like a womanizer. Don't misjudge him.

huà cāo lǐ bù cāo 话糙理不糙 (話糙理不糙)
"The words may be crude but the logic is not"; pay attention to the substance, not the form

♦ "哎，你怎么这么粗野？""对不起，老马，我说顺嘴了，可**话糙理不糙**。"
(From the novel 我是你爸爸)
"Oh, why are you being so rude?" "I'm sorry, Lao Ma, it's just a habit of speaking. The expression is coarse, but the idea is not."

♦ 你也说句实话，别逗得我们孩子把一颗心都挂在你身上，**赶明儿菜篮子打水一场空**。大姨没上过几年学，是个粗人，说话不会拐弯抹角，可这**话糙理不糙**，你说是不？
(From the novel 魔鬼与天使)
Give it to us straight. Don't string our kid along so she hangs on your every word, and then the next day when she wakes up, she's like someone who tried to scoop up water with a basket, but there's nothing there. I'm your oldest aunt and I don't have much education. I'm a simple woman who doesn't know how to beat around the bush. But even if my speech is crude, my meaning isn't. Right?

huà dōu ràng nǐ shuō le 话都让你说了 (話都讓你說了)
"You have all the words"; you can't argue from both sides

♦ "好歹儿的，先让她睡睡石板再说，没准儿真能睡成个死猪。""里外里**话都让你说了**。"
(From the novel 混在北京)

"Anyhow, let her sleep on the stone slab for the time being. Maybe she'll sleep like the dead." "You sure know how to talk out of both sides of your mouth." [An exchange between a husband and wife. Their nanny complained that her bed wasn't hard enough; she was used to sleeping on hard surfaces. The husband didn't believe her and suggested sleeping pills, but later changed his mind and agreed to let her try sleeping on a stone slab. Hence the jab from his wife.]

♦ "小王儿这个人儿确实有才，可是他的缺点也真够多的。" "话都让你说了，咱们到底要不要他？你得拿个准主意啊！"

"Xiao Wang is talented all right, but he's got a lot of weaknesses too." "You're talking out of both sides of your mouth. Do we want him or not? You have to make a decision one way or the other!"

huà shì zhè me shuō 话是这么说 (話是這麼說)

You can say that, but…; you're right, but …

♦ "你总不能怀疑到刘队的头上吧？" "话是这么说，可你知道聂总和刘震汉的关系也是兄弟。"

(From the TV series 黑洞)

"Don't tell me you're suspicious of Chief Liu!" [刘队 is short for 刘队长.] "Well, you've got a point. But you know Manager Nie and Liu Zhenhan are like brothers." [There is a suspicion that Liu, the police chief, has leaked information to Nie, who is suspected of economic crimes.]

♦ "不是有规定吗？每天的零售款必须上缴。" "话是这么说，可是有时候为了工作，也可以灵活一点儿。"

"There are rules, aren't there? You're supposed to report the retail intake every day." "That's what they say, but sometimes you've got to bend the rules a little for the sake of getting the work done."

huà yòu shuō huí lai le 话又说回来了 (話又說回來了)

"(But then) one has to take back what one has just said"; but then; on the other hand

♦ 把儿子送到农村去我确实觉得心疼，可是话又说回来了，让他去锻炼锻炼也有好处。

My heart aches sending our son to the country. But then again, it'll be good for him to experience some hardship.

♦ 这喷漆车间污染是有点儿污染，可话又说回来了，每个月还有38块岗位津贴呢！外带四条儿肥皂，两包儿洗衣粉。

(From the TV series 贫嘴张大民的幸福生活)

"The spray paint workshop is a bit polluted, but then, you get 38 yuan in extra pay, plus four bars of soap and two bags of laundry detergent."

huān shi 欢势 (歡勢)

"Happy posture"; happy; have a great time doing something

♦ 志河是当年吕建国和妻子下乡那个村的团支部书记，这几年在村里办厂，闹腾得挺欢势。

(From the novel 大厂)

Zhihe was the youth league secretary in the village where Lü Jianguo and his wife were sent [during the Cultural Revolution]. The last few years he's been running a factory in the village and he's having a great time.

♦ 别看他们现在折腾得挺**欢势**，过不了多久他们的公司准得破产。

Forget about the fact that right now they're having such a great time. Their company is sure to fold pretty soon.

huǎn guò jìnr lai 缓过劲儿来 (緩過勁兒來)

Have a respite; recuperate

♦ 上次出了碎玻璃的事儿，我们半年多才**缓过劲儿来**。

(From the TV series 大赢家)

It took us more than six months to recover from that broken glass incident. [People were harmed by pieces of broken glass found in a dairy company's milk. Sales plummeted as a result.]

♦ 你千万别手下留情，要是让他**缓过劲儿来**，说不定就该轮到咱们倒霉了！

Don't go soft on him. If you let him recover, it could mean trouble for us.

huàn tāng bú huàn yào 换汤不换药 (換湯不換藥)

"Change the hot water without changing the (herbal) medicine"; make a superficial change

♦ 这两本过去是被批判的，就像某些人一样被批判被打入另册，所以你父亲故意这样伪装它们。尽管换了书皮，但书还是原来的书，这叫**换汤不换药**，这就是一个人的外表不代表他的内心。

(From the novel 耳光响亮)

In the past, these two books were denounced, just as some people were denounced and blacklisted ["be put in another register"], so your father disguised them. He just changed the binding, but they were the same books. You could call it "changing the hot water without changing the medicine." In the same way, a person's outward appearance tells you nothing about his true character.

♦ "这回经理一换，咱们公司该有希望了吧？" "没用，**换汤不换药**。要想把公司搞好就得把整个儿体制都改一改才行。"

"Now that we have a new manager, there's hope for our company yet?" "Don't bet on it. Nothing has really changed. You'd have to change the system to turn things around."

huáng 黄

"Yellow"; fall through

♦ 他说给咱们拉的那个赞助**黄**了。

(From the TV series 祥符春秋)

The sponsorship that he promised to line up for us fell through.

♦ 你能把张大庆他们折腾那么多天才拿到的东西轻轻松松地搅和**黄**了，我真佩服你。

(From the TV series 天堂鸟)

Zheng Daqing and the others worked so many days to set this up, and you wrecked it with a wave of your hand. I've got to hand it to you. [Zhang Daqing wanted to buy a plot of land, but failed.]

huáng guā/huā cài dōu liáng le 黄瓜菜都凉了/黄花菜都凉了 (黃瓜菜都凉了/黃花菜都凉了)

"The food ('citron daylily') has gotten cold"; the opportunity is lost

♦　要是他们再商量商量，**黄瓜菜都凉了**。

(From the TV series 大雪无痕)

If they keep on talking about it, we'll lose our chance. [They will miss a good opportunity to solve a case.]

♦　等你想好了，**黄花菜都凉了**！

(From the TV series 红色康乃馨)

By the time you've thought it through, it'll be too late.

huáng liǎn pó 黄脸婆 (黃臉婆)

"Sallow-faced old woman"; unattractive old wife

♦　多丑呀！ 象我妈戴的！ 给你家那个**黄脸婆**吧。

(From TV drama 老宋和他的女儿)

They're so ugly! They're' the sort of thing my mother would wear. Why not give them to your old bag at home? [Talking about earrings.]

♦　你嫌我老了，不喜欢我这个**黄脸婆**了，是不是？

You think I'm too old. You don't love me anymore because I'm over the hill, right?

huáng shǔ láng gěi jī bài nián 黄鼠狼给鸡拜年 (黃鼠狼給雞拜年)

"The weasel pays a New Year's call on the hen"; harbor an ulterior motive; have a hidden agenda (The expression often finishes with 没安好心, which makes the meaning explicit, as in the second example below.)

♦　纪汉扬双臂盘在阔胸前，脊梁靠回牛皮椅背上，一脸似笑非笑。萌萌送礼给他？这种场面如果不叫"**黄鼠狼给鸡拜年**"，他可就找不着更适切的形容词了。

(From the novel 茂盛少女心)

Ji Hanyang folded his arms across his broad chest and leaned back in the leather chair with a fixed smile on his face. Mengmeng giving him a gift? If that wasn't a Trojan horse, he didn't know what it was.

♦　他们的总经理要参加咱们商场的开业典礼，我看他这是**黄鼠狼给鸡拜年**，没安好心。

Their general manager wants to attend our store's grand opening. If you ask me, that's like a cat dropping in on the mice, not really a friendly call.

huáng shǔ láng zhuān yǎo bìng yā zi 黄鼠狼专咬病鸭子 (黃鼠狼專咬病鴨子)

"The weasel makes a point of biting sick ducks"; prey on someone vulnerable; misfortunes never come singly

♦　"**黄鼠狼专咬病鸭子**，公司三个月没开资，文武的孩子还病了。"

(From the novel 剑胆琴心)

"It never rains but it pours. The company hasn't paid its workers for three months. On top of that, Wenwu's kid got sick."

♦ 这么个节骨眼儿上，车偏偏坏了，真是**黄鼠狼专咬病鸭子**。

Right at the crucial moment, the car breaks down. Troubles never come singly!

huáng yú nǎo dài 黄鱼脑袋 (黃魚腦袋)

"The brains of a yellow croaker" (a type of fish)"; stupid

♦ 你学也不像，真是**黄鱼脑袋**。

(From the short story 家庭风景二十章)

No matter how hard you try, you're too thick to get it. [Referring to learning English.]

♦ "你跟方雨林说了没有？马局找他。"那个办事员一拍脑袋，叫了声："哎哟，我怎么给忘了。""你真是个**黄鱼脑袋**！"

(From the novel 大雪无痕)

"Did you tell Fang Yulin? Bureau Director Ma [马局 is short for 马局长] is looking for him." The office worker slapped his head and cried, "Damn it, how could I forget!" "You're really spacy."

huī sūn zi 灰孙子 (灰孫子)

"Distant junior members of an extended family"; at the bottom of the totem pole

♦ 这种工作就是看人家脸色，做人家**灰孙子**！

(From the TV series 天下第一情)

When you do this kind of work [door-to-door peddling], you just have to get used to dirty looks. You have to grovel.

♦ 明天我要再出工就是**灰孙子**。谁出工谁就是**灰孙子**。

(From the short story 暧昧的关系)

If I show up for work tomorrow, I'm dirt. Whoever shows up for work is dirt. [The speaker swears not to go out and work in cold weather and get frostbitten again.]

huí mén 回门 (回門)

A bride's return to her parents' home (a ritual visit with her new husband, usually three days after the wedding)

♦ 三天回门的时候，瑞霞不愿意和丈夫并排走。

(From the novel 锁链，是柔软的)

On the way to her parents' home for the three-day visit, Ruixia refused to walk at her husband's side.

♦ 今儿不是回门的日子，他干吗往丈母娘家跑啊？

This isn't the day for the bride's visit. Why is he going to his mother-in-law's house?

huí qu 回去

"Go back"; regress

♦ 越大越回去，怎么连架都不会打了？

(From the TV series 今生是亲人)

The older you are the more useless you get. How come you can't even start a rumble?

♦ 都病了三天了，还不请大夫？林总管，你越活越回去了！

(From the novel 霸主不领情)

He's been sick for three days, and you still haven't called a doctor? Steward Lin, you're really losing it! [The young master has been sick for three days and the steward hasn't tried to get a doctor to check on the child.]

huí tóu 回头 (回頭)

Later; afterwards

◆ 你说，回头咱们把这个龙腾集团查趴下了，得有多少人下岗啊？
(From the TV series 黑洞)
Tell me, if the Longteng Group later falls apart as a result of our investigation, how many people will lose their jobs?

◆ 说吧，说吧！不说回头有人把你当哑巴卖了。
(From the TV series 贫嘴张大民的幸福生活)
Go ahead, talk. If you don't speak, afterwards people will think you don't know how. [A man is being sarcastic to his big-mouth brother.]

hùn chū ge rén yàngr lai 混出个人样儿来 (混出個人樣兒來)

Manage to make something of oneself

◆ 不混出个样儿来，也对不住自己啊！
(From the TV series 黑洞)
If you don't get it together, you're selling yourself short.

◆ 我是想混出个人样儿来再回来见你。
(From the TV series 一年又一年)
I just wanted to accomplish something before coming back to see you. [A husband is explaining to his wife why he disappeared to Hainan for a year before coming home.]

hùn hunr 混混儿 (混混兒)

Rover; idler; loafer; bum

◆ 咱们还真别小看了他们，别把他们都想成土头土脑的小混混。
(From the novel 永不瞑目)
Let's not underestimate them. Don't think they're all just crude punks. [A policeman is talking about drug pushers.]

◆ 现在这世道真是变了，原来胡同儿里的小混混儿现在都人五人六儿的当上经理了。
The world has really turned upside down. All those two-bit layabouts in our alley have now cleaned up and become company managers.

huó bú jiàn rén, sǐ bú jiàn shī 活不见人，死不见尸 (活不見人，死不見屍)

You don't see the person dead or alive; no sign of the person; gone without a trace

◆ "咱中国的哪座城市的辉煌后面没有一大批这样那样的好同志呢？他们真是在流血流泪呀！远的不说了，就说咱面前的，像孙亚东，像田立业……"高长河叹息道："是啊，可代价太大了，一个植物人，一个活不见人死不见尸！"
"Which city in China doesn't have many good comrades behind the scenes of their dazzling glory? They've shed their blood and tears! Forget about the ones who are far away; I'm just speaking about the ones who are right here, like Xun Yadong, or Tian Liye...." Gao Changhe sighed and answered, "True, but the price is too great. One is a

vegetable and the other has disappeared without a trace." [Two party leaders are talking. Sun Yadong, director of a supervisory committee, was run over by a group of criminals. He survived, but went into a coma. Tian Liye died during a flood trying to save other people.]

◆   他这一去八年了，连个信儿也没有，**活不见人，死不见尸**，也不知道到底是怎么会回事儿。

> He's been gone for eight years without even a letter. You don't know if he's dead or alive. Who knows what's become of him?

huó de zī rùn 活得滋润 (活得滋潤)

Live well (滋润: moist, moisten)

◆   人家**活得多滋润**啊！

(From the TV series 贫嘴张大民的幸福生活)

> That's the life! [Fishing, raising birds, and chatting with friends.]

◆   瞧瞧你的学生，成**大款**的，自备车的，买房子的，人家**活得多滋润**！

(From the TV series 田教授的二十八个保姆)

> Look at your students. They've gotten rich, fixed themselves up with cars, and bought houses. They're living the good life!

huó fan 活泛

Have flexibility; be alive or alert; flexible

◆   这两年，老太太和当年逃台的一个小叔子**接上了头**，又送了一个儿子去日本打工，手头**活泛**了，家里的吃穿摆用、行为举止也有点侨眷的劲儿了。

(From the novel 我是你爸爸)

> In the last couple of years the old lady reconnected with a brother-in-law who fled to Taiwan, and sent a son to work in Japan, so she has a little financial flexibility. Now when it comes to eating, clothes, furniture, and even behavior, she's a bit like someone with rich relatives abroad.

◆   到了公司你得**活泛**着点儿，多跟上上下下联系。

> At the company you have to be alert and open to opportunity. You have to network with supervisors and with coworkers.

huó gāi 活该 (活該)

Fully deserve; serves someone right

◆   你这小子，送上门的好事你不要，**活该**。

(From the novel 永不瞑目)

> You bastard, a golden opportunity lands on your doorstep and you let it go. You got what you deserve!

◆   我跟你说不能去，你非去。看，现在后悔了吧！　**活该**！

> I told you not to go but you went anyway. Now you're sorry! Serves you right.

huó jiàn guǐ 活见鬼 (活見鬼)

"See a ghost while still alive"; weird; uncanny

◆   真是**活见鬼**了，门窗都好好的，被害人却死了，凶手也不见踪影，真他妈的**邪门**！

(From the novel 魔湖惊魂)

Well, I'll be damned. The doors and windows are shut tight, but the victim is dead. There are no traces of the killer anywhere. This is fucking weird.

♦   我们正在设计的东西已经被他们给做出来了，真是**活见鬼**了！

We're still working on the design and they've succeeded in making the product. Blows my mind.

huó rén hái néng ràng niào biē sǐ 活人还能让尿憋死 (活人還能讓尿憋死)

"A living person can't let himself die from holding back pee"; there's an easy way out; don't just give up, but find the obvious solution

♦   怕啥，**活人不会让尿憋死**，自己想办法。

(From the novel 锁链，是柔软的)

What's there to be afraid of? There's always a way out; we'll think of a solution.

♦   你发哪门子愁啊？把股票抛出去，开个餐馆不就得了。**大活人还能让尿憋死**？

What are you worried about? Sell the stocks, open a restaurant, and you'll be all set. You can't just give up when you hit a roadblock.

huǒ 火

"Be on fire"; do a roaring business

♦   "'帝都夜总会'，听说过吗？生意**火**得不行。你喜欢唱卡拉OK吗？"肖童说："唱歌不行，**蹦迪**还凑合。"

(From the novel 永不瞑目)

"The Empire Nightclub, heard of it? A business can't get any better than that. Do you like Karaoke?" Xiao Tang replied, "Well, I can't sing, but I'm not bad at disco dancing."

♦   现在北京的汽车市场**火**得不能再**火**了，短短六年的时间汽车就多了一百万辆。

The car market in Beijing can't get any hotter. There are over a million more cars than there were just six years ago.

huǒ dōu shàng fáng le 火都上房了

"The fire has reached (the upper part of) the house"; things have reached a critical point

♦   我说**火都上房了**，你还不急啊！

(From the novel 远在天边)

We're in water up to our necks, and you're not even worried!

♦   你这儿还有心听音乐呢，我那儿**火都上房了**。

You can still bring yourself to listen to music over there, and here I can feel the wolves at my back.

huò xī ní 和稀泥

"Mix thin mud"; appease everyone involved; smooth things over; sidestep difficult issues in order to avoid conflict

♦   "你就会**和稀泥**！""本来就是一摊稀泥！一个乡下丫头，您跟她**较什么真儿**啊？！"

(From the TV series 大宅门)

"Count on you to smooth everything out.!" "Well, it wasn't such a big deal to begin with. She's just a country girl, so why quibble with her?" [An exchange between a mother and son. She just found out that her husband is having an affair with their maid.]

◆   要是没有我给你们**和稀泥**，你们早就吵翻了。

If I hadn't smoothed the waters between you two long ago, you'd have had a major run-in.

J

jī 鸡 (雞)

"Chicken"; hooker (野鸡: "wild chicken" or streetwalker)

◆   你要是万一碰上个**鸡**呢？　再弄上个什么病的。

(From the movie 有话好好说)

What if you run into a hooker and catch some disease?

◆   后来硕士生认识了一个舞女，此舞女纯属"**鸡**"。硕士生与"**鸡**"的事，被民警抓住了，这下在单位里搞得满城风雨，硕士生从此再也抬不起头来。

(From the short story 蚀杀)

Later on that guy with the M.A. degree met a taxi dancer who was really nothing but a hooker. The police caught them in the act, which set off a lot of gossip in the office. After that the graduate couldn't lift up his head.

jī dàn lǐ miàn tiāo gú tou 鸡蛋里面挑骨头 (雞蛋裏面挑骨頭)

"Pick out bones in an egg"; find fault where none exists; be overly critical; nitpick

◆   刀疤子笑了笑说："我说老赵，你别**鸡蛋里面挑骨头**好不好？"

(From the novel 假凤虚凰)

Scarface laughed, "Hey, Lao Zhao, stop the nitpicking, OK?"

◆   我看这篇文章挺好的，你不要**鸡蛋里面挑骨头**嘛。

I think this article isn't half bad. Don't be so critical.

jī fēi dàn dǎ 鸡飞蛋打 (雞飛蛋打)

"The chicken flies away and the egg falls to the ground"; "lose both the chicken and the egg"; lose everything

◆   我会出最高的价钱请律师，让你们**鸡飞蛋打**。

(From the TV series 今生是亲人)

I'll get the best lawyer money can buy. I'll make sure you lose it all. [In this custody fight, the speaker threatens, "you'll lose both the money and the child."]

♦ 我觉得咱们最好接着卖摩托车，不要插手汽车市场。虽说卖汽车利润高，可是风险也大，弄不好鸡飞蛋打。

I think we'd better stick to selling motorbikes and not dabble in the car market. Cars have a higher profit margin, but the risks are higher, too. If you're not careful, you could lose it all.

jī yì zuǐ, yā yì zuǐ 鸡一嘴，鸭一嘴 (雞一嘴，鴨一嘴)

"A word from the chicken and a word from the duck"; interruptions from all around; incoherent interruptions

♦ 他气恼地埋怨妻子：你能不能好好开你的车？ 跟我瞎搅和什么？ 让你鸡一嘴，鸭一嘴的，我的思路全乱了。

(From the novel 刮痧)

He was irritated and took it out on his wife, "Could you please keep your mind on your driving? Why are you bugging me? With all your yammering, I can't think straight."

♦ 你们这么鸡一嘴，鸭一嘴的，我到底听谁的啊？

When you're all jabbering at once, who am I supposed to listen to?

jí bìng luàn tóu yī 急病乱投医 (急病亂投醫)

"When an illness is urgent, seek a doctor at random"; look for help even from the unqualified; any port in a storm (also 病急乱投医)

♦ 小林绞尽脑汁想人，把京城里的同学想遍，没想出与这个单位有关系的人。也是急病乱投医，小林想不出同学，却突然想起门口一个修自行车的老头。

(From the novel 一地鸡毛)

Xiao Lin racked his brains to come up with someone. He thought about all of his Beijing classmates, but none of them had anything to do with that place. As a last resort, since he couldn't come up with any classmate, he suddenly remembered the old bicycle repairman near his home. [He is trying to find connections to get his child into kindergarten].

♦ 我知道你是主管后勤的，这生产的事儿不归你管，可我实在是没有别的办法啊，俗话说，急病乱投医。我们公司就等着你们厂的机器才能开工啊！

I know you're in charge of logistics. Production isn't your responsibility, but I'm out of ideas. As the saying goes, "any port in a storm." The company can't start work without your machinery.

jí yǎn 急眼

"Desperate eye"; desperate; very upset; very angry

♦ 狗急了还跳墙呢，大活人没饭吃还能不急眼？

(From short story 披露)

Even a dog will jump over the wall when he's cornered. How can a starving man not be desperate?

♦ 他两笔大买卖都让你给搅黄了，我看他是**急眼**了，你得防备着点儿。

You wrecked two of his business deals. I think he's mad as hell. You better watch out.

jǐ dui / jǐ da 挤兑/挤搭 (擠兌/擠搭)

Pick on; embarrass

♦ 人家是学生，你们**挤兑**她干什么？

(From the novel 都市危情)

She's a student. Why are you picking on her? [The person being addressed has been using coarse language to abuse someone.]

♦ 你别总**挤搭**人，其实你自己的毛病多着呢，我不爱说你就是了。

Don't always pick on people. To tell the truth, you've got plenty of faults yourself. I just don't like mentioning them to you.

jì chī bú jì dǎ 记吃不记打 (記吃不記打)

"Remember the eating but not the beating"; do not learn one's lesson

♦ 你他妈的真是**记吃不记打**！ 问那么多干什么？

(From the TV series 黑冰)

You never fucking learn, do you? Why ask so many questions? [The director of an underground factory is telling off a new employee.]

♦ 这些小混混**记吃不记打**，刚放出去没几天又在那儿卖上走私光盘了。

Those little punks never learn. They've been out on the street a few days and they're already selling smuggled CDs.

jiā chǒu bù kě wài yáng 家丑不可外扬 (家醜不可外揚)

(Proverb) "Family scandals should not be revealed to outsiders"; don't air your dirty laundry in public

♦ 算啦算啦，**家丑不可外扬**。说实话，我都发愁，明儿法院来了，叫我怎么张口！

(From the novel 找乐)

OK, OK. No need to air our dirty laundry in public. To tell the truth, I'm worried sick. Tomorrow when the court officers come, what am I going to say?

♦ 俗话说，**家丑不可外扬**。你这个副总经理私拿公司的钱，我当然要处罚，不过你放心，我是不会把你告到法院去的。我要是那样做咱们公司的股票非得跌到底不可。

As they say, don't air your dirty laundry in public. You're the deputy general manager and you embezzled the company's money. Of course I have to punish you. But don't worry; I won't take you to court. If I did that, our stocks would sink like a stone.

jiā dǐr 家底儿 (家底兒)

"Family foundation"; family fortune; family heritage

♦ 你就这么折腾，徐家这点儿**家底儿**非得让你给折腾光了！

(From the movie 活着)

If you keep screwing around, you're bound to run through the whole Xu family fortune. [A son is gambling.]

◆   不像过去靠俸禄，现在啊，就只有靠**家底**儿了。

(From the TV series 古城童话)

It's not like before when you could count on an imperial salary. Now you have to rely on family resources.

jiā huo 家伙 (傢夥)

"guy"; weapon; tool

◆   我要拉着他，跟我一起毁灭！ 带上**家伙**，玩命去！

(From the novel 都市危情)

I am going to drag him in and we can all go down together. Get your weapons. We'll put our lives on the line!

◆   哥几个跟我去教堂救火，带**家伙**！

(From the novel 神灯前传)

Brothers, some of you come with me to put out the fire at the church. Bring some weapons! [A conflict between the Boxers, who had set fire to a church, and militia members hired by the missionaries to protect the church.]

jiā jiā yǒu běn nán niàn de jīng 家家有本难念的经 (家家有本難念的經)

(Proverb) "Each family has a difficult sutra to recite"; every family has its own problems

◆   家家有本难念的经，你说是不是？

(From the movie 有话好好说)

All families have their problems, don't they?

◆   你别诉苦了，我也正和我老婆闹离婚呢。这就叫**家家有本难念的经**。

Stop complaining. My wife and I are getting a divorce. Every family has its own problems.

jiā mǎr 加码儿 (加碼兒)

"Add more chips"; raise the ante; raise prices or quotas

◆   我说差不多就行了，可是她老给自己加码儿。

(From the TV series 将爱情进行到底)

I tell her it''s good enough and she should be satisfied, but she always demands more of herself. [She wants to expand her car repair business].

◆   头儿，我们都累吐血了，您可千万别给我们再**加码儿**了！

Boss, we're so exhausted we could spit blood. Don't pile any more on us!

jiá bǎn qì 夹板气 (夾板氣)

"Get anger from both sides"; be sandwiched between two opponents

◆   都以为五好家庭靠当婆婆的和当儿媳的创造出来，岂不知若没有个忍辱负重甘受**夹板气**的儿子和丈夫，能有婆媳和睦的大好局面吗？

(From the short story 家庭风景二十章)

Everybody thinks that the "model family" is the creation of the mother-in-law and daughter-in-law. How come they don't realize that if there isn't a son-in-law and husband willing to endure suffering and gladly accept being caught in the middle, there's not much chance of harmony between mother-in-law and daughter-in-law? [五好家庭 refers

to a household which meets all the five criteria of a good family and is awarded a
certificate by the neighborhood committee.]

◆ 咱们自己租房搬出去住吧！ 你和我妈天天埋怨，这**夹板气**我实在受够
了！

> Let's rent our own place and move out. You and my mom complain every day. I've had
> enough of being caught in the middle!

jiǎ zhāo zi 假招子

"False banners/placards"; false advertising; hypocritical politeness

◆ 要不您就别来这**假招子**，咱们还回老样子，我比现在这么成天谢您还
省点儿力气。

(From the novel 我是你爸爸)

> How about stopping all that polite crap. Let's go back to the way it was. That way I won't
> have to say thank you all day and I can save a little energy.

◆ "婶，您甭忙，"我客气着，接过了粥，"我又不是外人，见天
来…""吃吧，吃……别来这套**假招子**。"

(From the novel 玩水之夏)

> "Auntie, don't trouble yourself." I tried to sound polite and took the porridge. "I'm not a
> stranger. I come here all the time." "Go ahead and eat. Quit the fancy talk."

...jià zi ...架子

"Shelf"; "scaffolding"; airs; pretenses

◆ 成了名人了，怎么了？ 跟妈也**拿上架子**了？

(From the TV series 北京女人)

> So you're famous now. What's wrong with you? Putting on airs with your own mother!

◆ 朕跟你们说过多少次，出宫以后不能**摆架子**。

(From the TV series 康熙帝国)

> How many times have we told you? When you're outside the palace you can't act high
> and mighty. [An emperor is lecturing some eunuchs.]

jiǎn le zhī ma diū le xī gua 捡了芝麻丢了西瓜 (撿了芝麻丟了西瓜)

"Pick up the sesame seed but lose the watermelon"; penny-wise and pound-foolish

◆ 你总干那**丢了西瓜捡了芝麻**的事儿。

(From the movie 大腕)

> You're always penny-wise and pound-foolish.

◆ 你以为赚了那几个小钱儿是好事？ 小心**捡了芝麻丢了西瓜**。

> You think earning that pittance is such a big deal? Watch out, don't lose your chance to
> make real money.

jiǎn yáng lào 捡洋落 (撿洋落)

"Pick up a 'foreign' treasure (left behind by others)"; get a windfall; hit the jackpot

◆ "**捡洋落**"起家的炮兵像个学步的孩子，在黑土地上的风雪中摸索着
学足、投步，踉踉跄跄。

(From the novel 血红雪白)

> Artillery troops who got started on foreigners' leftovers are like children learning to walk.
> On the black earth, in the middle of wind and snow, they grope and try to learn how to do
> it, plant their footsteps, stagger along. [After the Japanese were defeated and surrendered

in World War II, they left behind a lot of equipment. The artillery division of the Chinese Communist Northeastern Army came into possession of the artillery pieces. Because of its rich soil, Manchuria is often called "the black earth" in China.]

◆　"老张送给我的这辆车太费油了，空调也不管用。" "你白捡了这么个洋落，还不知足啊？"

"That car Lao Zhang gave me is real gas-guzzler. The air-conditioning doesn't work either." "Don't look a gift horse in the mouth! Be glad you got it for free."

jiàn gú tou 贱骨头 (賤骨頭)

"Cheap bones"; someone lacking in self-regard

◆　赵向东这个贱骨头，把公司的股票卖了换回你这么个东西！

(From the TV series 手心手背)

Zhao Xiangdong is such a sucker. He sold company stocks to rescue an asshole like you. [Zhao Xiangdong paid back money the man embezzled, but instead of feeling grateful the man did something damaging to his benefactor.]

◆　妈妈："我生来就是当佣人的命。" 儿子："贱骨头！"

(From the TV series 田教授的二十八个保姆)

Mother: "I was born to be a servant." Son: "Loser!"

jiàn hǎor jiù shōu 见好儿就收 (見好兒就收)

"Get out while the getting is good"; quit when you're ahead

◆　像你这样聪明的姑娘，应该有个比较好的处境。我虽然帮不了你，但我希望你能见好就收，以后还是做点别的事，吃青春饭不是长久之计。

(From the short story 吃花酒)

A clever girl like you should have a better future. I can't help you, but I hope you get out while the getting is good. Find something else to do from now on. You're not going to be young forever. [Spoken to a taxi dancer.]

◆　我看这价格让咱们压得差不多了，见好儿就收吧！

I think we've pushed the price down as far as possible. We better quit while we're ahead.

jiàn le dà tóu guǐ le 见了大头鬼了 (見了大頭鬼了)

(Shanghai dialect) "ran into a big-headed monster"; be possessed; what got into you?

◆　儿子好不容易找回来，结果又让你给骂走了，你见了大头鬼了？

(From the TV series 天下第一情)

It took us forever to find our son, and you drive him away? What got into you?

◆　见你的大头鬼啦，整天就知道酒，酒！不喝死你才怪呢！

(From short story 醉酒)

Are you crazy? All you know is drinking, drinking! You're going to drink yourself into the grave—see if I'm wrong!

jiàn miànr fēn yí bànr 见面儿分一半儿 (見面兒分一半兒)
"Meet and go halves"; divide the loot

♦ "拐子，有好处别**独闷儿**，你要人家事主一万银子，这里有我多少？""什么话，这里有你什么事儿？""见面儿分一半儿。""**门儿都没有**！有本事自己去绑一票儿。"

(From the TV series 大宅门)

"Gimpy, don't hog it all. You want them to pay 10,000, but how much do I get?" "What are you talking about? What's it got to do with you?" "Come on, go splits and give me half." "No way. Pull off a kidnapping yourself if you can."

♦ "这钱是你拼命挣来的，我怎么能要呢？""客气什么？有福同享，有难同当，**见面儿分一半儿**嘛！""

(From the novel 山水狂飙)

"You worked yourself to death to make this money. How can I take it?" "Don't stand on ceremony. We go through good and bad together. Whatever I have, you get half."

jiàn pú sa jiù bài 见菩萨就拜 (見菩薩就拜)
"Worship every Bodhisattva that comes one's way"; be deferential

♦ 这几年来，我说过你多少次，你那里搞得不错嘛，处于全市领先位置！该吹的就要吹，该跑的就要跑，该送的一定要舍得花本钱去送，要**见菩萨就拜**。钱又不花你自己的，你就是不听。

(From the novel 欲望的旗杆)

How many times have I told you over the last few years, you're doing great. You [your company] have a commanding lead in the city. When you need to boast, boast. When you need to do legwork, do it. When you need to give bribes, spend your capital and bribe. You have to be deferential in the right places. It's not your own money anyway. You just didn't listen.

♦ 我是**见菩萨就拜**，才要来这两万多块钱，离我们的二十万的缺口差得远呢！

I begged everyone in sight and barely managed to scrape up twenty thousand. It's a long way from the two hundred thousand we need.

jiàn qián yǎn kāi 见钱眼开 (見錢眼開)
"Open one's eyes when money is in sight"; see, and care about, nothing but money

♦ 你们别胡说，佟佟不是那种**见钱眼开**的人，这里边说不定有什么原因。

(From the novel 掠风)

You're talking nonsense. Dong Dong isn't the type who'd do anything for money. He must have a reason. [Everyone assumes that Dong Dong agreed to a divorce for the sake of money.]

♦   你大哥这人见钱眼开，往后少搭理他。

    Your brother only cares about money. After this, stay away from him.

jiàn tiānr 见天儿 (見天兒)

Every day at the crack of dawn; every day

♦   他见天儿地去**搓麻**，一搓就是两三点才回来。

(From the TV drama 眢兑胡同)

    He goes out to play mahjong at sunrise and doesn't get back till two or three in the morning.

♦   在这条胡同里的人眼里，列车员就是个很了不起的职业了，穿著制服，戴着袖标，**见天儿**价坐火车，上海、广州，专跑大地方。

(From the novel 红尘)

    For people in this alley, being a train conductor is an impressive job. You get to wear a uniform and an armband, and every day you travel to big places like Shanghai and Guangzhou.

jiāng jiu 将就

Make do

♦   丛小姐，我们这里没有象样的椅子，你就只能**将就**着在地上坐一会儿了。

(From the novel 爱上爱情)

    Miss Cong, we don't have any decent chairs here. You'll have to make do with sitting on the floor, I'm afraid.

♦   我们这个穷地方比不了大上海，菜不好，您**将就**着吃吧。

    You can't compare our poor area to Shanghai. The food''s not great. Just bear with it.

jiàng yǎn zi 强眼子

Someone willful, a bullheaded person

♦   他从小就是个**强眼子**，没有人能扭得过他。

(From the novel 空洞)

He's been bullheaded ever since he was a little kid. No one can get him to change his mind.

◆ 那个**强眼子**，非要把工作辞了去做买卖，谁劝他他都不听。

He's so pigheaded that he insists on quitting his job and going into business. He won't listen to anybody.

jiāo dài 交待/交代

Hand over

◆ 二十万，你的小命就**算交待**了。我知道，你不止这个数。

(From the novel 都市危情)

Embezzle two hundred thousand, and you risk the death penalty. I know you didn't stop at that. [The person being addressed has embezzled a substantial amount of money and could land himself in serious trouble.]

◆ 卖什么不行，头儿非让咱们卖毒品，我看这回我这一百八十多斤就**交代**在这儿了。

The boss won't let us sell anything but drugs. I think I'll just have to put my life on the line ["hand over this 180 jin"]. [One hundred eighty jin, or 198 pounds, is the speaker's body weight.]

jiáo qū 嚼蛆

"Chew a maggot"; spew nonsense

◆ 你少**嚼蛆**！姓金的老坟地里没有长当官的蒿子，我也不想朝高枝上飞。

(From the novel 锁链，是柔软的)

Stop talking nonsense! The Jins' backs aren't broad enough to carry me to high office—not that I would want to do that anyway. ["In the Jin family graveyard there aren't any tall wormwood trees I could climb on to reach high office, and anyway I don't want to fly up to a high branch."]

◆ 他老人家虽然家境富足，却能够杀富济贫，对抗官府，现在到哪里找这样的好汉去？ 说乐老头受了招安？ **嚼蛆**！ 满嘴**嚼蛆**！

(From the novel 流泪的淮河)

Although he's from a rich family himself, he's still willing to rob the rich, help the poor, and oppose the government. Where can you find a good man like that these days? You say Mr. Le surrendered to the government? Nonsense! Sheer nonsense!

jiáo shé tou 嚼舌头 (嚼舌頭)

"Chew the tongue"; gossip; talk idly

◆ 出牌！ 【注：正在打扑克牌】别烂**嚼舌头**。

(From the TV series 今生是亲人)

Play a card! Stop talking! [Spoken during a poker game.]

◆ 全是多少年的老邻居了，谁会去**嚼舌头**？ 比方阿姨你吧，你晓得了也不会去讲的，是吧？

(From the short story 家庭风景二十章)

We've all been neighbors for so long. Who's likely to tell tales? Auntie, for example, you wouldn't go talking, even if you knew about it, would you? [Talking about raising chickens illegally.]

jiǎo cǎi liǎng zhī chuán 脚踩两只船 (腳踩兩隻船)
With one foot in each boat; sit on the fence

♦ 我虽然看似**脚踩两只船**，重点可放在贵党这边。我跟国民党打交道，是为了赚他们的钱，而我跟贵党的交往，是重义轻利的。
   (From the novel 地火)
   It may look like I'm sitting on the fence, but my real sympathies are with your party. I deal with the KMT because I want to make money off them. In my dealings with your party I put principles ahead of profit.

♦ 姐，我觉得你不应该**脚踩两只船**，弄不好两只全跑了。
   Sister, I think you can't keep a finger in both pies. If you don't watch out, both of them will take off. [The sister is dating two men at the same time.]

jiǎo dǐ bǎnr shang dōu zhǎng zhe xīn yǎnr 脚底板儿上都长着心眼儿 (脚底板兒上都長著心眼兒)
"Calculating down to the soles of the feet"; extremely calculating

♦ 现在的人，脚底板儿上都长着心眼儿。
   (From the TV series 蓝色马蹄莲)
   Nowadays everyone watches out for himself.

♦ 老韩那人油着呢，**脚底板儿上都长着心眼儿**，你哪儿是他的对手啊？
   Lao Han is a slippery character, calculating within an inch of his life. You're no match for him, not even close.

jiǎo dǐ xia mǒ yóu 脚底下抹油 (脚底下抹油)
"Smear oil on the bottom of one's feet"; flee

♦ 霍天行点点头道："兵贵神速，谭北斗心眼儿多，别让他悟出来**脚底下抹油**溜了，傅大侠以为怎么样？"
   (From the novel 雍干飞龙传)
   Huo Tianxing nodded, "Speed is essential in war. Tan Beidou is very sly. Make sure he doesn't figure out our strategy and slip away. What do you think, Master Fu?"

♦ 我一看不好，就**脚底下抹油**，溜出来了，要不然非得让他们打得鼻青脸肿的。
   It didn't look good to me, so I gave them the slip right away. Otherwise I would have been beaten to a pulp for sure ["beaten until my nose was blue and my face swollen"].

jiǎo he 搅和 (攪和)
"Mix and blend"; hang out with; mix with

♦ 为了那么几个臭工资，就跟他们**搅和**在一起瞎胡闹，你说这值得吗？
   (From the TV series 问问你的心)
   You're hanging out with them and raising hell just for these stinking wages? Is it worth it?

♦ 你能把张大庆他们折腾那么多天才拿到的东西轻轻松松地**搅和**黄了，我真佩服你。
   (From the TV series 天堂鸟)

Zheng Daqing and the others worked so many days to set this up, and you wrecked it with a wave of your hand. I've got to hand it to you. [Zhang Daqing wanted to buy a plot of land, but failed.]

jiǎo jú 搅局 (攪局)

"Disrupt a round of a game"; disrupt; make trouble; interfere

♦   朱茜，你跑到这里搅什么局啊？

(From the movie 唐伯虎点秋香)

Zhu Qian, why did you come here to make trouble?

♦   李先生，我们今天晚上的慈善舞会是为了给得了癌症的儿童募捐的。这样的场合你也来搅局，是不是想和那些孩子过不去呢？

Mr. Li, this evening's charity ball is to raise funds for children with cancer. You want to disrupt that as well? Do you have something against those children?

jiào bǎn 叫板

"Cry out the tempo"; challenge someone (板 or 板眼: tempi in Beijing Opera)";

♦   你们在绿化带上盖房，这不是明摆着跟市政府叫板吗？

(From the TV series 天堂鸟)

You're building on the green belt. Are you trying to face off with the city government?

♦   老弟，你的汽车生意做得不错，为什么非要挤到这房地产市场上来，和我的公司叫板呢？

Brother, your automobile business is doing well. Why do you have to push your way into real estate and go head to head with me?

jiào fènr 叫份儿 (叫份兒)

Challenge; take on

♦   十四阿哥一抱拳："这位师傅，请借个路。"了因冷笑一声："我倒好说，"一摆手里的禅杖："你问它肯让不肯让？"众侍卫听了大怒："秃驴，你想找死么！""疯和尚，皮子痒了想找打不是？""你小子活腻歪啦，敢和爷们儿叫份儿！"

(From novel 夜探红楼)

Brother Fourteen clasped his hands together respectfully. "I ask the gentleman to let me pass." Liaoyin laughed coldly, "Fine with me." He waved the abbot's staff in his hand. "But you'd better ask my staff if it is willing." Hearing this, the guards were enraged [and took turns shouting at him]. "You bald donkey, you want to die soon?" "You crazy monk, is your skin itching for a beating?" "Are you tired of life? You dare to challenge us?" [Soldiers are angry with a Buddhist abbot who is blocking the road.]

♦   你的公司赚了几百万，就想和大华公司**叫份儿**，太自不量力了！ 人家有几十亿的资产啊！

Your company makes a few million and you want to challenge Dahua head-on? You're getting ahead of yourself! They have billions in assets.

jiào jìngr 叫/较劲儿 (叫/較勁兒)

"Compete to see who is stronger"; compete

♦   老顾本身就看你不顺眼，要不是郎院长出面给你说话，你是无论如何也回不了普外的。你以后少和他**较劲儿**，胳膊拧不过大腿，你当面顶撞他，别看他嘴上不说什么，心里肯定又记住你了。

(From the novel 疑是故人来)

Lao Gu didn't like you much to begin with. If Director Lang hadn't put in a word for you, there's no way you could have come back to General Surgery. Stop trying to compete with him. Little guys can't take on big ones. When you contradict him to his face, he may not say anything, but he's going to remember it.

♦   你是个小小的科员，别净想着跟处长**叫劲儿**。

You're just a low-level employee in the department. Don't keep trying to take on the boss.

jiào tiān tiān bù yīng, jiào dì dì bù líng 叫天天不应，叫地地不灵 (叫天天不應，叫地地不靈)

"Appeal to Heaven and Heaven doesn't respond; appeal to Earth and Earth can't help"; totally helpless; on one's own

♦   走到这一步，真是叫天天不应，叫地地不灵了。

(From the TV series 古船、女人和网)

At this point, the situation is beyond repair. [A shrimp farm's stock, bought on credit, all died.]

♦   如果我够聪明的话就应该在天黑之前离开这里，可是我现在是一动也不能动，在这叫**天天不应叫地地不灵**的鬼地方。

(From the short story 雨夜)

If I'm clever enough, I should be out of here before dark. But right now I can't make a move; I'm stuck in this godforsaken place.

jiào zhēnr 叫真儿/较真儿 (叫真兒/較真兒)

Be unnecessarily serious, literal-minded, or intransigent

♦   他受不了你这**较真儿**的脾气。

(From the TV series 大雪无痕)

He can't abide your uptight personality. [Speaking of the company's general manager. The fired employee refused to tolerate dishonest practices.]

♦ "你们卖的计算机到底是不是进口原装的？" "嘿，这小伙子还挺叫真儿。告诉你吧，进口没错，原装不原装就说不准了。"

"Are the imported computers you sell assembled abroad?" "Hey, this guy really knows how to split hairs. I can tell you, they're definitely imported, but whether or not they're assembled abroad I'm not sure."

jiē bu kāi guō 揭不开锅 (揭不開鍋)

"Can't open a pot lid"; out of food

♦ 要叫我说，你这是拿钱烧的。要是如今还穷得揭不开锅，也不会去找这困扰。

(From the novel 阴阳八卦)

If you ask me, too much money has made you lose your mind. If you were still dirt poor, you wouldn't have gone looking for this kind of trouble.

♦ 你开着豪华车还喊穷？ 我这儿都揭不开锅了！

You're driving a luxury car and you still complain that you're poor? I'm down to my last crust here!

jiē chár 接茬儿 (接茬兒)

"Connect the stubble"; continue

♦ 那你就接茬儿哭！

(From the TV series 今生是亲人)

All right, keep on crying! [Spoken to someone who refuses to listen to advice.]

♦ 你甭瞧他这会儿老实了，醒了以后还会犯瘾接茬儿折腾。

(From the novel 百年德性)

Don't be fooled by his good behavior. When he wakes up the addiction will take hold again and he'll be back to his old ways.

jiē (jié) gu yǎnr 节骨眼儿 (節骨眼兒)

"At the point where the bones meet;" at the critical juncture (节骨: joints; 眼: "moment" in colloquial Chinese)

♦ 那你也不能在这焦头烂额的节骨眼儿上跟他离婚啊！

(From the TV series 今生是亲人)

Even so you can't divorce him at a time like this, when he's up to his neck in trouble.

♦ 这满朝的文武，在节骨眼儿上能帮你的只有他。

(From the TV series 天下粮仓)

Out of all the civil and military officials at court, he's the only one who can help you in a crisis.

jiē lǎo dǐr 揭老底儿 (揭老底兒)

"Tear away the old bottom"; expose someone's dark secret

♦ 干什么？ 我也要揭他的老底儿，让他惨不忍睹！

(From the TV series 天下第一情)

What am I doing? I'm going to expose him, too. He'll be sorry he was ever born. [He intends to expose the illegal business operations of an uncle who cheated him.]

♦ 你别总跟我过不去，小心我在经理那儿**揭你的老底儿**！
Stop picking on me or I'll tell the manager what's been going on!

jiē líng zi 接翎子

(Shanghai dialect) get the drift; take a hint

♦ 他们想，母亲看见他们睡小床，一定会说："你们小夫妻天天分开睡
怎么行？还是我和冬冬一人睡一张小床吧。"这样隔离老人与儿子的
目的就可以不费口舌地达到了。偏偏老太太不**接翎子**，只叹了一句：
"现在的小囡真像个小皇帝，做爷娘的为他们啥事情都可以牺牲。"
便**没有下文**了。
(From the short story 家庭风景二十章)
> They thought if his mother saw them sleeping in single beds she'd be bound to say, "How can a young couple like you sleep in separate beds every night? Let Dongdong and me take the single beds." That way they could separate her and their son without wasting a breath. Who knew, the old lady couldn't take a hint. She just sighed and said, "Kids nowadays really are little emperors. Parents will sacrifice everything for them," and stopped at that. [the grandmother's sleeping with her grandson and the parents would like to separate them without hurting the grandmother's feelings.]

♦ 他使了个眼色，王五权乖巧，立刻**接了翎子**，带着手下的一批人就退
了下去。
(From the novel 不夜之侯)
> He shot [Wang Wuquan] a glance. Wang Wuquan was smart and got the message right away. He left with his people.

jiě mènr 解闷儿 (解悶兒)

"Dissipate boredom"; out of boredom; for fun

♦ 他们早就不是**解闷儿**了，完全是专业写作的架式，这不是**戗行**吗？
(From the novel 一点正经没有)
> Used to be they were doing it out of boredom, but that stopped long ago. Now they've got all the trappings of professional writers. This amounts to encroaching on our turf. [A professional writer is objecting to the increasing success of amateurs.]

♦ "大人，不将她赶出去吗？"一旁的仆从问道。"不必，看她的样子
也不像当刺客的料，留下来**解解闷儿**也好。"
(From the novel 勾魂使者)
> "Shouldn't we kick her out, Sir?" asked one of the nearby servants. "No need. She doesn't look like assassin material. Why not keep her around and have some fun?"

jiè huā xiàn fó 借花献佛 (借花獻佛)

"Borrow a flower to present to the Buddha"; recycle a gift

♦ 好！那我就**借花献佛**，请田兄干上一杯。
(From the TV series 笑傲江湖)

Good! Then I'll take advantage of your gift and invite you to have a drink with me, Mr. Tian. [Mr. Tian has just given him some wine.]

◆ 这东西你收下吧，其实不是我买的，是别人送我的。我这是**借花献佛**。

> Please take this. Actually, I didn't buy it. Someone gave it to me. I'm just recycling it.

jiè sb ge dǎnr yě bù gǎn 借Sb个胆儿也不敢 (借Sb個膽兒也不敢)

"Wouldn't dare even if you lent him some courage (an extra gallbladder)"; wouldn't dare in a million years

◆ 若在过去，你一个小经理，敢在我面前这么说话吗？**借你一个胆子怕也不敢**的！

(From the short story 还原)

> In the old days, would a low-level manager like you dare to speak like that to my face? Not in a million years!

◆ 你别听他瞎咋呼，说什么要到法院去告咱们。这儿是咱们的天下，**借他个胆儿他也不敢**真的上法庭。

> Don't listen to his empty threats about taking us to court. This is our territory. He wouldn't dare go to court, not on his life.

jīn guì 金贵 (金貴)

"Gold precious"; "as precious as gold"; extremely precious or valuable

◆ 这么**金贵**的东西，你说，他交给谁放心啊？

(From the TV series 黑洞)

> Such a precious thing. Tell me, to whom could he entrust it with confidence?

◆ 人家部长的女儿**金贵**着呢，咱们可不敢高攀。

> She's a government minister's daughter, a princess. She's way out of our league.

jǐn zhe 紧着 (緊著)

Give priority to

◆ 我带回来的钱也不多，先**紧着**给娘看病吧。

(From the movie 活着)

> I didn't bring back much money. Take Mother to the doctor first.

◆ 我中午回家再吃，先**紧着**人家。

(From the TV series 其实男人最辛苦)

> I'll eat when I go home at noon. Let her have it; she needs it more. [While bringing food to his ex-wife in the maternity hospital, a man gives his own meal to another patient who has no one to care for her.]

jīng shen tóur 精神头儿 (精神頭兒)

Energy level, energy

◆ 他嘟哝着："那损失的**精神头儿**，半个稗子面馍馍都补不过来…"

(From the novel 绿化树)

He mumbled, "When you've spent that much energy, half a millet bun won't replace it."
[稗子面馍馍: steamed bread made out of millet]

♦ 老爷子八十多岁了，可**精神头儿**还真不错。

Grandpa is over eighty, but he's still vigorous.

jǐng shuǐ bú fàn hé shuǐ 井水不犯河水

"The well water doesn't invade the river water"; steer clear of someone else's territory; have nothing to do with someone

♦ 你答应我一句话，见到他时，千万不要提我，不要说这个地址是我告诉你的。我跟他已经一刀两断，**井水不犯河水**。

(From the novel 百年德性)

Promise me one thing. When you see him, be sure not to mention me. Don't tell him I gave you his address. I've broken with him completely. We don't have anything to do with each other anymore.

♦ 你卖你的菜，我卖我的鱼，咱们**井水不犯河水**。

You sell your vegetables. I sell my fish. We don't step on each other's toes.

jìng jiǔ bù chī chī fá jiǔ 敬酒不吃吃罚酒 (敬酒不吃吃罰酒)

"If you won't drink out of respect, you'll have to drink as a punishment"; not know when to quit; turn down a good offer and then have to take a bad one

♦ 那个书呆子**敬酒不吃吃罚酒**，该！

(From the TV series 康熙帝国)

That bookworm let his opportunity slip by, and now he'll have to suffer! Serves him right! [A princess is infatuated with a young scholar, but he treats her coldly. The emperor punishes him and he thus loses an opportunity for advancement.]

♦ 我告诉你，你不要**敬酒不吃吃罚酒**！我出三千块钱买你这个饭馆儿已经是抬举你了，你要是敢卖给别人小心你的狗命！

I'm telling you, you'll suffer if you pass up this opportunity. I'm already doing you a favor by offering three thousand yuan for your restaurant. If you dare to sell it to anyone else, watch out for your life.

jiū zhù xiǎo biàn zi 揪住小辫子 (揪住小辮子)

See 抓住小辫子 zhuā zhù xiǎo biàn zi

jiù jí bú jiù qióng 救急不救穷 (救急不救窮)

(Proverb) "Save from immediate need, but not save from poverty"

♦ 这自古以来都是**救急不救穷**啊！

(From the movie 活着)

It's always been the case. You can help out with the immediate need, but that doesn't get someone out of poverty. [A poor man asks for a loan. The rich man refuses the loan, but instead gives him some shadow puppets and props and tells him to earn his living that way.]

♦ 我们这钱是给困难户取暖的，不是给你们拿去作买卖的。**救急不救穷**，你们别瞎伸手。

This money of ours is to provide heat for poor families, not to help you start a business. We can help out with an urgent need but we can't offer a ticket out of poverty. Don't expect handouts.

jiù nàme huí shì 就那么回事 (就那麼回事)

Just so-so; not so great

♦ "那你和他的关系…" "就是那么回事儿。"

(From the movie 有话好好说)

"And your relations with him...?" "Not that great."

♦ "那电影怎么样？" "就那么回事儿。"

"How's that film?" "Not all that great."

jiù qiàn 就欠

"All it lacks is"; what we need is...

♦ 挖煤怎么了？比别人矮半截儿？**欠**给他们来次能源危机，都把咱矿工当宝贝了。

(From the novel 丹凤眼)

So what if I'm a coal miner? Does that make me worse than other people? All it takes is an energy crisis, and we miners will be national treasures.

♦ 这么好的条件你还嫌苦，**就欠**把你送到大西北待上两年，回来你就老实了。

Such good conditions, and you complain! What you need is to be sent to the Northwest for a couple of years. When you come back you'll shut up.

jiù shǒur 就手儿 (就手兒)

While you're at it; without going out of one's way; without extra effort

♦ 就像他过去上班的时候坐在诊室里一样，一听到病人的诉说就把自己的事儿忘了。他**就手**把漱口盂扔到水龙头旁边，对马三胜说："走，我去看看！"

(From the novel 红尘)

It's like in the old days when he was at work. He'd sit in the consulting room and the moment he heard the patient's story, he'd forget his own affairs. [This time] he threw the rinsing bowl down next to the sink and said to Ma Sansheng, "Let's go, I'll have a look!"

♦ 哎，我这儿有一封信，你出去的时候**就手儿**给我扔信筒里去行吧？

Oh, I have a letter here. Could you put it in the mailbox on your way out?

jiù zhàng yì bǐ gōu xiāo 旧账一笔勾销 (舊賬一筆勾銷)

"The old accounts will be wiped out in total"; the past will be erased

♦ 这几十年的旧账，就凭你这几句话就一**笔勾销**了吗？

(From the TV series 今生是亲人)

Do you think a few words from you can settle accounts that have been mounting up for decades?

♦ 只要你把那小子交出来，咱们旧账一笔勾销。不然的话，可别怪我对你不客气。

So long as you hand over that bastard, we'll forget about the past. Otherwise don't blame me if I don't treat you with kid gloves.

jiù zhī dao 就知道

1. knew all along 2. all one knows is…

♦ 我就知道你不能往死里挤兑我们。

(From the TV series 手心手背)

I knew all along you couldn't do something that would embarrass us so much.

♦ 你个狗东西就知道贫嘴！你在我眼皮底下待了五年，你有多深水，我想还能看个八九不离十。要是没把握考到良好以上，趁早算了吧。

(From the novel 突出重围)

You asshole, you sure know how to talk a good game. I've observed you closely for five years now, and nine times out of ten I could say how much you know ["how much water you hold"]. If you're not sure you can get a B or better on the exam, give it up before it's too late.

jú qi 局气 (局氣)

(Originally gangster/mafia jargon) play by the rules; play by the book

♦ 我说你们也忒不局气，人家女孩，累坏了以后谁教你们。

(From the short story 我的羽毛球教练)

I think you guys have really crossed the line. It's not fair. She's just a girl. If you wear her out, who's going to teach you? [Several health club members have insisted on playing in turn with a young badminton coach, denying her a chance to rest.]

♦ 如果我们就这么一走了之，而把个烂摊子丢给你们，让你们替我们顶缸，未免显得我们太不局气。以后没脸见人！

(From the novel 一级恐惧)

If we just drop everything and leave, so that you've got a total mess to deal with and have to take the rap for us, we'd sure end up looking like cheaters. Afterwards we wouldn't be able to face people.

juǎn pū gai 卷铺盖 (卷鋪蓋)

"Roll up the bedding (and go home)"; be fired

♦ 一号病人是你负责的，如果出了问题，你就准备卷铺盖回家吧。

(From the novel 龙鳞道传奇)

Patient No. 1 is your responsibility. If there are any problems, you can expect to be sacked and go home.

♦ 你在技校学了三年，怎么这么简单的零件也做不好？ 听着，再把东西做坏了立马儿给我**卷铺盖走人**！

You've been at the vocational school three years and you still can't make a simple spare part like this? Listen, if you screw up one more time, you're out of here immediately!

jué huór 绝活儿 (絕活兒)

Unsurpassed, unsurpassable skills; exclusive or special skills

♦ 我说老余，我觉得你就像手里有**绝活**，却不肯传给徒弟的老艺人。你有这么好的主意，为什么不早说呢！

(From the novel 最后的荣耀)

Lao Yu, I think you're like those old artisans with first-class skills who aren't willing to pass them on to apprentices. If you had such a great idea, why didn't you tell me earlier?

♦ 这菜不错吧？ 告诉你，这可是我太太的**绝活儿**。

This dish isn't half bad, right? 'You know, this is my wife's specialty.

K

kāi gōng méi yǒu huí tóu jiàn 开弓没有回头箭 (開弓沒有回頭箭)

(Proverb) "Once you release the bow, the arrow is not coming back"; there is no turning back

♦ "丹红，这开弓可没有回头的箭啊！" "我知道，但这别无选择。"

(From the TV series 大赢家)

"Danhong, once you do this, you've burned your bridges." "I know, but I don't have any choice." [Danhong, the general manager of a company, is preparing to take a big risk by building new facilities and replacing outdated equipment.]

♦ 你也想下海做生意？ 我劝你再好好想想，**开弓没有回头箭**。万一你生意做不好，还想回来当教授，学校恐是怕不会同意的。

You want to take the plunge and go into business, too? I advise you to think it over. There's no turning back once you get started. If your business doesn't go well and you want to be a professor again, the university is not likely to agree.

kāi kǒu zi 开口子 (開口子)

"Make a breach"; set a precedent

♦ 北京的跳蚤市场最早是在东城开办的，据说是东四十条那儿的一家中学先开了口子。

(From the novel 耍叉)

Beijing's flea markets first started in the eastern part of the city. Supposedly, a high school on the Tenth Lane in Dongsi was the groundbreaker.

◆ 你想想，要是把公司的钱借给了他去买个人的房子，别人准得跟着学，咱们哪有那么多的资金啊？ 这口子绝对不能开。
   Just think, if we let him borrow money from the company to buy an apartment, others will surely want to follow his example. Where would we get that kind of money? There's no way we can set this kind of precedent.

kāi lǜ dēng 开绿灯(開綠燈)
"Turn on the green light"; consent to

◆ 你要是真想报答我，报到你们那儿的审批书开个绿灯就行了。
   (From the TV series 天堂鸟)
   If you really want to pay me back, just give a green light to the applications that land on your desk. [A government official asks how he can repay a businessman's gifts.]

◆ 你明明知道他们卖的是假冒伪劣产品，为什么还要开绿灯？
   You knew perfectly well they were selling counterfeit and shoddy goods. Why did you still give them the green light?

kāi xiǎo chāir 开小差儿 (開小差兒)
Desert or decamp; play hooky; be absent-minded

◆ "有事吗？ 我今天忙着呢。" "坐下！ 开会儿小差儿吧你！"
   (From the TV series 今生是亲人)
   "What is it? I'm really busy today." "Sit down. Take a break."

◆ "你刚才说什么？" "看，你又开小差儿了。注意力集中一点儿好不好？"
   "What did you just say?" "See, your mind wandered again. Try to concentrate, OK?"

kāi xiǎo zào 开小灶 (開小竈)
"Fire up the small stove (to prepare special dishes for someone)"; give special favors or privileges to someone

◆ 我们家老爷子从我进刑警队那天，就跟老杜挑明了：工作上的事儿，你要对他有偏有向，让他开小灶吃独食，我可不饶你。
   (From the novel 百年德性)

The day I joined the crime team at the police department, my old man gave it to Lao Du straight, "If you give him any special favors or special treatment, I won't forgive you."

♦ 你知道王新为什么这次考得这么好吗？我告诉你个秘密。老师天天给他开小灶儿！
   You know why Wang Xin did so well on the exam this time? I'll let you in on a secret. The teacher gave him special attention every day!

kāi/kuān xīn wán 开/宽心丸 (開/寬心丸)
"Reassurance pill"; reassurance

♦ "建军，你别瞎着急。现在医院瞎眼大夫特多，我们一个街坊就是给检查坏了，硬给开了刀，屁事没有。倒把一个什么零件给误切了去。你说坑人不坑人啊？现在还打着官司呢。"袁建军叹口气："你别给我吃开心丸了，昨天在省城都确诊了。没跑了。"
   (From the novel 天下大事)
   "Jianjun, don't get upset over nothing. These days lots of the hospital doctors don't know their business ["are blind"]. One of our neighbors was misdiagnosed. They even operated on him, and there wasn't a thing wrong. They took out one of his spare parts. That's doing people harm, right? He's suing them as we speak!" Yuan Jianjun sighed, "Don't try to cheer me up. Yesterday the provincial hospital confirmed the diagnosis. I'm afraid it's definite." [Jianjun's child was diagnosed with leukemia.]

♦ 我给你吃颗宽心丸吧，局长亲口跟我说了，这次精简不会简到你的头上，而且他还要提拨你呢！
   I'm going to tell you something to ease your mind. The bureau director told me himself. The downsizing won't affect you this time. What's more, he's going to give you a promotion!

kāi yǎn 开眼 (開眼)
"Eye opening"; an eye-opening experience

♦ 要不您给他们露两声，让他们开开眼。
   (From the movie 活着)
   How about singing a few bars to show them what you can do? [Asking someone to provide vocals for a shadow-puppet theater.]

♦ 这次去北京，我可真是开了眼了。别说是生意人和机关干部，就连街上收破烂儿的都有手机。
   This trip to Beijing was really an eye-opener. Not just business people and government officials but even the garbage collectors on the street all had cell phones!

kāi yáng hūn 开洋荤 (開洋葷)
"Taste foreign meat"; have a new experience; a novel experience (荤: meat or strong-tasting foods such as onions)";

♦ 我实在很难回答，因为我对此道是门外汉，以前从来没去过那种地方，今天还是第一次开洋荤。
   (From the novel 第一次任务)

It's really hard to answer, because I'm a complete newcomer at this. I never went to that kind of place before. Today is a first. [He was asked to give his opinion of a brothel.]

♦   老王以前连北京上海都没去过，这次却被人家请到欧洲去转了一圈
儿，真是大开洋荤。

Lao Wang had never even been to Beijing or Shanghai. This time he was invited on a tour of Europe. It was an eye-opening experience for him.

kāi yóu 揩油

(Shanghai dialect) "wipe grease"; swipe or filch

♦   我们骗的是那些想揩中国油的老外，骗的是那些想靠走私国家文物发
横财的鬼家伙，骗他们不光没罪还有功呢！

(From the novel 女性写真)

The ones we're cheating are those foreigners who try to rip China off, and those bastards who want to get rich smuggling out our national treasures. Cheating those guys isn't a crime—it's a service to the country. [Referring to those who make fake cultural relics.]

♦   他老想到我们这儿来揩油。我们这个小时装店哪有那么多的油水？ 下
次他再来你就说我不在。

He's always trying to get something from us for free. We're just a small dress shop; how can we come up with so much to give away? Next time he shows up, just tell him I'm not here.

kǎi zi 凯子 (凯子)

(Taiwan expression) gigolo

♦   今天晚上有个凯子陪我吃饭。

(From the movie 台北爱情故事)

Tonight I'm having dinner with a guy from an escort service.

♦   聊天去找三姑六婆不就行了，网上都是有知识有学问的人，谁会跟你
这老太婆有话聊啊！凯子就钓凯子嘛，你敢做干吗不敢承认，只是看
不出，一大把年纪了还色心不死！

(From the novel 水晶缘)

If you're just looking for someone to chat with, find some old hen and you're set. On the web everyone's knowledgeable and educated; who has anything to discuss with an old woman like you? But if you're looking for a boy toy, then say so. If you have the guts to do something, have the guts to admit it. Who knew, at your age you're still interested in sex!

kān jiā de běn shì dōu shǐ/ná chū lái le 看家的本事都使/拿出来了 (看家的本事都使/拿出来了)

"Bring out all one's house-guarding skills"; bring out the best you have

♦   今天来的客人都是我的高朋贵友，你要拿出看家的本事来侍候他们。

(From the novel 孽海)

Today's guests are important contacts ["my honorable friends"]. Pull out all the stops for them. [The manager of a club is speaking to a young female employee.]

♦ 这笔生意看来很难谈下去了。昨天老曹把**看家的本事都使出来了**，可对方就是不松口。

It looks like talks on the deal are off. Yesterday Lao Cao did everything he could, but the other side just wouldn't budge.

kàn bǎ nǐ v de 看把你V的

"Just look at how you..."

♦ 孙凯：她不知道我是谁吧？　陶涛：（不耐烦地）不知道！**看把你吓的**！

(From the TV play 朗朗星空)

Sun Kai: "She doesn't know who I am, right?" Tao Tao (impatiently): "No, she doesn't! Just look at how scared you are!"

♦ **看把你能的**！　跟你的死老子一样，小嘴巴巴巴地说不完的话。

(From the novel 锁链，是柔软的)

Look at you showing off! You're just like your lousy old man. Your little mouth just goes blah, blah, blah, and never stops.

kàn shénme kàn 看什么看 (看什麼看)

"What's there to look at!"

♦ **看什么看**！　该干什么干什么去！

(From the TV series 走过花季)

What's there to look at! Go back to what you're supposed to be doing! [The board chairman and general manager are arguing; employees are taking a lively interest.]

♦ **看什么看**！　没看过你爹你妈结婚呐？去去去！回去问问你爹你妈去！

(From the movie 牧马人)

What are you looking at? Is it because you missed your mom and dad's wedding? Go away! Go home and ask your mom and dad about it! [Kids are crowding around a window to watch a wedding ceremony, and the production brigade chief tries to shoo them away.]

kàn tòu le 看透了

Saw through; wised up; became disillusioned

♦ 我算**看透了**，想客客气气的，什么都办不成。

(From the novel 一点正经没有)

I've learned my lesson. Politeness gets you nowhere.

♦ 把王经理撤掉了，换了李经理，大家原来以为公司会好起来，谁知道姓李的手脚更不干净。我算**看透了**，现在当头儿的没有不为自己打小算盘的。

> After Manager Wang was sacked we had Manager Li. We all thought the company would turn around. Who knew! That Li's fingers are even stickier. My eyes have been opened. These days anyone in a position of power just looks out for himself.

kàn zài yǎn li bá bù chū lái 看在眼里拔不出来 (看在眼裏拔不出來)

Something gets into your eye and you can't get it out; become fixated on something

♦ "我哪有那眼福啊？ 回头您那黄麻头〖蟋蟀品种〗我**看在眼里拔 不出来**了。" "你不想看**拉倒**啊！ 还小肚鸡肠，还记仇儿了。"

(From the movie 洗澡)

> "Do my eyes deserve to see such a thing? Besides, what if I did get to see your Jutehead [species of cricket] and then coveted it?" "If you don't want to look, then forget it. I didn't expect you to keep score and hold grudges like that." [The two older men had had an argument over some crickets the previous day.]

♦ 别看了，小心**看在眼里拔不出来**了！ 再说了，这计算机再好你也买不起啊！

> Don't look any more. Watch out, don't get obsessed. Besides, no matter how great this computer is, you still can't afford it.

kàn zěnme shuō le 看怎么说了 (看怎麼說了)

"It depends on how one puts it"; it depends on how you look at it

♦ 大姑娘道："想必这件事很严重。"李克威道："那要**看怎么说了**，可以说很严重，也可以说根本没什么。"

(From the novel 玉翎雕)

> The young woman said, "This must be something serious." Li Kewei replied, "That depends on how you look at it. You could say it's really serious. You could also say it's no big deal."

♦ "这本书有用吗？" "**看怎么说了**，初学的人可能有点儿用，您要是想搞专业就差远了。"

> "Is this book of any use?" "That depends. It may be of some use for beginners, but if you want to specialize [in the field], then not by a long shot."

kàn zhe v 看着 V

Do something at one's discretion

♦ "水工，这次部里给咱们项目发了两千块钱的奖金，你说怎么个分配法？" "你**看着**办吧。"水工一副不在意的样子。

(From the novel 薄奠)

"Shui Gong, the Ministry gave our project [team] a bonus of two thousand yuan. How should we split it?" "Any way you want." Shui Gong seemed totally indifferent.

♦ "你想让我捐多少钱？" "一百万不多，一万不少，您**看着给**吧。"

    "How much would you like me to donate?" "A million's not too much, and ten thousand's not too little. It's up to you."

kàn zǒu yǎn 看走眼

    Misjudge

♦ 行，我真没**看走眼**。你是条汉子。

    (From the TV series 手心手背)

    OK! I didn't misjudge you. You are a good man.

♦ 我这回算是**看走眼**了，这个穿西服的敢情是个骗子。

    This time I really made the wrong call. That man in the suit turned out to be a con artist.

kāo 拷

    From English "to call"; call on a beeper

♦ 这是老爷子〖律师事务所的领导〗**拷**我，叫我立即赶回大华总部。

    (From the TV series 红色康乃馨)

    That's the boss ["old man," the head of the law firm] beeping me. He wants me to go back to Dahua's headquarters right away.

♦ 她说："那好，我以后有了生意需要用车，一定找你。"司机赶紧递给她一张自制的名片，上面只有一个拷机号码。司机说："**拷我就行**。"

    (From the novel 风中黄叶)

    She said, "All right, then. When my business gets off the ground, I'll look for you when I need a car." The driver quickly gave her a homemade card with only a beeper number and said, "Just page me."

kào 靠

    (Vulgar) Fuck; same as 操 (cào); no shit

♦ A: 行为艺术！ 够酷的啊！B: 还是你在这儿行为吧！ A: **靠**，整个他妈的艺盲！

    (From the TV series 手心手背)

    A: "Performance art! How cool is that!" B: "No, maybe you're performing!" A: "What a fucking philistine!" [A saw B throwing paper planes and thought that was a kind of performance art. But actually B was upset after losing his girlfriend. 行为 is short for 行为艺术, performance art. Here the noun is used as a verb to show his anger. 艺盲 describes someone ill-informed about art, and is patterned after 文盲: an illiterate, somebody who is "blind to letters."]

♦ "我开'丰田佳美'，是公司给配的车。" "**靠**！ 行啊你！这才叫蔫人出豹子！女强人！"

    (From the short story 无为在歧路)

"I drive a Toyota Camry. The company lets me use it." "No shit! Good for you! Still water runs deep [an unassuming person turns to out be a leopard]. What a superwoman!"

kē 嗑

Chatter; talk idly

♦　你说你这么好一姑娘，要模样有模样，要人品有人品，跟我**嗑**什么终身啊！

(From the TV series 手心手背)

> You're a girl who's got everything—both looks and character. Don't give me that "I'll wait for you" talk. [The speaker is about to go to jail. His girlfriend says she'll wait for him.]

♦　甲："我一**嗑**就能**嗑**上，信不信？"乙："我不信。"丙："我也不信，反正吹牛不用上税。"

(From the TV series 将爱情进行到底)

> A: "I can get any girl the moment I try. [嗑: to accost, "I can chat up any girl I want."] Believe it or not!" B: "I don't believe it." C: "Me neither. Talk is cheap."

kě jìngr 可劲儿 (可勁兒)

With all one's strength

♦　现在有什么珍珠护肤霜、抗皱美容霜，都买点儿，**可劲儿**地擦！

(From the TV series 一年又一年)

> Buy whatever kinds of pearl cream, or anti-wrinkle cream, are on the market. Buy them all, and slather them on! [Now that they have some money, a husband would like his wife to look younger and prettier.]

♦　人家城里人多有钱啊，炖肉粉条子**可劲儿**造，哪像咱们乡下，不到过年的时候吃不上肉。

> City folks have tons of money. They can have all the pork and bean noodle stew they want, not like us peasants. No meat for us unless it's Chinese New Year.

kě sǎng zi 可嗓子

"The throat makes as much sound as possible"; at the top of one's lungs

♦　他**可嗓子**呼唤着："你在哪儿！你在哪儿！咱俩回去！咱俩回去--"

(From the novel 阴阳界)

> He shouted as loudly as he could, "Where are you? Where are you? Let's go home."

♦　干什么呢你这儿？出了点儿事儿就**可嗓子**嚷嚷，怕别人不知道怎么着？

> What are you doing here? Some little thing happens, and you have to scream at the top of your lungs? Worried that someone might not know about it?

kě xī liǎor de 可惜了儿的 (可惜了兒的)

"Pity the…"; pity about the…

♦　我说，**可惜了儿的**这把岁数，你怎么没羞没臊啊你？

(From the movie 洗澡)

> I think it's really pathetic, at your age! Don't you have any shame at all? [Spoken about a foul play during a match.]

♦　您要么不搁盐，要么搁三回盐，**可惜了儿的**这菜了。

(From the TV series 贫嘴张大民的幸福生活)

Either you don't use any salt or you use three times as much as necessary. What a shame—the dish is wasted.

kě zhēn xíng a 可真行啊

(Often sarcastic) You're great! I've got to hand it to you!

♦ 阿玲你可真行啊，一下就赚了这么多，而且人家还表扬了我们！

(From the novel 桑拿小姐)

Ah Ling, you're really something. You made a bundle in no time, and then on top of that, you got them to sing our praises!

♦ 你可真行啊！ 写了三天的检查就写了一行字。

You're unbelievable. You spend three days writing a self-criticism and come up with just one line.

kèn jiěr 肯节儿 (肯節兒)

(Beijing dialect) critical moment (肯=裉 kèn, armhole)

♦ 这叫墙倒众人推，凡是在这肯节儿上折我郎健的主儿，有朝一日我挨个儿拾掇他们。

(From the TV series 手心手背)

This is hitting a man when he's down. Anyone who grabs the opportunity and tries to do me (Langjian) some damage will get his payback sooner or later.

♦ 我觉得这是个肯节儿。

(From the TV series 大雪无痕)

I think this is the key [to solving the police case].

kēng shēng 吭声 (吭聲)

Utter a sound or word

♦ 我这儿说了半天了，你们倒吭个声儿啊！

(From the TV series 康熙帝国)

I've been talking forever. Why don''t you say something!

♦ 我说大小姐，行还是不行您倒吭个声儿啊！ 人家还等着回话儿呢！

My fine lady, will it be yes or no? Just say the word! People are waiting for your answer. [A match-maker is speaking.]

kōng shǒu tào bái láng 空手套白狼

"Trap a white wolf with one's bare hands"; profit without investment of one's own

♦ 这几年他一直在玩这种空手套白狼的把戏。

(From the TV series 大雪无痕)

For the past few years he's been playing this kind of game, making profits off other people's investments.

♦ 你懂得做无本生意，别人难道不懂 "空手套白狼" 的道行？

(From the novel 浮沈商海)

If you understand how to start a business without capital, what makes you think others don't also know how to make money without investing anything?

kōu ménr 抠门儿 (摳門兒)

Stingy

♦ "老头补（车胎）忒贵，我回家自个儿补去。" "抠门儿！"
(From the TV series 贫嘴张大民的幸福生活)
"That old man charges too much for fixing tires. I'll go home and do it myself." "What a cheapskate!"

♦ 嘿，现在的司机可是真抠门儿呀，空调坏了，也不修，只有个小电扇在车里摇头晃脑一个劲地傻吹。
(From the novel 少年方唐－鸭子的故事)
Cab drivers are really stingy these days. The air-conditioner's broken and they don't get it fixed. There's just a little fan in the cab, looking very pleased with itself and blowing its stupid air.

kòu shǐ pén zi 扣屎盆子

"Dump the chamber pot over someone"; make someone else take the rap; falsely accuse someone else

♦ 万钢是她喜欢的男人，她能往她喜欢的男人的头上扣屎盆子吗？ 那样做可太缺德了。
(From the novel 大雪作证)
Wan Gang is the man she loves. Could she spread lies about the man she loves? That would be too rotten a thing to do. [Someone asked her to say she had slept with Wan Gang.]

♦ 我说，你怎么总往别人脑袋上扣屎盆子？ 这房子倒了完全是因为你买了不合格的水泥，可你却说是设计师的问题，这太不讲理了！
I'm asking you, why do you always blame someone else? The building collapsed because you bought substandard cement, and you blame the architect! It's totally unreasonable.

kòu zāng shuǐ/dào zāng shuǐ 扣脏水/倒脏水 (扣髒水/倒髒水)

"Pour dirty water over someone"; pin the blame on someone

♦ 你你你，你凭什么把这桶脏水扣在我的头上，你有什么权利！
(From the novel 永不瞑目)
You bitch! What grounds do you have to drag me through the mud like this? What right do you have? [A young woman lied about having slept with the man.]

♦ 那家伙特别坏，总是自己做坏事，再往别人身上倒脏水。
That guy is really bad news. He always does rotten things and makes someone else take the rap.

kù bì le 酷毙了

(Portmanteau word) can't be any cooler; extremely cool (transliteration of "cool" plus 毙, "to execute," as an intensifier)

♦ 这过程对我来说，绝对是酷毙了！谁让我这狐狸吃不着葡萄呢！
(From the TV series 手心手背)
The process was way cool. Absolutely! Can't complain if I'm not meant to have you ["if the fox is not allowed to have the grapes"]. [A young woman is repeatedly rejected by the

man she loves. He apologizes to her for being unable to reciprocate her feelings. She tries to put on a brave face and replies that she doesn't regret having pursued him. She jokes that she is like a fox craving a bunch of grapes out of her reach.]

◆ 这身儿西服再配上这副墨镜，**酷毙了**！可惜这双皮鞋差了点儿。

If you wear that suit and those sunglasses, you'll be really cool! Too bad your shoes don't quite make it.

kuài duīr 块堆儿 (塊堆兒)

(Beijing dialect) together

◆ 我那师哥，当年跟我**块堆儿**穿的警服，后来念了几年大学，最后熬成了副部级。

(From the novel 百年德性)

My classmate started wearing the police uniform at the same time as I did. Afterwards he went to college for a few years. He ended up being promoted to deputy minister.

◆ 我也想去逛街，咱们**块堆儿**去吧？

I feel like taking a walk down the street, too. Want to go together?

kǔn bǎng bù chéng fū qī 捆绑不成夫妻 (捆綁不成夫妻)

(Proverb) "Tying two people up together doesn't make them a couple";" you can't force an alliance or relationship

◆ "老夫子，树还没倒，猢狲就要散了！" 师爷不怒，只是谦恭地笑着。"**捆绑不成夫妻，**" 知县道，"既然要走，留也无趣。"

(From the novel 檀香刑)

"Old teacher, as they say, the tree has yet to fall, but the monkeys are already running away." The master did not get angry, but smiled modestly. "I can't compel you," the county magistrate replied. "Since you want to leave, there's no point keeping you here."

◆ 我看咱们既然不是一条心，不如趁早散伙，俗话说得好，**捆绑不成夫妻**。

I think that since we're of different minds, we might as well part ways right now. As they say, "tying two people up together doesn't make them a couple."

L

lā bú xià liǎn 拉不下脸 (拉不下臉)

"Can't pull down the face"; can't bring oneself to do something (for fear of embarrassment, either one's own or others')

◆ 有件事我想了很久了，像我们这种做学问的人，出力的活干不了，干别的又**拉不下脸**，所以我想办所学校，孔兄意下如何？

(From the short story 戏说古今)

There's something I've been thinking about for a long time now. Intellectuals like us can't do manual jobs and we're ashamed to do anything else, so I'm thinking about opening a school. What do you think, Brother Kong?

♦   我知道修公路必须要拆那座房子，但是你可能不知道，房主是我二大爷，还是你去说吧，我拉不下脸来。

> I know we have to tear down that house to build the highway, but there's something you may not know. The owner is my uncle. It'd be better for you to talk to him. I haven't the heart.

lā chě 拉扯

"Pull and tear"; raise a child (usually under difficult circumstances)

♦   梅生娘，你才三十几岁的人，可别说这丧气话，咬咬牙，把孩子拉扯大了，你就熬出头了。

(From the short story 粮食)

> Meisheng's Mom, you're barely past thirty. 'Stop talking doom and gloom. Bite the bullet, bring the kid up, and you'll see light at the end of the tunnel. [Meisheng's mother doesn't have any food, and thinks it would best to die and put an end to her misery.]

♦   你妈一把屎一把尿的把你们拉扯大，容易吗？

(From the TV series 空镜子)

> Your mother brought you all up, wiping your bottoms one by one. You think that was easy?

lā chū lái de shǐ 拉出来的屎

"The shit you put out"; one's word or commitment

♦   你们怎么又不干了？ 拉出来的屎哪能缩回去啊？

(From the TV series 古船、女人和网)

> You're quitting? You're going back on your word?

♦   如今的头头，" 拉出来又坐回去 " 的事儿可太多啦！

(From the novel 空洞)

> Bosses these days break their promises much too often. [A promised bonus failed to materialize.]

lā dǎo 拉倒

"Pull down"; forget it

♦   "我哪有那眼福啊？回头您那黄麻头〖蟋蟀品种〗我看在眼里拔不出来了。" "你不想看拉倒啊！ 还小肚鸡肠，还记仇儿了。"

(From the movie 洗澡)

"Do my eyes deserve to see such a thing? Besides, what if I did get to see your Jutehead [species of cricket] and then coveted it?" "If you don't want to look, then forget it. I didn't expect you to keep score and hold grudges like that." [The two older men had had an argument over some crickets the previous day.]

◆ 什么，卖进口的旧服装？ **拉倒**吧你！我才不会跟你去卖哪种东西呢！

What? Sell imported second-hand clothes? You can forget that! No way am I going to sell that kind of thing with you!

lā jiā dài kǒu 拉家带口

"Drag along the family and all its members"; be burdened with a family

◆ 你可别害我，让我往枪口上撞。我这小命不值钱，但也**拉家带口**呀！

(From the novel 都市危情)

Don't harm me, don't push me to suicide ["make me throw myself against the muzzle of the gun"]. My own life is worth nothing, but I have a family.

◆ "下班儿怎么还不走啊？" "我还有点儿事儿。" "你不像我们啊，**拖家带口**的。明儿见。"

(From the TV series 手心手背)

"Time to quit work. How come you're still here?" "I still have a few things to do." "You're not like the rest of us. We have families."

lā láng pèi 拉郎配

"Rope in someone for a bridegroom"; force a marriage

◆ 不是强迫？你眼前这个方案不就是**拉郎配**吗？

(From the TV series 大赢家)

You're not trying to strong-arm us? If this plan isn't a shotgun marriage, what is it? [A third party tries to get two competitors to cooperate.]

◆ 现在无论是外国还是中国，企业兼并都是大势所趋。但是你让我们这个汽车修理厂和儿童自行车厂合并，这也差得太远了，简直是**拉郎配**！

In China or overseas, mergers are the wave of the future. But you want our automobile repair factory to merge with the children's bicycle factory. That's too much of a stretch—it's apples and oranges!

lā pí tiáo 拉皮条 (拉皮條)

"Pull the leather strap"; work as a pimp

◆ "那个男的和那两个女的是什么关系？" "是干那个的。" "哪个？" "嗨，**拉皮条**的。"

(From the TV series 黑洞)

"What's the relationship between that man and those two women?" "He's one of those." "Those?" "Well, he's a pimp."

◆ 你他妈少给我乱当红娘，**拉皮条**你岁数还小点儿。

(From the novel 我是你爸爸)

You fucking better stop playing matchmaker with me. You're too young to be a pimp. [A son wants to play matchmaker for his father. 红娘 was a maid in the famous Yuan play 西厢记 (*Romance of the Western Chamber*) who succeeds in bringing her young mistress and her lover together.]

lái bù lái 来不来 (來不來)

At any given moment; frequently; any old time

♦ 有两把吉他，有一个破锣嗓子，就能凑合出一个摇滚乐队，**来不来**还他妈的什么"后现代"，你说这不整个儿一个**玩儿闹**吗？

(From the novel 百年德性)

Two guitars and a bad singing voice, and you've got a rock group. And they're always ready to give you that "postmodern" bullshit. If that isn't a bad joke, I don't know what is.

♦ 经理，你把李刚给我调走吧，这小子**来不来**的就骂人，昨儿还把小张打了一顿。

Manager, do me a favor and transfer Li Gang somewhere else. That bastard sounds off at people whenever he feels like it. Yesterday he even beat up Xiao Zhang.

lái de bú shì shí hou 来的不是时候 (來的不是時候)

Didn't come at the right time

♦ 真对不起，我**来的不是时候**，刚才那位也是崇拜你的研究生吧？

(From the TV series 一年又一年)

Sorry, it seems I came at the wrong time. Was that also one of your adoring graduate students? [An ex-wife saw a young woman at her former husband's house.]

♦ "老张在吗？" "嗨！ 你**来的不是时候**。老张天天都在，就是这会儿出去了。"

"Is Lao Zhang home?" "Oh, bad timing. Usually Lao Zhang's always home, but this time he just stepped out."

lái jìn 来劲 (來勁)

Get overly excited (after misunderstanding a situation or reading too much into it)

♦ "快把刀放下！" "不！" "还**来劲**了你！"

(From the movie 有话好好说)

"Put down the knife!" "No!" "Don't get so worked up!"

♦ "他拿二百凭什么就给我一百啊？" "**来劲**了是不是？ 给你一百就是抬举你了。不想干**立马儿**给我走人。"

"He gets two hundred. How come I only get a hundred?" "You're getting carried away, aren't you? A hundred is more than you're worth. If you don't want to do it, do me a favor and get lost right now."

lái shìr 来事儿 (來事兒)

"Make things come"; make things happen

♦ 还有一些人穿得整整齐齐，透着许多经验，也会找座位，坐下就聊个没完，跟自来熟似的。这种人一般都坐长途，会**来事儿**，是不错的旅行伙伴。

(From the novel 火车快开)

Then there are some well-dressed people who have experience finding seats. The minute they sit down they'll talk for hours. They seem at home right away. People like this are usually traveling long distances. They can make things happen and are good traveling companions.

♦   小李那人特能**来事儿**，要不然局长能那么**待见**他吗？
     Xiao Li is a player. Otherwise would the bureau chief like him?

lái tóur 来头儿 (來頭兒)

"The way someone has been coming on"; judging from the way someone has been behaving; backing

♦   你看那姓彭的**来头儿**，跟小玉已经是板上钉钉了，你去找又有什么用呢？
     (From the TV series 北京女人)
     That Peng guy has been acting as if he and Xiaoyu are already a definite item. What good will it do you to go after her?

♦   "这个姓王的底细你了解不？" "不太清楚，但是听他说话的口气挺有**来头儿**的。"
     "Do you know that Wang guy's background?" "Not exactly, but he sounds like he has some serious backing."

...lái zhe ...来着 (...來著)

Used after a verb in some northern dialects to indicate an ongoing action

♦   你现在着急上火，当时干什么**来着**？
     (From the TV series 大雪无痕)
     Now you're worried! What were you doing then? [Spoken to someone under investigation for taking bribes.]

♦   昨天下属守夜，看见这些刁民掘坟**来着**。
     (From the TV series 康熙帝国)
     Yesterday, your humble servant was on night guard duty and saw that mob robbing the grave.

lái zhèi yí tào 来这一套 (來這一套)

"Give me this routine"; (don't) give me that

♦   小林子，你少跟我**来这一套**，要说法律，我比你懂。咋的，我说话不好使啊？ 你这公安局长咋当上的不知道吗？
     (From the novel 使命)

Xiao Linzi, don't give me that. When it comes to law, I know more than you do. What? You don't like what you're hearing? Did you forget how you got to be police chief? [咋的: zǎdi, what? 不好使: "not good to use," hard to take. A superior is threatening the police chief who took his son into custody.]

♦ "这不是大民吗？我票忘带了，让我进去吧，下次我请你吃饭。"
"少跟我来这一套。别说我们只是街坊，就是我爸爸来没有票也不能进去看球。"

"Aren't you Damin? I forgot my ticket. Let me in. I'll take you to dinner next time."
"Don't give me that. Besides the fact that we're just neighbors, even my dad wouldn't get in to watch the ball game without a ticket."

lài há ma xiǎng chī tiān é ròu 癞蛤蟆想吃天鹅肉 (癩蛤蟆想吃天鵝肉)

"A toad eying swan meat"; desire something out of one's reach

♦ 我就真有那心不也是癞蛤蟆想吃天鹅肉吗？
(From the TV series 一年又一年)
Even if I wanted to try, she's way out of my league. [The speaker doesn't think the girl would be interested in him.]

♦ 你这是癞蛤蟆想吃天鹅肉！你一没关系，二没文凭，人家怎么会把总会计师这个肥缺给你呢？别做梦了！
That's just a fantasy! You don't have connections or academic credentials. Why in the world would they give you that cushy chief accountant job? Stop daydreaming!

làn zài dù zi li 烂在肚子里 (爛在肚子裏)

"Rot in one's stomach"; (let a secret) die with you

♦ 你跟别人也别说，就让这事儿烂在你肚子里。
(From the TV series 手心手背)
Not a word to anyone. Take this matter to the grave.

♦ 你别问了，他跟我说的话我绝对不会跟任何人说，只能烂在我肚子里。
Don't ask me. I absolutely won't tell anyone what he said. My lips are sealed.

làng zi huí tóu jīn bú huàn 浪子回头金不换 (浪子回頭金不換)

(Proverb) "The return of a prodigal is more precious than gold"

♦ "我这手，要是再碰麻将就拿电锯给锯了！""好啊，浪子回头金不换。"
(From the TV series 一年又一年)

"If these hands ever touch Mahjong again, I'll cut them off with an electric saw." "Good for you! You're turning over a new leaf. That's the best news I could hear."

◆ 我觉得可以让他来当车间主任，过去他做的那些坏事儿我不是不知
道，可俗话说得好，**浪子回头金不换**啊！

I think we could make him the workshop steward. It's not that I don't know about his past actions. But as they say, heaven loves a repentant sinner."

lāo yì bǎ 捞一把 (捞一把)

"Scoop up a bundle"; make off with a pile (of money)

◆ 别以为你的心思我不懂，想趁机**捞一把**，对不对？ 我就想不通你为什
么不能过安分点？

(From the novel 有我是谁)

You think I don't know what's on your mind? You want to grab the chance to pick up a bundle, right? I just don't understand why you can't just live your life in peace.

◆ 公司都快散伙了，谁不想趁机**捞一把**啊？

The company is about to break up. Who doesn't want to grab what he can?

lǎo bí zi 老鼻子

A great deal of; a great deal

◆ 我花了多大劲儿才让你搬到这儿来住，钱都花**老鼻子**了！

(From the TV series 黑冰)

I went to a lot of trouble getting you relocated here. I had to pay through the nose!

◆ 你别骗我，虽然你们卖的这种机器也是进口的，但是质量跟人家东方
公司的比起来差**老鼻子**了。

Don't try to cheat me. The equipment you're selling may be imported, but the quality can't compare with the Orient Company's, not by a long shot.

lǎo bù sǐ de 老不死的

"One who refuses to die"; damned old

◆ 小玲，我的"地图"喂了没有？ 别给我饿着，**赶明个我也整两条**
"银龙"，省得那**老不死**的金大头总在我面前臭显。

(From the novel 东北一家人)

Xiao Ling, did you feed the Map? Don't let it starve. Soon I'll get a couple of Silver Dragons just so that damned old Big Head Jin will stop showing off in front of me. [Map (Oscar cichlid) and Silver Dragons (Asian Arowana) are different varieties of tropical fish.]

◆ 你个**老不死**的，一辈子**死心眼**，就差吃枪子了，到老了还不知道改一
改！

(From the short story 传达三题)

You old wreck, you've been pigheaded your whole life. You just missed swallowing a bullet! Old as you are, you don't know how to change. [The husband almost got the death penalty.]

lǎo diào yá 老掉牙

"So old that the teeth are falling out"; old and outdated

◆ 就会唱那**老掉牙**的玩艺儿！ 你就不会唱点新的？

(From the TV drama 朗朗星空)

Is that all you can sing—chewed-over oldies? Why can't you sing something new?

◆ 你以为这是什么新鲜东西呢？ 告诉你吧，这在人家外国**老掉牙**了，都
没什么人用了！

You think that's something new? I'm telling you, it's ancient history abroad. No one uses
it anymore.

lǎo hú li 老狐狸

"Old fox"; a cunning guy

◆ 那**老狐狸**不但自己装病功夫一流，而且还会联合一家子人一起演戏，
上从我大舅舅一家人、管家、家庭医生，下到佣人们全都**一个鼻孔出
气**，所以我就算明知道他是在装病也**没辙**。

(From the novel 烈火青春)

That old fox is not only a real expert at faking illness, but he knows how to get the whole
family into the act. Everyone in my uncle's family—the housekeeper, the family doctor,
all the servants—will sing the same tune. Even if I know for sure he's just pretending to
be sick, there's nothing I can do. ["The old fox," the maternal grandfather, lives with the
uncle's family.]

◆ 这个**老狐狸**，做了坏事儿你还就是抓不到他的把柄。

That old fox, even when he does something really bad you can't find a way to pin it on
him ["can't find a handle to grab"].

lǎo hǔ yě yǒu dǎ dǔnr de shí hou 老虎也有打盹儿的时候 (老虎也有打盹兒的時候)

"Even the tiger takes a nap sometimes"; even the tiger lets his guard down sometimes; be
caught napping

◆ 他留神观察，警察们虽然防范极严，但**老虎也有打盹的时候**，啥时候
警察交接班，啥时候警察疲劳容易松懈，他都摸了个一消二楚。

(From the novel 噬血逃亡)

He observed carefully. The police kept close watch, but even tigers nap sometimes. He
learned all the details about when the police changed shifts and when they were likely to
get tired and let down their guard.

◆ **老虎也有打盹儿的时候**，难道他孙膑就不会有过错？

(From the TV series 孙子兵法)

Everyone has off-days. Don't tell me Sun Bin never makes a mistake!

lǎo huáng lì 老皇历 (老皇曆)

"Old imperial calendar"; ancient history

◆ "小虎子和小燕不是住在未来路2000号吗？" 我问。"那是**老皇历**
啦。他们早搬家了。"

(From the novel 小灵通漫游未来)

"Tiger Cub and Swallow live at 2000 Future Road, right?" I asked. "That's ancient history. They moved a long time ago."

◆   "你们不是每礼拜二休息吗？" "那是**老皇历**了，现在改星期四了。"

"Don't you have Tuesdays off?" "Not anymore. We switched to Thursdays."

lǎo liǎn 老脸 (老臉)

"Old face"; (for an older person) to lose face

◆   我舍开**老脸**跟你说吧！

(From the TV drama 昏晃胡同)

Even though I'm ashamed, I'll tell you. [Asking for a bigger apartment because his unwed daughter is pregnant.]

◆   让外人知道李大局长有个成天就知道跟乱七八糟的人厮混的女儿，您这张**老脸**还往哪儿搁呀！

(From the short story 失足少女)

Bureau Chief Li, if people find out your daughter hangs out with scumbags all day, where will you hide your face?

lǎo mēi kā chi yǎn 老眉咔嗤眼

"Old eyebrows and ugly eyes"; old and ugly

◆   我们从街西一直溜到街东，终于钻进了一家叫男孩女孩的酒吧。其实我实在不想进这家，你想我们**老眉卡嗤眼**的，冒充什么男孩女孩啊。

(From the short story 第一次进酒吧)

We wandered down the street from east to west, and finally went into a bar called Boys & Girls. Actually, I didn't really want to go in. Think about it, old bags like us passing for boys and girls!

◆   你们照吧，我这**老眉咔嗤眼**的，照出相片儿来也不好看。

Take a picture if you want. With an old bat like me, you can take photos but they're not going to look too good.

lǎo mén kǎn 老门槛 (老門檻)

(Shanghai dialect) "old threshold"; a shrewd old person

◆   放心吧，娘舅是个**老门槛**了，这种事错不了。

(From the TV series 天下第一情)

Relax, your uncle is a shrewd old guy. You can't go wrong with him. [An uncle asked his nephew to manage a restaurant; the nephew's mother is reassuring him.]

◆   这个**老门槛**，让我们两家打破头，他自己把好处都捞走了。

That old fox, he plays us off against each other and grabs all the good stuff.

lǎo wáng mài guā, zì mài zì kuā 老王卖瓜，自卖自夸 (老王賣瓜，自賣自誇)

"Old Wang praises the melons he sells"; blow one's own horn

◆   他长得帅极了！ 这可不是他**老王卖瓜，自卖自夸**，凡是见过悟轩的女人莫不被他迷去三魂七魄，只乞求他能看她们一眼。

(From the novel 鸡腿美人)

He's drop-dead handsome, and you don't have to take his word for it. Once a woman lays eyes on him she's head over heels. She just prays he'll glance her way.

♦ 你呀，光说你们的优点了，这叫**老王卖瓜，自卖自夸**。

Don't just tell us about your strengths. Don't blow your own horn.

lǎo yóu tiáo 老油条 (老油條)

"Old deep-fried dough"; an old, very slippery person

♦ 马驰骋耍嘴皮子逗不过这个**老油条**，只得嘴上服输，说："我把这个七品之下的县委副书记让给你吧！"

(From the novel 这个年月)

When it came to twisting words, Ma Chicheng was no match for that old weasel. He just had to admit defeat and say, "OK, I'll give you my lousy deputy county party secretary post!" [七品: seventh rank under the imperial system]

♦ 咱们谢经理可是个**老油条**了，你跟他说什么他就是不上你的套。

Our manager, Mr. Xie, is a shrewd old guy. No matter what you tell him he won't take the bait.

lǎo lao 姥姥

"(Maternal) grandma"; fuck; shit

♦ 房子刚修好，我还没享受几天，就让我拆？ **姥姥**！

(From the TV drama 耷儿胡同)

I just fixed up the house, and I haven't had very long to enjoy it. And now they want me to tear it down? Bastards!

♦ **姥姥**的，不分我个四居老子不干！

(From the TV series 贫嘴张大民的幸福生活)

No fucking way! Not unless they give me a four-bedroom apartment!

lǎo lao bù téng jiù jiu bú ài 姥姥不疼舅舅不爱 (姥姥不疼舅舅不愛)

"Beloved by neither grandma nor uncle"; loved by nobody

♦ 我们姐几个还没到了那**姥姥不疼，舅舅不爱**的份上，用不着别人赏饭吃！

(From the novel 狗不理传奇)

We sisters are not all alone in the world. We don't need people's handouts!

♦ 咱们这办公室真够可怜的，谁也不把咱们当回事儿，**姥姥不疼舅舅不爱**的。

Our office is really pitiable. No one takes us seriously. No one cares about us.

lǎo lao jiā 姥姥家

"Grandma's home"; God knows where; God knows how much

♦ 咱这回赔**姥姥家**去了。

(From the TV series 今生是亲人)

This time we're going to lose our shirts. [Two private contractors took on a remodeling project, did a poor job, and were asked to redo the work without extra pay.]

♦ "他们的投资是两千万，你前两天怎么说是二百万？" "哦，差了那么一点儿。" "哪儿是一点啊？ 都差**姥姥家**去了。"

"They're investing twenty million. How come you said two million the other day?" "Oh, my figure was a bit off." "A bit off? Off by several miles."

lào kēr 唠嗑儿 (嘮嗑兒)

(Northeastern dialect) talk; chat (also 唠唠)

♦ 今儿晚上上我们家，咱们老哥儿俩好好**唠唠嗑儿**。

(From the TV series 激情燃烧的岁月)

Come to our house tonight. We can have a good chat like the two old friends we really are.

♦ 大伙儿要继续努力，明天要做得更好！ 有不足的地方要改进，好的地方要发扬！ 我就总结这些了，我陪老舅**唠嗑**去了。

(From the novel 东北一家人)

Let's keep trying. We'll do better in the future. We'll correct our shortcomings and develop our strengths. OK, that sums it up. I'll go talk with my old uncle now.

lào mán yuan 落埋怨

End up being blamed

♦ 反正白天房子**闲着也是闲着**。不过有些事儿还是得事先跟你说说明白，免得到时候**落埋怨**。

(From the novel 牵手)

The room is vacant during the day anyway, but there are some things I'd better make clear in advance. I don't want to end up being blamed later.

♦ 你又不是领导，最好别乱出主意，省得将来**落埋怨**。

You're not in charge. Don't make any suggestions. You don't want to be blamed later.

lào xia huà bàr 落下话把儿 (落下話把兒)

"Provide a handle for criticism"; leave oneself vulnerable to criticism

♦ 今天要是醉倒在林府，晚上叫人抬回家去，还不知道到了谁的家，愣管自己的老婆叫大嫂， 那不就**落下话把**了吗？

(From the novel 括苍山恩仇记)

If I get falling-down drunk today at the Lin's and have to be carried back home at night and call my wife "Ma'am" because I don't know whose house I'm in, then I'm really giving her an opening, right? [A guest at a wedding banquet is reminding himself not to get drunk.]

♦ 让你负责招聘工作，结果你把自己的亲朋好友都招到咱们公司来了。你这么做不怕**落下话把儿**吗？

You were in charge of hiring new people, and you ended up recruiting your friends and relatives for our company. Aren't you afraid of leaving yourself open to trouble?

...le qù le ...了去了

Very much; extremely

♦ 这里面的学问可**大了去了**！

(From the TV series 其实男人最辛苦)

This [stock trading] is a vast field of knowledge.

◆ "我说，你真相信那个算命的老头儿的话？""人家是按照《周易》算的，那道理**深了去了**，我哪儿敢不信啊？"

"Tell me, do you really believe that old fortune-teller?" "He followed the *Book of Changes*; that's a very deep source of wisdom. I wouldn't dare not believe him!"

lè dé 乐得 (樂得)

Would be happy to; might as well

◆ 她也笑了："你敢乱来，我让你再躺半年。"我说："你要是愿意天天伺候我，我还**乐得**这么躺着呢。"

(From the novel 玉观音)

She laughed, too: "Stop messing around or I'll make you stay in bed for another six months." I replied, "If you're willing to wait on me day in and day out, I'm happy to lie here."

◆ 好不容易全家人聚会一次，没坐几分钟都说工作太忙得走。好！你们都走吧，我这个老头子还**乐得**耳根子清净呢。

It's not easy to get the whole family together, and then you sit a few minutes and everyone says they have to go because of work. OK, go on, all of you. At my age I might as well enjoy a little peace and quiet.

lè zi 乐子 (樂子)

Fun; pleasure

◆ 客人花钱是来找**乐子**，不是来听你失恋的牢骚！

(From the novel 女朋友)

The customers are spending money to have some fun. They don't want to hear about your lost loves! [The proprietor of a cabaret is criticizing a singer for singing too many songs about lost love, which customers find depressing.]

◆ 张局长正在组织人调查李副局长贪污的问题，不知道是谁给市里写了举报信，说张局长自己贪污得更多。市里已经派工作组下来了，看吧，这回咱们局里的**乐子**可大了！

Bureau Director Zhang was appointing people to investigate Deputy Bureau Director Li for embezzlement. Someone wrote an anonymous letter to the city accusing Zhang of being an even bigger embezzler! The city sent a working team to look into it. You just watch, we're going to have some real fun in our office this time.

léi zi 雷子

(Gangster/mafia jargon) policeman

◆ 你琢磨呀，抽"白粉"，可比上牌桌和上酒桌往里"吃"钱。你是当"雷子"的，应该门儿清呀！

(From the novel 百年德性)

Think about it. Smoking heroin burns up your money faster than gambling or drinking. You're a cop. You should know better than that!

♦ 我一早见雷子找上门来，心里还真**捏了一把汗**，可见他们审了你半天，连正眼都没看我就走了，就知道你没出卖我，可打心眼儿里感激你哩。

> I saw the police knocking on your door this morning. I was really sweating, but they grilled you for hours and left without even looking in my direction, so I know you didn't sell me out. I'm grateful from the bottom of my heart.

lěi cháng chéng 垒长城 (壘長城)
Building the Great Wall"; play mahjong

♦ 你是不是又**垒**了一宿**长城**？

(From the TV series 今生是亲人)
> Did you play mahjong all night again?

♦ 你三十多的人了，除了**垒长城**还有没有别的本事？

> You're over thirty. Is there anything else you can do besides play mahjong?

lěng bu dīng 冷不丁
Suddenly; when one least expects it

♦ "有事儿吗？" "我没事儿。**冷不丁**地想起你来了，过来看看老街坊。"

(From the TV series 手心手背)
> "Anything wrong?" "No. I just suddenly thought of you and decided to drop in on an old neighbor."

♦ 你这**冷不丁**的一声喊，真把我吓了一跳。

> Yelling like that out of the blue, you really scared me.

lèng 楞
Recklessly; rashly; for no reason

♦ 到底是怎么回事？ **楞**是谁都不放在眼里？

(From the TV series 编辑部的故事)
> What's the real story? Somehow no one is good enough for you. [A young man has rejected every woman he has been introduced to.]

♦ 越来越回去了，怎么架都不会打了，**楞**让人把脸给打了？

(From the TV series 今生是亲人)
> The older you are, the more useless you get. You forgot how to put up a fight? How come you just stood there let people smash in your face?

lèng tóur qīng 愣头儿青 (愣頭兒青)
A rash, reckless young man

♦ 你这个**愣头青**，你是捧着个金菩萨，还把它当作黄泥巴人哩！

(From the novel 曾国藩)

You're an idiot! You have a treasure in your hands, and you think it's trash. ["You have a golden Bodhisattva, and you think it's a clay doll."]

♦ 我们现在需要的是一个心细手勤的笔杆儿作秘书，你怎么找来这么一个愣头儿青？

What we need now is a meticulous, hardworking secretary who can write. How come you hired such a fool?

li ger lōng 哩格隆

Gibberish

♦ "人家说下岗就是作贡献。" "甭听他这**哩格隆**，他们就是欺负你这老实人。"

(From the TV series 一年又一年)

"He says being laid off is also making a contribution." "Don't listen to his baloney! They take advantage of honest citizens like you."

♦ "爸爸，我知道你特别开明。年轻人的心你最理解。" "你少来这**哩格隆**，我绝对不会让你跟那个小**混混儿**结婚！"

"Dad, you're very enlightened. You really understand young people." "Don't give me that crap. There's no way I'm going to let you marry that punk!"

lí le shéi dì qíu dōu zhuàn 离了谁地球都转 (離了誰地球都轉)

"No matter who leaves the earth still turns"; no one is indispensable

♦ 虽然说，**地球离了谁都照转**，大山子离了谁也一样日月争辉，但这个时候换将，总是兵家大忌吧？

(From the novel 省委书记)

No one's indispensable. It doesn't matter who decides to leave; the sun and moon will still shine over Dashanzi. But you don't change horses in the middle of a stream ["to change generals at this point would be violating military strategy"]. [The new mayor of a city is implementing radical reform. Suddenly, he receives a notice that the leadership of the province has decided to relocate him to another city. He is not happy and is complaining to the provincial party secretary.]

♦ "谢主任，您一走咱们专题部就没特色了。" "没关系，没关系，**地球离了谁都照样转**。"

(From the TV series 走过花季)

"Director Xie, if you leave, our special features department will lose all its flavor." "Not really. No one is indispensable. You can do without me."

lí pǔr 离谱儿 (離譜兒)

"Deviate from the score"; out of line; far-fetched

♦ "一旦真相揭开，必然会牵涉你爸爸的，所以你要杀人灭口。" "你越来越**离谱**！"

(From the novel 都市危情)

"If the truth comes out, your father will be implicated. That's why you want to kill people to shut their mouths." "You're getting more and more farfetched." [The accuser was in a horse riding accident. He thinks that the other person planned it because his father is being investigated for his involvement in a murder case.]

♦ 你说的也太**离谱**儿了，一个工厂的总工程师，怎么会到街上去捡破烂儿呢？

What you're saying is off the wall. Why would the chief engineer of a factory collect trash on the street?

lǐ duō rén bú guà 礼多人不怪 (禮多人不怪)

"No one objects to getting too many gifts"; there's no such a thing as too much when it comes to bribery

♦ **礼多人不怪**，他们知道葛明礼就喜欢这一套。

(From the novel 夜幕下的哈尔滨)

As they say, "you can't give too many gifts." They knew what Ge Mingli likes.

♦ 只带那条洋烟不够，把这洋酒也给他带去，常言道，**礼多人不怪**。

A carton of foreign cigarettes isn't enough. Take this bottle of foreign liquor as well. As they say, "there's no such thing as too many gifts."

lǐ qīng rén yì zhòng 礼轻人意重 (禮輕人意重)

"The gift is not much, but it means a lot"; it's the thought that counts

♦ 灵均，拿上，这是大家的心意嘛，**礼轻人意重**，不收下可不好。

(From the movie 牧马人)

Lingjun, take it. It's a gesture. It may not be much, but it's the thought that counts. You can't turn it down.

♦ 我这点儿东西实在拿不出手，我知道你也不缺这个，不过**礼轻人意重**嘛。

I'm embarrassed to give you this, and I know you don't need it, but it's the thought that counts.

lǐ wài bú shì rénr 里外不是人儿 (裏外不是人兒)

"Not seen as human by one's own or outsiders"; misunderstood by everyone; get no respect
(This is an abbreviated form of the phrase 猪八戒照镜子，里外不是人儿: "The Pig [one of the characters in the novel *Journey to the West*] looks in the mirror. He doesn't look good either in or outside the mirror.")

♦ 为了这次门票的分配，学生会**里外不是人**了。

(From the novel 清华美眉)

The way the Student Association allocated the tickets has alienated everyone.

◆ 我好心好意给你掩着盖着，你倒好，一下子就全都说出去了，弄得我里外不是人儿。

I kept it under wraps for you out of the goodness of my heart, but then you go and tell the whole world. You turned everyone against me.

lǐ wài lǐ 里外里 (裏外裏)

"Inside and out"; altogether

◆ 因为着急进货又经验不足，穗珠回来上班以后，发现全部是假的，这两天才搞清楚，要货的和卖货的是一伙人，里外里亏大了！

(From the novel 掘金时代)

When Huizhu got back to work, she found that the new stock was all counterfeit because of the buyer's haste and inexperience. Only in the last couple of days did it become clear that the buyer and the seller were in cahoots. It was a total loss.

◆ "好歹儿的，先让她睡睡石板再说，没准儿真能睡成个死猪。" "里外里话都让你说了。"

(From the novel 混在北京)

"Anyhow, let her sleep on the stone slab for the time being. Maybe she'll sleep like the dead." "You sure know how to talk out of both sides of your mouth." [An exchange between a husband and wife. Their nanny complained that her bed wasn't hard enough; she was used to sleeping on hard surfaces. The husband didn't believe her and suggested sleeping pills, but later changed his mind and agreed to let her try sleeping on a stone slab. Hence the jab from his wife.]

lì mǎr 立马儿 (立馬兒)

Right away; immediately

◆ 不想干立马儿走人，对工人你不能惯着。

(From the TV series 问问你的心)

If they're not willing to work, let them go right away. You shouldn't coddle workers.

◆ 小唐乐不滋儿地去了，一看立马儿愣了，敢情是单元楼两居室。

(From the novel 百年德性)

Xiao Tang left with a big grin on his face. He was stunned the moment he saw the apartment. It was a two-bedroom! [The apartment turned out to be better than expected.]

lián guō duān 连锅端 (連鍋端)

"The pot disappeared (as well as the food)"; completely; lock, stock, and barrel

◆ 这人搁别人那儿可能会把公司连锅端了老板还帮着数钱，但在严寒冰手下不可能。

(From the novel 浮沈商海)

Anywhere else this guy could sell the company down the river and have the owner happily count the money. But under Yan Hanbing, he doesn't have a chance. [搁: put; put someone in a position]

♦ 他的公司财大气粗，没过两天就把竞争对手连锅端了。

His company was rolling in money. In no time at all the competitors were totally blown out of the water.

liǎn shàng guà bú zhù 脸上挂不住 (臉上掛不住)

"Can't hang on the face"; be embarrassed or humiliated

♦ 下午，学区的岳校长来检查工作。例行公事后，在雷雨田房里喝酒，喝的半潮上，老岳在酒桌上开起了荤笑话。林燕**脸上挂不住**，什么也不说，拉着国天仙回自己房里去了。

(From the novel 断线的风筝)

That afternoon Principal Yue from the school district came to inspect the school. After the routine formalities, he started drinking in Lei Yutian's room. Pretty soon, they were half drunk and Lao Yue started cracking dirty jokes. Lin Yan was embarrassed. She took Guo Tianxian's hand and without saying a word they went back to their room. [Lin and Guo are young female teachers.]

♦ 你以后别去捡破烂儿了。我**好歹**是个主任，自己的老婆去捡破烂，我的**脸上**真有点儿**挂不住**。

Stop scavenging garbage. I've got my position to think about. No matter what, I'm still the director. If my wife goes and picks through trash it's too embarrassing.

liǎn shàng tiē jīn 脸上贴金 (臉上貼金)

"Gild the face"; praise oneself (or someone else); toot one's own horn

♦ "你就是长得老点儿。" "谁说老，那叫成熟。" "你可真会给自己**脸上贴金**啊！"

(From the TV series 失乐园)

"You're a little bit over the hill." "You call it over the hill, but I call it mature." "You sure know how to toot your own horn!"

♦ 企业家？ 你别往他**脸上贴金**了！ 他只不过是个个体户。

"Entrepreneur? Don't exaggerate on his behalf. He's just a small businessman."

liàn tānr 练摊儿 (練攤兒)

(Facetious) "practice the market"; open a small vending stand

♦ 我妈**练摊儿**去了。

(From the TV series 今生是亲人)

My mom went to her stand on the street.

♦ 没有你哥啊，你姐夫〖自称〗还**练摊儿**呢！

(From the TV series 一年又一年)

If it weren't for your brother, I [your brother-in-law] would still be a street peddler.

liáng cháng zi 凉肠子 (涼腸子)

"Turn one's bowels cold"; greatly disappoint; a downer

♦ 你大哥这句话真让人**凉肠子**。

(From the TV series 至爱亲朋)

What your older brother said was really a downer. [All the family members supported the younger brother's decision to open a restaurant, but the older brother insisted he needed the family savings to go abroad.]

♦   大家本来都憋足了劲儿，想大干一场，但是听了经理的这几句话，真是**肠子都凉**了。

Everyone was pumped up and ready to go for it, but after listening to the manager, they lost their spark.

liáng xīn bèi gǒu chī le 良心被狗吃了

"One's conscience was eaten by the dog"; unconscionable

♦   哼，你哪来这么多钞票？好呀，我为这个家累死累活，你倒也藏起私房钱来了，**良心被狗吃掉**了呀！

(From the short story 家庭风景二十章)

My God, where did you get this much cash? Damn it, I worked my ass off for this family of ours. And all the time you were stashing away your own money. It's unconscionable!

♦   你花钱给二奶买了一栋小洋楼儿，却让父母住在这四面透风的破屋子里，你的**良心**是不是**被狗吃**了？

You bought your mistress a fancy house, but you let your parents live in this broken-down, drafty dump. Where's your conscience?

liǎng qīng 两清 (兩清)

"Clear on both sides"; mutually free of (financial or ethical) obligations

♦   我们两个已经恩断义绝，**两清**了，还怕你什么？

(From the novel 空洞)

We're quits now; we don't owe each other anything. Why should I be afraid of you? [The two used to be father- and son-in-law.]

♦   您把东西拿好，咱们这**两清**了。

Take the merchandise. Now we're even. [Spoken during a sales transaction.]

liǎng/shuāng shǒu zuàn kōng quán 两/双手攥空拳 (兩/雙手攥空拳)

"Two hands clenching hollow fists"; empty-handed

♦   他现在**两手攥空拳**，正等着钱呢！

(From the TV series 一年又一年)

Right now he's broke. He's waiting for the money!

♦   宁寒林确实感到了自己的软弱，他一直有种**双手攥空拳**的感觉。

(From the novel 书惑)

Ning Hanlin really felt powerless. It was like clutching at empty air. [An educated man realizes his poverty.]

liǎng yǎn yì mō/mǒ hēi 两眼一摸/抹黑 (兩眼一摸/抹黑)

In the dark; in total ignorance; blindly

♦   你**两眼一摸黑**，一脚踩进去，想拔出来就难了。我是关照你一声，怕你撞到南墙上。

(From the novel 都市危情)

If you plunge ahead blindly and get in too deep, you won't be able to get out. I'm just trying to warn you. I don't want you to bang your head against the wall.

♦ 我初来乍到，**两眼一摸黑**，还靠大哥您多指教。

I'm new here, so I don't know anything. I'm depending on you to teach me.

liàng dǐ pái 亮底牌

"Show the bottom card"; give the bottom line

♦ 我今天给你们**亮个底**。

(From the TV series 黑洞)

I'll give you the bottom line today. [A police chief warns his subordinates not to act rashly; the case they are handling is very serious.]

♦ 我把**底牌亮**给你吧，我这次不仅是代表大华公司来跟你们谈生意的，我也是代表美国的亨特公司来的。

I'll lay it all on the table. This time I'm not only negotiating with you on behalf of Dahua. I also represent the American company, Hunter.

liàng sb yě bù 量Sb也不

"I think (somebody) won't dare"; I don't think/suppose somebody would

♦ 我**量她也不敢**怎么着。

(From the movie 洗澡)

I don't think she'd dare try anything further. [A wife seeks out her husband at a public bathhouse and stands outside calling him names.]

♦ 你这个小警察真是不知道天高地厚。别说是市公安局长，就是省公安厅长也要让我三分。超速有什么了不起的，罚单你随便开，**我量你也不敢**把我扣在这儿。

You're a rookie cop; you don't know who you're dealing with. ["You don't know that Heaven is high and Earth is thick."] Never mind the city police chief, even the provincial police chief doesn't step on my toes. So what if I was speeding? Ticket away. Be my guest. I dare you to detain me here.

liǎng shuō zhe 两说着 (兩說著)

"There are two sides to speak of"; there are two sides to the story; you can go about it two ways

♦ "去你的小不忍则乱大谋吧！你倒是忍了，马车不照样叫他们砸了！""事情得**两说着**。"

(From the TV series 大宅门)

"Forget about tolerating the small stuff for the sake of the larger picture! That's what you did, and they smashed the horsecart just the same." "Well, that's one way of looking at it."

♦ 你是问高标准还是低标准？这得**两说着**。高，可就高得没边儿，你们同学他妈肯定不够；低，不够判刑的就成。

(From the novel 我是你爸爸)

You want to know whether my standards are high or low? There are two ways of looking at it. High standards means out of reach; your classmate's mom definitely won't meet them. Low standards—as long as the woman stays out of prison—that's good enough. [A son tries to find a girlfriend for his father and wants to know what kind of person his father is looking for.]

liào huà 撂话 (撂話)

"Lay down the word"; announce; let it be known

◆ 神枪三炮把人绑走了，当时就**撂下话**了，说拿钱来领人。

(From the movie 红高粱)

Magic Gun Three Shots took the person away and let it be known right then and there that he expected ransom.

◆ 你不信没有关系，今天我把**话撂**在这儿了，这个公司不出三天就得垮。

I don't care if you don't believe me. I'm going on record today: this company will collapse within three days.

liào tiāo zi 撂挑子

"Put down the shoulder pole"; quit

◆ 开始我是想戏弄一下你们两个人，但是后来一想，你这个人是什么事儿都干得出来，**没准儿**一赌气给我**撂挑子**不干了。

(From the TV series 北京女人)

At first I was just teasing you two. Afterwards I thought, I wouldn't put anything past you. Who knows, you could get pissed and walk off the job. [A company boss has assigned a subordinate's ex-husband to work under her; now he is explaining that he changed his mind because he was afraid she would quit.]

◆ 公司的新产品马上要上市了，你在这关键时刻**撂挑子**，是不是故意跟我过不去？

The company's new product goes on the market right away, and you choose this moment to quit? Are you deliberately trying to make my life difficult?

līn bù qīng 拎不清 (拎不清)

(Shanghai slang) "can't tell the weight of what one is holding"; can't quickly assess a situation; slow-witted

◆ 我是不会看错人的，你要是个**拎不清**的人，跟你生意也不会做这么多年了，今朝也没啥好东西送给你，这只雷达表是我从德国带来的，一点小意思。

(From the novel 寻呼惊魂)

I'm a good judge of character. If you were stupid I wouldn't have done business with you for so many years. I don't have much to give you. Here, I got this Rado watch in Germany. A small token.

◆ 你告人家私自养鸡，人家反过头来到供电局告你私装空调，罚起款来价钿远远超过两只鸡！ 姆妈你怎么越来越**拎不清**了？

(From the short story 家庭风景二十章)

If you turn in the people who are raising chickens illegally, they'll report you to the electric company for having an illegal air-conditioner. The fine will be a lot bigger than the one for raising a few chickens! Mom, you're getting more and more foolish! [价钿: *Shanghai dialect*, "price;" 姆妈: *Shanghai dialect*, "m ma" or "mom"]

lín liǎor 临了儿 (臨了兒)

At the end of it; on top of it all

◆ 临了儿，您还让您爱人开着三轮儿车送我回家的。

(From the TV series 今生是亲人)

On top of it all, you got your husband to take me home in the sidecar of his motorcycle. [三轮车: "a three-wheeler;" here it refers to a motorcycle with a sidecar.]

◆ 检查团的那帮人真够黑的，大鱼大肉吃着，临了儿还把酒都带走了。

The people on the inspection team were really greedy. They wolfed down all the meat and fish. Not only that, but they took all the wine away with them too.

lín shí bào fó jiǎo 临时抱佛脚 (臨時抱佛腳)

"Cling to the Buddha's feet right before (one needs his help)"; start preparing right before an important task

◆ 林凡一直都不算一个好学生，也是个临时抱佛脚的主。但凭着他的聪明，成绩却也一直不错。

(From the short story 昨日情怀)

Lin Fan was never really a serious student. He would only hit the books before an exam. But he was smart, so his grades were always good.

◆ 你平常连个电话也不给我打，现在缺钱想起找我来了，这不是临时抱佛脚吗？

Usually you don't even call, but now that you're short of cash you seek me out and ask me to help you at a moment's notice? I call that cupboard love.

lín zi dà le, shénme niǎor méi yǒu a 林子大了，什么鸟没有啊 (林子大了，什麼鳥沒有啊)

(Proverb) "If the forest is big enough, what bird will it lack?" There will be all sorts of (strange) creatures if a place is big enough.

◆ 城里的人很多，象鸟；林子大了，自然什么鸟都有。

(From the short story 后街)

People crowd the city like a flock of birds. Of course, if a forest is big enough, there's no kind of bird you won't find.

◆ 这林子大了，什么鸟儿都有，你们俩倒互助上了。

(From the TV series 其实男人最辛苦)

Well, it takes all kinds. Imagine, you two working together! [The two used to be rivals in love.]

lǐng qíng 领情 (領情)

"Accept the feeling"; appreciate the gesture

◆ 我相信你，也领你这个情。

(From the movie 有话好好说)

I believe you, and I appreciate what you're trying to do.

◆　王哥，你的**情我领**了，工作不工作也没啥重要，说实话，把我拘在一
个地方，天天准点上班准点下班，看人脸色听人呼来唤去我还真难
受。

(From the novel 越轨诉讼)

> Brother Wang, I'm grateful for your efforts. I don't really care so much about having a
> job. To tell the truth, I find it hard to take being pinned down to one place, punching a
> clock, hanging on to people's expressions, and getting bossed around. [Brother Wang
> helped the speaker get a job.]

liú yì/liǎng shǒur 留一/两手儿 (留一/兩手兒)

"Conceal a hand or two or several"; hold back; not reveal everything; keep something in
reserve

◆　肥龙，听我说，人家今天没查你，恐怕不是不敢查你，而是跟你这儿
留了**一手**。

(From the novel 黑血)

> Feilong, listen to me, if they didn't investigate you today it's probably not that they were
> afraid, but that they didn't want to show you their hand yet.

◆　哎呀，不**留两手儿**不行啊，我要是把什么都教给他，老板还不立马儿
叫我走人？

> Well, I've got to hold something back. If I teach him everything I know, the boss will
> give me the boot right away.

liù gòu 六够/溜够 (六夠/溜夠)

(Northern dialect) thoroughly; through and through

◆　把我们折腾一**六够**，到了儿又说不干了。

(From the TV series 今生是亲人)

> They really put us through the mill. Now they say they're not going through with it. [The
> other party originally said they wanted to exchange their sons, who were switched at
> birth, but later changed their minds.]

◆　孙家权这叫来气，折腾了**六够**，挨了老爷子一顿骂，又碰上国强这么
个倔驴，到了啥也没弄成。

(From the TV 多彩的乡村)

> Sun Jiaquan was furious. He went to a great deal of trouble, got told off by the old man,
> and ran into that mule Guoqiang, but in the end he still got nowhere. [He wanted to buy
> some land to start several business enterprises, but he incurred his father-in-law's anger
> and was blocked by an inflexible rural official, Zhao Guoqiang.]

lòng zi de ěr duo, bǎi she 聋子的耳朵，摆设 (聾子的耳朵，擺設)

"The ears of a deaf man—just a decoration"; have no substance or serve no real purpose

◆　我只是**聋子的耳朵**，当**摆设**，充炮灰。

(From the novel 寻鼎记)

I'm not worth your attention; I'm just cannon fodder. [He was mistaken for a high-ranking minister.]

♦ 你以为工会真能代表工人的利益呐。告诉你吧，那叫**聋子的耳朵，摆设**。

You think the union represents the workers' interests? I'm telling you, it's just window dressing.

lòu liǎn 露脸 (露臉)

"Show one's face"; win face or public recognition

♦ 干得真脆！ 你为咱们刑警队**露了脸**，我无论如何也要给你请功。
(From the novel 百年德性)

That was brilliant. You did our crime unit proud. I'll insist that you get recognized.

♦ 千人公司的副总经理，虽然不是最有实权，他也还管辖着几个部，比起普通职工来，自己占的便宜也不少，在老百姓面前还是挺**露脸**的。
(From the novel 欲狂)

He's the deputy general manager of a company with a thousand employees. Even though he's not the most powerful in the company, he still has a few departments under him. He gets a lot more perks than ordinary employees, and he can lord it over the common folk.

lòu mǎ jiǎo 露马脚 (露馬腳)

"Reveal the horse's hooves"; let the cat out of the bag; give oneself away

♦ 罗正天瞒天过海，也有**露马脚**的时候。
(From the novel 花开的声音)

Luo Zhengtian tries to fool everyone, but sooner or later he'll show his true colors.

♦ "我走了。对了，请你把这封信留给小梅。" "你刚才说你不是为她来的，看，这下**露马脚**了吧？"

"I'm off. Oh right, please give this letter to Xiao Mei." "You just said that it wasn't because of her you came. You gave yourself away!"

lòu qiè 露怯

"Reveal one's timidity"; show one's ignorance; blunder through ignorance

♦ 观众……啊不，听众朋友们好。您看，一开始我就**露怯**， 我是第一回坐在主持人的位置上。
(From the TV drama 朗朗星空)

Hello, viewers—I mean, listeners. You see, I goofed right off the bat. This is my first time as host.

♦ 你又**露怯**了，这水不是喝的，是洗手的！

What a hick. That water's not for drinking; it's for washing your hands. [Referring to a finger bowl on a banquet table.]

lòu xiànr 露馅儿 (露餡兒)

"Reveal the filling"; reveal the truth; can't keep up a pretense

♦ "不行！ 我不准任何人欺负她。" "哈哈哈，我看你能撑多久？ 这下**露馅**了吧，还说你不喜欢人家。"
(From the novel 傲慢青春)

"No way. I won't allow anyone to take advantage of her." "Ha! I wondered how long you could keep it up! Now the secret is out! And you said you didn't like her!"

♦ 他说得跟真的似的，什么遇到了歹徒把钱抢走了。我一细问就**露馅儿**了，他是去了赌场把钱给输光了。

He made up a plausible story about running into some bad guys and getting robbed. But when I questioned him closely, his story fell apart. He actually went gambling and lost all the money.

lòu yì/liǎng shǒur 露一/两手儿 (露一/兩手兒)

"Show a hand or two"; show what one can do

♦ 今天在毕家我还不**露两手**？

(From the TV series 今生是亲人)
I'll show them a thing or two at the Bi's today. [The speaker wants to show off his culinary skills.]

♦ 我给你们**露一手儿**，我可是正经八板拜师学的变戏法。

I'll show you what I can do. Mind you, I learned my magic tricks from a master. [正经八板: seriously; 拜师: formalize a disciple-teacher relationship with a kowtow ceremony]

lú chún/tóu bú duì mǎ zuǐ 驴唇/头不对马嘴 (驢唇/頭不對馬嘴)

"Donkey lips or head do not fit a horse's mouth"; a non sequitur; illogical or contradictory; incoherent

♦ "西方现代化哲学的思维是非客观与主观形式的相交。"董客老爱说这种**驴头不对马嘴**的话，他一张嘴就让人后悔来找他。

(From the novel 你别无选择)
"Western philosophical discourses on modernity intersect non-objectivity with subjectivity." Dong Ke loves to sound off with that kind of incoherent babble. The moment he opens his mouth, everyone is sorry they invited him to speak.

♦ 他说得**驴唇不对马嘴**，警察怎么会相信呢？

His story didn't hold together. How could the police buy it?

lù zi yě 路子野

"(Travel down) a wild path"; well-connected

♦ 你的**路子真野**，莫非卖白粉的你也熟？

(From the short story 二乔的自由)

You really have gotten in with some shady company. Don't tell me you're also friendly with heroin pushers!

♦ 他的**路子可野**了，三教九流没有不认识的，你有什么事尽管找他。

He has connections everywhere. There's no one from any quarter he doesn't know. If you have a problem, he's the one to ask. [三教九流: the Three Religions (Buddhism, Daosim, and Confucianism) and the Nine Philosophical Schools (the Legalists, the Confucianists, the Daoists, the Mohists, the Yin-Yang, the Agriculturalists, the Political Strategists, the Eclectics, and the Logicians); people of all persuasions]

luàn chéng yì guō zhōu 乱成一锅粥 (亂成一鍋粥)

"Messy like a pot of rice porridge"; messy; chaotic

♦ 赵芬芳笑眯眯的："哎，善本，你也一起听听嘛，怎么一见我来就要走？"周善本笑了笑："不了，手上一摊子事呢，都**乱成一锅粥**了！"

(From the novel 绝对权力)

Zhao Fenfang was beaming, "Shanben, stay and listen a bit. How come you want to leave the moment you see me?" Zhou Shanben smiled and said, "I can't. I have my hands full. Everything's a mess."

♦ 既然上帝创造了男人和女人，那社会分工就会不同。只有大家共同努力，社会才会进步。如果男人打压女人，女人又不服男人，大家你争我斗，世界必定**乱成一锅粥**，还怎么发展呀？

(From the short story 我想当二奶)

Since God created male and female, naturally society must have division of labor. Only if everyone works hard can there be social progress. If men oppress women and women won't tolerate it, everyone will be at each other's throats. The world will be in chaos. How can we move ahead like that?

luàn tán qín 乱弹琴 (亂彈琴)

"Play a musical instrument chaotically"; act or talk nonsensically

♦ 简直是**乱弹琴**！你一个副厂级领导，到车间去当工人，你这是想告诉别人什么？

(From the novel 我本好色)

What a joke! A deputy director executive working as a factory hand. What are you trying to tell people?

♦ **乱弹琴**！这么重要的事怎么能交给那个毛孩子做呢？

Nonsense! How could you give such an important matter to an inexperienced kid?

luàn tào 乱套 (亂套)

"Mess up a set"; make a mess of something

♦ 这事儿啊，让向娜一**搅乎**，全**乱套**了！

(From the TV series 手心手背)

That deal? Once Xiangna got involved, it was totally messed up. [The speaker invited guests to a cabaret to discuss business, but the hostess Xiangna quarreled with the guest and nothing was accomplished.]

♦ 现在部队全**乱套**了！纵队找不到师，师找不到团。

(From the movie 大决战·辽沉战役)

Now the troops are in complete disarray. The corps can't find the division; the division can't find its regiments.

M

mā ma bù téng jiù jiu bú ài 妈妈不疼舅舅不爱 (妈妈不疼舅舅不爱)
See 姥姥不疼舅舅不爱 lǎo lao bù téng jiù jiu bú ài

má li/līr 麻利/利儿 (麻利/利兒)
Deft; dexterous; fast and neat

♦ 我下手是非常**麻利**的，我像当年屠宰牲口似的宰了我心中的仇人。
(From the novel 百年德性)
I moved like lightning and wiped out my enemy like a butcher slaughtering a beast.

♦ 我说您**麻利**儿地快睡觉去！
(From the TV series 手心手背)
I think you should hop right into bed.

mǎ dà hā 马大哈 (馬大哈)
A careless person; an absent-minded professor

♦ 哼，我看我们家马锐才没准儿呢，整个一个**马大哈**，二百五，让人当**枪使**。
(From the novel 我是你爸爸)
Crap. This Ma Rui of ours is not someone to count on. He's slipshod, impulsive, and putty in anyone's hands."

♦ "坏了，我把自行车落医院了！" "你真是**马大哈**！"
(From the TV series 其实男人最辛苦)
"Shit, I left my bike at the hospital." "You'd forget your head if it wasn't attached."

mǎ pì pāi zài mǎ tí/tuǐ shàng 马屁拍在马蹄/腿上 (馬屁拍在馬蹄/腿上)
"Get kicked while stroking a horse's backquarters"; an attempt at flattery backfires and instead offends its object

♦ 人家越不会抽烟越往人眼前送，拍马屁拍到了马蹄上。
(From the novel 赤橙黄绿青蓝紫)

You know he doesn't smoke and you still offer him cigarettes? You sure know how to butter someone up!

♦ 我本来是想讨好我们经理，说他的女朋友比电影演员还漂亮。谁知道那个女的刚把他甩了，我的话让经理满肚子不高兴，这可真是**马屁拍在马腿**上了。

> I meant to suck up to our manager when I told him his girlfriend was prettier than a movie star. Who knew, she'd just dumped him. What I said really put him in a bad mood. Flattery sure can backfire.

mǎ wáng yé sān zhī yǎn 马王爷三只眼 (馬王爺三隻眼)

"This prince has three eyes"; I'm somebody you don't want to mess with; you don't know who you're dealing with (马王爷: a Taoist deity born with three eyes)

♦ 黄毛丫头，我叫你**要贫嘴**，看爷爷的刀吧！ 要不**给你点儿颜色看看**，你也不知道**马王爷三只眼**！

(From the novel 百年风云)

> Baby, this is what you get for running off at the mouth. Watch the sword! If I don't teach you a lesson this time, you won't know who you're dealing with.

♦ 他必须**找茬儿**树立一下自己的权威，也好让施工队知道**马王爷是三只眼**。

(From the novel 空洞)

> He's got to find fault here and there to establish his authority. He's sending the construction team a message that he's not a pushover.

mǎ zǎi 马仔 (馬仔)

Henchman; underling; errand boy

♦ 我跟你这么多年的交情，到头来还不如一个**马仔**！

(From the TV series 问问你的心)

> We've been friends for so many years, and here you trust an errand boy more than me! [A lover complaining.]

♦ 你这样身份的人怎么能没有**马仔**呢？

(From the TV series 黑冰)

How could someone of your status not have a gofer? [The addressee is a big boss.]

mái tai 埋汰

(Beijing dialect) Dirt; treat like dirt; insult; dirty and messy

♦ "沈小姐是摇滚歌坛的一朵花呢。"范惠泽恭维道。别**埋汰**人了，老范。我还是花儿呢，狗尾巴花儿吧。"

"You, Miss Shen, are a beautiful flower in the world of rock music." Fan Huize said fawningly. "Stop making fun of me, Old Fan. Me, a flower? A dog's tail of a flower, perhaps."

♦ 瞧你这儿**埋汰**的，这么大的人了怎么还不会照顾自己？

This place of yours is a pigsty. How come at your age you still don't know how to take care of yourself?

mǎi zhàng 买账 (買賬)

Acknowledge seniority; accept authority; buy an argument; cave in to pressure

♦ 她本想说"男朋友"，又怕"男朋友"关系太远，概念模糊，人家不**买帐**，话到嘴边把"男朋友"改成了"爱人"。

(From the novel 越轨诉讼)

She was about to say "boyfriend," but then she worried that "boyfriend" sounded remote and fuzzy, and people might not take her seriously. So she quickly swallowed "boyfriend" and said "husband" instead.

♦ 那小子仗着他姐夫是市委常委，谁的**帐也不买**。

(From the novel 大厂)

Just because his brother-in-law is a member of the Municipal Party Standing Committee, that bastard won't take orders from anyone.

mài guān zi 卖关子 (賣關子)

"Pause at a critical moment (in storytelling) for suspense"; keep the audience guessing; show off; be coy

♦ "怎么不敲门就进来？" "那我出去了。" "你别跟我这儿**卖关子**。"

(From the TV series 黑洞)

"How come you walked in without knocking?" "Oh, want me to leave?" "Stop playing those games with me."

♦ 天明，你小子**卖了半天关子**，到底现在怎么样？

(From the novel 浮沈商海)

Tianming, you son of a bitch, you've kept us on tenterhooks long enough. Just tell us how things stand right now.

mǎn dì zhǎo yá 满地找牙 (滿地找牙)

"Look for one's teeth all over the floor"; beaten to a pulp

♦ 前两天有一小子就摸了（那个女孩）那么一下，结果怎么样？ **满地找牙**，抬着出去的。

(From the movie 有话好好说)

Only a few days ago, a guy just felt that girl up a little. Guess what? He got beaten so badly he had to be carried out.

◆ 大哥一出手，管保打得那小子**满地找牙**。

The moment you lift your hand, you'll knock the living daylights out of that bastard.

màn bàn pāi 慢半拍

"Slow by half a beat"; one step too slow

◆ 聪明的家伙开始在女生中物色女友了，这方面我总是**慢半拍**。

(From the novel 逃往中关村)

The smart guys began looking over the girl students. But I'm usually a bit slow in that regard.

◆ 别的咱们不说，在这股票市场上你要是**慢半拍**就等于是把大把大把的钞票送给人家了。

Forget about the other stuff, but if you miss a beat in the stock market, it's like giving away stacks of money.

màn shuō 漫说/慢说 (漫說/慢說)

Let alone; to say nothing of; not to mention the fact that…

◆ **漫说**法院怎么断还不一定，要真是那样，您还有五个女儿呢！

(From the TV series 今生是亲人)

Besides the fact that no one knows how the court will rule, even if it goes against you, you still have your five daughters! [The court is ruling on custody of the addressee's son.]

◆ **慢说**她瞧不上我们刚子，她就是瞧上我们刚子，我们刚子妈还瞧不上她呢。

(From the TV series 编辑部的故事)

Quite aside from the fact that she doesn't fancy our Gangzi; even if she did, Gangzi's mother might not fancy her.

māo 猫

"Crouch like a cat"; dodge; hide; hunker down

◆ 都什么时候了，你还**猫**在这儿读书？

(From the TV series 康熙帝国)

You hole up and read at a time like this? [A war is going on.]

◆ 让你蹲坑儿，别说四天，就是四个星期、四个月你也得在那儿**猫**着啊！

(From the TV series 大雪无痕)

You were told to stake him out, and it's only for four days. Even if it were four weeks or four months, your job is to lie in wait! [A plain-clothes policeman is ordered to keep watch on a suspect.]

māor nì 猫儿腻 (貓兒膩)

Scheme; scam; hanky-panky

◆ 咱们住房让公家花钱，不整个儿一**猫儿腻**吗？

(From the TV drama 眷見胡同)

We live in the house, and the taxpayers pay for it. Isn't this a scam?

◆ 你们自己去大吃大喝，把帐单拿回来报销，说是接待客户，这点儿**猫儿腻**骗得了别人骗不了我。

You went out for fancy food and drinks and put in for reimbursement, claiming you were entertaining clients. Maybe you can fool some people with this scam, but not me.

máo jiǎo nǚ xù 毛脚女婿 (毛腳女婿)

(Shanghai dialect) a new or prospective son-in-law

◆ 不知你爹爹喜欢什么东西，我这个**毛脚女婿**第一次上门见老丈人总不好意思空着手去罢？
(From the novel 鹰刀传说)

I don't know what your dad likes. But on my first visit as a prospective son-in-law, I can't just go empty-handed. [老丈人: father-in-law]

◆ 他是陈主任的**毛脚女婿**，分配工作的时候你得照顾着点儿。

He's Director Chen's new son-in-law, so when you pass out work assignments you'll have to give him a bit of special treatment.

máo máo yǔ 毛毛雨

"Drizzle"; a drop in the bucket; a piece of cake

◆ 北京有这么多人，五百台，**毛毛雨**啊！
(From the TV series 一年又一年)

There are so many people in Beijing. Five hundred sets are a drop in the bucket. [A television wholesaler is reassuring a retailer.]

◆ 我要是有了洛克菲勒的实力，竞选州长也不过是**毛毛雨**了。
(From the novel 浮沈商海)

If I had the clout of a Rockefeller, running for governor would be a breeze.

máo piānr 毛片儿 (毛片兒)

Porn flicks

◆ 大哥，这些都是美国、日本的顶级毛片，真的！
(From the TV series 都市情感)

Brother, these are the top porn flicks from the U.S. and Japan. For real!

◆ 他买来毛片儿不说，还借给别人看，结果让警察给抓起来了。

No only did he buy porn movies, he also lent them to other people. So he was picked up by the police.

mǎo/mǒu jìnr 卯/铆劲儿 (卯/鉚勁兒)

"Rivet or focus one's attention/strength"; put out all one's effort; do one's best

◆ 我这老弟是个好心眼儿，我看出来他是**铆足了劲**要给我上一堂生活课。
(From the TV drama 朗朗星空)

This buddy of mine is a really nice guy. I could tell he was doing his very best to teach me what life is about. [The friend took the speaker to a sauna and a bowling club, new experiences for him.]

♦   头儿，咱们的设备实在太旧了，就是**卯足了劲儿**干也没有人家快啊！

  Boss, our equipment is really too old. Even if we kill ourselves we can't compete!

mào liáng qì 冒凉气 (冒涼氣)

"Feel the cold air"; send a shudder up one's spine

♦   可千万别提那段儿。想起那段儿我就**冒凉气**，我是一遭被蛇咬，十年怕井绳。

  (From the TV series 一年又一年)

  Don't ever mention that episode to me again. Just thinking about it sends shudders up my spine. Once bitten, twice shy. ["Once bitten by a snake, for ten years you're afraid of a rope."] [Referring to stock market losses.]

♦   听了总经理关于精简机构的报告，老陈觉得后背直**冒凉气**。办公室里他的年龄最大，又没有学位，看来这次是在劫难逃了。

  The manager's report on downsizing made Old Chen's blood run cold. He's the oldest in the office and has no credentials. Looks like chances are against him this time.

mào shǎ qì 冒傻气 (冒傻氣)

Act silly or stupid; talk silly

♦   我那**冒傻气**儿的大外甥哎！脸儿有这么个要法吗？清白能这么着往回捡吗？

  (From the novel 与死共舞)

  I've got an idiot for a nephew! Is this how you get your dignity back? Is this how you clear your name? [脸儿=脸面. The nephew wants to commit suicide by jumping off a building to prove his innocence.]

♦   毕业后你要去当中学老师？儿子，你别**冒傻气**了，你的同学哪个不憋着出国啊！即使出不了国也得找个外资公司干干，现在没有钱可不行。

  Graduate and teach middle school? Come off it, son. Look at your classmates, they're all dying to go abroad. If you can't go abroad, at least find yourself a job with a foreign company. Nowadays, you can't get anywhere without money.

méi bǎ..sǐ 没把...死

...to death

♦   不就欣欣小姐吗？太嗲了，**没把我恶心死**！

  (From the TV series 其实男人最辛苦)

You mean Miss Xinxin? She's so syrupy I could die puking. [Miss Xinxin is a radio show host.]

♦ 我那儿子真不争气，别说重点高中了，就连普通高中也没考上，**没把我气死**。

My son is hopeless! Forget about an elite high school; he can't even get into an ordinary one. He's going to drive me to my grave.

méi chéng xiǎng 没成想/没承想

Did not expect

♦ **没成想**刚到这庙门口，电话就打过来了。

(From the TV series 黑洞)

What do you know, the moment I got to the temple door, my phone rang. [He went to a temple to burn incense, but was interrupted.]

♦ 我们寻思检查的已经走了，就又赌了起来，**没成想**那帮警察又杀了个回马枪，把我们的麻将和钱全都没收了。

We thought the cops had already left so we started gambling again. Who knew, the police make a reverse attack and confiscated all our money and our mahjong pieces too. [杀回马枪: strike backwards on horseback]

méi chī guò zhū ròu hái méi jiàn guò zhū pǎo 没吃过猪肉还没见过猪跑 (沒吃過豬肉還沒見過豬跑)

"I may not have eaten pork, but I've certainly seen pigs run"; I may not have hands-on experience, but I still know something

♦ 我虽没生过孩子，但对妇产科还是很熟的。**没吃过猪肉，还没见过猪跑**吗？

(From the novel 血玲珑)

I've never delivered a baby, but I know all about obstetrics. I'm not wet behind the ears.

♦ "这个活儿，我有点担心，咱们一直是盖四五层的楼房，从来没建过摩天大楼啊！" "怕什么？ **没吃过猪肉还没见过猪跑**？"

"I'm a little worried about this job. We've been working on four- or five-story buildings but we've never had any experience with skyscrapers!" "What are you afraid of? We know construction work. A building's a building, isn't it?"

méi de shuō 没的说 (沒的說)

"Have nothing to say about"; as good as can be; simply the best

♦ 他这个人是**刀子嘴豆腐心**，尤其是对下面的干警，那真是**没的说**。

(From the TV series 大雪无痕)

He's got a heart of gold under a rough exterior. When it comes to how he treats his cops, he's the best there is.

♦ "明天能借辆大奔吗？" "管车的老张跟我**没的说**，这事儿您就放心吧。"

"Can I borrow a Mercedes tomorrow?" "Old Zhang is the one in charge of the cars, and we're like brothers. So don't worry, it's a done deal."

méi hǎo qìr 没好气儿 (沒好氣兒)

Displeased; upset; obnoxious; obnoxiously

♦ "我要结婚了。" 我**没好气儿**对着小薛说了一声。

(From the short story 结婚)

"I'm getting married," I said to Xiao Xue as nastily as I could. [Xiao Xue is the speaker's ex-boyfriend who's been carrying a torch for her.]

♦ 我不是不愿意去请教那位计算机专家，可是因为上次的财务纠纷，他一见我就**没好气儿**，还是您亲自出马吧！

I don't mind asking the computer guru for help. It's just that ever since that financial ruckus last time, he gets huffy whenever he lays eyes on me. You'd better go yourself.

méi mao hú zi yì bǎ zhuā 眉毛胡子一把抓 (眉毛鬍子一把抓)

"Grab hold of anything and everything, from the eyebrows to the beard"; handle everything from A to Z; do it all; take care of everything

♦ 〖公司〗管理上没有层次，**眉毛胡子**都由他秦冀平**一把抓**。

(From the TV series 大赢家)

There's no hierarchy in the [company's] management. Qin Jiping has taken everything on. [Qin is the party secretary.]

♦ 你是一个现代化的企业的总经理，不能**眉毛胡子一把抓**。

You're the general manager of a modern enterprise. You can't attend to every detail.

méi ménr 没门儿 (沒門兒)

No way!

♦ 把我儿子当你儿子使唤？ **没门儿**！

(From the TV series 贫嘴张大民的幸福生活)

Order my son around as if he were yours? No way!

♦ 你想作我的女婿？ **没门儿**！ 我女儿是硕士学位，你呢，连大学都没读过，这也太不般配了！

You want to be my son-in-law? Fat chance! My daughter has a master's degree and you didn't even go to college. It would be a terrible match.

méi pǔr 没谱儿 (沒譜兒)

"Without a score or recipe"; clueless; silly

♦ "你们一个月能挣多少钱啊？" "**没谱儿**，活儿不好找。"

(From the TV series 今生是亲人)

"How much money can you make in a month?" "No clue. Jobs are hard to find."

♦ 我明天没功夫陪你啊！ 净干这**没谱儿**的事儿。

(From the movie 爱情麻辣烫)

I'm too busy to waste time with you tomorrow. You're always screwing things up. [They went to get a divorce, but the husband forgot to bring the marriage certificate.]

méi qǐ sè 没起色

No improvement; no progress

◆ "妹妹近来身子好些了吧。""还是**没什么起色**。"

(From the novel 李莲英)

"Sister, are you feeling any better now?" "No, still no better."

◆ "我好好努力，以后跟上不就成了？""你跟得上吗？ 高一的时候就这么说，都两年了，有**起色**吗？""瞧您说的，怎么**没起色**？ **没起色**还一直上到高三都没留级？"

(From the novel 心动少年时)

"I'm really going to work hard and catch up now, that's all." "Really? That's what you said when you started high school. Do you think you've improved in the last two years?" "Listen to you! How can you say I haven't improved? I made it all the way to senior year without flunking out, right?"

méi shénme dà bù liǎo de 没什么大不了的 (沒什麼大不了的)

There's nothing to worry about; no big deal

◆ 这次空手而归**没什么大不了的**。

(From the TV series 康熙帝国)

So we came back empty-handed this time. It's no big deal. [The speaker led a failed attack on Taiwan.]

◆ "哎哟，新车撞成这样子了，咱们怎么和经理交待呢？""**没什么大不了的**，天天在路上跑难免有个磕磕碰碰的。"

"Oh no! A new car bashed up like this—how are we going to tell the manager?" "It's not the end of the world. We're on the road day in and day out. A few dents and scrapes are inevitable."

méi shìr rénr 没事儿人儿 (沒事兒人兒)

"Someone who's not involved"; a carefree or blindly happy person

◆ 明儿就高考了，你这乐乐呵呵的跟**没事儿人儿**似的。

(From the TV series 今生是亲人)

The college entrance exam is tomorrow and you're as carefree as if it had nothing to do with you.

◆ 也就是你，没皮没脸跟个**没事人儿**似的，把你妈的脸，把你妈的脸都给丢尽了！

(From the TV series 北京女人)

You're too much! You're as brazen as if it had nothing to do with you. You've made your mother a laughing-stock.

méi tóu cāng ying 没头苍蝇 (沒頭蒼蠅)

"A headless fly"; someone who doesn't know which way to turn

◆ 他明天一早就要飞离北京了，我想事不宜迟，所以急得**没头苍蝇**似的；满世界找你！

(From the novel 栖凤楼)

He's flying out of Beijing tomorrow morning. I figured this couldn't wait, so I was running around like a chicken with its head cut off looking for you. ["He" is a foreign investor whose departure may mean the end of a business deal.]

♦ 他家出了麻烦，这两天他跟**没头苍蝇**似的，到处乱撞。

His family's in trouble, so for the past few days he's been running around like a chicken with its head cut off, looking for help everywhere.

méi wán 没完

"No end"; endlessly

♦ 我丑话说在前头，要是让我吃一点儿带荤腥儿的我跟你**没完**！

(From the movie 甲方乙方)

Let me tell you upfront, if I find a trace of meat in the food, I'll be on your case forever. [A wealthy businessman is fulfilling his dream of eating simple vegetarian peasant food.]

♦ 你有完**没完**？ 我都听你说了一个上午了！ 让我清静一会儿行不行？

Are you done yet? I've been listening to your yammering for a whole morning! Leave me in peace for a while, OK?

méi xì 没戏 (沒戲)

No hope; hopeless; no way; impossible

♦ "咱们使使劲儿能挣出来吗？ " "**没戏**，除非印一期反动黄色的。 "

(From the TV series 编辑部的故事)

"Can we make that much if we put in the effort?" "No way. Unless we publish an issue that's all counter-revolutionary politics, or maybe pornography." [The editors of a magazine are talking about how to get the money for a robot.]

♦ "你说老许能把高校长请来吗？ " "**没戏**！这年头没红包儿谁来啊？ "

"Do you think Old Xu could invite Principal Gao?" "Impossible! These days no one comes without being paid off." [红包儿: hóng bāor, red envelope, the traditional way of offering a bribe or reward money]

méi xīn méi fèi 没心没肺

"Without heart or lungs"; heartless; ungrateful; careless; indiscreet

♦ 刘震这孩子不是**没心没肺**的白眼儿狼。

(From the TV series 今生是亲人)

This kid Liu Zhen is not a heartless monster. [Liu Zhen just found out that he was adopted. He was so shocked that he left home. The speaker thinks that Liu will come back.]

♦ 他这个人就是这么**没心没肺**的，别跟他一般见识。

He's always shooting his mouth off like that. Don't take it seriously.

méi yǐngr 没影儿 (沒影兒)

"Not even a shadow (of truth)"; there's no such thing; fictitious

♦ 有吃有穿，有穿有戴就是福气。说那些**没影儿**的事干啥？

(From the novel 锁链，是柔软的)

You have food and clothing; with clothes on your back you should count yourself lucky. Why bother with rumors? [The head of a large family tries to put a stop to speculations about a possible marriage into wealth that will bring the family a change in fortune.]

◆   你们别听他这儿胡咧咧，**没影的事**！
(From the TV drama 朗朗星空)
Don't listen to his nonsense. It's a lot of hot air. [Talking about a man who claims to have had an unusual romantic experience when sent down to the countryside during the Cultural Revolution.]

méi yǒu bú tòu fēng de qiáng 没有不透风的墙 (沒有不透風的牆)

"There are no walls that are impenetrable"; walls have ears

◆   他也知道**没有不透风的墙**，一旦有人举报，上边知道了，怎么办呢？
(From the novel 红与黑)
He also knows that the walls have ears. Once someone talks and the higher-ups hear about it, what's he supposed to do?

◆   俗话说**没有不透风的墙**，在咱们这个办公室你做什么事也保不了密。
As they say, walls have ears. You can't do anything and keep it a secret in this office.

méi yǒu guò bú qù de kǎnr/qiáo 没有过不去的坎儿/没有过不去的桥 (沒有過不去的坎兒/沒有過不去的橋)

"There's no ridge you can't climb over/there's no bridge you can't cross"; there's no difficulty that can't be overcome; nothing is impossible

◆   人活着吧，就**没有过不去的桥**。
(From the TV series 今生是亲人)
In this life nothing is impossible.

◆   你别犯愁了，钱丢了也没什么大不了的，世上**没有迈不过去的坎儿**。
Stop worrying. So you lost the money, big deal! For every problem there's a solution.

méi yǒu jīn gāng zuànr, bié lǎn cí qì huór 没有金刚钻儿，别揽瓷器活儿 (沒有金剛鑽兒，別攬瓷器活兒)

(Proverb) "If you don't have the right tools, don't try to fix fine porcelain"; don't take on a job that's beyond your abilities (金刚钻: diamond bit)

◆   **没有金刚钻**，干吗**揽这瓷器活**？这不是耽误我们做生意吗！
(From the novel 透支爱情)
If you don't have the stuff, why did you come to us? Don't you see you're holding up our business? [The addressee wanted a business deal but doesn't have the necessary cash.]

◆   常言道：**没有金刚钻儿，别揽瓷器活儿**。既然你没有学过计算机，为什么还要申请我们这个高科技公司的工作？
If you don't have the qualifications, don't take on the job. Since you've never studied computers, why apply for work at a high-tech company like ours?

méi zhé 没辙 (沒轍)

No way out; at the end of one's rope

◆   我去找他是因为我真的**没辙**了。
(From the TV series 大雪无痕)

I went to him because I was really at the end of my rope. [A daughter is trying to explain to her angry mother why she turned to her divorced father as a last resort.]

♦ 新来的警官真厉害，给红包不要，说好话不听，硬是把老张给抓走了，我看，咱们现在是一点儿**辙都没有**了，只有请律师去法庭打官司了。

> That new policeman is too much. He won't take bribes and won't listen to pleas, and he took Old Zhang away just like that. I think we're out of options. We've got to hire a lawyer and take the matter to court.

méi zhì 没治

"No cure"; No question about it; super; awesome

♦ "看哪，人家这才叫自行车！" "骑上去真轻啊！" "其实就是钢好。" "谁说的？ 这漆也烤得**没治**了…。"
(From the novel 空洞)

> "Look, this is what I call a bike!" "It's like riding on a cloud." "It's just that the steel is good." "Says who? The paint job is awesome too…"

♦ "昨儿的电影怎么样？" "**没治**了，特棒！"

> "How was the movie yesterday?" "Awesome! Out of sight."

méi zhǔnr 没准儿 (沒準兒)

There is the possibility that…; possibly; perhaps

♦ 开始我是想戏弄一下你们两个人，但是后来一想，你这个人是什么事儿都干得出来，**没准儿**一赌气给我**撂挑子**不干了。
(From the TV series 北京女人)

> At first I was just teasing you two. Afterwards I thought, I wouldn't put anything past you. Who knows, you could get pissed and walk off the job. [A company boss has assigned a subordinate's ex-husband to work under her; now he is explaining that he changed his mind because he was afraid she would quit.]

♦ "老刘怎么没来啊？" "**没准儿**他家里有事儿。"

> "How come Old Liu isn't here?" "Maybe something came up at home."

měi de sb/měi si sb 美得Sb/美死Sb

You wish!; be extremely happy and complacent

♦ "妈妈你是给爸爸化〖妆〗吗？" "**美得**他！"
(From the TV series 黑洞)

> "Mom, are you dressing dad up?" "He wishes!"

♦ "你们都说李刚长得丑，可我觉得就是他有男人味儿。" "你这话要让他听见得**美死**他。"

> "You all say Li Gang is ugly, but I think he's the one who looks like a real man." "If he heard you, he'd be walking on air."

mèi liáng xīn 昧良心

Against one's conscience

♦ 你既然都**昧**了**良心**了，还顾什么脸面？
(From the TV series 失乐园)

Now that you've trampled on your conscience, why worry about saving face? [He has blackmailed his friend for money.]

◆　我虽然穷，但是绝不会昧着良心去赚黑钱。

　　I may be poor, but I've got a conscience and I'm not going to make money illegally.

mén fèngr lǐ kàn rén , bǎ rén kàn biǎn le 门缝儿里看人把人看扁了（门縫兒裏看人把人看扁了）

To look at someone through the crack of a door (and get a distorted image); underestimate; look down upon

◆　你说这种话，简直是门缝里看人，把人看扁了！

　　(From the novel 情剑无刃)

　　Your remark just shows that you have no respect for me. [He is accused of frequenting whorehouses.]

◆　"你要能解这道数学题，我当场死给你看。" "你别门缝儿里看人！我可是去年数学竞赛的冠军。"

　　"If you can solve this math problem, I'll drop dead." "Don't underestimate me. Last year I got first place in the math contest."

mén kǎnr gāo 门槛儿高（門檻兒高）

"High threshold"; beyond the reach of common people; inaccessible

◆　我知道你们这儿门槛儿高，门槛儿太高了！ 我无事不登三宝殿。

　　(From the TV series 手心手背)

　　I know your place is hard to get to. In fact, I'd say it's impossible! But I wouldn't have come without a good reason. [三宝殿: sān bǎo diàn, Three Treasures Hall, a Buddhist temple. The expression 无事不登三宝殿 is also used to describe an opportunist who "comes to pray at the temple only when he/she has a favor to ask of the gods."]

◆　你要真的看不起我，我就把木料当场放把火烧了，日后我也再不敢登你的高门槛。你要认我这个小老弟，就把木料留下，你做家具也行，当柴火烧也行，随你便。

　　(From the novel 越轨诉讼)

　　If you think I'm not worthy of your friendship, I'll set fire to this wood right now and burn it up, and never darken your noble door again. But if you're willing to accept me as a younger brother, please keep the wood. You can make furniture or use it as firewood, whatever you want. [A gift-giver is speaking to the recipient who has politely refused the gift.]

mén kǎn jīng 门槛精（門檻精）

(Shanghai dialect) too smart or calculating when self-interest is at stake (门槛: smarts)

◆　碰到媳妇很晚回来还到食柜里翻小菜，好婆的脸就不由自主地拉得老长，心想媳妇是门槛精，自己掏钱在外面吃顿饭都舍不得。

　　(From the short story 家庭风景二十章)

　　If she runs into her daughter-in-law coming back late and looking for food in the cupboard, Grandma pulls a long face. She thinks her daughter-in-law is too tight to spend her own money eating out.

◆　这台湾老板的门槛也太精了，每个月只给两千工资，多五百也不干。

　　(From the TV series 走过花季)

This Taiwanese boss really counts every penny. He pays only two thousand a month and won't put in another five hundred no matter what.

ménr qīng 门儿清 (門兒清)
Know all about

♦ 这片儿的人儿，别说四十多岁的，就是四十多岁的妈八十多岁的我们也门儿清。

(From the TV series 今生是亲人)

Someone in this neighborhood over forty? Well, we're over eighty. We can even tell you everything about the mothers of the forty-year-olds. [An old man answers someone inquiring about a woman over forty who lived in the neighborhood.]

♦ 别看他是老外，对咱们北京的胡同儿可门儿清了，全北京的胡同名儿，他差不多都能背出来！

OK, so he's a foreigner, but he knows the Beijing alleys like the back of his hand. He can name almost all the Beijing alleys from memory.

ménr yě méi yǒu 门儿也没有 (門兒也沒有)
No way! also see 没门儿

♦ 明说了吧，我得让那些骚娘儿们知道知道我的厉害。想把你从我这儿弄走？门儿也没有哇！

(From the novel 找乐)

Let me give it to you straight. I have to let those sluts know who the hell they're dealing with. They want to hire you away from me? No way!

♦ 你要让他帮你的忙？门儿也没有啊！

Ask him to help you out? Forget it!

mèn hú lu 闷葫芦 (悶葫蘆)
"Noiseless gourd that keeps everything inside itself"; a mystery; a person of few words

♦ 既然把话捅出来了，咱们都说开，别叫他钻在闷葫芦里了。

(From the novel 萧尔布拉克)

Now that it's out in the open, let's all speak frankly. Don't leave him in the dark. [The speaker revealed that the wife of one of the listeners has been unfaithful.]

♦ 唐吴茜向来时髦，总觉得自己会有个像闷葫芦似的女儿很奇怪。

(From the novel 木头空姐)

Tang Wuqian has always been a fashionable woman, so she thinks it's strange that her daughter is as dumb as a post.

méng zài gǔ li 蒙在鼓里 (蒙在鼓裏)
"Kept inside a drum"; kept in the dark

♦ 全班四十多个同学未见得都让她蒙在鼓里，唯独你跳了出来捅破了这层窗户纸。

(From the novel 我是你爸爸)

There are forty kids in your class. It's not too likely she fooled them all, and you had to be the one to point out that the emperor had no clothes. [A father is scolding his son for pointing out a teacher's mistake.]

◆   我们都让他**蒙在鼓里**了，要不是昨天他太太来单位找他我们还以为他真是单身汉呢！

> He sure did a number on us. If his wife hadn't come to the office looking for him, we'd still think he was single.

miàn 面

"Mushy"; "doughy"; weak; wimpy; like a jellyfish

◆   太面了，面得都能蒸包子了！

(From the TV series 今生是亲人)

> Cream puffs! They're so soft they'll get steamed like buns. [蒸包子: zhēng bāo zi ,steamed stuffed buns made from wheat dough. Soccer fans are complaining about the performance of a team.]

◆   王经理这个人太面了，对那些闹事儿的工人就应该一律开除，跟他们没有什么可啰嗦的。

> Manager Wang is such a wimp. Right off the bat, he should have fired the workers who made trouble. What's there to talk about with them?

miè 灭 (滅)

"Exterminate"; kill off; zap; attack

◆   你赶快找几个人上北京，把廖红宇给我**灭**了。这回你要是再办不利索，我就把你**灭**了！

(From the TV series 大雪无痕)

> Get a few guys to Beijing right away, finish off Liao Hongyu for me. If you don't do a clean job this time, I'll have you offed instead.

◆   他这个电影批评家专门跟**大腕儿**过不去，谁火就**灭**谁，就连在国外拿了大奖的演员也被他说得一无是处。

> This film critic makes it his mission to take superstars down a peg. Whoever's hot gets it from him. Even with actors who've won big prizes abroad, he'll say they're totally worthless.

míng bǎi zhe 明摆着 (明擺着)

"Prominently displayed"; evidently; obviously

◆   这段时间正严打赌博，这群小子敢顶风作案并且还把场子摆在十字路口，这不是**明摆着**想跟咱们干警对着干吗！

(From the short story 牛所长抓赌)

Right now there's a big crackdown on gambling. These guys not only have the nerve to commit the crime anyway, but they even set up shop right at the intersection. They're clearly trying to fight the police head-on.

♦ 你问我为什么炒他的鱿鱼，这道理不是**明摆着**的吗？短短两个星期他就和顾客打了三次架，这样下去谁还会到咱们这儿来买东西？

You want to know why I fired him? Isn't it obvious? In two weeks, he had three fights with customers. Any more of this, and who's going to come and shop here?

míng rén bù shuō àn huà/míng rén bú zuò àn shì 明人不说暗话/明人不做暗事 (明人不說暗話/明人不做暗事)

"An honest or innocent person doesn't speak in riddles/an honest or innocent person doesn't do shady things"; get straight to the point

♦ 既然您明白，我**明人也就不说暗话**了。我请他来就是要把他的手剁掉。

(From the movie 有话好好说)

Since you know all about it, I don't have to beat about the bush. I asked him to come so I could chop off his hand. [The person in question has stolen the speaker's girlfriend.]

♦ 我**明人不做暗事**。我告诉你：我不光是一个人，我还有一些分布在全国各地的弟兄。

(From the TV series 黑冰)

An honest person has nothing to hide. I assure you I'm not alone. I have buddies all over the country. [A drug dealer is trying to convince his supplier that he is well-connected.]

míng xì 明戏 (明戲)

Understand

♦ 虽说退休前是个派出所所长，但是他也**明戏**，这多少有点儿照顾情绪的意思，穿了小四十年警服，临完闹个"白板"，面子上挂不住。

(From the novel 百年德性)

Before he retired he was a precinct police chief, but he knew very well this offer was just meant to make him feel good. After all, he wore the police uniform for nearly forty years. If he didn't have some sort of title when he left it would be humiliating. [A former police chief is offered a titular position to maintain his status after retirement.]

♦ "哎，有一点我一直不明白，为什么管蹬板车的叫'板爷'，管你们出租司机却叫'的哥'呀？""那还不**明戏**吗，我们这行才几年呀，人家打前清那会儿就干上了。"

(From the short story 的哥)

"There's one thing I've wondered about for a long time. Why are the tricyclists called 'Board Grandfathers' and you cabbies are called 'Taxi Brothers'?" "What's so hard to understand? We've only been around a few years, but they go back to the Qing Dynasty."

mó pò/báo zuǐ pí zi 磨破/薄嘴皮子/磨嘴唇

"Grind one's lips"; implore through nonstop talking (variation: 磨嘴唇)

♦ 我实在没有办法，这是我**磨破嘴皮子**才找来的活儿。

(From the TV series 今生是亲人)

I was really out of options. I talked my head off begging people to get this job.

◆ 我和他娘把**嘴唇都磨薄**了！这孩子，从小主意大，认准了理儿，十头老牛也拉不回来。

(From the short story 天才)

His mother and I begged him until our tongues dropped out of our mouths. Ever since he was little this kid's had a mind of his own. Once he believes in something, a team of oxen couldn't drag him away.

mó yáng gōng 磨洋工

Loaf on the job; goldbrick; slack

◆ 你怎么现在才来啊？**磨洋工**啊？

(From the TV series 新七十二家房客)

How come you're so late? Trying to avoid work? [A grandmother has called on her whole family to search for treasure hidden in her house. The grandson was late.]

◆ 你**磨洋工**我就有权管理！现在就通知你，这个月的奖金你没有了！

(From the novel 村女窈窕)

If you loaf on the job, it becomes my business. Let me tell you right now, you're not getting your bonus this month.

mó zheng 魔症

"Possessed by the devil"; spellbound; obsessed

◆ **魔症**了，我瞧这是恩是仇都少不了。

(From the TV series 今生是亲人)

She's possessed. I think she's bound to end up with hate as well as love. [Describing a woman's obsessive attempt to find a friend she has not seen for twenty years. She stands on a street corner hoping the friend will pass by.]

◆ 因为叠页子不用动脑筋，所以就在脑子里走棋，有的时候，**魔症**了，会突然一拍书页，喊棋步，把家里人都吓一跳。

(From the novel 棋王)

Since I could fold the book pages for the publisher without thinking, I spent the time figuring out chess moves in my head. Sometimes I got so wrapped up in the game I would slap the page and call out a move, making my whole family jump.

mǒ bó zi 抹脖子

"Cut one's own throat"; kill oneself

◆ 算了！我不活了，干脆死个痛快。现在谁知道我在这儿呢？我要饿死那是什么滋味？不如**抹脖子**痛快。

(From the novel 童林传)

OK, I'll just die. The quicker the better. Who has any idea that I'm stuck here? If I die of hunger, what would that feel like? Better just cut my own throat, short and sweet. [A martial arts master has fallen into a pit and can't get out, so he is considering suicide.]

♦ 真没想到他一时想不开就**抹脖子**了。

I never thought he'd commit suicide just because he felt trapped for one moment.

mò bù kāi miàn zi 磨不开面子 (磨不開面子)

Too shy or embarrassed to lift one's face; hide one's face

♦ 遇上这样的好事，怎么倒**磨不开面子**了？

(From the novel 魔鬼与天使)

Such a good opportunity and you suddenly get shy? [A smooth talker gets tongue-tied when she tries to find her daughter a boyfriend.]

♦ "你怎么不在饭店干了？" "厂里请我回去，**磨不开面子**。"

(From the TV series 贫嘴张大民的幸福生活)

"How come you're not working at the hotel anymore?" "The factory asked me back. I didn't have the heart to say no." [The second speaker was laid off by the factory temporarily and was recently called back.]

mò ji 磨唧

Drag one's feet; approach indirectly

♦ 火车都快开了，你怎么还这儿**磨唧**呢？

(From the TV series 激情燃烧的岁月)

The train's about to leave. Why are you still dragging your feet here?

♦ 他说他再也不理那个姑娘了，可是没过两天就又**磨磨唧唧**地去找人家了。

He said he'd never speak to that girl again. Now, just two days later he's trying to sidle up to her again."

mǔ yè cha 母夜叉

"Female Yaska" (Hindu demon); shrew; vixen

♦ 哪他妈有你这小**母夜叉乱掺和**的？滚一边去，急了我连你一起抽！

(From the novel 我是你爸爸)

Who the fuck are you to stick your nose in? Little bitch! Get lost, or I'll beat the shit out of you too! [A hoodlum is threatening a teenage girl who is trying to stop him from beating up her classmate.]

♦ "我告诉你，这儿是北大，想骂街回你们自己的地盘儿！" "我就骂！" 勺子说："气死你！ 你也**没辙**！**母夜叉**，母老虎，**母夜叉**，母老虎！"

(From the novel 我的出头之日)

"Let me tell you something. This is Beijing University. If you want to swear in public, do it on your own turf!" "If I want to swear, I'll swear," said Spoon, "I want to make you mad enough to croak, and there's nothing you can do about it. Vixen, shrew! Vixen, shrew!

N

ná bù qǐ gèr 拿不起个儿 (拿不起個兒)

See 拾不起/成个儿 shí bù qǐ/chéng gèr

ná de qǐ lái fàng de xià qù 拿得起来放得下去 (拿得起來放得下去)

"(Someone who can both) pick it up and put it down"; someone who is able to take it or leave it; a person of courage and determination under any circumstances

♦ 卫大哥，你一向是个**拿得起放得**下的人，我问你，你究竟是要死要活？

(From the novel 幻剑灵旗)

Brother Wei, you've always been a man of resolution. I'm asking you, do you want to live or to die?

♦ "听说老陈下岗了，他受得了吗？" "他是个**拿得起来放得下去**的人，你不用替他担心。"

"I heard that Lao Chen was laid off. Do you think he can take it? "He's a man who can deal with anything. You don't have to worry about him."

ná huà tián hu rénr/ná huà tián ke rénr 拿话甜乎人儿/拿话甜可人儿 (拿話甜乎人兒/拿話甜可人兒)

Sweet-talk;, butter up;, blandish

♦ 嘿，你这猴崽子，就会**拿话甜可人**！

(From the novel 狗不理传奇)

You son of a bitch! All you're good for is buttering people up.

♦ 我说，你别光**拿话甜乎人儿**啊，现在办什么事儿都讲究实惠，不出点儿血不行。

Sweet-talking won't cut it. Nowadays everyone wants to see tangible benefits. If you don't put your money where your mouth is, forget it. [出血: to part with money or something precious]

ná sb kāi shuàn 拿Sb开涮 (拿Sb開涮)

Make fun of somebody; make a joke at somebody's expense

♦ 女儿："您再老也是大家闺秀，这美女是没有年龄的。" 妈妈："你这疯子，**拿你老妈开涮**。"

(From the TV series 问问你的心)

Daughter: "No matter how old you are, you're still the daughter of a respected house. Beauty is not limited by age." Mother: "Are you crazy, making fun of your poor old mother?"

♦ 这不是**拿人开涮**吗？ 他可认真了，咱们这样做道德吗？

(From the movie 甲方乙方)

Aren't we going to make a fool of him? He's really literal-minded. Do you think what we're doing is ethical? [Talking about making friends based on false identity.]

ná táng 拿搪

Put on airs; be arrogant and difficult

♦ 受了点儿处分，就**变了方**的跟领导**拿搪**？

(From the TV series 大雪无痕)

You're disciplined a little, and you pull one trick after another to make life difficult for your superior?

♦ 遇到有些**拿搪**的厂，小赖搬出部生产局的牌子，说是要核对产品手册上的技术资料，几下就把对方镇住了。

(From the novel 向上爬)

If a factory was uncooperative, Xiao Lai would mention the Production Department of the Ministry, saying that some of the data in the product manual would have to be verified. They straightened things out pretty soon.

ná zhú yi 拿主意

Come up with a plan or make a decision (usually on somebody's behalf); make up one's mind

♦ 医院想让家属**拿个主意**。

(From the TV series 贫嘴张大民的幸福生活)

The hospital wanted the patient's family to make a decision [about the treatment plan.]

♦ 厂长，明天早上人家就会上门儿来要债了，还说不还钱就把咱们的机器搬走，怎么对付他们您得赶快**拿主意**啊！

Director, tomorrow they'll come looking for the money we owe them. They even threatened to take our machinery away if we don't pay. You've got to come up with a plan to deal with those people.

nǎ bèi zi 哪辈子

"In which lifetime?" For a lifetime; forever; when

♦ 你们俩给我买这么多营养品，我得喝到**哪辈子**去啊？

(From the TV series 今生是亲人)

You two bought me so much power food, it'll last me a few lifetimes. [Parents bought their son nutritional supplements to take while studying for the college entrance exam.]

♦ 早回来了，为什么不做饭？ 就等人待候呢？ 我是**哪辈子**欠你的？

(From the novel 剑胆琴心)

You got home early, so why didn't you cook dinner? Waiting for someone to serve you? Just remind me, since when did I become your slave? [A wife talking to her husband.]

nǎ miào de hé shang 哪庙的和尚 (哪廟的和尚)

"The monk of which temple?"; Who the hell...?

♦ "于观回来马上让他去见我。" "你是**哪庙的和尚**？" "我是他爸爸！"

(From the movie 顽主)

"Tell Yu Guan to come see me the moment he's back." "Who the hell are you?" "I'm his father." [Yu Guan is a company manager. His father is talking to one of Yu Guan's employees.]

◆ 你算是**哪**庙的和尚啊？ 凭什么查我们的账啊？

Who the hell do you think you are? What gives you the right to audit our books?

nǎr de huà 哪儿的话 (哪兒的話)

Don't even mention it! It was nothing!

◆ "这回多亏你了，谢谢！" "**哪**的话！"

(From the novel 碎雪)

"I really owe you for this. Thank you." "Oh, don't be silly. It was nothing."

◆ "这次多亏了你帮忙，不然我非得赔大发了。" "**哪儿**的话，咱们的关系也不是一天两天了。"

"Without your help this time, I really would have lost everything." "Come on, it was nothing. You and I have been friends for so long!"

nǎr hàn/gén nǎr 哪儿和/跟哪儿 (哪兒和/跟哪兒)

Where's the connection? What does that have to do with anything? What do you mean?

◆ "打扰你休息了？" "**哪儿**跟**哪儿**啊？"

(From the TV series 今生是亲人)

"Am I interrupting your break?" "What are you talking about! Not at all."

◆ "听说许主任和陈总闹崩了？" "**哪儿**和**哪儿**啊？刚才俩人还一起 喝酒呢。"

"I heard that Director Xu and Manager Chen had a fight." "What gave you that idea? They were having a drink together just a moment ago."

nǎr liáng kuai nǎr wánr qù 哪儿凉快哪儿玩儿去 (哪兒凉快哪兒玩兒去)

See 哪儿凉快哪儿歇/呆/待着去 nǎr liàng kuài nǎr xié/dāi zhe qù

...nǎr qù le ...哪儿去了 (...哪兒去了)

"Why go there?" What's that got to do with anything? You're off by a mile.

◆ "〖我〗也许会输给这个刚刚坐在你身边的女孩子。" "你想**哪**去了？"

(From the TV series 红色康乃馨)

"Maybe I'm going to lose out to that girl who was sitting next to you." "Where'd you ever get that idea?" [The first speaker suspects her boyfriend is romantically interested in someone else.]

◆ "你别拿你媳妇儿打马虎眼！" "妈，您扯**哪儿**去了？"

(From the TV series 贫嘴张大民的幸福生活)

"Don't use your wife as an excuse!" "Mom, how could you say such a thing?" [The mother is discussing money matters with her children. Her second son claims his wife handles their money matters.]

nǎr liáng kuai nǎr xiē/dāi zhe qù 哪儿凉快哪儿歇/呆/待着去 (哪兒凉快哪兒歇/呆/待著去)

"Go someplace cold!" Go to hell! Get the hell out of here! Stop bugging me!

♦ "豆豆，嫁给我吧。" "不嫁，哪儿凉快哪儿待着去！"

(From the novel 一见钟情)

"Doudou, marry me." Doudou was opening a letter, and without even looking up she said: "No way. Get the hell out of here!"

♦ "头儿，咱们这辆车太旧了，您修了半天了也没修好，咱们干脆买辆新的算了。" "你小子懂什么，就知道乱花钱。去，哪凉快哪歇着去！"

"Chief, this car of ours is too old. You've been fixing it forever and it's still on the fritz. Why don't we just buy a new one?" "What the hell do you know except how to waste money? Go back to your toys."

nà jiào yí ge 那叫一个...(那叫一個...)

Nothing can beat (something); nothing is more...than...; something is really...; talk about...

♦ 勇哥爱踢足球，球技没说的，那叫一个臭，平时没人爱和他踢。

(From short story 非常教师)

Brother Yong loves soccer; but his technique – talk about awful! Usually no one wants to play with him.

♦ 那叫一个火啊！ 买什么涨什么，今天又涨了小一千。

(From the TV series 一年又一年)

Talk about being hot! Whatever she buys goes up. The stocks she bought today went up nearly a thousand yuan for her again. [An old woman struck it rich in stocks.]

nà mènr 纳闷儿 (納悶兒)

Be bewildered; be dumbfounded; find something hard to understand

♦ 我就纳了闷儿了啊，看你们家的条件也不像供不起你上学啊！

(From the TV series 今生是亲人)

I just don't get it. Seems to me your family could afford to pay for college. [Commenting on a college student's choice to work as a railroad porter.]

♦ 哎，我就纳了大闷儿了，你们霞光〖公司〗干什么要来连云山掺和啊？ 中国这么大，到什么地方不行啊？

I'm stumped. Whatever brought your Xiaguang (Company) here to mess around at Mount Lianyun? China's so big; why couldn't you find someplace else to go?

nǎi yóu xiǎo shēng 奶油小生

A young man of butter-colored skin (or complexion); a fair-skinned young man; a pretty boy

♦ 两个化妆陪着扮演司机的演员来了，这是个细皮嫩肉的奶油小生。

(From the movie script 顽主)

Two makeup artists came with the actor who played the driver. He was a pretty boy.

◆ 我不喜欢**奶油小生**，男人就应该有点儿粗劲儿。

I don't like wimps; men should be a little bit rough.

nán wei 难为 (難爲)

Give someone a difficult task; give someone a tough nut to crack; make things difficult for someone

◆ 从一千多万人里把他找出来，这也真**难为**你们了。

(From the TV series 今生是亲人)

Searching for him out of ten million people! That was really a tough one for you. [Talking about finding a son switched at birth twenty years before.]

◆ 既然你们觉得资金有困难，我就不**难为**你们了，想和我们合作的人有的是。

Since you're having problems with capital, I won't give you a hard time. There are a lot of people who want to go into business with us.

nāo zhǒng 孬种 (孬種)

"A bad seed"; a loser; a coward

◆ 牧民们谁也不愿意要我，牧民一提到我，就说是个"**孬种**"。

(From the novel 血色黄昏)

None of the herdsmen wanted me. Whenever my name was brought up, they'd say, "He's a loser."

◆ 你姓黄的要不是**孬种**就站出来！

You, Huang! If you're not a coward, come out!

náo yǎng yang 挠痒痒 (撓癢癢)

"Scratch an itch"; only touch the surface of something; an ineffective measure

◆ 那没劲，那不**挠痒痒**吗？

(From the movie 有话好好说)

That's really ho-hum. Just like a slap on the wrist, isn't it? [Referring to hitting a person with a brick, as opposed to hacking him up with a cleaver.]

◆ "你的玩笑都是伤人的。""我伤你哪儿？胳膊还是腿？伤人？你还有地方怕伤？你早成铁打的了，我这几句话连你**挠痒痒**都算不上。"

(From the novel 动物凶猛)

"Your jokes hurt people." "Oh, where did I hurt you? On your arm, or your leg? Hurt people? Are you still capable of being hurt anywhere? You became an iron man long ago. My remarks didn't even amount to a mosquito bite."

nǎo dai diào le wǎn dà de bā 脑袋掉了碗大的疤 (腦袋掉了碗大的疤)

"If the head falls it leaves only a wound the size of a bowl"; death is nothing to me

◆ **脑袋掉了碗大的疤**，老子这辈子死了好几回了，反正这条命是白捡的。

(From the novel 亮剑)

I'm not worried about losing my head. I've already died many times in this one lifetime. Any time I have leftover is like icing on the cake.

♦   怕什么？ 工作丢了就丢了，**脑袋掉了**也**不过碗大的疤**，我豁出去了！就是告到北京去我也要把咱们市的这几个贪官告倒。

> What's there to be afraid of? So I lost my job. Even if I lose my head, so what? I'm going all out! Even if it means appealing all the way to Beijing, I'm going to take this city's corrupt officials to court and bring them down.

nǎo dai shuān zài kù yāo dài shang 脑袋拴在裤腰带上 (腦袋拴在褲腰帶上)

"Have one's head tied to a belt loop on one's pants (where it may be lost at any time)"; live on the edge of death; be in the line of fire; put one's life on the line

♦   这算什么？ 像咱们这行人，哪个不是把**脑袋拴在裤腰带上**，整天在刀尖上混日子？
(From the novel 白眉大侠)

> What's the big deal? People like us all risk death every day; we live on a knife's edge.

♦   大哥，自从三年前我跟你做第一笔白粉生意，就把**脑袋拴在裤腰带上**了。现在钱赚了不少了，咱们能不能换点儿正经的生意做？

> Boss, ever since our first heroin deal I've been living on a precipice. Now that we've managed to make quite a pile, why can't we switch to some kind of respectable business?

nǎo zi/dai jìn shuǐ le 脑子/袋进水了 (腦子/袋進水了)

"Brain-flooded"; brain-damaged or brain dead; have a hole in one's head; have rocks in one's head

♦   你**脑袋**肯定是**进水了**，那女孩儿是雨森带来的，跟我有什么关系啊？
(From the TV series 将爱情进行到底)

> Have you gone off the deep end? That girl came with Yusen. What connection does she have with me? [Talking to a jealous girlfriend.]

♦   什么？ 地下赌场还要搞开业典礼？ 你的**脑袋进水了**吧？

> What? You want to have a grand opening for an underground casino? You must have rocks in your head.

nào bēng/fān le 闹崩/翻了 (鬧崩/翻了)

Quarrel to the point where a relationship is broken off; reach a showdown

♦   绿叶跟立秋**闹崩了**，所以立秋才一个人跑回来，他们俩怕还要离婚哩！
(TV series script 百姓)

Luye and Liqiu had a meltdown. That's why Liqiu came back alone. Maybe they're even going to want a divorce.

◆ "你怎么这么快就回来了？" "我跟我们头儿闹崩了，他把我给炒了。"

"How come you came back so soon?" "I had a showdown with my boss and he sacked me."

nào/nòng/gǎo bu hǎo 闹/弄/搞不好 (鬧/弄/搞不好)

If anything goes wrong; if somebody botches it up; in the worst case scenario; possibly

◆ 开车，闹不好就撞死一口子；做买卖，闹不好就打一架。

(From the short story 前科)

Be a taxi driver? Well, if you mess up you could kill someone. Be a street vendor? Well, if you mess up you could get into a fight.

◆ 这次不但不会裁我，搞不好，还会升我一下子。

(From the TV series 手心手背)

Not only am I not going to get sacked, but I might even get promoted.

◆ 别碰你老板的那小骚货，弄不好，你小命可就没了。

Keep your hands off your boss's little bimbo. If anything goes wrong, you're dead meat.

nào le bàn tiān 闹了半天 (鬧了半天)

After wasting a lot of time; at the end of the day; it turns out

◆ 闹了半天，你新潮来新潮去，骨子里还有这么多的封建积垢。

(From the novel 一半是火焰一半是海水)

Never mind all this talk about new ideas. At the end of the day you still have the old ones in your bones.

◆ 嗨！ 闹了半天你不是厂长，你怎么不早说呢？

Hey! After all that, turns out you're not the factory director. Why didn't you tell us before?

nào zháo le/dǎi zháo le 闹着了/逮着了 (鬧著了/逮著了)

"Got it"; got lucky; struck it rich; got it made

◆ 这回你可闹着了！

(From the TV drama 杳見胡同)

You hit it this time! [Speaking of winning a lottery.]

◆ "她生了个孩子，你说我该怎么办？" 葛东生一脸忧愁。 "嘿，这你可闹着了。" 方林毅来了情绪， "你有儿子啦！"

(From the novel 天津大战)

"She had a baby. What am I supposed to do now?" Ge Dongsheng looked really worried. But Fang Yiling was all worked up, "Wow, you hit the jackpot! You've got a son!"

něi hú bù kāi tí něi hú 哪壶不开提哪壶 (哪壶不開提哪壶)

"Lifting the pot where the water is not boiling"; someone who's always putting his foot in his mouth; touch a sore spot

◆ "你结婚了吗？" "你怎么哪壶不开提哪壶啊？ 哪有你这么幸运啊？"

(From the TV series 天堂鸟)

"Are you married?" "You really know how to touch a sore spot, don't you! No, I don't have your marvelous good fortune."

♦ 人家小王总共就出过那一次事故，你倒好，老把这件事挂在嘴边上，真是**哪壶不开提哪壶**。

> Xiao Wang had just one accident the whole time. But you can't seem to have a conversation without bringing it up. You're a master at saying the wrong thing!

něi mén zi 哪门子 (哪門子)

Why in the world? (rhetorical question)

♦ 嘿！我还没愁呢，你摇什么脑袋犯的**哪门子**愁啊？ 一个羊也是放，一群羊也是赶。

(From the novel 空洞)

> Hey! If I'm not worried, why are you shaking your head and agonizing like that? If you can take care of one sheep, you can manage a herd. [The wife is pregnant with a second child.]

♦ "你说谁会是下届美国总统啊？" "管你屁事！你操的**哪门子**心啊？"

> "Who do you think will be the next US president?" "Is that any fucking business of yours? Why the hell are you bothering about a thing like that?"

néng ger 能格儿 (能格兒)

Capable; resourceful; crafty

♦ 刚才还听罗丁吹你**能格儿**呢。说你半个月前刚帮罗丁救出了几百万的货。怎么才几天就不敢顶风作案了？

(From the novel 浮沈商海)

> Luo Ding was just carrying on about how you've really got the stuff—said you saved goods worth millions for him two weeks ago. How come after a few days you're backing away from a job just because it's difficult?

♦ 你总是说你多**能格儿**，你**能格儿**怎么还是小科长一个？

> You're always saying how capable you are. If so, how come you're still a lowly section chief?

nǐ hái bié shuō 你还别说 (你還別說)

Now that you mention it; you may find this hard to believe, but...; believe it or not

♦ **你还别说**，这公安局还非得买你们的东西。

(From the TV series 黑洞)

> Believe it or not, the Security Bureau is required to buy your products. [Prison supplies must be products made by ex-labor camp prisoners.]

♦ **你别说**，真把我这馋虫儿给勾出来了。

(From the movie 甲方乙方)

> Believe it or not, it really made my mouth water. [The speaker was too busy to eat, but later found he had an appetite.]

nǐ nǎr nàme duō fèi huà 你哪儿那么多废话 (你哪兒那麼多廢話)

"Where did you find so much nonsense to say?" Stop yakking; shut up

♦ **你哪儿那么多废话**，我就问你干还是不干？

(From the TV series 黑洞)

Spare us the nonsense. I just asked whether you were in or not.

◆　"局长，刚才找你的那个女的我怎么有点儿眼熟啊，是不是电视台的？" "你哪儿那么多废话，该干什么干什么去。"

> "Director, the woman who came looking for you seems a bit familiar. Is she from the TV station?" "Shut up! Get on with your work."

nǐ yě yǒu jīn tiān 你也有今天

Your day has come (a vengeful remark); it's your turn now; what goes around, comes around; here's a dose of your own medicine

◆　"哈，哈，哈，想不到**你也有今天**。" 震兴又发出了近乎变态的笑声。

(From the novel 大雪山)

> "Hah, hah! You never thought it would be your turn someday. Zhenxing's laugh sounded almost perverse. [The speaker has just taken his revenge after years of being bullied and humiliated.]

◆　向问天，天网恢恢，**你也有今天**！

(From the TV series 笑傲江湖)

> Xiang Wentian, justice has a long arm, and what goes around, comes around. [A villain is being besieged.]

nǐ zǒu nǐ de yáng guān dào, wǒ zǒu/guò wǒ de dú mù qiáo 你走你的阳关道，我走/过我的独木桥 (你走你的陽關道，我走/過我的獨木橋)

"You take your broad avenue, and I'll cross over my log bridge"; let's go our separate ways

◆　我不会再拦着你，也请你不要再打扰我。从今以后，**你走你的阳关道，我过我的独木桥**，咱们分道扬镳。

(From the novel 敌人的诱惑)

> I won't stand in your way anymore, and I ask you not to bother me again, either. From this point on, you go your way and I'll go mine. Let's part company for good.

◆　既然咱们谈不到一块儿去就算了。往后**你走你的阳关道，我走我的独木桥**。

> Since we can't agree, let's just forget it. Goodbye and good luck!

nì wai 腻歪

1."intimate"; indecently intimate or excessively sentimental behavior 2 "sticky or greasy"; too much of something; be tired of

◆　你还当着我的面儿，跟那女的**腻腻歪歪**的不正经。

(From the TV drama 贫嘴胡同)

> Making out with a woman like that right in front of me! It's indecent. [A roommate's complaint.]

◆　我说你活**腻歪**了，看见红灯还往前开？

> I'd say you're tired of life, ignoring a red light like that.

niǎo 鸟 (鳥)

"Dick"; frigging; asshole (also pronounced diǎo)

◆　你怎么能相信那些**鸟**玩意儿呢？

(From the TV series 康熙帝国)

How could you believe in those fucking toys? [Referring to foreign cannons.]

◆ 工人们都骂，说办公室老郭带人去OK，还嫖，给抓起来了。厂里用的
这叫什么鸟人？

(From the novel 大厂)

The workers were all grumbling, saying Lao Guo from the General Office took people to karaoke joints and even to hookers, and that they got arrested. What kind of assholes does the factory hire as managers?

niǎo qiāng huàn pào 鸟枪换炮 (鳥槍換炮)

Birdhunting guns replaced by cannons; dramatic improvement

◆ 咱们家怎么了？ **鸟枪换炮**了？

(From the TV series 一年又一年)

What's up with our place? Did it just get a major upgrade? [Referring to the sudden appearance of many home appliances.]

◆ "嘿！ 你也用上计算机了！" "是啊，**鸟枪换炮**了。"

"Wow! Even you use a computer now!" "That's right. I've joined the modern world."

niào 尿

(Vulgar) "piss"; give a damn; care about; be afraid of (used with a negative)

◆ 不要把自己看的太高了，你想学海子那个**傻逼**做文学的圣徒啊，告诉
你，你就算死十趟八趟也没人**尿**你，除了你父母和我们这些哥们伤心
谁把你当个鸟？ 操，简直是有神经病。

(From the short story 绝望与迷惘)

Don't take yourself so seriously. Are you trying to copy that asshole Haizi and be a literary martyr? Let me tell you something. Nobody would give a shit if you killed yourself eight or ten times. Except for your parents and a few buddies like us who'd feel sad, who cares about you? Fuck, this is totally nuts. [Spoken to someone who is contemplating suicide. Haizi was a poet who committed suicide.]

◆ 您用不着吓我。现今这社会里，谁**尿**谁呀？

Don't try to scare me. Nowadays, no one is fucking afraid of anyone.

niào bú dào yí ge hú li 尿不到一个壶里 (尿不到一個壺裏)

Can't piss into the same pot; don't see eye to eye; don't get along

◆ 班子里，他跟贺玉梅挺团结，纪委书记齐志远和赵副厂长几个都跟他
尿不到一个壶里。老齐和老赵原来都憋着要当书记当厂长的，恨吕建
国抢了饭碗，总跟他弯弯绕。

(From the novel 大厂)

On the leadership group, he and He Yumei are a team. Qi Zhiyuan, the head of the Disciplinary Commission, and Deputy Director Zhao, along with some others, don't get along with him. Qi and Zhao both coveted the directorship for a long time, so they hate Lu Jianguo for getting the job and always try to undercut him.

◆　咱俩怎么能一块儿写本书啊？　什么事上都**尿不到一个壶里**。
　　How could we write a book together? There's not one thing we agree on.

niē le yì bǎ hàn 捏了一把汗

"Have a handful of sweat"; so worried that one's sweating; worried; scared

◆　我一早见**雷子**找上门来，心里还真**捏了一把汗**，可见他们审了你半天，连正眼都没看我就走了，就知道你没出卖我，可打心眼儿里感激你哩。
　　(From the novel 心动少年时)
　　I saw the police knocking on your door this morning. I was really sweating, but they grilled you for hours and left without even looking in my direction, so I know you didn't sell me out. I'm grateful from the bottom of my heart.

◆　我一听是你老婆的电话，心里还真**捏了一把汗**，谁知她没问我你昨晚去哪儿了，而是要跟我老婆说话。这样，我才松了一口气。
　　When I realized it was your wife on the phone, I sweated blood. But she didn't ask me where you were last night. Turned out she just wanted to talk to my wife. Then I was able to relax.

nín/nǐ zhè shi mà wǒ 您/你这是骂我 (您/你這是罵我)

You're just making fun of me; you might as well call me names; why not just say it to my face

◆　"外边儿有高就了吧？" "二奶奶，**您这是骂我**，我不是那见利忘义**攀高枝儿**的人！"
　　(From the TV series 大宅门)
　　"So you have a high position somewhere else?" "Madam, you're mocking me. I'm not such a social climber that I'd sacrifice my principles for money." [A pharmacist is speaking to the manager of a family pharmaceutical business.]

◆　"您来了以后，咱们村的面貌真是焕然一新。" "**您这是骂我呢**。有意见您就直说吧。"
　　"Ever since you came our village looks brand-new and shiny." "You're making fun of me. Just tell me straight out what's bugging you."

níu 牛

Arrogant; someone whose qualities or achievements give him/her the right to be arrogant or insolent; full of oneself; amazing; awesome

◆　"方达已经跟我说了，她可能不大愿意配合。" "还那么**牛气**？"
　　(From the TV series 红色康乃馨)
　　"Fangda already told me she might not be willing to cooperate." "She's still on her high horse?" [Fangda has a husband in jail. She is supposed to be cooperative when her husband is already convicted of a crime.]

◆　小姨，你真**牛**，跟姥爷平起平坐了！
　　(From the TV series 今生是亲人)

Auntie, you're awesome. You're right up there with grandpa now. [Both are professors.]

níu bī 牛逼

Similar to 牛 but vulgar

♦   您特美，特得意，**屁颠儿屁颠儿的，人五人六的，牛逼烘烘的。**
(From the novel 耍叉)
You're very pleased with yourself, smug, complacent, and genteel. You think your shit doesn't smell.

♦   我叫东狮，是东半球最**牛逼**的诗人。
(From the movie 北京乐与路)
I'm Dongshi, the hottest poet of the Eastern Hemisphere.

níu pí dēng long 牛皮灯笼 (牛皮燈籠)

A lantern made of cow hide (no light can come through); not capable of being enlightened; thick; thick-headed

♦   你这小**牛皮灯笼**怎么透亮了？
(From the TV series 今生是亲人)
What penetrated your thick little head so you suddenly saw the light?

♦   我就知道她们是**牛皮灯笼**，怎么点都不明！ 真是气死人了！
(From the short story 渴望和睦)
I just knew they were really thick and would never get it. It's so frustrating!

P

pá yáng fēn 扒洋分

(Shanghai dialect) rake together; make foreign money

♦   许静为了**扒洋分**，把袁方给甩了。
(From the TV series 天下第一情)
Xu Jing dumped Yuan Fang so that she could (go abroad and) make foreign money. [Yuan was Xu's boyfriend.]

♦   C家好婆(Mandarin=姥姥)说：“隔壁大外孙强强签证已经签出来了，听讲立时三刻就要走的，总归要送点东西意思意思。”媳妇嘴巴一撇：“用不着的，他是出国**扒洋分**，又不是插队落户。”
(From the short story 家庭风景二十章)
Grandma of Apartment C: "Qiangqiang, the oldest grandson of our next door neighbor, got his visa. I hear he's leaving right away. We ought to give him some kind of gift in any case." Her daughter-in-law sneered and said, "No need. He's going abroad to soak up dollars; it's not as if he were being sent down to the countryside to live with peasants."

pāi xiōng pú zi 拍胸脯子

Pat one's chest as a gesture of confidence or to make a vow

♦   我跟他说不要拿冯祥龙的东西，他**拍着胸脯子**跟我保证过。结果还是拿了一套房子。这下有好戏看了。
(From the TV series 大雪无痕)

I told him not to accept anything from Feng Xianglong and he swore up and down he wouldn't. Now it turns out he accepted an apartment from him. Sit tight, there's going to be some interesting times ["a good show"] ahead.

♦ 十年前他彭东东说可以给小玉一生的幸福，我二话**没说**就离开了。可是今天，我可以**拍着胸脯**对您说，我能给小玉一生的幸福。

(From the TV series 北京女人)

Ten years ago, this guy Peng Dongdong promised Xiaoyu a lifetime of happiness, so I backed off without uttering a word. But today, I can swear on all I hold sacred that it is I who will give Xiaoyu a lifetime of happiness. [The speaker is asking Xiaoyu's mother for permission to marry Xiaoyu after her divorce from Peng Dongdong.]

pài yòng chǎng 派用场 (派用場)

Put to good use

♦ 他是块黄金，可惜**派**不上什么**用场**。

(From the short story 人不是黄金)

He's pure gold, but unfortunately you can't put him to good use here. [The country town is too small to take advantage of the literary talent of the young man in question.]

♦ 你别看这些旧机器在我们城里**不起眼**，送到乡下去能**派大用场**呢！

These old machines don't look like much in the city, but take them to the countryside and they can be put to great use.

pān gāo zhīr 攀高枝儿 (攀高枝兒)

Climb to a taller branch (of a tree); put oneself under the patronage of a powerful person

♦ 你不是撇下大可**攀高枝儿**了吗？ 怎么又回来了？

(From the TV series 其实男人最辛苦)

Didn't you ditch Dake for someone more powerful? What brought you back? [Speaking to Dake's ex-wife.]

♦ 我自己的女儿我还能不了解吗？ 你们别相信那些闲言碎语，她绝对不会**攀高枝儿**嫁给市长的儿子。

I know my own daughter! Pay no attention to the gossip. There is no way she is going to marry the mayor's son and be a social climber.

pánr liàng 盘儿靓 (盤兒靚)

Pretty face; good looks (盘儿=脸盘儿, face)

♦ 这几天我主要跟两个女的，就是朱妮和沙莉，不但**盘儿靓**，身条也好。

(From the novel 都市危情)

I spent the past few days for the most part with two girls, Zhuni and Shali. Not only are they pretty, but their figures are nice too.

♦   什么？ 省话剧团把小玉选去当演员，这不可能啊！ 她的个儿这么矮，盘儿也不够靓啊！

What? The provincial drama troupe is making Xiaoyu an actor. That's impossible! She is so short; and besides, she's not that pretty.

pàn xīng xing pàn yuè liang 盼星星盼月亮

Wait eagerly for the light of the stars and the moon; look anxiously forward to an event or to someone's appearance

♦   我就**盼星星盼月亮**似的盼你。

(From the TV series 花非花)

I was longing for your visit like someone longing for water in the desert.

♦   大家都**盼星星盼月亮**似的盼着工作组来，没想到这个工作组和那帮黑心的老板**穿的是一条裤子**。

They longed for the arrival of the investigation team as their saviors. They never imagined that the investigation team members themselves were working together with the black-hearted bosses.

páo de liǎo hé shang páo bù liǎo miào 跑得了和尚跑不了庙 (跑得了和尙跑不了廟)

A monk can get away, but not his temple; you can run, but you can't hide

♦   他拿出一副手铐，说道："用不用给你戴上？" 阿兰结结巴巴地问道："什么？" 小警察说道，"你想不想跑？" 阿兰答道："不…不。" 小警察说："那就用不着了。就该是这样，**跑得了和尚跑不了庙** 嘛。"

(From the novel 东宫西宫)

He took out a pair of handcuffs and said, "Shall we put these on?" Ah Lan stammered, "Wh……what?" The young policeman said, "You're not going to run away on me, are you?" "No, oh, no." The policeman said, "We don't have to do it then. That's right. You can run, but you can't hide."

♦   老板不在？没关系，**跑得了和尚跑不了庙**。两天之内不把钱还给我，我就把你们这商店砸了。

Your boss isn't in? That's Ok. He can run, but he can't hide. Give me my money back within two days or I'll smash this store of yours to pieces.

pǎo lóng tào 跑龙套 (跑龍套)

Be a stagehand; be a spear-carrier; play an insignificant role

♦   我看这样好了，让他给大伙做点**跑龙套**的工作，大家有多余的饭，赏给他一口。

(From the short story 从卡尔大街向左一拐弯)

What about this? We'll hire him for odd jobs and if there is leftover food, we'll throw him a few scraps. [Speaking of an unemployed homeless man.]

◆ "听说你混得不错，进了有名的海山公司了！" "哪里哪里，我在公司里只是**跑跑龙套**，说不定什么时候就会让人家炒了。"

"We heard you're doing all right and have joined the famous Haishan Company." "Not really. I just run errands for them. They could sack me at any time."

pào mó gu 泡蘑菇

Dunk the mushroom to get it soft; dawdle away one's time; kill time

◆ 到底是怎么了？ 我没时间跟你**泡蘑菇**，快说。

(From the novel 苍天在上)

What's wrong with you? I haven't got time to waste with you. Spit it out!

◆ 不让进就是不让进！ 少在这儿**泡蘑菇**，泡也没用！

(From the novel 我是你爸爸)

I'm not letting you in and that's final. Don't waste your time here—there's no point. [The words of a gatekeeper at the entrance to a stadium.]

pào niur 泡妞儿 (泡妞兒)

Womanize; flirt with young girls

◆ 你啊，就是**泡妞儿**的时候精神！

(From the movie 一见钟情)

The only thing you've got energy for is chasing girls! [An employer speaking to an employee.]

◆ "你看这个经理让小谢当怎么样？" "他啊，除了**泡妞儿**什么本事都没有？"

"How about giving Xiao Xie that manager position?" "Him? What's he good for besides chasing girls?

pào tāng 泡汤 (泡湯)

Fail; to fall through; fall apart

◆ 现在倒好，让你们这么一搞，全部**泡汤**！

(From the TV series 新七十二家房客)

So now look what happened! Once you guys laid a hand on it, everything fell apart. [Plans for a neighborhood election fell through.]

◆ 不管您怎么去讲，反正您得赶快把人帮我们弄出来，那小子手里有咱们一千多万合同呢，不能为这事**泡了汤**啊。

(From the novel 大厂)

Tell them anything you want, but you've got to catch him as soon as possible. That bastard has our ten million yuan contract in his hand. We can't let the deal go bad because of this mess. [An important business client has been picked up by the police for visiting a prostitute.]

pào tǒng zi 炮筒子

A cannon barrel; a straight shooter

◆ "你们有什么话就说出来嘛！" "我是个**炮筒子**，我什么也不怕，我来说！"

(From the TV series 问问你的心)

"If you have something to say, out with it." "I'm a straight shooter. I have nothing to be afraid of. So, let me do the talking."

♦ 李云龙是个**炮筒子**脾气，不高兴了谁都敢骂，过后就完。

(From the novel 亮剑)

Li Yunlong is like a loaded gun; he'll chew out anyone when he's angry. But once his anger is past, it's past.

péi bǎng 陪绑 (陪綁)

A prisoner who has not been condemned to death but is taken to the execution grounds as a deterrent; share the responsibility; be lumped together with wrongdoers

♦ 用不着二团三团一起**陪绑**。我的错误，组织上可以做降职、撤职处分。

(From the novel 突出重围)

You shouldn't extend the blame to the second and third regiments. I am the one at fault. The authorities can punish me with demotion or dismissal.

♦ 后来我才知道，他们早就选好经理了，让我去应试不过是**陪绑**。

I only found out later that they had already chosen a manager. They only had me take the exam for show.

péi běnr zhuàn yāo zi/zhuàn yāo he 赔本儿转幺子/赚吆喝 (賠本兒轉麼子/賺吆喝)

Lose money only to prove you're in business; pay money and get nothing in return; get a rotten deal

♦ 这么作不是**赔本转幺子**吗？ 您作生意**图**什么啊？

(From the TV series 手心手背)

Are you throwing away money just to show you're in business? What's the point of doing business in the first place? [Criticizing a reckless lowering of prices.]

♦ 这么办吧，我好人做到底，我**豁**出去了。我给您十五块，我**赔本赚吆喝**认了。

(From the novel 天桥演义)

OK, I'll be a good guy and go for broke. Here's fifteen kuai. I'm willing to lose money so the deal will go through. [The speaker is bargaining over the price of a young girl he is buying.]

pèi 配

Match; be qualified to do something; be in the position of doing something

♦ 后生，你也**配**吃牛肉？牛肉是给三炮留的。

(From the movie 红高粱)

Young man, I'm afraid you don't rate high enough for beef. The beef is reserved for Sanpao. [A restaurant owner is speaking. Sanpao is the head of a group of bandits.]

♦ 我耍弄你？ 我今儿把话搁这儿了，给她**打下手**你都不**配**！ 那已经是抬举你了！

(From the TV series 北京女人)

You think I'm taking you for a ride? I'm just going to say this: you're not even good
enough to be her assistant. Even that would be more than you deserve. [A manager is
speaking to a newly hired employee who complained about being assigned to work under
his ex-wife.]

pèng dīng zi 碰钉子 (碰釘子)

Hit a nail that's in the way; come up against a wall; hit a snag; meet with resistance or
rejection

◆   大哥，我从来没有追求过明星，而且，追求她的人又那么多，我怕碰
    钉子。

(From the novel 豪门奇谭)

Brother, I've never been a superstar groupie. And besides, she has so many admirers
chasing her, I'm afraid I just won't meet with her approval.

◆   到了新学校，你人生地不熟，得捡人家爱听的话说，要不然肯定碰钉
    子。

When you get to the new school you'll be a stranger in a strange place. So watch your
mouth and say only what people want to hear. Otherwise, you'll have problems for sure.

pèng yì bí zi huī 碰一鼻子灰

"Get a noseful of dust"; run into a blank wall; be rejected

◆   你少去碰一鼻子灰了！他是高人，能给你一叫就来吗？

(From the novel 从阴间来)

Don't go down that blind alley! He's no ordinary man. Do you expect him to just come
when you call?

◆   他拿着三千块钱想把那位大歌星请到咱们的小县城来演出，结果呢，
    碰了一鼻子灰。这点儿钱，给明星的跟班都不够。

He took three thousand kuai and thought it was enough money to bring a famous singer
for a performance in our little town. Turned out he really missed the boat. It wasn't even
enough to pay her entourage.

pèng yùn qi 碰运气 (碰運氣)

Try one's luck; give something a shot

◆   "可是，办公室没人，都去开会了，你也办不了事啊。"警卫说。
    "我去碰碰运气吧！"没等警卫允许，我就骑上车，直朝里面冲过
    去。

(From the novel 浪－－一个叛国者的人生传奇)

"But there's no one in the office; they're all at a meeting. You can't get anything done," said the security guard. "Just let me give it a shot." I didn't wait for the guard's permission—just got on my bike and rushed in.

♦ 我知道北京电影学院很难考，我自己的条件也不怎么好，但是还是想**碰碰运气**。

I know how hard it is to get into the Beijing Film Academy, and my qualifications aren't that impressive. But I still want to try my luck.

pí 皮

Thick-skinned; shameless; mischievous

♦ "听话个什么！ **皮**死了，我不要他了！"

(From the novel 本次列车终点)

A nice boy? He's a pain in the butt! I'd like to disown him! [A mother replying to someone who complimented her son.]

♦ 我是董老师！叶子同学，你上课睡觉，还给老师起外号，真是太**皮**了！放学后到我办公室来！

(From the short story 沉重的灵魂)

I'm Dong, your teacher, and I'm talking to you, Yezi! You dozed off in class and you thought up insulting names for your teachers. What a troublemaker! Come to my office after school!

pí shi 皮实 (皮實)

Tough-skinned; tough; sturdy

♦ "里边怎么没声儿了，这小子真够**皮实**的。"

(From the TV series 大宅门)

"Why is it so quiet in there? This kid is a tough one."[A comment about a kidnapped boy who shows no fear.]

♦ 妈呀，我看这人挺**皮实**的，别再挑了。

(From the novel 二劳改和女人们)

Come on, Mom, I think this guy has staying power. Stop looking. [A daughter is helping her mother select a boyfriend.]

pí xiào ròu bú xiào 皮笑肉不笑

The skin smiles but not the flesh; put on a false smile; be insincere

♦ 他们早听说过我，大约有点排斥，只**皮笑肉不笑**地握握手，只叫声："经理！"就**没下文**了。

(From the novel 舞夜游侠)

They heard about me long ago and were probably prejudiced against me. So they just shook my hand with a forced smile and said, "Mr. Manager." That was the extent of it.

◆ 你看他那**皮笑肉不笑的德性**，真让人恶心！
Just look at his hypocritical smile. Makes me want to puke!

pì diānr pì diānr 屁颠儿屁颠儿 (屁顛兒屁顛兒)

1. (run so fast that) the buttocks shake up and down; behave obsequiously; fawn on someone
2. elated, complacent; overjoyed

◆ 因为他**屁颠儿屁颠儿**地交涉，文化站至少由每月的逢单日开门，改为天天大门洞开了。
(From the novel 找乐)
Because he kept sucking up to the guy, at least the Cultural Center is open every day now. Before it was only open on odd-numbered days.

◆ 老刘住了三十多年小平房，现在分到了一套两室两厅的单元房，给他美得**屁颠儿屁颠儿**的。
Old Liu lived in same tiny house for over thirty years. Now his work unit has finally given him an apartment with two bedrooms and two living rooms. He feels as if he had died and gone to heaven.

pì gu chén 屁股沉 (屁股沈)

Heavy-assed; overstay one's welcome

◆ 好啦，我在你这儿不能**屁股太沉**，"中心"还有许多口啰嗦事儿等着我去伤脑筋呢。我们一言为定，红妹治疗的事，我明后天等你的回话。
(From the novel 百年德性)
All right. I can't sit here all day. I've still got a lot of pesky problems to handle back at the Center. Let's shake on it. I'll wait for your word on Hongmei's treatment plan tomorrow or the next day.

◆ 德子今晚晌儿一直气儿不顺，早盼着这俩**屁股沉**的主儿快走。
(From the novel 红尘)
Dezi was in a foul mood all night and couldn't wait for those two to leave, but they seemed glued to their chairs.

pì yě bù/méi gǎn fàng 屁也不/没敢放

Not even (dare to) release a fart; not say a word

◆ 赵明是个**滚刀肉**，厂里没人敢惹他。前年的承包费就没交，说是赔了。前任许厂长**屁也没敢放**一个，就算**拉倒**了。
(From the novel 大厂)
Zhao Ming is a bully. Nobody at the factory dares to provoke him. Two years ago he didn't pay the required fee for his contract, claiming he lost money. The former director let it go without daring to say a word, and that was the end of it.

◆ 你姐夫不在那时，你们新闻界连**屁也没放**一个，人死一年多了才来瞎起哄。
(From the novel 有我是谁)

When your brother-in-law passed away, you media people didn't report one word about it. And now that the man has been in his grave for a year, you're making all this noise?

pīn fèngr/pī fènr 拼缝儿/批份儿 (拼縫兒/批份兒)

A plug or wedge that makes up for what's missing; a connection/connector; a go-between; liaison

◆ 那么这个胡大庆，也许只是整个毒品销售网络中的一个骨干销售人员，也就是这圈子里的人说的那种 **"批份儿"** 的角色。

(From the novel 永不瞑目)

In that case, this Hu Daqing may be a major pusher in the drug trafficking network, or a "liaison" as they call it in those circles.

◆ 找不到水泥对不对？找我啊！有我当**拼缝儿**什么东西都搞得到。

Couldn't get cement? Come to me! Use me as your connection and you'll get whatever you want.

pīn yí ge gòu bēnr pīn liǎ zhuàn yí ge 拼一个够本儿拼俩赚一个 (拼一個夠本兒拼倆賺一個)

"Kill one and you break even, kill two and you make a profit"; go all out; risk everything

◆ 他们死得惨，可说是粉身碎骨，但值，值疯了，咱们多打死多少敌人啊—战友们这一冲。我们很算的过这笔帐：**拼一个够本，拼俩赚一个**。

(From the novel 看上去很美)

They died a terrible death—they were blown to pieces. But it's worth it beyond our wildest dreams if we count how many enemies died in this round of attack. The bottom line is in our favor. Killing one is breaking even and killing two is making a profit.

◆ 我跟日本人拼了！**拼一个够本儿拼俩赚一个**！

I'll go down together with the Japanese. Killing one is breaking even and killing two is making a profit.

píng tóu lǎo bǎi xìng 平头老百姓 (平頭老百姓)

"People with flat haircuts"; common folks

◆ 我要非想给人治病也不是不可以，刚一上手应该先给一些**平头老百姓**小的溜地看看，担的风险小一些。

(From the novel 空洞)

It's not that I couldn't treat patients if I insisted, but when I'm starting out, it's a better idea just to treat common folks on the street. It's less risky.

◆ 咱们是**平头百姓**，人家是当官的，你根本别想跟人家比。

We're just common folks and he's a government official. There's no comparison at all.

pō léng shuǐ 泼冷水 (潑冷水)

Pour cold water on; be a wet blanket; discourage

◆ 小绢嗔道："你就会**泼冷水**，这不成那不成，那么，你来拿个主意，可好？"

(From the novel 锈剑瘦马)

Xiaojuan pouted as she said, "The only thing you're good at is being a wet blanket. This won't work; that won't work. Well, why don't you come up with an idea!"

◆   人家热情这么高，你偏偏去**泼冷水**，安得什么心啊？

I was so excited, but you insisted on being negative. I wonder what you've got up your sleeve?

pò gǔ zhòng rén chuí 破鼓众人捶 (破鼓衆人捶)

Join with others in beating a broken drum; to betray or join in the persecution of a person already in distress; sharks flocking to the smell of blood (*see also* 墙倒众人推 qiàng dǎo zhòng rén tuí)

◆   真是**破鼓众人捶**，咱们个体户可不敢出事儿，出了事儿就是假冒伪劣典型。

(From the TV series 大赢家)

It's like sharks flocking to the smell of blood. Small private businesses like ours can't afford to make mistakes. One mistake and you're held up as a bad example for selling shoddy or fake products. [A private milk farm was shut down because of quality problems.]

◆   现在的人心太坏，平常跟你有说有笑，但凡出点差错，就来个**破鼓众人捶**。

Nowadays people are too mean-spirited. One minute they're talking and laughing with you; but the next minute, if you're in a bit of trouble, they join the crowd against you.

pò guàn zi pò shuāi 破罐子破摔

A cracked pot can afford more cracks; a hopeless or desperate person can afford to act recklessly; to have nothing to lose

◆   去他妈的，**破罐子破摔**，反正是个破了。

(From the novel 平凡的事业)

The hell with it! A dead man has no shame, and I'm a dead man. [Since people call him a loafer, he has decided to give up the effort to work altogether.]

◆   警长让咱们审这个犯人的时候要耐心点儿，要不然他**破罐子破摔**，这线索就断了。

The police chief asked us to use patience in interrogating this prisoner. Otherwise he might feel his situation was so desperate that he had nothing to lose, and he would refuse to give us a lead.

Q

qī cùn 七寸

"The seventh inch"; fatal spot; to hit the vital spot; to hit the nail on the head; to hit where it hurts most (from the expression 要打蛇就要打七寸: if you want to kill a snake, hit the seventh inch)

◆   "你是生个女儿不**过瘾**，还想生个儿子！" "你算打他的**七寸**上了！"

(From the TV series 贫嘴张大民的幸福生活)

"Having a daughter isn't enough for you. You still want a son." "You're right about him. You hit the nail on the head."

◆　俗话说**打蛇要打七寸**，你要想挤垮这家公司就得从降低价格上下手。

As the saying goes, you've got to hit them where it hurts the most. If you want to crush this company, you have to start by lowering your prices.

qī lǎo bā shí 七老八十

Very old; a very old age; aged

◆　爹啊！你都**七老八十**了，这话亏你说得出口！

(From the novel 鸳莺梦)

Oh, Dad! Talking about such things at your age! [The daughter is surprised that her father is discussing her love affair.]

◆　都**七老八十**的还离什么婚？也不怕别人笑话？

Getting divorced at your age? Aren't you afraid people will laugh at you?

qī qī sì shi jiǔ tiān 七七四十九天

For forty-nine days; for a long time; forever (The number refers to the cycle of days in Buddhist mourning ritual.)

◆　谈吧，咱们谈上个**七七四十九天**。

(From the TV series 黑洞)

Keep beating around the bush if you want. We can shoot the breeze till the cows come home. [A suspect is resisting interrogation.]

♦ 下雨怕什么？下他个七七四十九天才好呢！不用去外边干活了，反正咱们干多干少都拿一样的工资。

So what if it rains? It can rain for forty days and forty nights for all I care. We don't have to go outside to work, and anyway we get paid the same no matter how much we work.

qí huó 齐活 (齊活)

Be done, be complete, be all set

♦ 你就把我当你的一个小哥们儿对待就**齐活**了。

(From the novel 我是你爸爸)

Just treat me like one of your little buddies and we're all set.

♦ 和姑娘约会有啥难的？先要电话号码，然后打个电话，约个时间吃顿饭或看个电影不就**齐活**了？

What's so hard about asking a girl out? Get her phone number, give her a call, and set a date for a dinner or a movie. Then you're in business.

qí lú kàn chàng běn, zǒu zhe qiáo 骑驴看唱本，走着瞧 (騎驢看唱本，走著瞧)

See 等着瞧 děng zhe qiáo

qí mǎ zhǎo mǎ 骑马找马 (騎馬找馬)

Use temporarily while seeking something better; interim; fallback, make-do

♦ 我有些觉得他的心计过甚，他竟然是在**骑马找马**，说实在的，我的思想深处有些忿忿不平，但不是为他，而是为什么我就没有这么一个机会呢？

(From the novel 从一到十)

Somehow I felt he was a schemer. Turned out he was using me as a fallback until he found the right woman. To be honest with you, deep down I resented it. Not so much because of him—but why can't I have the same opportunity? [A man who already has a girlfriend keeps looking for others on the Internet.]

♦ 我干的这话儿算不上什么正经工作。**骑着马找马**吧。

This job isn't any kind of career. It's just a transition until I find the real thing.

qǐ dà zǎo gǎn wǎn jí 起大早赶晚集 (起大早趕晚集)

To get up very early but arrive late at the market; to start early but finish late

♦ 看来我是**起个大早儿，赶了个晚集**啊！

(From the TV series 大赢家)

Looks like I had a headstart but finished last. [The speaker has an early start on planning and yet failed to beat his competitor.]

♦ 我等于是**起了个大早，赶了个晚集**。的哥带我兜了两小时的圈子。这不现在才到。

> I set out early but arrived late. The taxi driver drove me in circles for two hours, and as you can see I just got here.

qǐ hòng jià yāng zi 起哄架秧子

To facilitate something or to encourage somebody by making a lot of noise; to cheer or boo

♦ 我哪能跟你比，你这是真本事，著名足球运动员，又出名又出国，现今还能挣大钱，哪像我们只能**起哄架秧子**，给你们球星叫好。

(From the novel 足球黑字)

> How can I compare myself to you? You have the real stuff; you're a famous soccer player and you've even played abroad. You can make big bucks now. People like us can't do anything but cheer for stars like you.

♦ 我只希望这场比赛在我俩之间进行下去，不要任何观众，我既不需要他们的呐喊助威，也不需要**起哄架秧子**。

(From the short story 无果之恋)

> I only hope that match takes place just between the two of us. No spectators. I don't want either their cheers or their booing.

qǐ xiān 起先

At first; in the beginning; originally

♦ 我开小饭馆和便民店，**起先**呐，是被逼的。

(From the TV series 大赢家)

> When I first opened the restaurant and convenience store it was because I had no other choice. [The speaker was laid off and had to start a small business, but later she came to enjoy it.]

♦ 他**起先**也不是这个**德性**，就是有了几个钱儿以后，脸儿就变了。

> He wasn't such an asshole at first, but as soon as he had a little bit of money he became a different person.

qì bú fènr 气不忿儿 (氣不忿兒)

Cannot tolerate or suppress one's anger

♦ 打小我也以为自个是个文曲星下凡。好长时间**气不忿儿**，他董永凭什么呀？

(From the TV series 编辑部的故事)

Even as a kid, I thought I was a literary genius. I was resentful for a long time. What did Dong Yong have that I don't? [文曲星 is the celestial deity or star associated with literature. Dong Yong is the famous lover who marries a female immortal because of his filial piety.]

♦　我炒他的鱿鱼是因为他出了事故，你要是觉得**气不忿**可以把你自己的工作让给他嘛。
　　　I fired him because he got into an accident. If you're so worked up about it, give him your own job.

qì guǎnr yán 气管儿炎（妻管严）(氣管兒炎（妻管嚴）)

"Inflammation of the trachea"; henpecked (This is a pun, because 气管儿炎 or tracheitis is homonymous with 妻管严 or "tightly controlled by the wife.")

♦　从现在起我就算得了**气管炎**（妻管严）啦！
　　(From the novel 空洞)
　　　From now on, consider me henpecked. [The speaker has just gotten engaged.]

♦　你还不知道吗？老李那人整个儿一**气管儿炎**，哪怕是花五块钱也得经过老婆批准。
　　　Don't you know Lao Li is completely under his wife's thumb? If he wants to spend five yuan, she has to OK it first.

qì sǐ huó rén bù cháng mìng 气死活人不偿命 (氣死活人不償命)

"Making someone die of anger is not a capital offense"; to be so angry you could die

♦　**气死活人不偿命**，是吧？而且，气死活人的事儿也有，是吧？
　　(From the novel 不良父母)
　　　You don't have to pay with your life for annoying someone to death, right? Besides, it actually happens that people die of pure irritation, isn't that so?

♦　托福差一分上录取线，这可真是**气死活人不偿命**。
　　　I was just one point short of the TOEFL score I needed for admission. I was ready to die of anger.

qì tóur shàng 气头儿上 (氣頭兒上)

In a fit of anger; at the peak of one's anger

♦　他这个人性子直，**气头儿上**说了些不合适的话，大家不要介意。
　　(From the TV series 孙中山)
　　　He's a straight shooter. If he made some inappropriate remarks in a fit of anger, I hope you won't take offense.

♦　你**气头儿上**咱不讨论离婚的事好不好？
　　　Since you're in such a rage, we won't talk about the divorce right now, OK?

qiā 掐

Quarrel; wrangle

♦　你们俩一天不**掐**就闷得慌。
　　(From the movie 洗澡)
　　　If you two go one day without fighting, you're bored to death. [Two good friends meet and quarrel every day in a public bath.]

♦　我跟他再怎么**掐**，我们是哥儿俩。
　　(From the TV series 手心手背)

No matter how we quarrel, he and I are brothers.

qiǎ bó zi 卡脖子

To have a stranglehold on; to choke the life out of

♦ 还有五十万两军饷卡着咱们**脖子**呐！

(From the TV series 大宅门)

They've got us in a stranglehold with this 500,000 of military pay and provisions we have to supply! [The military government ordered the business to supply 500,000 taels of soldiers' pay and provisions.]

♦ 我看咱们得换个地方摆摊了，东城工商局的那帮家伙总卡我们的**脖子**。

I think we should set up our stand somewhere else. Those guys from the Industry and Commerce Bureau of the East District are always squeezing us to death.

qiān tóur 牵头儿 (牽頭兒)

To take the lead; to make the connections; to take the initiative; to bring something together

♦ 老实告诉我，这事是不是你**牵的头儿**啊？好汉作事好汉当，你就等着处理吧！

(From the TV series 大赢家)

Tell me honestly, were you the ringleader? A real man accepts the consequences of his actions. You can count on being punished.

♦ 全是我**牵的头儿**，我认了。

(From the TV series 黑洞)

I was the one who started it all. I admit it. [The speaker is taking the responsibility in order to exonerate his accomplices.]

qiān wàn bié zhènme shuō 千万别这么说 (千萬別這麽說)

Don't talk that way! Don't ever say that!

♦ "你真善良，可我马上就要成残废了，你对我这么好有什么用呢？""你**千万别这么说**，捐了肾的人同样可以很健康地活着。"

(From the novel 红披巾)

"You're very kind, but why be so nice to me when I'm soon going to be crippled?"
"Don't talk that way! Kidney donors can usually lead a perfectly healthy life."

♦ "要不是你帮我，这次我就完了。""**千万别这么说**，咱们共事多年了，我不能看着您倒霉啊。"

"If you hadn't helped me out, I'd be finished this time." "Don't ever say that! We've worked together so many years. There's no way I could watch you go down the drain."

qián duō bù yǎo shǒu 钱多不咬手 (錢多不咬手)

"A big chunk of money won't bite your hand"; big dough never hurts anybody; money doesn't bite; money doesn't hurt

♦ 这买卖大了，**钱多了又不咬手**！

(From the TV drama 耷晃胡同)

We're talking big business here. Don't be afraid of big bucks! [A pep talk on increasing the scale of the business.]

◆ 以前没钱的人贪多，都说钱不咬手，我现在感觉，**钱多不是咬手的事，而是咬心**。

(From the novel 红马)

Used to be people without money longed for it. They said, "Big dough never bites anyone's hands". Now I know it's not your hand but your heart that gets chewed up

qián jiǎo zǒu hòu jiǎo jiù... 前脚走后脚就···(前腳走後腳就···)

On the heels of someone else; right after; as soon as; immediately

◆ 你爸爸**前脚走**你**后脚就**跑，被他看见怎么办？

(From the TV series 天下第一情)

You're running out right at the heels of your dad. What if he sees you? [A child is grounded by his father.]

◆ 他知道辛守笃这个人靠不住，**前脚走后脚就**去卖他。

(From the novel 欲狂)

He knows how unreliable Xin Shoudu is, and that as soon as he turns his back Xin will sell him down the river.

qián pà láng hòu pà hǔ 前怕狼后怕虎 (前怕狼後怕虎)

"To be afraid of the wolf/dragon in front and the tiger behind"; to be afraid of taking actions for fear of unpleasant consequences; excessively cautious; indecisive; hesitant

◆ 你不总是**前怕狼后怕虎**的吗？这回怎么下决心了？

(From the TV series 今生是亲人)

Haven't you always been really cautious? How come you made the decision [to divorce] this time?

◆ 你要是这么**前怕狼后怕虎**的，什么也干不成。做生意嘛，总会有赚有赔的。

If you always hesitate to act, you'll never accomplish anything. That's business; you win some and lose some.

qiàn le yí pì gu zhài 欠了一屁股债 (欠了一屁股債)

To be deeply in debt; to be in the red

◆ "她那个修理厂要是没有杨铮撑着早就垮台了。" "就是到现在还**欠了一屁股债**呢！"

(From the TV series 将爱情进行到底)

"If she didn't have Yang Zheng to prop it up, that repair center of hers would have gone under long ago." "The fact is, even now it's really in the red."

◆ 别看他一口气买两辆新车，他**欠着一屁股债**呢。

Forget about the two new cars he bought, one right after the other. He's up to his neck in debt.

qiàn sb bā/èr bǎi diào/qián 欠Sb八/二百吊/钱 (欠Sb八/二百吊/錢)

To owe somebody money

◆ 那天，我见着了刘能，他不理人，气鼓鼓的，像谁**欠着他二百钱**。

(From the short story 星期日的野餐)

I saw Li Neng the other day. He ignored me and looked really mad, as if I owed him a bunch of money.

◆ 老王一天到晚总沉着脸，好象别人欠了他八百吊似的。
　　Lao Wang always has a long face, as if everyone owed him eight hundred kuai.

qiáng dǎo zhòng rén tuī 墙倒众人推 (牆倒衆人推)

To join others to topple a falling wall; to betray or join in the persecution of a person already in distress; sharks flocking to the smell of blood

◆ 他现在也够可怜了，要是**墙倒众人推**，他往后可怎样活下去呀？
　　(From the novel 人生)
　　He's miserable enough now. If you hit him while he's down, how do you expect him to survive? [A student is sent back from the city to his village; his ex-girlfriend takes pity on him.]

◆ 这叫**墙倒众人推**，凡是在这坎节儿上折我郎健的主儿，有朝一日我挨个儿拾掇他们。
　　(From the TV series 手心手背)
　　This is called collective persecution. When the day comes, I will take care of each and every one of those who tried to ruin me [Langjian] at this critical juncture.

qiáng niǔ de guā bù tián 强扭的瓜不甜

(Proverb) "The melon that you rip from the vine (as opposed to the one that falls to the ground naturally when it's ripe) doesn't taste sweet"; some things can't be forced

◆ 阿肖，你都看到了！这次，你就彻底死心吧！你喜欢的人根本不爱你，你又何必强求？**强扭的瓜不甜**啊！
　　(From the novel 蝴蝶公主)
　　Ah Xiao, you saw it all. This time I hope you'll give it up for good. The one you like doesn't like you. Why try to force it? Some things can't be forced.

◆ **强扭的瓜不甜**，如果他们不想和我们联合投资，我们就自己干。
　　You can't force them. If they don't want to be our investment partners, we'll go it alone.

qiàng háng 戗行 (戧行)

To go beyond one's professional duties and intrude on someone else's turf

◆ 他们早就不是**解闷**儿了，完全是专业写作的架式，这不是**戗行**吗？
　　(From the novel 一点正经没有)
　　Used to be they were doing it out of boredom, but that stopped long ago. Now they've got all the trappings of professional writers. This amounts to encroaching on our turf. [A professional writer is objecting to the increasing success of amateurs.]

◆ 电影导演**戗行**拍电视广告？那要我们广告公司做什么？
　　Film directors producing commercials? That's our turf! What are we advertising companies supposed to do?

qiāo biān gǔ 敲边鼓 (敲邊鼓)

"To beat the drum at the side"; to back someone up; to speak on someone's behalf; to egg someone on

◆ 我也不好，不该阴一句阳一句地**敲边鼓**，人家都是补台，偏我拆台。
　　(From the TV series 编辑部的故事)

I wasn't blameless either. I shouldn't have egged them on. I made gratuitous remarks, directly and indirectly. Everyone else was trying to make it work while I was messing it up.

◆ 私营在经济舞台上永远是个配角，只要**敲好边鼓**就行了。
(From the TV series 大赢家)
Private business always plays a supporting role on the economic stage. If they swell the chorus, that's enough.

qiāo dǎ 敲打

To shake somebody up; to knock sense into somebody; to criticize; to scold

◆ 我的脾气急，您多**敲打**着我点儿。
(From the novel 百年德性)
I can be hot-tempered. Hope you'll rein me in a bit.

◆ 你儿子这么胡涂，你得**敲打敲打**他。
You son is so clueless. You've got to knock some sense into him.

qiāo zhú gàng 敲竹杠

To extort; to fleece

◆ 大庆，她这完全是在**敲竹杠**！
(From the TV series 天堂鸟)
Daqing, this is highway robbery! [The price for a piece of land suddenly jumped from fifty million to one hundred million kuai just before a contract was to be signed.]

◆ 你不要以为我这是在**敲你竹杠**，原来就是这么贵。
Please don't think I'm fleecing you. It's always been this expensive.

qiào yǐ (wěi) ba 翘尾巴 (翘尾巴)

"To carry one's tail high"; to have a swelled head; to be cocky and self-important

◆ 不就一破副段长吗？你让我当厂长这**尾巴**也**翘**不到天上去。
(From the TV series 贫嘴张大民的幸福生活)
You're only a lousy deputy section chief. I wouldn't be this cocky if you made me head of the whole factory.

◆ 刚做点儿事就**翘尾巴**了？你要学的还多着呢！
One small accomplishment and you get cocky. You have a lot to learn!

qiě 且

It will be a long time before...

◆ 我儿子去南方出差了，**且**回不来呢。
(From the TV drama 两个人的婚礼)

My son went to the south on business. He won't be back for a long time.

◆ 功课我刚开始做。要做完啊，且着呢！

I just got started on my homework. I won't be done for quite a while.

qīn xiōng dì míng suàn zhàng 亲兄弟明算帐 (親兄弟明算帳)

(Proverb) "Even blood brothers keep clear accounts"; No matter how close your friendship, in financial matters it's better to have everything spelled out

◆ 他跟我说了，这不是徒弟和师傅的问题，是公司对公司，必须**亲兄弟明算账**，按国家制订的《公司法》办事。

(From the novel 省委书记)

He told me that this matter wasn't between a master and an apprentice, but between two companies. Financial arrangements must be made according to national corporate law, whatever our personal relationship. [The former master and apprentice now each head a company. The apprentice's company is about to take over the company of his former master.]

◆ "这是还你的五万块钱。""算了吧。""哪有借钱不还的道理，**亲兄弟还要明算帐**呢！"

(From the TV series 失乐园)

"Here's the fifty thousand kuai I borrowed from you." "Oh, forget it!" "It's not right to borrow money and not pay it back. Even between brothers financial matters should be clear."

qīng guān nán duàn jiā wù shì 清官难断家务事 (清官難斷家務事)

(Proverb) "Even the most upright judge can't handle family quarrels"; don't get involved in a family dispute

◆ **清官难断家务事**，这事你管不了。

(From the TV series 都市情感)

Even the most upright judge can't handle family quarrels. You'd better stay out of this.

◆ 俗话说**清官难断家务事**，这两口子打架很难分出对错来。

As the saying goes, no outsider, no matter how impartial, can settle a family dispute. Between husband and wife, it's hard to decide who's right and who's wrong.

qīng yí sè 清一色

Uniformly; consistently; completely

◆ 进了小楼后我才发现，这里面更具梦幻色彩，墙壁是肉红色的，玻璃和镜子是**清一色**的深蓝，连地毯都是淡灰绿色，人在里边有一种恍恍惚惚的感觉。

(From the novel 我和我的小白鼠妻子)

When I got into the building I found the colors were even more hallucinatory. The walls were painted meat-red. The windowpanes and mirrors were uniformly dark blue. Even the carpet was grayish-green. It made your head swim.

◆ 人家公司**有的是**钱，汽车就有十几辆，而且是**清一色**的大奔。

  The company is swimming in money. They own a dozen cars and every last one is a Mercedes.

qǐng 擎

To wait without doing anything; to sit around until things happen

◆ "找到了她千万别惊动她，回来告诉我她在哪儿在干什么就行
  了。""得嘞，您**擎**好儿吧！"

  (From the TV series 手心手背)

  "When you find her, make sure that you don't do anything to alarm her. Just come back and tell me where she is and what she's doing." "All right, just sit tight." [The first speaker is asking his subordinate to locate a missing sister.]

◆ "你说的是真的？""你就放心回去，**擎**等着抱儿子吧！"

  (From the TV series 古船、女人和网)

  "Are you for real?" "Rest assured. All you have to do is go home and wait for the birth of your son." [A fortuneteller answers the question of whether an expected child is male or female.]

qǐng biàn 请便 (請便)

Go ahead. do as you please; be my guest

◆ 你们觉得该怎么处理我，就**请便**吧。

  (From the TV series 今生是亲人)

  Punish me as you see fit. Go ahead. [The speaker has failed to finish his work on time.]

◆ "你要是这么说，我们真得到法院去起诉你们了！""**请便**。"

  "If that's all you have to say, we'll just have to take you guys to court." "Be my guest."

qǐng shén róng yi sòng shén nán 请神容易送神难 (請神容易送神難)

(Proverb) To invite a god (guest) is easy, but to get rid of him is hard; something is easy to get but hard to get rid of; someone who is here to stay; an easy entry but a difficult exit

◆ 嘿嘿嘿嘿，小哥，**请神容易送神难**！咱们兄弟好歹也有十年没见了，
  我们多住些日子，你会死啊？

  (From the novel 情惑那西色斯)

  Ha! Brother, guests are easy to invite but hard to get rid of. For better or worse, we haven't seen each other for at least ten years. Would it kill you if I stay a few more days?

◆ 我这还**请神容易送神难**了？你还赖上我了？

  (From the TV series 手心手背)

  Looks like I'm stuck with something I can't get rid of. Are you just going to hang around me?

qióng guāng dàn 穷光蛋 (窮光蛋)

Pauper; ne'er do well

◆ 跟你实说吧，如果我男人他现在成了个**穷光蛋**，我肯定会跟个有钱的
  野男人私奔的。

  (From the novel 女性写真)

Let me level with you. If my man turned out to be a ne'er do well, I'd run off with any guy who had money.

♦ 真没想到她会嫁给那个**穷光蛋**，这不是**鲜花插在牛粪**上了吗？

I never expected her to marry a pauper like that. It's like a fresh flower stuck into a cowpie, isn't it?

qióng jiā fù lù 穷家富路 (窮家富路)

Economize at home but spend while traveling

♦ 你再带点儿钱吧，**穷家富路**的，带点儿。

(From the TV series 今生是亲人)

Take a bit more money. You can economize at home, but there's never enough money when you travel, so take a bit more.

♦ 俗话说**穷家富路**，出远门多带点儿钱是应该的，别太寒酸了。

As they say, you can save at home but you have to spend on the road. For such a long trip you have to take more money. You don't want to look too shabby.

qióng...shénme 穷...什么 (窮...什麼)

Why the hell (do you keep doing this)? Stop it!

♦ "您不是要一身清白吗？ 咱爷儿们就还您个一身清白，还**穷嚷嚷个什么**？"

(From the novel 与死共舞)

"You wanted a clear conscience, right? OK, I'll let you have a clear conscience. So why the hell do you keep bitching?" [In order to avoid investigation into an old law case, a false certificate of death has been provided for "you."]

♦ **穷打扮什么**？是人家小赵儿结婚又不是你结婚。

Why do you keep primping? It's Xiao Zhao's wedding, not yours!

qiū hòu de mà zha, bèng da bù liǎo jǐ tiān le 秋后的蚂蚱，蹦达不了几天了(秋後的螞蚱，蹦達不了幾天了)

Like a locust when autumn has passed, its days are numbered

♦ 大爷，您放心，刘黑七是秋后的蚂蚱，蹦达不了几天了。

(From the novel 乱世黑客)

Don't worry, Grandpa. Liu Heiqi is like a locust in winter; his days are numbered.

♦ 日本鬼子是秋后的蚂蚱，蹦达不了几天了。

The Japanese devils are like locusts in winter; their days are numbered.

qiú 球

(Vulgar) balls; what the hell; my ass; bullshit

♦ "刘队长饶了我吧，我家里有八十岁的老娘，靠我要饭养活。" "你娘早死个**球**了，还敢来蒙我！"

(From the short story 鱼市)

"Chief Liu, please let me off. I'm the sole support of my eighty-year-old mother."
"Bullshit! Your mother died a long time ago. You've got some nerve trying to put one over on me."

♦ "人家来了好几个电话了，我看你还是去吧。""去个**球**！"
"They called quite a few times. I think you'd better go." "No fucking way."

qíu yé ye gào nǎi nai 求爷爷告奶奶 (求爺爺告奶奶)

"Beg grandfather and ask grandmother"; treat everyone as a savior in order to get a favor; beg around; go to a great deal of trouble to accomplish something

♦ 嘿！这小子，我**求爷爷告奶奶**的才找来这么一个差事，你还不去？
(From the TV series 今生是亲人)
What a bastard! I went from pillar to post to get you this job. Why the hell did you turn it down?

♦ 我**求爷爷告奶奶**的才弄到这么点儿钱，您可得省着点儿用。
I went to a lot of trouble to scrape up these few pennies. You better make it last.

qù nǐ de 去你的

Stop the nonsense! Come off it! Go fuck yourself!

♦ "你这么喜欢孩子赶明儿自个儿生一个！""**去你的**！"
(From the TV series 古船、女人和网)
"Since you like children so much, why don't you have one yourself one of these days?" "Come off it!"

♦ "我们领导让我去西藏工作两个月，让我给推掉了，怕你看不见我心里难受。""**去你的**，你爱去哪儿就去哪儿，我才不在乎呢！"
"Our boss wanted me to work in Tibet for two months. I rejected the assignment. I was afraid you might miss me if you didn't see me around." "Bullshit. Go wherever you want; I don't care."

quē dé 缺德

"Lacking virtue"; mean-spirited; evil

♦ 将来让病人住在潮房子里，你们可是**缺了八辈子大德了**，绝不会有好儿。
(From the novel 空洞)

You're condemning the future patients to damp rooms. That's the lowest of the low. You won't get away with this! [Construction workers building a hospital are accused of shoddy work.]

♦   人家这钱是看病用的，可你却拿去赌。你忒缺德了吧？

This was the money they put aside for medical bills, and you take it for gambling! Don't you think that's contemptible?

R

rào wān zi 绕弯子 (繞彎子)

Speak in a roundabout way; beat around the bush

♦   您以后有话直说，我不会绕弯子。

(From the TV series 今生是亲人)

From now on if you have something to say, say it right out. I'm no good at talking in circles.

♦   你绕了这么大一弯子，原来还是来为他说情的。告诉你，我罚他罚定了，你怎么说都没用！

You beat around the bush for so long, and it turns out you just want to speak up for him. Let me tell you something. I mean to fine him, and fine him I will. Doesn't matter what you say.

rě bù qǐ hái duǒr bù qǐ 惹不起还躲不起 (惹不起還躲不起)

If you can't win a fight, you can always take your leave, right? Discretion is the better part of valor.

♦   不试了，惹不起还躲不起吗？

(From the TV drama 昝兒胡同)

I give up. I know when I've lost; I'll just gather my things and go, OK? [The speaker tried to test his new washing machine on a public water faucet. The neighbors protested.]

♦   这买卖我不做了，惹不起还躲不起吗？

(From the TV series 水浒传)

OK, I'll give up this business. Discretion is the better part of valor, right? [Spoken to a thug who is bullying people in the market.]

rě yì shēng xīng 惹一身腥

"Cause yourself to smell fishy all over"; inflict a bad reputation or pain upon oneself; invite or stir up trouble

♦   我明明警告过你没事别去招惹陌生人，你偏要强出头，惹一身腥，活该！

(From the novel 秀逗大侠)

I told you distinctly not to mix it up with strangers. But you just had to show off, and now you've gotten yourself into deep shit. Serves you right! [He lost a fight and now has to lie low.]

◆ 都说去广东可以赚大钱，可是我去了，结果一分钱没赚着，身上带的本钱还让人都给骗走了，真是没吃着鱼，倒惹了一身腥。

They all say you can make a pile in Guangdong, but I went and didn't make a cent. What's more, the money I brought got ripped off me. I really went for wool and came back shorn.

rén xīn dōu shì ròu zhǎng de 人心都是肉长的 (人心都是肉長的)

The human heart is made of human flesh. nobody is completely devoid of humanity; please have some compassion

◆ 人心都是肉长的。想当年把人家逼成那个样，现在说句好话，送点薄礼，还不应该？

(From the novel 锁链，是柔软的)

Have a little compassion! Back then you drove him to the wall. Now would it kill you to say a kind word and send her some sort of token?

◆ 他的心也是肉长的，礼也送了，好话也说了，他总不会对咱们孤儿寡母下毒手吧？

He's not made of stone. We've sent him gifts and begged him; after that he's surely not going to harm an orphan and a widow, is he?

rén xīn gé dù pí 人心隔肚皮

"The heart is hidden by the skin of the belly"; you can't see someone's heart; you can't know someone else's intentions

◆ 犯人："你们睡吧，我是不会跑的。"公差："人心隔肚皮，我们怎么能相信你？"

(From the TV series 水浒传)

Criminal: "You go ahead and sleep. I'm not going to run away." Officer: "Who knows what you have up your sleeve? Why should we believe you?"

◆ 我真怀疑他不保险，别看他是联队长，人心隔肚皮，谁猜得着？

(From the novel 平原枪声)

I'm really not so sure we can rely on him. So he's leading the allied commando team, OK, but who knows what's in his head?

rén yì zǒu chá jiù liáng 人一走茶就凉

"Once someone has left the tea gets cold"; out of sight, out of mind; people are fickle

◆ "喂，怎么样？女人来信了吗？我的三胜根本不给我来信，不过我也没给她写。""是吗？大概正在和第二个情人一边吃着团子一边赏月吧！""也许是那样。但是，我根本就无所谓。人一走茶就凉嘛！"

(From the novel 东史郎日记)

"Hey, what's up? Got a letter from your girlfriend? My Sansheng [Mikatsu] doesn't write me at all. I don't write her either." "Is that right? She's probably with her next lover right now, watching the moon and eating mooncakes." "Maybe so. But I don't care. Out of sight, out of mind." [A conversation between two soldiers away from home.]

♦ 原来我这儿门庭若市。现在呢，刚一从市长的宝座退下来就连个人影儿都看不见了，真是**人一走茶就凉**。

Used to be like Times Square at my house, but since I stepped down as mayor there's not even the shadow of a visitor here. People are fickle!

rén zhār 人渣儿 (人渣兒)

The dregs of humanity

♦ 天天跟这帮**人渣儿**在一起我可受不了！

(From the TV series 黑洞)

I can't stand living with this human scum every day! [A business manager is put into a prsion cell filled with convicted criminals.]

♦ 你说你的朋友都是大腕儿，依我看都是一些**人渣子**！

You told me your friends were all big shots. If you ask me, they're bums.

rèn (tóu) le 认(头)了 (認(頭)了)

Reluctantly accept something as inevitable or as a concession; cave in to the force of nature or circumstances; be able to live with something

♦ 我丢一个儿子我**认了**，我不能都丢了我！

(From the movie 洗澡)

I can accept losing one son, but I can't bear to lose both. [A father is angry that his estranged first son has allowed his retarded brother to wander off.]

♦ 打光棍我**认头了**，这年头儿还能包办婚姻吗？

(From the TV series 特勤中队)

If I never find a wife, I can live with that. Do you really think in this day and age it's still possible to arrange marriages? [A son is unhappy that his mother is arranging a marriage for him.]

ròu bāo zi dá gǒu 肉包子打狗

"Like scaring away a dog with a meat ball"; throw money to the winds

♦ 这一百万给了他，那可是**肉包子打狗**有去无回啦！

(From the TV series 大雪无痕)

If you give him this million, it'll be just like throwing it away.

♦ 你把钱借给他可得想好了，我看纯粹是**肉包子打狗**。

You'd better think twice before lending him money. If you ask me, it's throwing your money to the winds.

ròu téng 肉疼

Something pains/hurts somebody

♦ 这钱就算丢了。周卫东要是能还钱，母猪都会变成巩俐。他倒不是那种爱占人便宜的小气鬼，但忘性奇大，他有钱的时候，你跟他借钱，他也记不住。不过想起来还是**肉疼**，我现在一个月总收入才几千块，这下看来又要动用老本了。

(From the novel 成都，今夜请将我遗忘)

I consider the money gone. Expecting Zhou Weidong to pay back money is like expecting a slut to turn into a princess ["a sow to turn into Gong Li"]. It's not that he's greedy or stingy or likes to cheat people; it's just that he's so scatterbrained. If he lends money to you, he won't remember that either. But it hurts to think of it. My total monthly income right now is just a few thousand yuan. It looks like I'm going to have to dip into my savings again. [The speaker once loaned Zhou Weidong two thousand yuan.]

◆ 你看你看，真是三百多块钱，我是怕你**肉疼**钞票，才讲八十多块钱的。

(From the short story 家庭风景二十章)

Take a good look. Actually it cost three hundred kuai; I only said eighty because I was afraid my spending so much money would upset you. [The husband lied about the price of a sweater he bought his wife as a birthday present. He had to tell her the truth when she complained that it was too cheap.]

rù tǔ bàn jiér 入土半截儿 (入土半截兒)

"Halfway into the ground"; one foot in the grave

◆ 他都六十四了，半截儿入土的人。

(From the TV series 康熙帝国)

He's sixty-four; he already has one foot in the grave. [The Kangxi Emperor dismisses a recommended official as too old.]

◆ 你们想搬家你们搬，反正我就住这平房。我是入土半截儿的人了，经不起折腾了。

Move out if you want. I'm going to stay in this little house. At my age I can't stand so much change.

ruǎn mó yìng pào 软磨硬泡 (軟磨硬泡)

Use both soft and hard tactics to get what one wants; beg and implore incessantly; importune

◆ 这**狗日**的哪象个团长？ 无赖嘛，都象你们团这么**软磨硬泡**，我这后勤部长就别干啦。

(From the Novel 亮剑)

You bastard, what kind of a colonel are you? A real pest! If everyone hounded me the way your regiment does, I'd just resign as chief of logistics.

◆ 我跟他说你没时间，可是他**软磨硬泡**，非要见你。

I told him you were busy, but he just begged and implored, insisted on seeing you.

ruǎn shì zi 软柿子 (軟柿子)

Soft persimmon that can be squeezed into any shape; an easy mark; a pushover

◆ 红红不放心，怕人家**把你当软柿子**捏，让我来给你**戳**着。

(From the TV drama 耷兄胡同)

Honghong was afraid they'd think they could push you around, so she asked me to come back you up.

◆ 这姑娘也不是**好捏的软柿子**，真要放弃她，她**撕破脸**闹起来，自己不但名誉扫地，恐怕连这个厂长也当不成了。

(From the novel 魔鬼与天使)

This girl is no pushover. If you really dump her, she might forget about appearances and make a big stink. Not only would it ruin your reputation; it could cost you the factory directorship.

S

sā bǎor liǎ/yì dǎor 仨饱儿俩/一倒儿 (仨飽兒俩/一倒兒)
"Three meals and two (or one) naps"; enough food and sleep; a self-sufficient and regular life

◆ 〖你这小子〗工人当着，从外国进口的山地车骑着，每天**仨饱儿俩倒儿**，真不知道自己是**吃几碗干饭**的啦！
(From the novel 空洞)
[You bastard], you've got a worker's job, an imported mountain bike, three meals, and a warm bed. And so you think you're really hot stuff!

◆ 别看你是坐办公室的，整天得看领导的脸色行事，多没劲啊！还不如跟我一起当搬运工呢，天天**仨饱一倒**，省心，钱也不少挣。
OK, you work in an office, but you've got to check the boss's face before doing anything. What a drag! Why don't you come work as a porter with me? You'll have three squares, plenty of sleep, no worries, and enough money to get by.

sā guā liǎ zāor 仨瓜俩枣儿 (仨瓜俩棗兒)
"Three melons, two dates"; a trifling amount; a pittance

◆ 下岗就跟家待着吧，反正缺这**仨瓜俩枣儿**的，还不至于饿着。
(From the TV series 今生是亲人)
When I'm laid off I'll just stay home. Losing that pittance of a salary doesn't mean I'll starve.

◆ "回头我让朗健把钱还给你。" "**仨瓜俩枣儿**的，你随便吧！"
(From the TV series 手心手背)
"I'll have Langjian return the money to you later." "It's just small change. It's up to you."
[He is rich and doesn't care if the money is returned or not.]

sā huār/huānr 撒花儿/撒欢儿 (撒花兒/撒歡兒)
"Gambol"; have a ball; have a field day

◆ 他们有钱烧得没边没沿儿**撒欢儿**，咱们还得陪着他们。
(From the novel 百年德性)
They have money to burn, so they just party like there's no tomorrow. Unfortunately, we have to go along.

◆ 张老师说明天去春游不上课，孩子们一听乐得直**撒欢儿**。
As soon as Mr. Zhang announced that the next day's class was canceled for a spring field trip, the kids went wild.

sā jiǔ fēng 撒酒疯 (撒酒瘋)
Act drunk and crazy (either when actually drunk, or when under pretext of being drunk)

◆ "你撒什么酒疯儿啊？" "我就**撒酒疯儿**！"
(From the movie 有话好好说)

"Why do you have to act like a drunken fool?" "I'll act however I damn well please!"

♦   你可千万别喝了，您那酒量太小，一会儿喝醉了**撒酒疯**，不是给咱们全家人丢脸吗？

> No matter what, don't drink anymore. You haven't got much tolerance for alcohol. If you get plastered and make a scene, the whole family will look bad.

sā pāo niào zhào zhao 撒泡尿照照

"Take a piss and look at yourself in the reflection"; take a good look at oneself; don't flatter yourself; who the hell do you think you are?

♦   你也不**撒泡尿照照**，你哪点儿像会发财的样子？

(From the novel 重庆孤男寡女)

> Look at yourself in the mirror! Does that look like someone who's going to get rich?

♦   剪彩是人家当官儿的事儿，你去凑什么热闹？也不**撒泡尿照照**自己，还以为自己真是个人物呢！

> It's for big officials to cut the ribbons. What would you do there—just raise the headcount! Take a good look at yourself! You think you're a bigshot, but you're wrong.

sā yě 撒野

"Go wild"; act crazy or uncivilized

♦   "谁让你在这儿**撒野**？" "她是我老婆，我想怎么打就怎么打。"

(From the TV series 问问你的心)

> "Who says you can run amuck here?" "She's my wife. I can beat her up any way I want."

♦   你别跟我**撒野**，有道理就当着大家的面说清楚。

> Don't act like a mad dog with me. If you're in the right, you can make your case before the world.

sāi yá fèngr 塞牙缝儿 (塞牙縫兒)

"Fill the crack between the teeth"; smidgen; trifling amount

♦   您这点儿银子还不够**塞牙缝儿**的呢，起什么哄啊？

(From the TV series 大宅门)

> The silver you brought isn't even enough to fill the cracks between my teeth. What's all the fuss about? [The ransom money offered for a kidnapped child is not enough.]

♦   这点儿钱连**塞牙缝儿**都不够，您还想办公司？　门儿也没有。

> That's not enough money to get in the door, and you're thinking of starting a company? Forget it!

sān bā 三八

(Taiwan expression) impetuous; tactless; idiotic; loud

♦   我是不是太三八了？我小声一点就是。有些人是不好惹的。

(From the short story 脐)

> Am I talking too loud? OK, I'll be quieter. There are some guys here you wouldn't want to mess with. [Spoken in a bar.]

♦   她太开放，也太三八了，你要是跟她在一起啊，她一定会爬到你头上的。

(From the novel 亲亲我的爱)

She's very uninhibited and a bit too impetuous. If you live with her, she's going to walk all over you.

sān cháng liǎng duǎn 三长两短 (三長兩短)

"Three longs and two shorts"; unexpected and unfortunate event (usually death)

◆ 他已经不在了，你要是再有个三长两短的，这日子可怎么过啊？
(From the TV series 欲罢不能)
He's no longer with us, and if anything happens to you, what am I going to do? [A mother-in-law is speaking to her daughter-in-law after her son's death.]

◆ 大少爷，押运镖银可不是什么好玩儿的事儿，想劫道的多着呢！要是您有三长两短，我这个镖头儿可就担待不起了。
First Young Master, guarding money transports is not fun and games. A lot of people want to rob travelers. If anything happened to you, I'll have to take the responsibility since I'm the head of the guard service. It's more than I can handle.

sān jiǎo māo 三脚猫 (三腳貓)

"Three-legged cat"; a lame and incapable person

◆ 哎呀二叔，我就会那么三脚猫似的两下子，在村上胆大敢下手，可没进过正式的医院啊！
(From the novel 空洞)
Oh, Second Uncle, I'm not qualified; I just know a few medical tricks. I could be brave in the village, but I've never worked in a real hospital. [A "barefoot doctor" is offered a position as a hospital nurse.]

◆ 你用不着害怕和他较量，别看传得挺神，其实他只有三脚猫的本事。
Don't be afraid of testing your strength against him. Forget about his superhero reputation; actually his skills are pretty lame.

sān jù bù lí běn hángr 三句不离本行儿 (三句不離本行兒)

"Can't say three sentences without coming back to talk of one's trade"; return to one's favorite topic again and again

◆ 他三句不离本行，都是带色的笑话。
(From the novel 上海宝贝)
He always gives you the same line—nothing but dirty jokes.

◆ 你看你这个经纪人啊，本来不是给老爷子拜寿来了吗？怎么说着说着就又谈起股票来了？真是三句不离本行儿。
Stockbroking again! Didn't we come here to celebrate the old man's birthday? How come you managed to turn the conversation back to stocks? All you can do is talk shop.

sān qīng zi 三青子

A rash, impulsive and wild youngster; young and reckless

◆ 还别说，这小子真有点儿三青子劲儿。
(From the TV series 古城童话)
Believe it or not, this guy's as full of energy as a rash young punk.

◆ 走到陶然亭游泳池门口，碰见两个才十三四岁的小毛猴儿缠住一个山东口音的外地姑娘，一边说些下流的三青子话，一边跟她抢夺一个塑料丝儿编的茶杯套。
(From the novel 落魄英雄传)

When I got to the gate of the Carefree Pavilion Swimming Pool, I ran into two thirteen- or fourteen-year-old punks harassing a girl with a Shangdong accent. They were making obscene remarks to her while trying to grab a plastic tea cozy out of her hand.

sān shí nián hé dōng, sān shí nián hé xī 三十年河东，三十年河西 (三十年河東，三十年河西)

"East of the river for thirty years and west of the river for thirty years"; nothing remains the same; time changes everything

◆　三十年河东，三十年河西，凭你林教头这身本事，久后说不定会成大事呢！

(From the TV series 水浒传)

　　Time can change everything. With your skills, Master Lin, you could end up doing great things. [Master Lin is under police escort, going into exile.]

◆　三十年河东，三十年河西，你懂不懂？我的目标就是**打一枪换一个地方**，挣足了钱我就撤。

(From the TV series 大赢家)

　　You've got to keep moving, understand? I fire the first shot from one place and the second from another. As soon as I have enough money, I'll quit.

sān tiān dǎ yú liǎng tiān shài wǎng 三天打鱼两天晒网 (三天打魚两天曬網)

"Fish for three days and dry the net for two"; unable or unwilling to concentrate on something

◆　妈住院的日子初云上班**三天打鱼两天晒网**，有时点个卯就跑。

(From the novel 太阳雪)

　　When mom was in the hospital, Chuyun couldn't spend much time on her job. Sometimes, she just punched in and then slipped out.

◆　开汽车比骑自行车难多了，你这**三天打鱼两天晒网**的，什么时候才能学会啊？

　　Driving a car is a lot harder than riding a bike. If you don't put some time into it, how will you ever learn?

sān tiáo tuǐ de há ma zhǎo bu zháo, liǎng tiáo tuǐ de rén yǒu de shì 三条腿的蛤蟆找不着，两条腿的人有的是 (三條腿的蛤蟆找不著，两條腿的人有的是)

"Three-legged toads are hard to find, but two-legged humans are plenty"; there is no shortage of people; people are a dime a dozen (variation: 条腿儿的蛤蟆没有，两条腿儿的人有的是)

◆　你们走，你们都走！我就不信这个。三条腿的蛤蟆找不着，两条腿的人有的是！

(From the TV series 北京女人)

　　Go ahead and quit, all of you! I just don't believe this. There's plenty more where you came from! [A manager is speaking to employees who are quitting to protest bad treatment.]

◆　天底下两条腿儿的蛤蟆没有，两条腿儿的人有的是，干吗非找他啊？

(From the TV series 手心手背)

Men are a dime a dozen. Why chase after him? [A brother disapproves of his sister's choice of a boyfriend.]

sēng duō zhōu shǎo 僧多粥少
"There are more monks than porridge"; too many people competing for too few resources

◆ 当时有朋友劝他到台湾去图发展，他本能地感觉到台湾**僧多粥少**，老蒋惯于排斥异己，而且故土难离。

(From the novel 那方方的博士帽)

Back then some of his friends urged him to go to Taiwan for opportunities, but he knew instinctively that there was too much competition in Taiwan, and that old Chiang (Kai-Shek) routinely discriminated against outsiders. Besides, it's hard to leave your country.

◆ "房子分好了没有？" "**僧多粥少**，难啊！"

"Did all the housing get assigned?" "Not enough to go around. It's a tough one!"

shā huí mǎ qiāng 杀回马枪 (殺回馬槍)
"Strike backwards on horseback"; turn around for a surprise attack

◆ 这是在使用疲劳战术，把咱们拖垮！但我偏要去找，走，**杀他个回马枪**！

(From the novel 刑警手记)

They're waging a war of attrition to wear us down. But that's all the more reason why I have to find him. Let's strike when they least expect it! [The man he's seeking refuses to see him, always leaving word that he's away.]

◆ 我们看着警察走远了，想再搓一把，谁想到他们**杀了回马枪**。

We watched the cops until they were out of sight, and then went back for one more round of gambling. Never dreamed they'd make a surprise reappearance.

shā jī gěi hóu kàn 杀鸡给猴看 (殺雞給猴兒看)
"Kill a chicken to frighten the monkeys"; punish one as a lesson to many

◆ "你知道朕为什么要处罚你吗？" "懂了，皇上**杀鸡给猴看**。"

(From the TV series 康熙帝国)

"Do you know why I, your Emperor, want to punish you?" "I do. Your Majesty is making an example of me."

◆ 董事长撤你的职是**杀鸡给猴看**，你没做错什么事，不过替罪羊而已。

The chairman of the board removed you from your post as a warning to others. You didn't do anything wrong; you're just a scapegoat.

shā rén bú guò tóu diǎn dì 杀人不过头点地 (殺人不過頭點地)
"Killing a man is just letting his head hit the floor"; there are things worse than death; there's a limit to everything; don't go too far

◆ 哥几个，得了吧，**杀人不过头点地**，人家新来乍到，欺侮人家姑娘干嘛？

(From the novel 弧光)

Brothers, enough already. There's a limit to everything. This girl just got here, so why do you guys keep picking on her?

♦ "行了！**见好就收**吧！" "我也是这个意思，**杀人不过头点地**！这一年多，孙家上下使了银子无数，府台大人就是不结案，七爷这招儿够阴的！"

(From the TV series 大宅门)

"OK. Enough is enough!" That's what I think too. This is worse than murder! The Sun family has been pouring in money for over a year now, but the governor just refuses to close the case. Master Seven's strategy was really vicious!"[The governor and Master Seven are related and have ganged up against the Sun family.]

shā rén bú jiàn xiě 杀人不见血 (殺人不見血)

"Kill people without spilling blood"; kill or hurt somebody without leaving any evidence or by subtle means

♦ 她要**杀人不见血**。她要杀人而还要保持住一种优雅。

(From the novel 上官婉儿)

She is trying to slip the knife in without spilling blood. She wants to kill without spoiling her makeup. ["She wants to kill but keep her elegance."].

♦ 这种**杀人不见血**的主意一定是那个**老狐狸**出的。

Must have been that old fox who thought up such a deceptive and deadly idea.

shā rén cháng mìng, qiàn zhài huán qián 杀人偿命，欠债还钱 (殺人償命，欠債還錢)

"If you kill someone, you pay with your life; if you are in debt, you pay the money back"; debts must be paid

♦ 这有什么好说的，**杀人偿命，欠债还钱**，自古就是这么个理儿。

(From the movie 活着)

What else is there to say? You pay your debts. That's the way it's always been.

♦ 常言道**杀人偿命，欠债还钱**，你欠了我的钱，就得还。

As the saying goes, "a life for a life, and money for a debt." You have to pay back the money you owe me.

shá chén guāng 啥辰光

(Shanghai dialect) when; at what time

♦ 小**赤佬**瞎话三千，妈妈**啥辰光**讲过这种话啦？

(From the short story 家庭风景二十章)

You little jerk, you're lying. When did Mom ever say such a thing? [瞎话: *Shanghai dialect*, nonsense; lies; 三千: *Shanghai dialect*, numerous]

♦ 我不是嫌围裙乡气，我的意思是**啥辰光**啥个打扮，啥场合啥个打扮。围裙是下菜地、在灶披间里才好围的。

(From the novel 淡出)

I'm not saying aprons are for peasants. I'm just saying what you wear should suit the time and place. Aprons are for the vegetable patch or the kitchen.

shǎ bī 傻逼

(Vulgar)"stupid cunt"; asshole; jerk; idiot

◆   "现在我们民族的首要问题还不是个人幸福，而是全体腾飞。""为什么？"洋人不明白，"全体是谁？""就是大家伙儿——**敢情**洋人也有**傻逼**。"

(From the novel 一点儿正经没有)

> "Right now the most important issue for our country is not individual happiness, but rapid improvement for everyone." "Why?" The foreigner didn't understand, and asked, "Who is 'everyone'?" "'Everyone' means all of us, together—looks like foreigners can be stupid assholes too."

◆   王大头毕业后去了公安局，刚报到就坚决要求不坐机关，非要去当片警。当时我和李良都骂他**傻逼**，他说你们才是**傻逼**。

(From the novel 成都，今夜请将我遗忘)

> Bighead Wang got a job at the Public Security Bureau after graduation. The day he reported for duty he firmly requested not to do office work. He insisted on walking a beat. Li Liang and I both said he was an idiot. He said we were the ones who were idiots.

shǎ màor 傻冒儿 (傻冒兒)

Fool; idiot; jackass

◆   爱情？你别逗了。干咱们这行儿的，谁说爱情谁是大**傻冒儿**。

(From the TV series 手心手背)

> Love? Come off it. In our line of business, anyone who talks about love needs her head examined. [A remark made by an escort girl.]

◆   华兴公司的经理整个儿一**傻冒儿**！花一千万买的所谓先进设备其实是人家淘汰的旧生产线，倒找钱都没人要。

> The manager of Huaxing Company is a complete fathead! The so-called advanced equipment he bought for ten million turned out to be a second-hand, outdated assembly line, the kind of stuff nobody wants even if you pay them.

shǎ rén yǒu shǎ fú qi 傻人有傻福气 (傻人有傻福氣)

"A fool has a fool's luck"; a lucky dog

◆   能嫁给我不该羡慕？真是**傻人有傻福气**，居然能找着我这样儿的还不费吹灰之力。

(From the novel 过把瘾就死)

> Marrying me, what a coup! Some people really have all the luck. Imagine landing someone like me without even breaking a sweat.

◆   我一直都说大民这孩子**傻人有傻福气**，能娶你这么漂亮贤慧的老婆。

(From the TV series 贫嘴张大民的幸福生活)

> I've always said this kid Damin is a lucky dog to have a pretty, gentle wife like you.

shǎ yǎn 傻眼

"Dazzled"; dumbfounded; stupefied

◆   我早就说过，在我手底下找个事儿，这回**傻眼**了吧？

(From the TV series 手心手背)

Didn't I tell you long ago you'd better work for me? And now you're surprised at how it
turned out? [A friend went to work in a nightclub against the speaker's advice, and got
into trouble.]

♦ 他原来根本没把我看在眼里，我把钱往桌子上一拍，他一看就**傻眼
了**。

At first he didn't take me seriously at all. But when I threw the money on the table, he
was blown away.

shāi kāng 筛糠 (篩糠)

"Sifting chaff"; shake or tremble in fear

♦ 老季头儿哪有这胆儿啊，表面上没事，心里已经**筛了糠**了。

(From the novel 耍叉)

Old man Ji doesn't have the guts for that sort of thing. He may look calm, but he's
shaking like jelly inside. [Ji called somebody names on a bus; the other party has now
gotten off and is banging on the bus door calling on Ji to come out and fight.]

♦ "还是骑摩托车比较**来劲**。" "不成了，撞了你之后，一上摩托车就
筛糠。"

(From the movie 轮回)

"I think riding a motorcycle is more exciting." "Not anymore. Ever since I hit you my
legs are like jelly the moment I get on it."

shài tái 晒台 (曬臺)

"Expose"; make vulnerable

♦ 老乔陪着笑脸："你说…他吹，我不跟着吹那不是**晒人家台**么？"

(From the novel 希望的田野)

Lao Qiao smiled ingratiatingly, "You be the judge…he was talking big, and if I didn't
play along, I'd be hanging him out to dry, wouldn't I?"

♦ 你把我们哥几个**晒**在这儿，叫我们怎么办？

(From the novel 约会)

So you're just going to ditch your friends here? What are we supposed to do? [A mahjong player wants to leave, ending the game.]

shān bú zhuàn shuǐ zhuàn 山不转水转 (山不轉水轉)

"The mountain won't twist, but the river will"; nothing is fixed or irreversible; nothing is set
in stone; nothing is impossible; flexibility is a virtue or necessity; it's a small world

♦ 生意上的事，往往**山不转水转**，苦求无得。

(From the novel 你别无选择)

In business, you often have to be flexible. Rigidity gets you nowhere.

♦ 兄弟，**山不转水转**，咱们还有见面的时候。

Brother, it's a small world. We'll meet again somewhere.

shān gāo huáng dì yuǎn 山高皇帝远 (山高皇帝遠)

"The mountain is high and the emperor is far away;" a forgotten spot; a place beyond the
reach of the law (variation: 天高皇帝远 "heaven is high and the emperor is far away")

♦ 按说他是童工，违法，但这儿**山高皇帝远**，谁管你法不法？

(From the novel 黑星星)

Strictly speaking, he's a child laborer and that's illegal. But around here you can get away with it. Who cares if it's legal or not?

◆ 你当我们这儿天高皇帝远，京里什么消息都听不见？

(From the novel 地狱新娘)

You think this is some godforsaken spot where news from the capital never comes?

shǎn/shān shé tou 闪/扇舌头 (闪/扇舌頭)

"Break one's tongue"; have one's tongue cut off as a punishment for libel

◆ 背后讲人坏话闪舌头！ 以前我也那么看他，可相互一处，满不错呢。

(From the novel 罪鹰)

Don't badmouth people behind their backs! I used to feel that way about him too, but once I got to know him, it turns out he's a decent guy.

◆ 人家张经理为了把你招进公司得罪了不少人，你还说他成心欺负你，说这种话你也不怕闪着舌头？

Manager Zhang stepped on quite a few toes when he hired you for this company. And you say he's deliberately picking on you! How can you say that in good conscience?

shàng bu liǎo zhuō/tái miàn 上不了桌/台面 (上不了桌/臺面)

"Can't be put on a table"; unpresentable (variation: 摆不上桌面)

◆ "都明，你还真是个怪才！" "雕虫小技，上不了桌面。"

(From the TV series 大赢家)

"Douming, you're really some weird kind of genius!" "Just a few small tricks." [Douming used illegitimate means to gain the upper hand over his competitor.]

◆ "张经理收了我们钱，却把工程包给了别人，咱们可得跟他们好好理论理论。" "这事说出去也摆不上台面，还是算了吧，省得纪检部门找咱们的麻烦。"

"Manager Zhang took our money but gave the contract to someone else. We've got to have it out with him." "However you look at it, this deal is not above-board. Let's forget it. We don't want the Department of Discipline and Inspections giving us grief."

shàng dāo shān xià huǒ hǎi 上刀山下火海

"Climb a mountain of swords, plunge into an ocean of fire"; be willing to risk everything; be determined or prepared to go to any length; put one's life on the line

◆ "你能把合同签回来吗？" "咱是谁啊？我就善于干那种上刀山下火海的事情，你放心吧。"

(From the TV series 大赢家)

Do you think you can land the contract, signed, sealed, and delivered?" "You know me! Life-and-death matters are my specialty. Consider it done!"

◆ "我听你的，你说上刀山我就上刀山，你说下火海我就下火海，绝没二话。"

(From the novel 越轨诉讼)

I'll do whatever you say. I'll walk through flames or jump into the sea if that's what you want. No second thoughts."

shàng fáng jiē/xiān wǎ 上房揭/掀瓦
"Climb up the roof and tear off the tiles"; run wild

◆ 孩子毕竟是孩子，懂得什么好歹？平时一天三顿地给他讲道理，他还备不住要出点事，这回可好，大撒把没人管了，那他还不**上房揭瓦**？
(From the novel 我是你爸爸)
Kids are kids. What do they know? Even when I try to talk some sense into him three times a day, I still never know when he's going to get in trouble. Now that there isn't anyone to supervise him, he'll probably wreck the house.

◆ 这些猴儿崽子，三天不打，**上房掀瓦**。简直要造反了。
(From the novel 慈禧外传)
Those bastards, if you cut them a little slack they run wild. It's practically an uprising!

shàng gǎn zi 上赶子 (上趕子)
Pursue someone to gain favor; cozy up to someone

◆ 他不认我，我还不想**上赶子**高攀呢！
(From the TV series 今生是亲人)
If he's not willing to accept me, I don't intend to court him for the sake of social standing. [The speaker mistakenly thought his biological father was trying to shun him.]

◆ 别人躲都躲不及，你还**上赶子**去找他！
(From the TV series 失乐园)
Everyone else couldn't run away from him fast enough, but you're actually seeking him out! [He is an AIDS patient.]

shàng liáng bú zhèng xià liáng wāi 上梁不正下梁歪
(Proverb) "When the upper beam is not straight, the lower ones will go aslant"; subordinates will follow the example their superiors set; fish begins to stink at the head

◆ "你看你那不省事的样子！""我怎么了，还不是家传，**上梁不正下梁歪**不是？"
(From the short story 我的爱情)
"Look at your behavior!" "What's wrong with my behavior? It runs in the family! I'm just following your example, right?" [A mother and daughter are arguing about whether the daughter is dating at too young an age.]

◆ **上梁不正下梁歪**，他们公司出了那么多贪污犯，问题就出在公司的领导上。
Fish begins to stink at the head. That company of theirs has produced so many embezzlers, and it goes all the way up to the management.

shàng tàor 上套儿 (上套兒)
Set someone up; fall for someone's trap

◆ 我担心我是上了别人的套儿了。
(From the TV series 黑洞)

I'm afraid I was set up.

♦   小陈儿啊，你可得小心点儿，我觉得那个姓王的是在给你上**套儿**呢。
    Xiao Chen, you've got to be careful. I think that Wang guy is trying to set you up.

shàng xīn 上心

"Take to heart"; serious or enthusiastic about something; take an interest in something

♦   亏得同院儿的老街坊们**上心**，这要是搁楼里头，人早没了。
    (From the movie 甲方乙方)
    Lucky the courtyard neighbors kept their eyes open. If this happened in an apartment
    building, he would be dead for sure. [A suicide attempt was averted by neighbors.]

♦   小林这孩子工作吊儿浪当，成家立业的事儿他也不**上心**。
    This Lin kid goofs off at work, and he doesn't give any serious thought to starting a
    family or establishing a career, either.

shàng zéi chuán 上贼船 (上賊船)

"Board a pirate's boat (without a way to get off)"; go on a one-way trip; pass the point of no
return; go down the primrose path

♦   是她，这条母狗把我拉上了**贼船**。
    (From the novel 浮沈商海)
    That bitch was the one who boxed me into this hole. [Referring to an illegal maneuver to
    destroy a business competitor.]

♦   一旦上了**贼船**，想下来就不容易了。
    Once you start down the criminal path, it's hard to return.

shàng zhèn hái kào fù zǐ bīng 上阵还靠父子兵 (上陣還靠父子兵)

"To fight a real battle one needs one's own family army"; at critical moments you can only
count on your own

♦   打虎要亲兄弟，**上阵靠父子兵**。至于殷元中，到底隔了房，只能借
    助，信是信不过的。
    (From the novel 将军镇)
    When it comes to the crunch, blood is thicker than water. You can only trust your own.
    As for Yin Yuanzhong, he's not immediate family. You can use him, but you can't count
    on him.

♦   "你把这几个重要的职位都给了你那几个儿子，这样合适吗？""怕
    什么？俗话说得好，**上阵还靠父子兵**。"
    "You gave all the important positions to your own sons. Is that ethical?" "What's the
    problem? As the saying goes, 'blood is thicker than water.'"

shāo bāo 烧包 (燒包)

"Smug, showing off one's riches"; someone who is smug and showy because of their riches

♦   又是谁**烧包**了，想起请你吃饭？
    (From the TV series 大雪无痕)
    Now who's showing off, inviting you to dinner?

♦   "听说外国一家儿有俩电视。""那是老外有钱，**烧包**！"
    (From the TV series 一年又一年)

"I heard that in foreign countries every home has two TV sets." "That's because foreigners have money to burn. They like to flaunt it!"

shāo gāo xiāng 烧高香 (燒高香)

"Burn incense piously to have a wish granted"; grateful

◆ 要是真这样，我就上庙里**烧高香**去了。

(From the TV series 今生是亲人)

If that's really the case, I'll go to the temple to thank the gods. [The speaker's child changed his/her mind and is now willing to take driving lessons.]

◆ 咱是个粗人，三个饱一个倒，混吃等死，… 混饱肚皮就**烧高香**了。

(From the novel 赝人)

I'm just a simple man. Eat and sleep, and wait for the end. If my stomach is full, I'm grateful.

shào ye 少爷 (少爺)

"Young master"; waiter; service boy; escort (in Taiwan)

◆ **少爷**，送水果进来！

(From the movie 台北爱情故事)

Waiter, bring the fruit!

◆ 由于想赚更多钱，因此决定去酒店当个**少爷**。不但能领小费，还能看漂亮的酒店小姐，工作又不累。

(From the novel 瑶池夜影)

Since he wanted to earn more money, he decided to take a job as an escort in a nightclub. Not only could he get tips, but he could watch the pretty girls working there; and besides, the work wasn't very hard.

shē bu dé hái zi tào bu zháo láng 舍不得孩子套不着狼 (捨不得孩子套不著狼)

(Proverb) "You can't trap the wolf without sacrificing a child"; no pain, no gain

◆ 网站就得拿钱砸，**舍不得孩子套不着狼**啊！

(From the movie 大腕)

A website is just a money pit. You won't get anywhere without putting in some real investment. No pain, no gain.

◆ **舍不得孩子套不住狼**，何况几个西瓜。等咱孩子把事弄成了，咱就不用种地了。

(From the short story 地震)

You've got to be willing to sacrifice to accomplish something. Anyway, we're just talking about a few watermelons. If our kid pulls this off, it's goodbye to working in the fields. [The kid is a watermelon grower who's trying to invent a seismograph.]

shéi chéng xiǎng 谁承想 (誰承想)

see 没成想 méi chéng xiǎng

shéi ràng sb shì... 谁让Sb是... (誰讓Sb是...)

"Whose fault is it that somebody is..."; after all, you are my...

◆ 我给你一股，咱们一块儿干，**谁让你是我兄弟呢**？

(From the TV series 黑洞)

I'll cut you in on it; let's work together. We're buddies, aren't we? [Talking about setting up a company.]

♦ 我是关心你，我怎么不管大街上那些野小子在干吗？ **谁让你是我儿子的。**

(From the movie 顽主)

I'm just worried about you. How come you don't see me worrying about those wild kids on the street? I can't help it if you're my son.

shéi shuō bú shì a 谁说不是啊 (誰說不是啊)

"Who could dispute that?" Isn't it so? (variation: 可不是吗)

♦ "我说你也真够倒霉的，当上〖电影院〗经理了又没好电影了。" **"谁说不是啊！"**

(From the TV series 一年又一年)

"I think you've had bad luck. You finally made it to manager [of a cinema], and suddenly there are no more good movies." "You can say that again."

♦ "你要是早点儿下海，说不定现在已经当大老板了。" **"谁说不是啊！"**

"If you'd gone into business sooner, you'd probably be a big boss by now." "That's for sure."

shéi zhī dào 谁知道 (誰知道)

Who knows; who knew

♦ 这几年厂里效益不好，在厂门口盖了一个饭馆。来了业务在那儿招待，方便，也比在街上吃便宜。盖好了就让销售科承包了。**谁知道，**饭馆弄得不象样子，价钱还挺**宰人**。

(From the novel 大厂)

The factory wasn't doing well the last few years, so they built a restaurant at the entrance. We thought we'd take our business customers to eat there. It'd be convenient and cheaper than eating elsewhere. When it opened we let the Sales Department run it under a subcontract. Who knew, they did a bad job, and the prices are a ripoff.

♦ **谁知道**他一走之后，人也不来， 信也不来。

(From the novel 花国春秋)

No one dreamed that once he left he'd never come back. And not even a letter from him!

shēn zài fú zhōng bù zhī fú 身在福中不知福 (身在福中不知福)

"When you're in the midst of good fortune you don't realize it"; not know when you're well off; not know how good you have it

♦ "我怎么你了？我对你还不够好啊？你在医学院进修那会儿，谁天天接你送你风雨无阻的？不幸福？你是**身在福中不知福**啊你！"

(From the novel 纽约丽人)

"What did I do to you? I didn't treat you well? When you took refresher courses at the medical school, who took you and picked you up every day, rain or shine? You just don't know how lucky you are!

♦   你们这些年轻人啊，条件这么好，一天到晚还总是嫌这嫌那的，真是**身在福中不知福**。

You young people have it so good, and yet you complain all day long. You just don't know how well off you are!

shēn zi bǎnr/gǔr 身子板儿/骨儿 (身子板兒/骨兒)

"Body condition/body and bones"; physical condition

♦   等你们有钱的时候，再还我，嗯？我和老头子**身子骨**还挺硬朗的，这个钱可能好几年都用不着！

(From the novel 苍天有泪)

Pay me back when you have the money, OK? Your dad and I are in pretty good health. We probably won't need the money for several years.

♦   就他那**身子板儿**，不生闲气能活一百岁！

(From the TV series 大宅门)

Since he's in such good health, if he doesn't get worked up about things he could live to a hundred!

shén bù zhī guǐ bù jué 神不知鬼不觉 (神不知鬼不覺)

"Gods don't know, and ghosts don't notice"; absolutely clandestine; under the table

♦   能让你看出来？ 嘁，要的就是**神不知鬼不觉**。

(From the novel 我是你爸爸)

How's it possible for you to tell? No way. The whole idea was to keep it hush-hush.

♦   嘿！ 这小子**神不知鬼不觉**地就娶了个媳妇当上爹了。

Wow! This guy became a husband and a father before anybody knew it.

shén jīng xī xī 神经兮兮 (神經兮兮)

"The appearance of neurosis"; neurotic; weird; kooky

♦   你**神经兮兮**的，瞧你脸色，哭过了。

(From the novel 都市危情)

You look weird. Look at your face; you've been crying.

♦   她一天到晚**神经兮兮**的，不是说要给这个看病就是要给那个看病。"

(From the novel 混在媒体)

She always seems flaky, offering medical examinations to anyone she sees.

shén me fēngr bǎ nǐ gěi chuī lái le 什么风儿把你给吹来了 (什麼風兒把你給吹來了)

"What wind blew/brought you here?" Why are you here?

♦   田大哥，**什么风把您给吹来了**？

(虚拟剧《胖头鱼餐厅》)

Brother Tian, why are you here?

♦   我当是谁呢？原来是杨老弟。稀客呀稀客！ **哪一阵风把你刮来的**？

(From the novel 庚子风云)

What do you know! Turns out it's you, my old friend Yang. A rare visitor indeed! What brought you here?

shēng fen 生分

Become distant or estranged

♦   多上你二哥那儿走走，老不来往，一家人就生分了。

(From the novel 都市危情)

Call on your second brother a bit more often. Even family members can become strangers if they never see each other.

♦   "哎，大编剧。""别这么叫，叫同志。""同志？不，不能这么叫，生分。""那叫哥们儿。"

(From the TV drama script 爱你没商量)

"Hey, hot-shot scriptwriter." "Please don't call me that. Call me comrade." "Comrade? I can't call you that; it sounds so distant." "Well, call me buddy, then."

shēng mǐ zhǔ chéng shú fàn le 生米煮成熟饭了 (生米煮成熟飯了)

"Raw rice has been cooked"; what's done can't be undone; the die is cast

♦   我在想是不是应该把生米煮成熟饭。

(From the movie 大腕)

I was wondering if we should go ahead and set it in stone.

♦   不提他们了，生米已经煮成熟饭了。

(From the TV series 一年又一年)

Let's not mention them. What's done is done. [The speaker is unhappy with his son's marriage.]

shěng de 省得

Spare someone the trouble of; so as to avoid

♦   莫厂长的习惯，只要一打官腔，眼睛就看着别处，省得别人尴尬自己也尴尬。

(From the novel 魔鬼与天使)

The factory director, Mr. Mo, used to look aside whenever he had to talk like an official, in order to avoid embarrassing his listeners and himself.

♦   明天咱们也买辆车，省得那家伙总在我面前臭显。

Let's buy a car too tomorrow, to stop that jerk from showing off in front of me.

shěng yóur de dēng 省油儿的灯 (省油兒的燈)

"A lamp that burns less kerosene"; someone who's not easy to deal with (usually used with a negative)

♦   您这闺女，赶快抓空儿修理吧，这长大了，可不是一盏省油儿的灯啊！

(From the TV series 北京女人)

About this daughter of yours, you'd better hurry and nip the problem in the bud. When she grows up she's going to be a real handful. [The girl wants to start dating at the age of ten.]

♦ 你以为他是**省油的灯**？ 看吧！ 你要是不分给他一套房子他能把你吃了！

You think he's a pushover? You'll find out! If you don't assign him an apartment, he'll chew you up and spit out the pieces.

shī zi dà kāi kǒu/kāi dà kǒu 狮子大开口/开大口 (獅子大開口/開大口)

"The lion's mouth is wide open"; ask for too much; have insatiable demands; greedy

♦ 你别狮子大开口啊！

(From the TV series 祥符春秋)

Please don't go overboard with your demands.

♦ 他其实是来拉广告的，三千以内你就跟他定吧，**狮子开大口**，免谈。

(From the short story 爱又如何)

Actually he came to sell advertising slots. If it's under three thousand you can go ahead and sign; but if his prices are out of line, forget it.

shī zi duō le bù yǎo rén 虱子多了不咬人 (蝨子多了不咬人)

"When there are many lice, you don't feel the bite"; after enough pinpricks, you cease to feel it; after a while you don't notice it

♦ 老顾那边儿，天天五六个电话，**虱子多了不咬人**，我都习惯了。

(From the TV series 贫嘴张大民的幸福生活)

I get five or six calls a day from Lao Gu. After a while, it makes no impression on me. I've gotten used to it. [Lao Gu is calling to get a loan paid back.]

♦ 好在生活中几乎没有让人快乐的事儿，在失意中生活惯了，"**虱子多了不咬**，账多了不愁"，否则我该怎么办呢？

(From the novel 走向混沌)

Luckily, life has never been a bed of roses for me anyway, so being disappointed is nothing new to me. If you get beaten up often enough, nothing gets you down, and once your debts are large enough you stop worrying about them. Well, what else can I do?

shí bù qǐ gèr/ná bù chéng gèr 拾不起个儿/拿不成个儿 (拾不起個兒/拿不成個兒)

"Something you can't take or pick up in one piece"; cannot be whole or complete

♦ 钱满天觉得虽然胸口不那么憋闷了，但浑身酸痛酸痛的**拾不起个来**，只能瘫了一般躺着。

(From the novel 多彩的乡村)

Qian Mantian didn't feel he was suffocating anymore, but his whole body ached so that he thought he'd come apart if he stood up. So he just lay there as if paralyzed.

♦ 可别提了，一住进省医院我这身子就**拿不成个儿**了，躺着都累得慌，就好象看见鬼门关了，黑乎乎的冒凉风啊！

(From the novel 刘老根)

Don't even talk about it! As soon as I checked into the provincial hospital I thought my body was coming apart; I felt exhausted even when I lay down. It was as if the gates of hell had opened and gusts of cold wind were blowing right at me.

shí bu shí 时不时 (時不時)

From time to time; now and then

♦ 虽说成天跟著书记段长鞍前马后地跑，**时不时**还挨一顿熊，可大家都很融洽。

(From the short story 笔杆儿们)

Even though they run themselves ragged for the party secretaries and section chiefs all day long and still get told off sometimes, everybody gets along fine. [Describing people who work as secretaries for higher-ups.]

♦ 我是撒谎大王。撒的谎天衣无缝。**时不时**的，一天几次，事先想好或不假思索，出于本能或不顾羞耻，我瞪着又圆又亮的眼睛撒谎。

(From the novel 说谎的女人)

I'm the queen of lies. My lies are seamless. I lie often, several times a day. Whether premeditated or improvised, out of instinct or out of shamelessness, I just tell my lies with my big bright eyes open and without a blink.

shí sān diǎn 十三点 (十三點)

(Shanghai dialect) "Thirteen points"; an immature person; a nutcase; flighty

♦ 她不是十三点，是不拘小节，根本没想到男女有别。

(From the novel 戏子)

She's not flaky; she just doesn't pay attention to little things. She never thought about the difference between the sexes. [She entered a men's dormitory room without knocking.]

♦ 那个十三点阿钟，又在外面瞎说了。

(From TV series 涉外保姆)

That nutcase Ah Zhong is shooting off her mouth to outsiders again.

shí wén duàn zìr 识文断字儿 (識文斷字兒)

"Able to read and write"; literate; educated

♦ 秀秀没上过学，但自小对识文断字的人有好感。

(From the novel 乡村教师)

Xiuxiu never went to school, but from an early age she has had this liking for people who could read and write.

♦ 你是个识文断字儿的人，做事怎么这么不讲道理？

You're an educated man; how come you're so unreasonable?

shí xiàng 识相 (識相)

(Shanghai dialect) "read faces"; recognize other people's reactions and know when to stop; behave appropriately

♦ "识相点。" 老头子挑着寿眉说："别找不自在。"

(From the novel 一点儿正经没有)

"Behave yourself," the old man said, raising his shaggy eyebrows. "Don't ask for trouble." [寿眉: long and bushy eyebrows, considered a sign of longevity]

♦ 都怪我不识相，打扰你们了。

(From the TV series 编辑部的故事)

Sorry I misunderstood the situation and disturbed you all.

shǐ bù de 使不得

"Cannot be used"; useless; does not work; inappropriate; a bad idea; don't (do something)

♦ 使不得，皇上使不得呀！

(From the novel 顺治皇帝)
> Please don't. Your majesty, please don't do it. [A eunuch is trying to stop a child emperor from sleeping in the same bed with his mother.]

♦ 啊哟住手，这可使不得！ 这狗是老板的宠物，你打它不是炒自己的鱿鱼吗？

> Oh my God, stop it! You can't do this! This dog is the boss's pet. If you hit it, aren't you sure to get sacked?

shǐ huài 使坏 (使壞)

"Use dirty tricks"; play dirty tricks; sabotage

♦ 我看他是瞄上你了，你可别吃了他的亏，你跟我们不一样，你可是贵如千金的黄花闺女，该敲就狠狠地敲他，可是也要多留一万个心眼，防着他使坏。

(From the novel 越轨诉讼)
> I think he's got his eye on you. Don't let him take advantage of you. You're not like us. You're a young lady, precious as gold. When you have the chance, get as much as you can out of him. But you've also got to be really careful, in case he means you harm.

♦ 你这家伙，老给我使坏，今天是和你算总帐的时候了！

> You son of bitch, you're always playing dirty tricks on me. Today it's time to settle the score.

shǐ xìng zi 使性子

"Follow the dictate of one's temperament"; headstrong and stubborn; have a tantrum

♦ 虽然你爱使个小性子，你还是能让我们放心的。

(From the TV series 大雪无痕)
> Even though you can be temperamental, by and large we're not too worried about you.

♦ 你都十七了，还老使性子，爸怎么放心呢？

(From the TV series 失乐园)
> You're almost seventeen and you still throw temper tantrums. I'm your father; how could I not worry?

shì...de tiān xià 是…的天下

"Is the kingdom of…"; it is…that reigns or dominates…

♦ 现在是生猛海鲜美国芹菜橄榄菜的天下，谁还会来卖这个？

(From the short story 家庭风景二十章)

What's in now is live seafood, American celery, and rapini [a leafy green vegetable]. Who wants to sell something like this? [Referring to a kind of pickled vegetable.]

◆ 现在的音乐市场是流行歌曲**的天下**，你的那些古典玩意不吃香了。

Pop songs rule the music market these days. Your classical stuff is no longer in.

shì jie 世界

"World"; the whole wide world; all over

◆ 你开个破"二一二"（国产老式吉普车）绕**世界**转悠，人家不罚你罚谁啊？

(From the TV series 贫嘴张大民的幸福生活)

You rode that broken 212 [a brand of outdated, domestically made jeep] all over town. And you were surprised that you got a ticket?

◆ 可**世界**您放眼望去，冷眼向洋，人是不少，好的也有，可**归齐包圆**哪个不是人生爹妈养的？

(From the TV series 编辑部的故事)

Look at the world objectively. There are plenty of people and some of them are decent. But when all is said and done, which of them was not born of a woman and raised by a father and mother?

shì luó zi shì mǎ lā chu lai liù liu 是骡子是马拉出来溜溜 (是騾子是馬拉出來溜溜)

"Whether it's a mule or a horse, bring it out and put it through its paces"; action speaks louder than words; everything has to pass muster

◆ 训练两天，是骡子是马拉出来溜溜。

(From the TV series 祥符春秋)

Train them for two days, and see if they've got the stuff. [Referring to a process of admitting students.]

◆ **是骡子是马拉出来溜溜**，功夫不好就好好练！

(From the novel 天桥演义)

You've got to demonstrate your skills. And if you're not up to it, you have to practice harder.

shìr mā 事儿妈 (事兒媽)

"The mother of all (trifling) matters"; meddler

◆ 陶涛：（几分撒娇）你怎么那么事多呀！ 孙凯：你刚知道哇？ 我就是一**事儿妈**！

(From the TV drama script 朗朗星空)

Taotao (flirtatiously): "How come you're involved in so many things!" Sun Kai: "You only just found out? I'm the king of busybodies!"

◆ 芝麻大个巡按天下己任，**事儿妈**似的！ 蠢驴！

(From the novel 血晨)

A two-bit inspector who thinks everything under the sun is his business! What a snoop! Jackass!

shìr shìr de 事儿事儿的 (事兒事兒的)

Posing as someone important; have an air of importance; posing and meddling

◆　嗨！　事儿事儿的，跟真的似的！

    (From the TV series 贫嘴张大民的幸福生活)

       Look! He thinks he's really something! As if he's for real! [Complaining about a former apprentice who is now a manager.]

◆　李刚这人我实在看不惯，也不是领导，却总是**事儿事儿的**，好象别人都不如他。

       I can't stand the sight of Li Gang. He's not in charge of anything but he's so pompous, as if he's better than everyone else.

shǒu dào qín lái 手到擒来 (手到擒來)

"Stretch out your hand, and you've captured your man"; as easy as lifting one's finger; a piece of cake

◆　王爷，开封府那帮人看起来挺吓人，其实是一群酒囊饭袋，成不了事的，邓车一定能够**手到擒来**。

    (From the novel 包青天)

       Prince, those guys from Kaifeng Prefecture only look intimidating. Actually, they're a bunch of good-for-nothings. They're not going to accomplish anything. Deng Che can take care of them with one hand tied behind his back.

◆　"您能不能给我介绍个广告公司？" "这你算找对人了，**手到擒来**的事儿。"

       "Do you think you can find me an advertising company?" "You came to the right person. For me it's a piece of cake."

shǒu tóur 手头儿 (手頭兒)

"At hand or on hand;" financial condition at the moment

◆　眼下，**手头**实在太紧了。

    (From the TV series 古船、女人和网)

       Right now, things are tight. [There is no money available to buy equipment.]

◆　我**手头**太紧了，你再容我两个月，把这批货给倒腾出去。

    (From the TV series 贫嘴张大民的幸福生活)

       I'm strapped for cash right now. Give me two more months to get this batch of goods sold.

shǒu xīn shǒu bèi dōu shì ròu 手心手背都是肉

"The palm and the back of the hand are both (one's own) flesh"; both are equally important; it hurts to give up either

◆　嗨，老大老二都是我的儿子，**手心手背都是肉**嘛，我怎么会有偏心眼儿？

    (From the novel 魔鬼与天使)

Look, my first and second sons are both my children. They're both my flesh and blood. How can I favor one of them?

♦ 说实话，**手心手背都是肉**，我真不舍得把咱们的计算机部卖掉来维持房地产的运营，可有什么办法呢？ 咱们的资金只够一头儿啊！

To tell the truth, they're equally important to us. I really hate to sell the computer division in order to keep the real estate business going. But what choice do we have? We've only got enough capital for one of them.

shǒu yì cháo/shǒu cháo 手艺潮/手潮 (手藝潮/手潮)

"Damp skills/damp hand"; not skilled enough; green

♦ 他还跟踪了那家伙一段。可惜他刚学会开车**手太潮**，跟不上，半路给丢了。

(From the novel 永不瞑目)

He was tailing that guy for awhile. Unfortunately he'd just learned to drive and wasn't too good at it. He couldn't keep up and lost him after a bit.

♦ 你说老李干了三十多年木匠了，我说他**手艺有点儿潮**。

You told me Lao Li had been a carpenter for over thirty years. I'd say he's new at it.

shòu hóu 瘦猴

"Skinny monkey"; skinny as a monkey

♦ 没有水的农业就象没有娘的孩子，有了娘，这个娘也没有奶子，有了奶子，这个奶子也是个瞎奶子，没有奶水，孩子活不了，活了也象那个**瘦猴**。

(From the novel 透明的红萝卜)

Farming without water is like a child without a mother. Or if it has a mother, she has no breasts. Or if she does have breasts, they're dry. Without milk, the child can't live. Or if it lives, it looks like a little skeleton.

♦ 结婚前他跟**瘦猴**似的，现在可好了，躺着比站着还高。

He was as skinny as a rail before he got married. Now, look at him! He's taller lying down than standing up.]

shòu lèi le 受累了

Shoulder too much work or too many burdens

♦ "今天让你**受累了**，真有点过意不去。" "这是什么话呀，你来了你是客人，我总要尽地主之宜的呀。"

(From the short story 爱在远方)

"I put you to too much trouble. I'm really sorry." "Don't talk like that; you're a guest. I was just doing what any host does."

♦ "许老，让您**受累了**。" "没什么，这是我应该做的。"

"Lao Xu, sorry we laid so much on you." "It's nothing; I only did what I was supposed to do."

shòu yáng zuì 受洋罪

"Endure hardship of an alien kind"; go through an unfamiliar and consequently painful experience; a pain in the butt

♦ "搬楼房去不是挺好的吗？" "不习惯，也不愿意受那份儿洋罪。"

(From the TV drama 眷恋胡同)

"Wouldn't it be better to move to an apartment building?" "I can't get used to it, and I won't put up with that kind of change." [Moving from a house to a high-rise apartment building.]

♦ 咱们都老夫老妻的了，还过什么情人节啊？ **受这份洋罪！**

(From the TV series 一年又一年)

We've been married forever. What's the point of celebrating Valentine's Day? What a pain in the butt!

shòu sǐ de luò tuo bǐ mǎ dà 瘦死的骆驼比马大 (瘦死的駱駝比馬大)

(Proverb) "A starving camel is still bigger than a horse"; a bankrupt millionaire is still richer than a street beggar

♦ "你要多少钱？""瘦死的骆驼比马大，钱对我根本不是问题。"

(From the TV series 黑冰)

"How much money do you want?" "A bankrupt millionaire is still richer than a street beggar. I'm not at all here for money."

♦ "你根本没有盖大楼的实力！""这些年我虽然没做什么大项目，但是**瘦死的骆驼比马大**，你这不是**挤兑**我吗？"

(From the TV series 天堂鸟)

"You don't have the capacity to put up a large building." "It's true I haven't done a major project in the past few years, but a wounded lion is still a lion. Are you trying to put me down?"

shǔ huáng huā yú de 属黄花鱼的 (屬黃花魚的)

"Born in the year of the yellow croaker" (A yellow croaker is a fish symbolizing slipperiness and sneakiness. Here it is used satirically in place of a zodiacal animal for the year of one's birth.)

♦ 他是**属黄花鱼的**，只能溜边。

(From the novel 连环套)

He was born under the sign of the eel—good for nothing but slipping away. [He sneaked away when confronted by stronger kung-fu masters.]

♦ 我说你是**属黄花鱼的**？ 怎么一出点儿事就想溜啊？

I think you're an eel. The moment anything bad happens, you slip away.

shǔ luo 数落 (數落)

"Enumerate someone's wrongdoings"; scold; put someone down

♦ 我哗啦一声就把鱼网搋倒了，又**没鼻子没脸**地把他一顿**数落**。

(From the TV series 古船、女人和网)

With a swoosh, I yanked the fishnet down, and without sparing any words I really let him have it.

♦ 你就会**数落**人，有本事你自己干出个样儿来给我们瞧瞧。

The only thing you're good at is criticizing others. If you've got any ability, do something, and show us!

shuǎ huā zhāor 耍花招儿 (耍花招兒)

"Pull a deceptive move in a martial arts fight"; play a trick

♦ 郭丽冷冷地看着他，琢磨着他又**耍什么花招**。

(From the TV drama script 朗朗星空)

Guo Li was staring at him coldly, wondering what trick he was going to pull next.

♦ 在我面前**耍花招儿**？ 你还嫩了点儿。

Play tricks on me? You're still too green.

shuǎ pín zuǐ 耍贫嘴 (耍貧嘴)

"Play with one's lips/tongue"; garrulous; glib

♦ "妈妈，你的教诲我时刻记在心里。" "别跟我**耍贫嘴**，妈的话是当真的。"

(From the TV series 问问你的心)

"Mom, I will always keep your teachings in my heart and remember them." "Stop running off at the mouth. I was serious."

♦ 你个狗东西就知道**贫嘴**！你在我**眼皮底**下待了五年，你有多深水，我想还能看个八九**不离十**。要是没把握考到良好以上，**趁早**算了吧。

(From the novel 突出重围)

You asshole, you sure know how to talk a good game. I've observed you closely for five years now, and nine times out of ten I could say how much you know ["how much water you hold"]. If you're not sure you can get a B or better on the exam, give it up before it's too late.

shuǎ xiǎo hái zi pí qi 耍小孩子脾气 (耍小孩子脾氣)

"Act like a child"; act irrationally or stubbornly

♦ "好了，别**耍小孩子脾气**了，快2点了，回去吧。" 我帮她擦了擦脸，亲了一下她额头。"走吧，我送你。" 我拥着她站起来。

(From the short story 人生如梦，洗洗睡吧)

"OK. Don't act like a child. It's almost two o'clock in the morning. Please go home." I wiped her face and kissed her on the forehead, "Let's go. I'll take you." I helped her stand up. [A lover is reluctant to leave.]

♦ 二十几的人了，怎么还**耍小孩子脾气**？

You're over twenty already: how come you still act like a baby?

shuǎ xīn yǎnr 耍心眼儿 (耍心眼兒)

Play mind tricks or use secret schemes for personal gain or to outsmart others; play dishonest tricks

♦ 以前我可没少帮你，事情到我头上你跟我**耍心眼儿**？

(From the novel 黑学)

I've helped you a lot in the past. Now that I need help, how come all I get is clever excuses?

♦ 在爸爸面前你就别**耍心眼儿**了，到底闯了什么祸赶快说出来。

Don't try to be smart with your old man. Just tell me what kind of trouble you're in.

shuǎ zuǐ pí zi 耍嘴皮子

"Play with one's lips"; engage in empty talk to show off or to get one's way; pay lip service

♦ 我就不出来，我不愿意和你们这些**耍嘴皮子**的律师打交道。

(From the TV series 红色康乃馨)

Forget it, I'm not coming out. I don't want to deal with you fast-talking lawyers.

♦ 你得学一个硬碰硬的专业，不要学那些耍嘴皮子的东西。

Study some solid profession. Don't waste your time on anything that's just talk.

shuǎi liē zi 甩咧子

Throw someone a dirty look; show displeasure; sulk

♦ 喝就喝吧，甩什么斜咧子啊？

(From the TV series 其实男人最辛苦)

If you want to eat, eat. What's with all the sulking? [A husband made chicken broth for his wife who had just given birth. She was upset that he gave some of the broth to other women.]

♦ 你工作一共没几天，自己数数，甩了几回咧子了？

You've only been working here a few days, but count them yourself—how many times have you had the sulks?

shuǎi shǒu zhǎng guì 甩手掌柜 (甩手掌櫃)

"Hands-off manager"; one who gives employees a free hand

♦ 你倒是甩手掌柜做惯了。这么大一片店，扔给我，自家出去鬼混。

(From the novel 南方有嘉木)

Seems you're used to hands-off management. Such a big store, and you leave it all in my hands while you go out and fool around.

♦ 你这位老同志，在家一定是甩手掌柜吧？ 有你这么买东西的吗？

(From the TV series 大赢家)

"Comrade, old sir, I guess you don't help around the house much! I've never seen anyone shop like this before. [An old man is buying four different brands of milk at the store.]

shuài dāi le 帅呆了 (帥呆了)

"Drop-dead handsome"; gorgeous

♦ 你穿上这身大衣，简直是帅呆了！

(From the TV series 大雪无痕)

With this coat on, you look gorgeous!

♦ 你的这张照片照得真不错，帅呆了，不知道会迷倒多少年轻女孩儿。

This is really a good photo of you. Drop-dead handsome. No telling how many young girls will get a crush on you.

Shuàn 涮

"Dip (like sliced mutton) in a hotpot"; con; trick; rip off

♦ 让人家涮了一道，挺可惜的。

(From the TV series 贫嘴张大民的幸福生活)

She let someone con her; it's really a shame! [The speaker's sister was conned by a man and lost her virginity.]

♦ 他让那女的给涮了，又送钻石戒指，又买裘皮大衣，结果人家跟别的男人结婚了。

He was taken for a ride by that woman. He gave her a diamond ring, he bought her a fur coat, and she ended up marrying someone else.

shuāng dǎ le 霜打了

"Struck by frost"; withered; spiritless

♦ 怎么了？都跟**霜打了**似的？

(From the TV series 大雪无痕)

What's up? How come you all look like someone just died?

♦ 我说你啊，刚才还活蹦乱跳的，这会儿怎么跟**霜打了**似的？

You're impossible! A minute ago you were jumping around. How come you're suddenly bummed out?

shuǐ fèn 水分

"Moisture content"; water-diluted product or false information; fake or false element; exaggeration

♦ 我只是大华的法律顾问，根据大华方面提供的信息和资料考察是否符合法律法规。但是如果这些信息资料本身就掺杂着**水分**，甚至弄虚作假，那与本人无关。

(From the TV series 红色康乃馨)

I'm only the legal counsel of Dahua Company; my job is to check that Dahua provides information and data in accordance with the law and regulations. But if the information and data themselves are false or fraudulent, that has nothing to do with me.

♦ 现在连外行都看得出新星公司的经营状况糟透了，可你们却说他们的营业额不断上升，我觉得你们的调查报告里**水分**太大了。

shuǐ huò 水货 (水貨)

Smuggled goods

♦ "我的价比他们低百分之二十。""**水货**？""我从来不卖**水货**。"

(From the TV series 手心手背)

"My price is twenty percent lower than theirs." "Smuggled goods?" "I never sell smuggled goods."

♦ **不得了了**！他们的商店卖**水货**，他被警察抓走了！

Oh, my God! Their store sold smuggled goods, and the police have arrested them.

shùn gānr pá 顺竿儿爬 (順竿兒爬)

"Climb the pole"; ride someone's coattails; suck up to superiors; upward mobility

♦ 现在不偷不抢，不顺着竿子往上**爬**，就别想发财。

(From the novel 锁链，是柔软的)

Nowadays if you don't steal or rob, or if you don't ride someone's coattails, you'll never get rich.

◆ 那几个家伙就是顺竿儿爬，只要把姓王的解决了他们准得散伙。

Those guys only do other people's bidding. If we bring down that Wang guy, the whole gang will fall apart.

shùn yǎn 顺眼 (順眼)

"Easy on the eye"; not a welcome sight; a thorn in one's side (usually used with a negative)

◆ 经过大一一年的了解与摩擦，彼此之间由于新鲜和神秘而产生的友谊和尊敬消失殆尽了，谁看谁都不**顺眼**，谁也不服谁，暗地里都**较着劲**，吃饭, 起床, 自习, 活动, 工作谁也不愿意落在谁后面。

(From the novel 大学鲁鱼)

After a freshman year of acquaintance and some friction, their friendship and respect for each other, based on novelty and mystery, completely disappeared. Now they hate the sight of each other, and they have no more mutual respect. They are secretly competing in everything they do—eating, getting out of bed, studying, extra-curricula activities, and work; neither wants to lag behind the other.

◆ 我今天怎么了这是，你看我什么都不**顺眼**？

(From the TV series 失乐园)

What did I do wrong today? Why can't you stand the sight of me?

shuō bái le 说白了 (說白了)

"Put it plainly"; simply put; tell it like it is; call a spade a spade

◆ 丈夫："红花还得绿叶扶。"妻子："还绿叶呢！ **说白了**，跑龙套的！"

(From the TV series 五彩戏娃)

Husband: "Red flowers need green leaves to set them off." Wife: "A green leaf? Let's be honest, you're nothing but a spear-carrier." [The husband thinks his supporting role in a theatrical troupe is important, but his wife disagrees.]

◆ 把话**说白了**吧，您今天拿不出二十万块钱来就别想走了。

Let me spell it out for you. You're not going to leave here today unless you cough up twenty grand.

shuō Cáo Cao Cáo Cao dào 说曹操曹操到 (說曹操曹操到)

"Speak of Cao Cao and there he is"; speak of the devil (曹操: a politician, military strategist, and poet who lived from 155-220)

◆ **说曹操曹操到**，这位就是我刚才说的名角，我们团长。

(From the TV series 五彩戏娃)

Speak of the devil! This is the star I was talking about just now, the director of our theatrical troupe.

♦ 哟，**说曹操曹操就到了**，你不是问我谁是王主任吗？ 刚进来的就是。
Wow, speak of the devil! Didn't you ask me who Director Wang is? Well, he's the one that just walked in.

shuō de bǐ chàng de hái hǎo tīng 说得/的比唱得还好听 (說得/的比唱得還好聽)

"He talks more euphoniously than he sings"/"talking that sounds better than singing"; sweet-talk; talk a good game

♦ "我这不是为你么？你老一个人打光棍儿，我也不落忍。" "**说的比唱的还好听**，我看你是没人管着勒着难受，这责任我负得起来。"
(From the novel 我是你爸爸)
"It's all for your sake, right? I didn't have the heart to see you stay a bachelor for ever." "You talk a good game, but I think you just can't stand it if you're not under someone's thumb. I guess I'll just have to take on that responsibility."

♦ "过几天等生意做大了我给你在郊区买个别墅。" "得了吧你，**说得比唱得还好听**。"
"Wait a couple of days until my business picks up, and I'll buy you a house in the suburbs." "Come off it. Talk is cheap."

shuō de dào qīng qiao 说得倒轻巧 (說得倒輕巧)

It's easy to say; it's easier said than done

♦ "十年了！" "就当是一场恶梦吧。" "你**说得倒轻巧**，一个人一辈子有几个十年啊！"
(From the TV series 一年又一年)
"It's been ten years!" "Just look at it as a bad dream." "Easy for you to say! How many decades do you get in a lifetime?"

♦ "这首诗有什么难翻的？" "**说得轻巧**！ 你试试！"
"What's so hard about translating this poem?" "It's easier said than done. Try it yourself!"

shuō de guò qu 说得过去 (說得過去)

"Passable, so to speak"; justifiable; OK; not too bad

♦ 咱哥们儿对朋友真的**说得过去**。
(From the TV series 贫嘴张大民的幸福生活)
I don't really treat my friends too badly.

♦ "最近他的表现怎么样？" "还**说得过去**。"
"How's his performance lately?" "OK, I'd say."

shuō de shì 说的是 (說的是)

"That's right"; that it is; indeed; you said it!

♦ "为什么天下有情人都不能聚在一起啊？" "**说的是啊**！"
(From the TV series 手心手背)

"Why can't all the lovers in the world just be together?" "You said it!"

♦ "既然炒股来钱来得快，咱们不如也炒上一把。""说的也是，经营电子产品太辛苦，风险也不比炒股小。"

Since you can make money real fast in stocks, why don't we take a flyer in the market?"
"You're right. Dealing in electronics is tough and the risks aren't any less than in the stock market."

shuō huàr 说话儿 (說話兒)

"As we speak"; immediately; right away

♦ 我爸跟他们经理说话儿就回来了。

(From the TV series 一年又一年)

Their manager and my dad will be back right away.

♦ 说话儿就到春节了，有什么好电影没有？

(From the TV series 一年又一年)

Spring Festival's right around the corner. Are there any good movies?

shuō jù bú zhòng tīng de huà 说句不中听的话 (說句不中聽的話)

"Say something not pleasing to the ear"; This is not what you want to hear, but…; I'm sorry to say this, but…

♦ 说句不中听的话，他们既然敢做这第一回，说不定还会有第二回的。

(From the novel 红嘴绿鹦鹉)

I know this isn't what you want to hear, but since they had the guts to do it once, they may very well do it a second time.

♦ 说句不中听的话，你现在这个男朋友不像是个老实人。

Excuse me for saying so, but this boyfriend of yours doesn't look like an honest guy to me.

shuō jù tāo xīn wō zi de huà 说句掏心窝子的话 (說句掏心窩子的話)

"Say something that reveals the heart"; honestly; the truth is…

♦ 你少来这套吧！ 跟你说句掏心窝子的话，我信不过你！

(From the TV series 大宅门)

Enough of that! I'm going to level with you: I don't trust you!

♦ 说句掏心窝子的话，我真不愿意挣这种亏心钱，可是公司上上下下几十口子还指着我吃饭呢，没有办法啊！

To tell the truth, I'd rather not make money in a way that offends my conscience. But in this company there are dozens of mouths looking to me for food. I have no choice!

shuō le suàn 说了算 (說了算)

"Speak and it's done"; it's up to… the person who calls the shots

♦ 搬不搬家不能你说了算，我还是一家之主呢。你也得听听我的。

(From the short story 环绕我们的房子)

It's not just up to you whether we move or not. I'm a senior member of the family too. You must hear what I have to say.

♦ 昨天张经理在电话里说没问题，今天李主任又说还要研究研究，你们这儿到底谁**说了算**？

Yesterday Manager Zhang said on the phone there was no problem. But today Director Li said that we had to consider it further. Just who is it who calls the shots with you guys?

shuō nàr qù le 说哪儿去了 (說哪兒去了)

"Why do you say that?" What are you talking about? You're completely mistaken.

♦ "你给我站住！ 方晓玉！ 你这儿憋什么主意呢？" "没有啊！ 你**说哪儿去了**？"

(From the TV series 北京女人)

"Stop right there! Fang Xiaoyu! What schemes are you hatching?" "Nothing! What are you talking about?"

♦ "你要是离婚了孩子归谁呢？" "你**说哪去了**？我和他只是吵了一架，根本没想过跟他离婚。"

"Who gets custody of the child if you divorce?" "How did you ever get that idea? He and I just had one fight. Divorce never crossed my mind."

shuō nǐ...ba nǐ hái... 说你...吧 你还... (說你...吧 你還)

I told you...but you wouldn't listen

♦ 唉，**说你**胡涂，**你还**不乐意听！

(From the novel 黑色念珠)

Too bad! Didn't I say you were mixed up? But you wouldn't listen!

♦ **说你**傻吧**你还**不承认。看看，你都干了些什么！

I told you it was foolish but you wouldn't admit it. Now look what you did!

shuō nǐ ké sòu nǐ hái jiù chuǎn shang le/shuō nǐ pàng nǐ jiù chuǎn 说你咳嗽你还就喘上了/说你胖你就喘 (說你咳嗽你還就喘上了/說你胖你就喘)

"Someone says you have a cough and you start gasping right away/someone says you're fat and you start panting right away"; stop stretching my point; don't push it

♦ "你干得挺好。" "我啊，什么干得不好？" "别**说你胖你就喘**。"

(From the TV series 一年又一年)

"You did a pretty good job." "Me? Is there anything I don't do well?" "Don't push it."

◆　"小刘啊，有困难就言语啊！""头儿，我最近手头的确很紧，简直都揭不开锅了。""嘿，**说你咳嗽你还就喘上了**！"

"Xiao Liu, just let me know if you have any problems." "Well, Chief, I'm pretty strapped for cash lately. I don't know where my next meal is coming from." "Hey, don't push your luck!"

shuō nǐ shénme hǎo a 说你什么好啊 (說你什麼好啊)

"What do you want me to say about you?" I don't know what to say about you; what am I supposed to do with you?

◆　姐，让我**说你什么好啊**。姐夫干的是生意，生意场上的事离得开吃喝玩乐吗？

(From the short story 大厂)

Sis, what can I tell you? My brother-in-law [your husband] is a businessman. Business operations require a little wining and dining and entertainment.

◆　朱进啊朱进，让我**说你什么好呢**？你这个人岗位换了十几个，到哪儿都**捅漏子**，干不来，你除了能贡献点儿农田肥料还能干什么？

(From the TV series 大赢家)

Zhu Jin, my friend, what can I say about you? You've changed jobs a dozen times or more. At every single place, you weren't up to the job and left a mess behind you. What good are you, besides for churning out shit to fertilize the fields?

shuō shìr 说事儿 (說事兒)

"Use something as a talking point"; make a case out of something; use something as an excuse

◆　他〖前夫〗就是不能接受含青有男朋友，又知道自己无权干涉，只有拿孩子**说事**。

(From the novel 浮沈商海)

It's just hard for him [ex-husband] to accept that Hanqing has a boyfriend. He knows he has no right to interfere, so he uses their child as a pretext.

◆　"我们把工程给了他们公司是因为他们的工人比你们多四倍。""甭拿人多**说事儿**。我们的机械设备比他们先进多了！"

"We gave them the project because they have four times as many workers as you do." "Please don't use the workforce as an excuse. Our machinery is much more advanced than theirs."

shuō shùn zuǐ le 说顺嘴了 (說順嘴了)

"Speak out of habit"; not control one's speech

◆　"哎，你怎么这么粗野？""对不起，老马，我**说顺嘴了**，可**话糙理不糙**。"

(From the novel 我是你爸爸)

"Oh, why are you being so rude?" "I'm sorry, Lao Ma, it's just a habit of speaking. The expression is coarse, but the idea is not."

♦   "不是跟你说了吗？在这儿不能叫我杜哥，要叫我杜总。" "对不起，杜总，我刚才**说顺嘴**了。"

"Didn't I tell you before? You can't call me Brother Du here! You have to call me General Manager Du." "Sorry, General Manager Du, I just spoke out of habit."

shuō xià dà tiān/shuō pò tiān qù 说下大天/说破天去 (說下大天/說破天去)

"You can talk until the sky falls down/apart"; you can talk until you're blue in the face

♦   **说下大天来**，胳膊也拧不过大腿，你是当官的我是玩轮子的，不听你的不行，自己认倒霉吧！

(From the novel 赤橙黄绿青蓝紫)

Doesn't matter what I say; little guys can't take on big ones. You're a government official and I'm just a driver. If I don't listen to you I'm in trouble. That's just my luck.

♦   没错，**说破天去**，我也就是抗震的后妈。

(From the TV series 今生是亲人)

That's right. You can talk until you're blue in the face, but I'm still only Kangzhen's stepmother.

shuō xián huà 说闲话 (說閒話)

"Talk idly"; gossip

♦   过去跟你说你都不听，怕人**说闲话**，今天这是怎么了？

(From the TV series 花非花)

You wouldn't listen when I talked to you about it before; you were afraid people would gossip. So what's changed now?

♦   自从那次在画室中对张宇吐露心声之后，沈奕就没有来过这里。因为张宇担心会有人**说闲话**。

(From the novel 爱在边缘)

After he confessed his love to Zhang Yu in the studio, Shen Yi stopped coming here. It was because Zhang Yu worried that people might gossip [about their homosexual relationship].

shuō yì qiān, dào yí wàn 说一千，道一万 (說一千，道一萬)

"Say it a thousand times or ten thousand times"; say what you want, but...

♦   **说一千，道一万**，这死老汉是个好人！要么我能等他八年，跟他过一辈子！

(From the short story 传达三题)

Say what you want, but this old guy is a good person. If not, would I have waited eight years, and be willing to spend my whole life with him?

◆ 说一千，道一万，现在这年头儿，没有钱什么事情都办不成。

Talk all you want, but in this day and age, you can't do anything without money.

sī fáng qián 私房钱 (私房錢)

Private money; savings

◆ 哼，你哪来这么多钞票？好呀，我为这个家累死累活，你倒也藏起私房钱来了，良心被狗吃掉了呀！

(From the short story 家庭风景二十章)

My God, where did you get this much cash? Damn it, I worked my ass off for this family of ours. And all the time you were stashing away your own money. It's unconscionable!

◆ 你别在意，男人有点儿私房钱是正常的嘛。

I hope you don't mind. It's pretty normal for a man to have some money of his own.

sī pò liǎn/zhuā pò liǎn 撕破脸/抓破脸 (撕破臉/抓破臉)

"Rip the face off"; have a face-off; have a confrontation

◆ 真要是撕破了脸儿，对大家都不好。

(From the TV series 黑洞)

If there were ever a showdown, it would be bad for everyone.

◆ 他心里着急，还得把火往下压压，脑袋得保持冷静，能不抓破脸就不抓破脸。

(From the novel 燕王扫北)

He's upset, but he had to control his anger and remain calm in order to avoid a confrontation.

sī zuǐ 撕嘴

"Rip off the lips"; punish the lips that say the wrong thing; cut out someone's tongue

◆ 待会儿人来了，〖你要是还这么说，〗看我撕你的小嘴儿！

(From the TV series 北京女人)

They'll be here in a minute, [and if you keep talking like this], I'll shut that mouth of yours!

◆ 你要是敢把这件事捅出去我就撕你的嘴。

If you ever dare to leak this, I'll cut your tongue out.

sǐ dào lín tóu le hái...死到临头了还... (死到臨頭了還...)

"Do something even when about to die"; do something despite the danger; unrepentant

◆ 何可待，你这条丧家犬，死到临头了，还玩阴谋？

(From the novel 都市危情)

He Kedai, you're like a lost dog. You're about to die, and you're still hatching plots?

♦ 我可不是危言耸听，你们这些人真是不知好歹，都死到临头了，还在
这儿寻欢作乐！

I'm not being sensational. You people are so clueless that you're still partying on the eve of your own destruction.

sǐ mǎ dàng huó mǎ yī 死马当活马医 (死馬當活馬醫)

"Treat a dead horse as if it were alive"; (forced by circumstances to) do the impossible

♦ 我知道这样风险很大，但是现在也只能死马当活马医了。

(From the TV series 蓝色马蹄莲)

I know the risk is high, but we don't have a choice now. We have to try the impossible.

♦ 这案子现在没什么更好的出路了，只能让肖童杀进去试试。死马当做
活马医吧。

(From the novel 永不瞑目)

With this case we don't have any better options now. All we can do is let Xiao Tong push his way in and give it a try. It's a real long shot, but it's all we can do. [Xiao Tong is being planted as a mole.]

sǐ nǎr qù le 死哪去了

"Where'd you go to die?" Where the hell were you?

♦ 你那个表哥也不知道死哪儿去了，整年见不到他。

(From the novel 下水道)

I don't know where the hell that cousin of yours is. Haven't seen him for a whole year.

♦ 你死哪去了？ 八点多才回家，连个电话也不来。

Where the hell were you? You didn't get home till eight, and you didn't even give me a call.

sǐ pí liǎ liǎn 死皮赖脸 (死皮賴臉)

"Thick-skinned and brazen-faced"; brazen; shameless

♦ "你这个人怎么这么野蛮啊？" 韩妍的眉头紧紧的皱起，对这种看起
来冷酷，其实却是死皮赖脸的人完全没辙。

(From the novel 笨女孩)

"How come you're so crude?" Han Yan scowled. She couldn't do anything with this guy. He seemed to be just insensitive, but he really was a brazen lowlife.

♦ 老头子，对门那小子死皮赖脸缠着咱们家闺女，你得想个办法啊！

Old man, the guy across the hall has been pestering our daughter shamelessly. You've got to think of something!

sǐ qi bāi liē/sǐ qi bái lài 死气掰咧(死气掰咧)

"Beg and grab like a scoundrel"; insist despite objections or protest; pester endlessly

♦ 人家说饱了就饱了，干吗死气掰咧地让人家吃？

(From the TV series 今生是亲人)

When people say they're full, they're full. How come you keep hounding them to eat more?

♦ 人家不让挑〖西红柿〗，你还在这儿死气掰咧地挑！

(From the TV series 一年又一年)

They don't let you pick and choose [tomatoes]. And you have to insist on doing it anyway!

sǐ rén shuō huó le 死人说活了 (死人說活了)
"Speak in a way that can raise the dead"; eloquent; speak with a magic touch

♦ 知青们即便能把**死人说活了**，他也无动于衷。

    (From the novel 将军镇)

    Even if the educated young people had golden tongues, he would remain unmoved. [A group of young people tried to get into an orchard to eat some fruit, but were turned away despite their eloquent appeals. [知青 literally means "educated youth," students sent to the countryside for re-education during the Cultural Revolution.]

♦ 他确实能干，外贸方面的知识非常专业，又会讲话，能把**死人说活了**，所以没多久就把他调到贸易部门了。

    (From the novel 洛杉矶蜂鸟)

    He's very capable indeed, an expert on foreign trade. He's also a smooth talker whose speech can move mountains, so he was quickly transferred to the trade department.

sǐ xīn yǎnr 死心眼儿 (死心眼兒)
"Dead-set in heart"; one-track mind; stubborn; inflexible

♦ 你怎么那么**死心眼儿**啊？ 把人喊出来你不就走了吗？

    (From the movie 有话好好说)

    How come you're so stubborn? Once your shouting gets her out, you can go, right? [The speaker has fallen in love with a woman who lives in a highrise building, but he doesn't know which apartment. He is trying to hire someone to shout her name until she comes down, but the prospective shouter is embarrassed.]

♦ 你这人就是**死心眼**，在哪儿赚钱不是赚钱，干嘛非教书不可呢？

    You're so stubborn. Money is money, wherever you earn it. Why do you insist on teaching?

sǐ yào miàn zi huó shòu zuì 死要面子活受罪
(Proverb) "Endure hardship for the sake of saving face"; value appearances over feelings; pay a high price for keeping up appearances

♦ 我就怕男人**死要面子活受罪**。

    (From the TV series 黑洞)

    I'm scared of men who care too much about appearances.

♦ 你觉得一个大学生去搞直销**寒碜**是不是？ 可**死要面子活受罪**啊！

    You think it's degrading for a college student to do direct marketing, don't you? But pride can be expensive.

sǐ zhū bú pà kāi shuǐ tàng 死猪不怕开水烫 (死豬不怕開水燙)
"A dead pig doesn't fear boiling water"; the dead have nothing to fear

♦ 别瞧这小子牙豁，嘴挺严实。小唐审了他两天，**愣**没从他嘴里抠出东西来。**死猪不怕开水烫**，"豁牙子"死活不开口。

    (From the novel 百年德性)

Despite that gap between his teeth, he's really very tight-lipped. Xiao Tang interrogated him for two days and didn't get a thing out of him. Dead men have nothing to fear. This Gaptooth won't open his mouth for anything.

♦ 小伙子劳改也劳改过了，活脱脱一副**死猪不怕开水烫**的样子："要钱没有！ 要命一条！ 听说你要到法院起诉，现在我就跟你走！"

(From the short story 辞职者)

This young guy has already been through labor-reform camp. His attitude is, he has nothing more to lose. "Want money? I haven't got any! Want my life? Be my guest. I hear you want to take me to court. Let's go right now!"

sì jiǎo cháo tiān 四脚朝天 (四腳朝天)

"Four feet pointing toward the sky"; fall over; kill; die (variation: 脚丫子朝天)

♦ "买卖怎么样啊？" "不太好，累得**四脚朝天**啊，也挣不着钱。"

(From the TV series 贫嘴张大民的幸福生活)

"How's business?" "Not too good. I work till I drop and still don't make money."

♦ 我这儿都忙得**脚丫子朝天**了，你们就知道催！

(From the movie 甲方乙方)

I'm so busy I could keel over, and you just pressure us to do more!

sōng kǒur 松口儿 (鬆口兒)

"Relax your jaws"; let go; relent

♦ 强！ 打烂了头他也不**松口儿**。

(From the TV series 康熙帝国)

A tough guy! You can beat him to a pulp and he still won't talk.

♦ 婆婆跟我借钱的事我一直也没**松过口**。所以她对我一肚子气。

My mother-in-law asked for money but I never gave in, so she's really pissed at me.

sòng shàng ménr 送上门儿 (送上門兒)

"Bring to someone's door"; volunteer; be a godsend

♦ 老佛爷正找不着替罪羊呢，你这不是**送上门儿**去吗！

(From the TV series 大宅门)

The Great Buddha can't find a scapegoat, and you're just falling into her lap! [老佛爷 is what Empress Dowager 慈禧 preferred to be called.]

♦ **送上门**的好事他不会拒绝，但**煮熟的鸭子飞了**，他也不会强求。

(From the novel 凝星蕴邪)

He wouldn't turn down a roasted pigeon if it flew into his mouth, but if it flew away again he wouldn't fall apart, either.

suí 随 (隨)

"Follow"; be like; resemble

♦ 你**随**你爸爸，抠门儿！

(From the TV series 贫嘴张大民的幸福生活)

You're a cheapskate like your dad!

◆ 这孩子的脾气又不随他爹，又不**随**他娘，倒有点儿像他那没见过面儿
的爷爷。

This kid's personality isn't like his father's, or his mother's, either. He's more like the grandfather he never met.

suí yuán 随缘 (隨緣)

"Follow one's destiny"; determined by fate

◆ 他的性格比较内向，但要是遇到**随缘**的人，也有说有笑的。

(From the TV series 花非花)

He's not very outgoing. But once he meets a kindred spirit, he can be talkative and witty.

◆ "老弟，你也三十出头儿了，真想独身一辈子吗？" "其实我一直在
找，可不是人家看不上我就是我看不上人家。唉！一切**随缘**吧！"

"My dear brother, you're over thirty. Do you really want to be single all your life?" "I'm actually always looking for someone. But either I'm not good enough for her or she's not good enough for me. Well, I guess it's in the hands of the gods."

suō tóu wū guī 缩头乌龟 (縮頭烏龜)

"A turtle that draws its head into its shell"; coward

◆ 我一直告诉你们，干什么事都得讲个韧劲儿，别像个**缩头乌龟**似的，
碰到一点什么难处，就赶紧地把头往回缩。

(From the novel 大雪无痕)

I keep telling you, whatever you do you've got to have persistence. You can't just bail out whenever you hit a problem.

◆ 公司的这几个领导平常总是争着出风头，可是现在公司遇到大麻烦
了，一个个都变成了**缩头乌龟**，谁也不想负责任。

The company brass usually loves the limelight. But now that the company has encountered some big difficulties, they all draw their heads in. Nobody wants to take any responsibility.

T

tái gàng 抬杠 (擡杠)

Bicker; argue for the sake of arguing

◆ "今天夜里肯定有情况。"小陈说："你咋就这么肯定?要是没情况
呢?" "你还别**抬杠**，我要说得不准，我那枝'勃朗宁'就归你。"

(From the novel 亮剑)

"Something will definitely happen tonight." Xiao Chen said, "How can you be so sure? What if nothing happens?" "Don't pick an argument. If I'm wrong, you can have my Browning. [Referring to a military exercise.]

♦ 这两口子一见面就**抬杠**，整天吵个不停。我看干脆离了算了。

Those two start fighting as soon as they see each other. They just never stop arguing. I think they should just get a divorce, and be done with it.

tái jiào zi 抬轿子 (擡轎子)

"Carry the sedan chair"; flatter; sing the praise of

♦ 看看你们两个人，一唱一和地给我**抬轿子**，好，我收下你们这一片孝心，谢谢你们啦！

(From the TV series 问问你的心)

Look at you, flattering me like two birds singing in unison. All right, I'll accept it as a token of your filial piety. Many thanks! [The speaker is accepting clothing that she considers much too flashy.]

♦ 你现在当领导了，身边一定会有**抬轿子**的人。对这些人，你要特别小心。

Now that you're in a leadership position, you've surely got some flatterers around. Those are the people you've got to watch out for.

tái tóu bú jiàn dī tóu jiàn 抬头不见低头见 (擡頭不見低頭見)

"If they don't see each other when they lift their heads, they see each other when they lower them" [or vice-versa]; bump into each other all the time; never out of sight of each other (variation: 低头不见抬头见)

♦ 我瞅着你俩，**抬头不见低头见**，总不得劲，总不是个事儿。

(From the novel 隐形伴侣)

I can see that being stuck with each other must feel pretty weird for both of you. It just can't go on like this forever. [A couple still work together after they separated.]

♦ 咱们街里街坊的，**低头儿不见抬头儿见**，你何必非跟我过不去呢？

We're neighbors and we can't avoid bumping into each other. Why do you always have to give me a hard time?

tái yang dǎ/cóng xi bianr chū lai 太阳打/从西边儿出来 (太陽打/從西邊兒出來)

"The sun rises in the west"; unbelievable; impossible; unexpected

♦ 今天是**太阳从西边出来**了，怎么做那么多好吃的？

(From the movie 爱情麻辣烫)

Today the sun rose in the west! How come you made so much delicious food? [The wife normally cooks only the simplest food.]

♦   哟呵！这太阳打西边出了吧？今天怎么想起来看我了？ 这三年你连个信都没有！

Well! So the sun rose in the west today? What made you decide to pay me a visit? For three years I haven't even gotten a letter from you!

tān duō jiáo bú làn 贪多嚼不烂 (貪多嚼不爛)

"Take too much food to chew it well"; bite off more than one can chew

♦   谁像你好胃口？ 家花、野花、喇叭花都好，小心**贪多嚼不烂**。

(From the novel 亲亲大色狼)

Who has an appetite like yours? In your own bed or someone else's, all women look good to you. Watch out you don't bite off more than you can chew. [家花: cultivated flower or legitimate relationship; 野花: wild flower or illicit relationship; 喇叭花: morning glory, added for rhythm]

♦   这学期你一下上六门课？ 当心**贪多嚼不烂**。

You're going to take six courses this semester? Careful, don't take on more than you can handle.

tān pái 摊牌 (攤牌)

"Show one's cards"; showdown

♦   我想他们早晚得知道，昨天晚上我跟他们**摊牌**了。

(From the TV series 走过花季)

I thought they'd find out sooner or later, so I broke the news to them last night. [She is in love with a much older man, and was afraid her parents would oppose the match.]

♦   你别太心急了，我觉得现在还不是跟他们**摊牌**的时候。

Don't be in such a rush. I don't think it's time for a showdown with them yet.

tān shang 摊上 (攤上)

"Have a share in"; receive something undesirable or unpleasant; be so unlucky as to get

♦   蓝月颖怎么**摊**上陈建国这么个丈夫？

(From the TV series 都市情感)

How in the world did Lan Yueying end up with a husband like Chen Jianguo? [Lan is a beautiful and successful woman; Chen is both unskilled and handicapped.]

♦   你还别瞧不起你爸，你**摊**上我这个爸还真算你有福气。换个人家试试，不说别的，就冲你和我说话这口气，早大耳刮子抢你了。

(From the novel 我是你爸爸)

Stop sneering at your dad! You're lucky you've got me for a father. Try someone else, and you'll see. Just the way you talk to me would get you a big slap in the face, not to mention everything els.

tān tái 坍台

(Shanghai dialect) "collapse the stage"; lose face; make someone lose face

♦   为上街摆摊卖馄饨，钱世丽的家里争论了几天。儿子奇奇坚决反对，吐出的全是短句：丢人。**坍台**。失面子。

(From the novel 转来转去 云阳)

Qian Shili's family debated for several days about setting up a street stand to sell wonton soup. Her son Qiqi was dead set against it. He just kept spitting out words like "embarrassing," "disgraceful," and "scandalous."

◆   我再三告诉你，今天的宴会是决不能迟到的，你到现在还没有准备好，难道一定要给我**坍台**？

(From the novel 紫贝壳)

I told you again and again, we absolutely can't be late for the banquet today. And you're still not ready! Are you trying to make me look bad?

tán bu shàng 谈不上 (談不上)

"Can't talk about"; nothing to speak of; it is inaccurate to say

◆   "我记得你曾对我讲过，你同乡党委赵书记熟悉。"三哥说："熟悉**谈不上**，一般认识，我在县财政下拨款上帮过他一点小忙。"

(From the novel 家丑)

"I remember you told me you know the township party secretary well." Third Brother: "Can't say I know him well; we're just acquainted. I helped him out a bit when the county finance authority was allocating funds."

◆   我写过两三本小说，**谈不上**经验，算是知道一点儿吧。

I wrote two or three novels. I wouldn't say I'm an expert; I just know how to do a few things.

tāng hún shuǐ 趟混水

"Wade in muddy water"; get involved in a mess; fish in troubled waters

◆   "你快走，别**趟**这混水！""前辈，这混水我今天**趟**定了。"

"Hurry up and leave. Don't get involved in this mess." "Sir, today I'm involved in this mess for sure." [The first speaker is being besieged by over a hundred people and the second speaker, a stranger, volunteers to help.]

◆   公司现在正乱着呢，工商局已经派人来查了，你还是躲远点，别来**趟**这混水。

The company's in chaos now. The Bureau of Industry and Commerce has already sent people to investigate. You'd better stay away and keep clear of this mess.

tǎng zài gōng láo bù shang shuì dà jiào 躺在功劳簿上睡大觉 (躺在功劳簿上睡大覺)

"Sleep soundly on the book of one's merits"; rest on one's laurels

◆   最难能可贵的是，他并没有**躺在功劳簿上睡大觉**，一双慧眼还在寻找未开发的市场。

(From the short story 猪.com)

What I most admire is that he didn't rest on his laurels but kept a sharp eye out for new potential markets.

- 谁都知道您过去是个英雄，可您也不能老**躺在功劳簿上睡大觉**啊！

  Everyone knows you were a hero in your day, but you can't just keep resting on your laurels.

táo bù liǎo gān xì 逃不了干系

"Can't avoid implication"; can't stay uninvolved; can't remain untouched

- 现在是没她什么事儿，但要是顺藤摸瓜的话，周怡就**逃不了干系**。

  (From the TV series 花非花)

  Now she's not implicated, but if someone follows the case to the bottom, Zhou Yi won't be able to stay out of it. [顺藤摸瓜: grope along the vine to find the melons]

- 这件事如果捅出去，我们大家谁都**逃不了干系**。

  If this business ever comes to light, none of us will get away unscathed.

táo huan 淘换 (淘換)

"Search and replace"; seek; find

- 打哪儿**淘换**这身外国行套？

  (From the TV series 一年又一年)

  Where on earth did you dig up that foreign outfit? [At the beginning of the period of economic reforms, a wife is amazed when her husband returns from the south in a Western suit.]

- 鼻烟壶这东西现在不好找了，您老想要，我会尽力去给您**淘换**。

  Snuff boxes are hard to come by these days. But if you really want one, I'll do my best to find one for you.

táo huār yùn/táo yùn 桃花儿运/桃运 (桃花兒運/桃運)

"Peach blossom luck"; luck with women; luck in love

- 小子，官运、**桃运**一块儿走啊！

  (From the TV series 手心手背)

  You bastard, you hit the jackpot in politics and love at the same time! [Spoken to someone who just got a promotion and is dating the bureau chief's daughter.]

- 听说这家伙让老板的女儿给看上了，怪不得这几天有事没事都笑颠颠的，原来是交上了**桃花运**！

  I heard the boss' daughter fell in love with this lucky bastard. No wonder he's had a shit-eating grin for the last few days. It's because he's lucky in love.

tǎo ge shuō fa 讨个说法 (討個說法)

"Beg for an explanation"; seek an official explanation or justification

- 我打这个官司不是为了钱，就是为了**讨个说法**。

  (From the TV series 欲罢不能)

  I didn't start this lawsuit for money, but to get an official explanation.

- 香港青年本意也不是奔钱而来，他们只是来**讨个说法**、讨个公道。

  (From the novel 布衣青天杨剑昌)

The young people from Hong Kong didn't come here for money. All they wanted was for someone to hear their grievances and treat them justly.

tào cí 套词/套磁 (套詞/套磁)

"Approach someone with sweet talk"; charm; butter up

♦ 少跟我这儿**套词**，其实我一分钱都不应该给你。

(From the TV series 今生是亲人)

Don't try to butter me up. Actually, I shouldn't have given you even one cent.

♦ 含青乐了，心想，这男人一副朴实样，还挺会和女孩"**套磁**"。

(From the novel 浮沈商海)

Hanqing was amused. She thought that this guy seemed simple and guileless, but he really knew how to charm the girls.

tào jìn hu 套近乎

"Draw near"; endear; cozy up to

♦ 都他妈滚，少跟我们**套近乎**！ 我们谁的同志都不是。

(From the novel 一点正经没有)

Get the fuck out of here, all of you! Don't try to cozy up to us. We're not anybody's comrades.

♦ 你跟我**套近乎**一点儿用也没有，所有的工人全部得下岗，这是总经理的主意。

Being friendly to me will get you nowhere. All of the workers must be laid off. This is the general manager's decision.

tí zhe tóu lái jiàn wǒ 提着头来见我 (提著頭來見我)

"Come see me carrying your head in your hands"; come back with your shield or on it; either get it done or kill yourself

♦ 如果再丢失一门〖大炮〗，你们两个就**提着头来见我**。

(From the TV series 康熙帝国)

If you lose just one more cannon, you two are history.

♦ 你要是不把张志刚给我抓回来就**提着头来见我**。

Either you come back with Zhang Zhigang, or I'll have your head.

tì sǐ guǐr 替死鬼儿 (替死鬼兒)

"Sacrificial ghost"; fall guy; scapegoat

♦ 上级指示，每个村要检那罪大恶极的阶级敌人处死三、五个。按照村庄大小，赵老运带回两个名额，这是个死数。赵老运犯了难，要说罪大恶极，王家庄要数杨乃谦。可他人去庙空，怎么办？拿他儿子当**替死鬼**？

(From the novel 地主的女儿)

The edict came down that each village should choose three to five flagrant class enemies for execution. Based on the size of the village, Mr. Zhao came back with a quota of two executions. Mr. Zhao found himself in a difficult spot. Given his nefarious crimes, Yang Naiqian was the first choice in Wang Village, but he was nowhere to be found. What to do? Take his son as a scapegoat?

♦ 那么，说起来，你提名我这次陪她去北京，是把我当**替死鬼**送的？

(From the novel 办公室的故事)

In that case, your suggestion that I escort her to Beijing makes me the sacrificial lamb?

tì tóu de tiāo zi, yì tóur rè 剃头的挑子，一头儿热 (剃頭的挑子，一頭兒熱)

"Like the barber's shoulder pole—only one end is warm"; one-way affection or enthusiasm (An itinerant barber carries his tools on a pole across his shoulders; on one end is a bucket of warm water.)

◆ 老黄，我看你是**剃头挑子一头热**，人家根本瞧不上咱们这样的人。
(From the novel 蛇神)
Lao Huang, I'd say this is a one-way romance. Women like her don't look at guys like us.

◆ 你喜欢她可她不喜欢你啊，算了，别**剃头的挑子，一头儿热**了！
You like her all right, but she doesn't like you. So forget it, and come off this one-sided infatuation!

tì zuì yáng 替罪羊

"Sacrificial lamb"; scapegoat

◆ 你放心，**替罪羊**我已经找好了。
(From the TV series 黑洞)
Don't worry. I've already found a scapegoat.

◆ 先开枪你也未必能把中国人打退，打不退中国人你就肯定会成为**替罪羊**。可如果眼睁睁看着中国人把路修通，你的下场也比当**替罪羊**好不了多少。
(From the novel 末日之门)
Even if you open fire first, you won't necessarily get the Chinese to retreat. And if the Chinese don't retreat, you'll be the scapegoat. But if you let the Chinese finish that road right before your eyes, you'll end up not much better than a scapegoat anyway. [The argument of an Indian military officer.]

tiān cǎir 添彩儿 (添彩兒)

"Add color"; enrich; glorify

◆ 这道药膳要是开发出来，肯定能给咱们餐饮部**添彩儿**。
(From the TV series 刘老根)
When this health food [food containing medicinal herbs] is developed, it'll definitely score one for our Food and Drinks Department.

◆ 这次王建国拿了个全国中学生作文一等奖，可给咱们学校**添彩**了！
Wang Jianguo won first prize at this year's national middle school writing contest. What a coup for our school!

tiān dì liáng xīn 天地良心

"Heaven and earth and my conscience (know)"; I swear to God; on my honor

◆ **天地良心**，我这货真是三块六进的。我这货真是三块六进的。
(From the TV series 今生是亲人)
I swear to God, I bought these goods at $3.60 a piece.

◆ 一分钱，二分货，三分心，他说这就是生意人的**天地良心**。
(From the TV series 问问你的心)

A customer who spends one yuan deserves two yuan worth of merchandise and three yuan worth of service.

tiān dǔ 添堵

"Add barriers"; irritate; annoy

♦ 行了行了！ 别说这个了，你是请我吃饭呢？ 还是来**添堵**的？
(From the TV series 天堂鸟)
> Enough already! Please change the subject. Are you treating me to dinner or are you trying to annoy me?

♦ 你们都出去，少在我这儿**添堵**！
> Get out, all of you! Stop hassling me here.

tiān shàng diào xiànr bǐng 天上掉馅儿饼 (天上掉餡兒餅)

"A pie falling from the sky"; good fortune falling into one's lap; pennies from heaven

♦ 我知道没有**天上掉馅儿饼**的事儿。
(From the TV series 花非花)
> I know good fortune doesn't just fall into your lap.

♦ 你瞧瞧你那副样子，哪像个劳动人民的孩子。好逸恶劳，游手好闲，坐在那儿等**天上掉馅饼**。
(From the TV series 编辑部的故事)
> Look at you. How can you call yourself a son of the working class! You want all pleasure and no work, you spend your days loafing around, and you sit there waiting for pennies from heaven.

tiān wáng lǎo zi 天王老子

"Father king of heaven"; the king of heaven; the heavenly father

♦ 别说神仙，就是**天王老子**，只要敢进我家门，我就拿他下马。进了我家门，就得服我管。
(From the TV series 编辑部的故事)
> He's some sort of god? Even if he were the King of Heaven himself, if he dares to enter my door I'll show him who's boss ["make him get down from his horse"]. In my house, I make the rules.

♦ 谁不交钱也不能进去。就是**天王老子**来了，也得照样买票。
> No one gets in without paying. Even if God himself turns up, he has to buy a ticket like everyone else.

tiān xià wū yā yì bān hēi 天下乌鸦一般黑 (天下烏鴉一般黑)

(Proverb) "All the crows in the world are equally black"; crooks are crooks everywhere

♦ 没劲，真没劲，**天下乌鸦一般黑**……怪谁呢？谁也不怪，就怪我自个。
(From the TV series 编辑部的故事)

Bummer! What a bummer! Crooks are crooks everywhere. Who should I blame? Nobody but myself.

◆ 天下乌鸦一般黑，所有的老板都一样坏。
    It's the same everywhere. All bosses are crooks.

tián tour 甜头儿 (甜頭兒)

"Sweet taste"; pleasant or positive experience; incentive

◆ 这些人，可怜不得，你放他这次，他得了甜头，下次还来，说不定还带着鱼网来。
    (From the novel 打鱼的和钓鱼的)
    Don't feel sorry for these people. You let them off once, and they get a taste for it. They'll be back, and probably with fishing nets too. [They are fishing where it's forbidden.]

◆ 找不到爱情？ 试试网上聊天室呀！ 你只要尝到一回甜头, 就上瘾了。
    Can't find romance? Give the chatrooms a try! One hit and you'll be hooked.

tiǎn zhe liǎn 恬着脸 (恬著臉)

"Shameless face"; show no shame when begging for favors; thick-skinned; have the gall to ask

◆ 她樊月娥没给齐家添置过一件象样的家当， 没往家交过一文钱工资，还隔三差五地恬着脸跟丈夫和叔叔要钱供她零花挥霍、贴补她的娘家。
    (From the novel 叔那方面不行)
    This Fan Yue'e woman never bought even one piece of furniture for the Qi household, and she never gave the Qi family one penny of her salary. But from time to time she had the gall to ask her husband and his uncle for pocket money, and funds to pay for her little luxuries and to support her own relatives.

◆ 上次的钱你还没还呢，还恬着脸子来跟我借，拉倒吧你！
    You haven't paid back the money you borrowed last time. And now you have the gall to ask for another loan? Get lost!

tiáo zi 条子 (條子)

Cop; fuzz

◆ 我看你是条子，到我们这儿来卧底的。
    (From the TV series 黑冰)
    I think you're a cop an undercover agent planted on us.

◆ 最近这市场上常有条子假扮的客人，我们的毒品买卖得先停两天了。
    Recently there've been cops in the market posing as customers. We better lay off the drug business for a few days.

tiǎo dà liáng 挑大梁

"Serve as the crossbeam"; assume a vital position; play the leading role

◆ 你这时候不挑大梁还等什么时候？海天〖公司〗未来的发展全寄托在你的身上。
    (From the TV series 失乐园)

What are you waiting for? Now is the time to step up and assume leadership. Haitian Company's future development depends entirely on you.

◆   他这个人吹吹喇叭，**抬抬轿子**还行，但绝对不是**挑大梁**的材料。

He'll do as a cheerleader ["blow the trumpet and carry the sedan chair"], but he's not at all leadership material.

tiǎo míng le 挑明了

"Make bright"; bring something out in the open; reveal a secret

◆   这个事儿还是早点儿**挑明了**好。

(From the TV series 今生是亲人)

It's best to bring this matter out in the open as soon as possible.

◆   今天我把话**挑明了**，我要状告你们龙腾集团走私贩私。

(From the TV series 黑洞)

Let me spell it out for you today: I'm going to turn your Longteng Group in for smuggling.

tiǎo tóur 挑头儿 (挑頭兒)

"Act as the head"; take the lead

◆   你要让我**挑头儿**，得给我点儿权力。

(From the TV series 黑洞)

If you want me to take the lead, you've got to give me some power.

◆   这件事的确是他**挑头儿**干的。

He really was the one who started all this.

tiào/táo chū sb de shǒu zhǎng xīn 跳/逃出Sb的手掌心

"Jump out of/escape the palm of somebody's hand"; escape somebody else's control

◆   我想**跳出**他的**手掌心**，躲得远远的。

(From the TV series 天下第一情)

I want to escape from his grasp and hide somewhere far away. [An overly strict father makes his son feel resentful.]

◆   你就是跑到天涯海角，也**逃不出我的手掌心儿**！

You can run to the ends of the earth but you'll still be under my thumb.

tiào jìn huáng hé xǐ bù qīng 跳进黄河洗不清 (跳進黃河洗不清)

"Even if you jump into the Yellow River, you can't wash yourself clean"; cannot escape guilt or responsibility

◆   到头来被人反咬一口，她就是**跳进黄河也洗不清**啊。

(From the TV series 大雪无痕)

In the end, someone could make a false countercharge against her, and there's no way she could clear her name, no matter how hard she tried.

◆   他还当着妻子的面儿说，他爱我，是因为我才要离婚的，我就是**跳进黄河也洗不清**了。

(From the TV series 失乐园)

Right in front of his wife, he said he loved me and it was only because of me he wanted a divorce. Now I'm disgraced, no matter what I say.

tiě 铁 (鐵)

"Iron strong"; strong (ties or bond)

♦ 谈也没用，别看你俩是老同学，关系又**铁**，现在社会都认钱了。

(From the novel 大厂)

No point talking, even though you two were classmates and your friendship is strong as iron. In today's society, people only recognize money. [The speaker thinks the listener's effort to persuade a friend not to change jobs will be fruitless.]

♦ "快走吧！老迟到小心让剧组开除了！" "放心，咱们跟导演**铁**着呢！"

(From the TV drama 夻兒胡同)

"Hurry up. You're always late; watch out you don't get fired from the crew of the TV show." "Don't worry, the director and I are thick as thieves."

tiě gōng jī 铁公鸡 (鐵公雞)

"Iron rooster (difficult to pluck)"; cheapskate

♦ 我没想到他是**铁公鸡**，一毛不拔。

(From the TV series 都市情感)

I didn't think he'd be such a cheapskate; you can't get a cent from him. ["I didn't expect him to be such an iron rooster; you can't even pluck out one feather."]

♦ 那家伙是只**铁公鸡**，你别想从他那儿借到一分钱。

That son of a bitch is a tightwad. Don't expect to borrow a penny from him.

tīng fēng jiù shì yǔ 听风就是雨 (聽風就是雨)

"Hear the wind and immediately expect rain""; think the sky is falling; take rumors as facts; jump to conclusions

♦ 我告诉你们，不要**听着风就是雨**。

(From the TV series 问问你的心)

I'm telling you, don't assume the sky is falling. [Advice given to shareholders who want to sell when they hear the company lost a lawsuit.]

♦ 你别**听风就是雨**，张局长一时半会儿调不走的。

Don't jump to conclusions. Director Zhang won't be transferred any time soon.

tīng hǎo le 听好了 (聽好了)

"Listen well"; listen up; listen carefully

♦ 他把我一下按在了椅子上说，你给我**听好了**，从今天开始，你就是老子的人了，什么你都给老子**听好了**，要不我杀了你！

(From the novel 幽灵小镇)

He pushed me into the chair and said, "You listen carefully. From this day on, you belong to me. Listen and remember every word I say, or I'll kill you."

♦ 你给我听好了，要是秀梅有个三长两短，我跟你没完！

    You listen up: if anything happens to Xiumei, I'll be on your case forever.

tīng là (lá) la gǔ jiào hái bú zhòng zhuāng jia le 听剌剌蛄叫还不种庄稼了 (聽剌剌蛄叫還不種莊稼了)

"If we hear the mole crickets chirp, should we stop planting crops?"; Don't let a trivial threat keep you from necessary action. (A rhetorical question; a mole cricket is an insect that feeds on the stems of crops.)

♦ 咱也不能叫坏人给吓住，听剌剌蛄叫还不种庄稼了。

    (From the TV series 祥符春秋)

    We shouldn't let the bad guys scare us away. Don't let their empty threats stop us.

♦ 他们的话根本不可信，你别二忽了，听剌剌蛄叫还不种庄稼了？

    Don't believe a word they say. And stop waffling—we can't give up just because we hear a bump in the night!

tīng sb yí jù 听sb一句 (聽Sb一句)

"Listen to a word (of advice) from somebody"; listen to somebody just once; give somebody's advice a chance

♦ 听妈一句，别再查下去了。

    (From the TV series 欲罢不能)

    I'm your mother; listen to me just this once. Don't investigate [the cause of the accident] any further.

♦ 听哥一句话，忘了他吧，好好地过自个儿的日子。

    (From the TV series 贫嘴张大民的幸福生活)

    I'm your brother; just listen to me this once. Forget him and go on with your life. [A brother is advising his sister after her fiancé was killed in an accident.]

tǐng bú zhù 挺不住

"Can no longer stand up"; can no longer hold; cannot sustain

♦ 我实在挺不住了。你输了有国家撑腰，我输了可就倾家荡产了！

    (From the TV series 大赢家)

    I really can't sustain any further losses. If you lose money, the state backs you up, but if I lose money, I lose everything. [The manager of a private business is talking to the manager of a state-owned enterprise.]

♦ 老王啊，我挺不住了，快来拉兄弟一把吧！

    Lao Wang, I can't hold on any longer. Quick, give your brother a hand, please.

tǐng yāo gǎn zi 挺腰杆子

"Keep one's back/waist straight"; hold one's head high; maintain one's dignity

♦ 要是没有这块利税，我们这些当头儿的去北京开会腰杆子就挺不起来。

    (From the TV series 大雪无痕)

Without those corporate income taxes, we officials simply can't hold our heads up when we go to meetings in Beijing. [A high-ranking local official tries to stop police from investigating a big company that pays high taxes.]

◆　要是没有**硬碰硬**的证据我能**挺着腰杆子**说话吗？

Do you think I'd be able to stand up straight and talk like this if I didn't have rock-solid evidence?

tǒng chū qu 捅出去

"Disclose to the outside"; leak information; bring something out in the open

◆　有一案子上面不让查，他给**捅出去**了。

(From the TV series 黑洞)

There was this case that the higher-ups said was off-limits, but he brought it out in the open.

◆　这件事儿是谁给**捅出去**的？　咱们一定得查清楚。

Who leaked this? We've got to get to the bottom of it.

tǒng lóu zi 捅漏/娄子 (捅漏/蔞子)

"Poke a hole in scuttle"; make a mess of; get into trouble

◆　我担心这么一个案子，他们弄不好**捅漏子**。

(From the TV series 黑洞)

I'm worried they'll sink a case like this if they handle it wrong.

◆　忙你是帮不上，别给我**捅漏子**我就**烧高香**了。

I certainly wouldn't expect you to help out. I'll give thanks if you just don't give me any trouble.

tǒng mǎ fēng wō 捅马蜂窝 (捅马蜂窝)

"Stir up a hornet's nest"; offend somebody or do something dangerous

◆　您怎么尽**捅马蜂窝**？那主考就是鳌拜的亲信！您取功名，管他什么圈地不圈地？

(From the TV series 康熙大帝)

Why do you always have to stir up a hornet's nest? That chief examiner is Aobai's trusted right-hand man. If you want to achieve honor and rank, what do you care whether Aobai is enclosing land or not? [Spoken to a friend who has criticized Aobai's land policy in his examination essay.]

◆　你们都不敢说，我说。我就不怕**捅**他这个**马蜂窝**。

None of them dared to speak up, so I will. I'm not afraid to face him and stir up this hornet's nest.

tǒng pò chuāng hu zhǐ 捅破窗户纸 (捅破窗戶紙)

"Poke a hole in the paper window"; bring what's understood or obvious out into the open

◆　我们已经是无话不说的朋友，就让我**捅破**这层**窗户纸**吧。虽然说我早已晓得你的真实身份，但是没把你当警察，我压根儿是把你看做朋友的。

(From the novel 百年德性)

We're already friends and there's nothing we can't talk about, so let me blow the lid off this subject. I knew your real identity all along, but right from the beginning I definitely considered you a friend rather than a cop.

◆ 这两个人在一起工作三年多了，情投意合，可谁都不好意思**捅破这层窗户纸**，向对方**挑明**爱慕之心。

These two have worked together for more than three years and gotten along pretty well. But they're both shy about tearing off the veil and revealing that they're in love.

tōu jī mō gǒu 偷鸡摸狗 (偷雞摸狗)

"Steal chickens and dogs"; commit petty thievery; pilfer

◆ 说话客气点！ 什么**偷鸡摸狗**的小偷本事？开锁，可是一门非常需要技巧的专业知识。

(From the novel 江湖风神帮)

Watch what you say! What do you mean, petty thievery? Locksmithing is a craft that requires plenty of professional knowledge.

◆ 你是有头有脸儿的人了，不能再干那种**偷鸡摸狗**的事儿了。

You're now a man of status. You can't engage in this kind of pilfering anymore.

tóu dǐng zhǎng chuāng, jiǎo dǐ xia líu nóng 头顶长疮，脚底下流脓 (頭頂長瘡，腳底下流膿)

"Scabies on the scalp and pus on the sole"; an out-and-out villain

◆ 这小子**头上生疮，脚底流脓**，坏透了，偷学我们家的武功不算，还想拐骗你，这种人留他不得。

(From the novel 武林痴小子)

This bastard is a total degenerate, rotten to the core. Not only did he secretly learn the martial arts of our house, but he even tried to lure you away. We can't keep a man like this.

◆ 城里那鬼地方，好人去了黑心窝，坏人去了**脚底流脓头顶生疮**。

(From the short story 1934 年的逃亡)

The city is a sinister place where the hearts of good people are corrupted, and bad people become monsters.

tóu dou dà le 头都大了 (頭都大了)

"Head swells"; blood rushes to the head; head explodes

◆ 她跳出窗户，又回过头来说："喂！下午到河边去游泳啊？ "我一听**头都大了**。去游泳！这是犯了错误反省的态度吗？

(From the novel 地久天长)

She jumped out the window, turned back and said, "Hey, let's go swimming in the river this afternoon, OK?" This suggestion just blew my mind. Go swimming! Is that the right attitude for someone who did wrong and should be repenting? [The woman is supposed to be writing a self-criticism.]

◆　老板说下个月还要裁员，我一听头都大了。

Our boss said there would be more layoffs next month. My head just exploded when I heard it.

tóu tóu nǎor nǎor 头头脑儿脑儿 (頭頭腦兒腦兒)

"Heads and brains"; leaders; honchos

◆　他躺在医院里，先是市里**头头脑脑**们，接下是部委办局头头脑脑们，再接下是各乡镇的头头脑脑们，再接下去是企业的**头头脑脑**们，不分白天黑夜逐一来访。

(From the novel 市委一号)

He lay in the hospital, and day and night a stream of important visitors came to see him. First were the officials of the municipal government; then there were chiefs of various municipal departments, commissions, offices, and bureaus; followed by township officials and then the heads of different companies and factories.

◆　"昨天你们那个会开得怎么样？""**头头脑儿脑儿**的倒是来了不少，就是没有一个愿意出钱的。"

"How was the meeting yesterday?" "Well, lots of bigshots showed up but none of them offered any money."

...tour 头儿 (...頭兒)

Worth doing

◆　建国，你跟我一块走吧。这个破厂有什么**呆头**啊？你这个破官有什么**当头**啊？

(From the novel 大厂)

Jianguo, let's leave together. What's there about this wretched factory that makes it worth staying? Is this lousy official post worthy of you?

◆　这个破电影实在没有什么**看头儿**。

This terrible film is really not worth watching.

tòu zhe 透着 (透著)

"Soaked in"; replete with; demonstrate

◆　自己的和公家的就是不一样，**透着**爱惜，打算使一辈子？

(From the novel 永失我爱)

You sure treat your own property and public property differently. You treat your own with care and love. Are you planning to hang onto it forever? [Spoken to someone who has just obtained his own apartment and is decorating it with loving care, in contrast to his behavior when he lived in a dormitory.]

◆　一看你就**透着**有学问，比别人的书卷气都浓。

(From the TV series 编辑部的故事)

It's easy to see you're steeped in erudition. No one else has such a bookish air.

tū lu 秃噜 (秃嚕)

Collapse; cannot sustain

♦ 也真邪了门儿，"豁牙子"碰上老杜便拉稀了。他扛了没多大工夫，就**秃噜**了。

(From the novel 百年德性)

It's really weird how Gaptooth got the runs when he saw Lao Du. He didn't hold out for long before he just caved in. [Lao Du is the police chief; previous investigators had gotten nothing out of Gaptooth.]

♦ 他开始装得挺像，后来一细问就**秃噜**了。

At first he did pretty well lying, but after some close questioning he fell apart and confessed.

tú 图 (圖)

"Covet"; hope to get; desire

♦ 人家**图**你什么啊，不就**图**你这个人吗？

(From the TV series 都市情感)

What do I hope to get out of you? You're what I hope to get!

♦ 人活一世**图**什么？不就**图**天天吃饱饭吗？

(From the TV series 一年又一年)

What is it that a human being wants in life? Nothing but a full stomach every day, right?

tǔ bāo/bào zi 土包子/土豹子

Country bumpkin

♦ 住在这里的老百姓，也都是没见过市面的**土包子**。

(From the novel 锁链，是柔软的)

The people who live here are all hicks who've never seen anything.

♦ 你是标准的**土包子**，妓女还真的会在眼睛上写着卖皮人？

(From the short story 冲突)

You're a total clodhopper. Would a prostitute write, "I sell my hide" on her forehead?

tǔ huáng di/shang huáng di 土皇帝/土皇上

"Local emperor"; local despot; neighborhood tyrant

♦ 地头蛇又找到了洋靠山，真是如虎添翼，成了北市场的**土皇上**。

(From the novel 夜幕下的哈尔滨)

Once this local bully found a foreign backer, he became a flying tiger. Now he was king of the North Market.

♦ 他啊，是我们这儿的**土皇帝**，你惹他，他能扒你一层皮！

This guy, he's our local tyrant. If you piss him off, he'll skin you alive.

tǔ lǎo màor 土老帽儿 (土老帽兒)

"Old country hat"; yokel; redneck

♦ **土老帽儿**一个。给我提皮包都不配。

(From the novel 都市危情)

What a hick! He's not even worthy of carrying my suitcase.

◆   像这样不知哪条地缝钻出来的经理，要长相没长相要风度没风度的土老帽儿，保不准是二道贩子变的呢！

(From the novel 浮沈商海)

Who knows what hole this manager crawled out of! He's a redneck without a decent appearance or manners. In all probability he only just moved up from being a petty speculator.

tù zi bù chī wō biān cǎo 兔子不吃窝边草 (兔子不吃窩邊草)

"The hare doesn't eat the grass around its burrow"; birds don't foul their own nests; one does not harm those close to home

◆   我找我的朋友怎么就是找了你的便宜？难道县医院的女人都是你的？**兔子不吃窝边草**，你有本事也到矿医院去找。

(From the novel 空洞)

I came here to see my friend. How can you claim I'm taking advantage of you? Are you saying that all the women in the County Hospital are your personal property? Isn't that fouling your own nest? If you think you're hot, why not come look for romance at the Miners' Hospital? [A doctor from the Miners' Hospital makes a rebuttal to the head of the County Hospital.]

◆   **兔子还不吃窝边草**呢，你倒好，偷东西偷到家门口来了。

Birds don't foul their own nests, but you steal things at your own doorstep.

tù zi jí le hái yǎo rén ne 兔子急了还咬人呢 (兔子急了還咬人呢)

"(Even) a rabbit will bite when it's cornered"; even a worm will turn; the most timid person will strike out if he or she has no alternative

◆   什么事也得不即不离儿的，这么**挤兑老娘**呀！**兔子急了还咬人**哪！

(From the novel 天桥演义)

You're really crossing the line. Picking on a lady like me! Watch out, even a worm will turn.

◆   他打人一点儿都不新鲜。**兔子急了还咬人**呢！

It's no wonder he hit someone. Even a worm will turn.

tù zi néng jià yuán 兔子能驾辕 (兔子能駕轅)

"(If) rabbits could pull carriages"; not cut out for; ask somebody to do the impossible (usually negative)

◆   要是**兔子能驾辕**咱还养什么马啊！

(From the TV series 红色康乃馨)

If rabbits could pull carriages, why would we need horses?

◆   什么，你让他当经理？不行，不行！**兔子驾不了辕**。

What? You want to make him the manager? No way! You can't make a silk purse out of a sow's ear.

tù zi yǐ (wěi) ba cháng bù liǎo 兔子尾巴长不了 (兔子尾巴長不了)

"(Like) the hare's tail—can't be long"; doomed

◆   别看何浩若趾高气扬，他是**兔子尾巴长不了**。

(From the novel 孔氏家族全传)

Even though He Haoruo is still riding his high horse, his days are numbered.

♦ 你别看他现在挺神气的，**兔子尾巴长不了**。

He may look cocky now, but his end is in sight.

tuī/tēi 忒

Too; very

♦ 您也别**忒**急了，过不了几天他准就搬回来了。

(From the TV series 今生是亲人)

Don't worry too much. He'll move back in a few days for sure.

♦ 小姐您这胆儿也**忒**大了，什么人都敢嫁！

(From the TV series 手心手背)

Miss, you really have a lot of guts. You'd dare to marry just about anyone!

tuì yí bù hǎi kuò tiān kōng 退一步海阔天空 (退一步海闊天空)

"Step one step back, and you will find the ocean is broader and the sky wider"; a little compromise goes a long way

♦ **退一步海阔天空**，何必把人往死里整呢？

(From the TV series 大雪无痕)

If you give in a little, you'll benefit too. Why drive a man to the wall?

♦ 老王啊，你别那么**较真儿**好不好，**退一步海阔天空**嘛！

Lao Wang, stop splitting hairs, all right? A little compromise goes a long way.

tuì yí wàn bù shuō/jiǎng 退一万步说/讲 (退一萬步說/講)

"Say you went back ten thousand steps"; in the unlikely event that…; for the sake of argument, let's imagine the unlikely scenario that…

♦ **退一万步讲**，就算他们抓住你什么了，也还有我挡着呢！

(From the TV series 黑洞)

For the sake of argument, let's say that they caught you. I'd still be there for you and shield you.

♦ 我觉得他们不敢**把我怎么样**。**退一万步说**，就是真的上了法庭他们也拿不出什么象样儿的证据。

I don't think they'd dare to touch me. Say they did, even if the case went to court they wouldn't be able to produce any decent evidence.

tuō hòu tuǐ 拖后腿 (拖後腿)

"Pull someone's leg back"; impede; hold up

♦ 这回她要再**拖后腿**，我就休了她。

(From the novel 突出重围)

If she holds me back once more, I'm through with her. [His wife twice prevented him from getting promoted.]

♦   我看得出来，你太太没少**拖你的后腿**，你要是真觉得为难就别跟我们干了。

I can see that your wife is a real impediment for you. If this is too awkward for you, we'd better part company.

tuō le kù zi fàng pì 脱了裤子放屁 (脫了褲子放屁)

"Take off one's pants in order to fart"; a procedure that makes no sense

♦   "算了，别**脱了裤子放屁**了。"

(From the movie 大腕)

"That's enough, stop wasting your breath!" [Translating unnecessarily for a foreigner who understands Chinese.]

♦   既然你要把工厂卖掉，为什么还要先让三分之一的工人下岗呢？这简直是**脱了裤子放屁**。

Since you're going to sell the factory anyway, why bother laying off a third of the workers? It's a completely wasted effort.

W

wā qiáng jiǎo 挖墙脚 (挖牆腳)

To sabotage; to undermine the foundation of something; to pull the rug out from under someone's feet

♦   我都明〖人名〗也是生在新社会，长在红旗下，**挖**国家**墙角**、拆社会主义大厦的事儿我能干吗？再说咱们**退一万步讲**，我都明就这么傻啊？明知道违法乱纪的事儿还要以身试法，我**有病**啊？

(From the TV series 大赢家)

I, [Douming], was born in the new society too and raised under the red flag. How could I undermine the foundation of the country and shatter the socialist structure? Besides, I would never be that stupid. Do you think I'd plunge into something I know very well is illegal? You think I'm crazy?

♦   张志文是我们好不容易才找来的网络奇才，刚来我们公司两天你们就想把他拉到你们公司去，这不是**挖**我们的**墙脚**吗？

Zhang Zhiwen is our Internet expert. We had to work really hard to get him. He's been here only two days and now you're hiring him away. Are you trying to pull the rug out from under our feet?

wà sài 哇塞

Wow; awesome

♦   许翰明做了一桌丰盛的晚餐，全是多多爱吃的菜。多多高兴地围着饭桌又蹦又跳："**哇塞**！太棒了！"

(From the novel 圣爱)

Xu Hanming cooked a sumptuous dinner with all of Duoduo's favorite dishes. Duoduo jumped up and down at the table: "Awesome! This is great!"

♦ "主任说了，明天每人发一台笔记本计算机。""**哇塞**！看来这个公司咱们真来对了。"

"The director said that everyone would get a laptop tomorrow." "Wow! We sure did the right thing when we signed on with this company."

wài kuài 外快

Money made on the side; outside income; fringe benefits

♦ 一点儿**外快**都没有，那叫**窝囊废**！

(From the TV drama 卷儿胡同)

Can't make anything on the side. What a loser! [Sneering at a poor middle school teacher.]

♦ 我姥姥有点儿**外快**。

(From the novel 我是你爸爸)

My grandma has a bit of income on the side.

wān wān ràor 弯弯绕儿 (彎彎繞兒)

Devious or indirect; to act deviously or indirectly; to maneuver

♦ 几天不见你还跟我**弯弯绕儿**了！

(From the TV series 手心手背)

It's just a few days since I last saw you and now you're being coy with me.

♦ 这人是我们公司有名的**弯弯绕儿**，他有什么话从来不会直接说出来。

The man is the most devious character in our company. He never tells you straight out what's on his mind.

wánr bú zhuàn 玩儿不转 (玩兒不轉)

Not able to manage, handle, or take care of

♦ 眼下只有两个孩子还**玩不转**呢，再添一张嘴可怎么办？

(From the novel 空洞)

Now we've only got two kids and we can't manage. What are we going to do with one more mouth to feed?

♦ 我看经理是**玩儿不转**了，这事儿除了大哥您亲自出马真没有别的办发。

Seems to me the manager can't handle it anymore. Unless you yourself fix it, there's no way out.

wánr huā huó 玩儿花活 (玩兒花活)

To play tricks; to pull a fast one

♦ 他在工地上，就没人敢**玩花活儿**。

(From the short story 村长陶醉)

Nobody dares to pull anything when he 's there at the construction site. ["He" is a tough village head.]

◆ 咱们既然是合作，就得一个心眼儿，谁也别**玩花活**。

Now that we're working together, we've got to have the same goals. No one pulls any fast ones.

wánr mìng 玩儿命 (玩兒命)

To risk one's life; to work like a dog

◆ 我要拉着他，跟我一起毁灭！ 带上家伙，**玩命**去！

(From the novel 都市危情)

I am going to drag him in and we can all go down together. Get your weapons. We'll put our lives on the line!

◆ 三十多岁的人了，何必呢？ 这么**玩儿命**干什么啊？

(From the TV series 一年又一年)

You're past thirty; why work like a dog? What's the point? [The husband is complaining that his wife works too hard.]

wánr nào 玩儿闹 (玩兒鬧)

A bad joke; a slacker, a good-for-nothing

◆ 有两把吉他，有一个破锣嗓子，就能凑合出一个摇滚乐队，**来不来还他妈的什么"后现代"，你说这不整个儿一个玩儿闹**吗？

(From the novel 百年德性)

Two guitars and a bad singing voice, and you've got a rock group. And they're always ready to give you that "postmodern" bullshit. If that isn't a bad joke, I don't know what is.

◆ 他不过是个小**玩儿闹**，没什么真本事。

He's just a slacker. He has no talent to speak of.

wánr nǐ de...ba 玩儿你的...吧 (玩兒你的...吧)

Go ahead and act like... ; go ahead and be...

◆ 好了，我的少爷，你还是回家去吹着空调，慢慢儿**玩你的深沉吧**。好狗不挡道，让我出去，我还得去挣我的五斗米呢。不陪你玩了啊。

(From the novel 兄弟)

All right, young master, go on back to your air-conditioned home and take your time playing at being a deep thinker. If you're a smart boy, you'll step aside and let me leave. I have to go and earn my next meal. I'm not going to play games with you anymore.

◆ **玩儿你的清高吧**！ 这一套在学校里还行，在公司里只能自讨苦吃！

Go ahead and be holier than thou. That might work with school kids, but in a business you 're just asking for trouble.

wánr qù 玩儿去 (玩兒去)

Go to hell!; Get out of here!

◆ "没错，"石静笑着说，"全都**玩去**。"

(From the novel 永失我爱)

"That's right." Shi Jing smiled, "Go to hell. All of you." [Shi Jing is being teased about her love life. Her statement confirms that they are right—she is in love with someone.]

◆ 让我当主编？**玩儿去吧你**，我肚子里有多少墨水我自己还不知道？
   Me? An editor-in-chief? Get out of here! I know my own capabilities perfectly well.

wánr wán 玩儿完 (玩兒完)

To die; to kick the bucket; to bite the big one; go down

◆ 他冲着话筒歇斯底里大叫："地下室里有四箱塑料炸药，如果你们坚持要搜就必须答应我的条件，不然我引爆它，咱们和这座酒店一块**玩儿完**。"
(From the novel 天若有情)
   He screamed hysterically into the microphone: "There are four boxes of plastic explosives in the basement. If you insist on searching there, you'll have to agree to my conditions. Otherwise I'll set them off and we'll all go down, along with this hotel."

◆ 你们别吵了，咱们要是自己掐起来准得一块儿**玩儿完**。
   Stop arguing. If we fight among ourselves, we'll all go down for sure.

wánr xū de 玩儿虚的 (玩兒虛的)

To play games; to pull tricks; to be dishonest

◆ "五年你都没来看我，今儿怎么想起来了。"王军说："**怪**想你的，就来看看。""少跟我**玩虚的**，我还不知道你。"陈茅说。
(From the short story 植物)
   "You haven't come to see me for five years. How come you just remembered me?" Wang Jun said, "I came because I really missed you." "Don't play games with me. I know you," Chen Mao replied.

◆ 你这就不对了，跟**铁哥们儿**不能**玩儿虚的**，有什么话直说。
   It's your fault. You can't pull tricks with your buddies. If there's a problem, just say it straight out.

wánr yīn de 玩儿阴的 (玩兒陰的)

To play dirty or mean tricks; to be devious or underhanded

◆ 他自称"姜太公"，就因为他办什么事儿都放在明面儿上，不**玩儿阴的**，也就是"愿者上钩"的意思。不信，明天一早你去找他试试，准保他不会一推六二五的。
(From the novel 九死还魂草)

He calls himself "Jiang Taigong" because he lays everything on the table and doesn't play dirty tricks. You take the bait willingly. If you don't believe me, give it a shot tomorrow morning. I guarantee he won't brush you off.

◆ 他那个人专门**玩阴的**。表面上看挺和气挺厚道，背地里净给你**使坏**。

　　He's a professional con man. He may look friendly and honest; but once your back is turned, he's plotting against you right away.

wàn jīn yóur 万金油儿 (萬金油兒)

Jack of all trades

◆ 我呢，在考察队里只能算是滥竽充数，文化馆的"**万金油干部**"嘛，文物、摄影、美术什么的都搞点儿。

(From the short story 古刹幻影)

　　As for me, I'm part of the expedition team just to make up the numbers. The usual Cultural Department "'jack of all trades." I do a bit of everything: cultural relics, photography, fine art, you name it.

◆ 老李这个人是**万金油儿**，什么都会一点儿，可是没有一样儿精通。

　　Old Li is a jack of all trades but master of none. He knows a bit of everything but has no particular expertise.

wàn wan méi yǒu xiǎng dào 万万没有想到 (萬萬沒有想到)

Not expected in a million years

◆ 我的故事也许你在电视里再也熟悉不过，我也一样。可是我却**万万没有想到**，这样的事情居然发生在我的身上。

(From the novel 我只愿，春暖花开)

　　You've seen this story many times on TV. Me too! But I never expected that it would happen to me. Not in a million years.

◆ 我**万万没有想到**，杀人犯竟然就是这个表面上看起来非常温柔的姑娘。

　　I would never have thought this girl who seemed so gentle could be the murderer. Not in a million years!

wáng bā dàn 王八蛋

Bastard; son of a bitch

◆ 畜牲，又是一夜！〖去赌博〗**狗改不了吃屎**，你这小**王八蛋**！

(From the movie 活着)

　　Another night of gambling, you animal! The leopard can't change its spots. Bastard!

◆ 哪个**王八蛋**把我汽车的玻璃砸了？**有种**的出来！

　　Which son of a bitch broke my car window? Come out if you've got the balls!

wáng dao 王道

Tyranny; tyrannical

◆ 哎，那年月就这么**王道**！谁让你不把帽子戴住了呢，帽子刮飞啦，脑袋也得跟着搬家！

(From the novel 官场斗)

　　Well, in those days there was tyranny. Whose fault was it if you couldn't keep your hat on your head? Now the hat has blown away. Next thing you know, your head is going to follow it. [A straw hat that blew away caused a disturbance among the queen's honor guard.]

♦ 监狱长也太王道了，你提点儿意见就关你的禁闭。

The warden's a tyrant. The slightest complaint, and he locks you in the cell.

wǎng huǒ kēng li tiào/tuī 往火坑里跳/推 (往火坑裏跳/推)

To jump (or push somebody) into a fiery pit; to put in harm's way

♦ 妈，你是把女儿往火坑里推，非让我犯错误。

(From the novel 都市危情)

Mom, if you force me to do something wrong, you put me in harm's way. [A mother forces her daughter to leak confidential information to people under investigation.]

♦ 你真不该让你妹妹去歌厅工作，去那种地方简直是往火坑里跳。

You shouldn't let your sister work in a karaoke joint. Working there is like jumping into a fire.

wǎng jué lù shàng bī 往绝路上逼 (往絕路上逼)

To force someone up against the wall; to push someone to the limit; to give someone no choice but to kill him/herself

♦ 这不是把我父母往绝路上逼吗？

(From the TV series 今生是亲人)

You are trying to force my parents up against the wall, aren't you? [The narrator is trying to stop someone from revealing his real biological identity to his parents.]

♦ 你把我肚子弄大了，现在又说要跟别人结婚，这不是把我往绝路上逼吗？

You knocked me up and now you're marrying someone else. You want me to kill myself?

wǎng shēn shang lǎn 往身上揽 (往身上攬)

To take something on your own back; to take credit; to shoulder responsibility

♦ 天下的不幸多着呢。都往自己身上揽，你还活不活了？

(From the short story 倾听夜色)

There's so much misery in the world. If you carry it all on your own shoulders, how can you keep on living? [The male character thinks the female character is too sentimental.]

♦ 你可真行啊！ 好事都往自己身上揽，麻烦都推给别人。

You're too much! You take credit for all the good things and let everyone else deal with the crap.

wèi nǎo dai 喂脑袋 (喂腦袋)

To eat

♦ 去吧，该喂脑袋了。

(From the TV series 大雪无痕)

Let's go. Time to grab a bite.

◆ "我实在没有时间跟你们去吃饭。""哪有这个道理？再忙这脑**袋也要喂啊。**"

"I'm too busy to eat." "What do you mean? No matter how busy you are, you have to refuel."

wō nāng (nang) fèi 窝囊废 (窩囊廢)

Good-for-nothing; loser

◆ 我是办错了事走错了路，嫁了你爸那个**窝囊废**，没有办法的了。

(From the novel 魔鬼与天使)

I made a big mistake marrying your father, that loser. Now there's no way out.

◆ 看你人模人样儿的，原来是个**窝囊废**！

You looked like a man. Turns out you're a real loser.

wǒ guò de qiáo bǐ nǐ zǒu de lù hái duō ne/ wǒ chī de yán bǐ nǐ chī de fàn hái duō ne 我过的桥比你走的路还多呢 /我吃的盐比你吃的饭还多呢 (我過的橋比你走的路還多呢/我吃的鹽比你吃的飯還多呢)

"I have crossed more bridges than you have walked roads"; "I have had more salt than you have had food"; I've forgotten more than you ever knew; I'm way out of your league

◆ 你懂什么？ 我过的桥比你走的路还多呢！

(From the TV series 激情燃烧的岁月)

What the heck do you know? I've forgotten more than you ever knew.

◆ 我吃的盐比你吃的饭还多，你用不着告诉我这活儿怎么干。

I've forgotten more than you ever knew. Don't you tell me how to do this job.

wǒ jiào/ràng sb v 我叫/让Sb V (我叫/讓Sb V)

This is what you get for (verb)…

◆ 〖一边打一边说〗你果然把金子私吞了，**我让你骗！ 我让你骗！**

(From the TV series 水浒传)

You're the one who took the money! This is what you get for cheating! This is what you get! [The speaker beat up a colleague who took more than his share of joint pay while claiming that the total amount he took was much less.]

◆ "**叫你耍流氓！ 叫你耍流氓！叫你耍流氓！** "每骂一句便踢他一脚，直到他瘫在地上。

(From the novel 永不瞑目)

This is what you get for hooliganism! This is what you get for hooliganism!" They punctuated each remark with a kick until he collapsed on the floor. [The victim was beaten up because he went out with his boss's daughter.]

wǒ shuō ne 我说呢 (我說呢)

No wonder; that explains it

◆ "那你也不是梦蝶了？""不是。""**我说呢**，我在台上还**纳闷**呢，梦蝶怎么换模样了，我记错了？ 别**露怯**。"

(From the movie 顽主)

"So you weren't Mengdie any more?" "No." "No wonder! I got confused on the stage, wondering why Mengdie looked like someone else, or whether I remembered it wrong. I'll be sure not to give it away!"

♦ "老陈最近怎么了，又买房子又买车的。" "你不知道？他中了个百万头彩。" "我说呢！"

"What's up with Lao Chen? He bought a house and a car?" "Didn't you hear? He hit the lottery for a million." "That explains it!"

wǒ shuō shénme lái zhe 我说什么来着 (我說什麼來著)

What did I tell you? I told you so.

♦ A："这球悬了！" B："我说肯定能进。" A："赌一杯酒的。" 〖球没进。〗A："我说什么来着？"

(From the movie 一见钟情)

A: "That ball is going to miss!" B: "I say it'll go in." A: "I'll bet you a glass of wine." (The ball misses the hole in a nightclub pool game.) Told you so!"

♦ "听说没有，老许把咱们公司的情报卖给对方了。" "我说什么来着，他这人根本靠不住。"

"Did you hear, Lao Xu sold company secrets to our competitor?" "What did I tell you? He's not someone you can trust."

wū yā zuǐ 乌鸦嘴 (烏鴉嘴)

A mouth like a crow; croaking doom

♦ "你们今天打算谈什么生意？如果两方无法达成协议怎么办？" "乌鸦嘴！" 他白她一眼。

(From the novel 不肯上车的新娘)

"What business deal are you discussing today? What if you can't reach an agreement?" "Stop croaking doom!" He gave her a dirty look.

♦ 你这个乌鸦嘴，今天商店刚开张你就说不吉利的话，我真该炒了你！

You're always croaking doom! Making such an unlucky remark on the store's grand opening day! I should have fired you!

wú lǐ jiǎo sān fēn 无理搅三分 (無理攪三分)

To act unreasonably; to pester; to harass; to make a scene without a reasonable cause

♦ 宋玉红是一头出名的母老虎，在厂子里都管她叫 "红辣椒"，仗着她嘴巴子厉害，一向是有理不让人，无理搅三分。

(From the novel 魔鬼与天使)

Song Hongyu is famous for being a shrew. They call her "Red Pepper" at the factory. She's got a nasty tongue. When she's in the right, she never gives anyone a break, and when she's in the wrong she just makes a scene.

◆ 厂里有明文规定，五十五岁退休，你却非要留下来，这不是**无理搅三分**吗？

> The factory has a very clear rule of retirement at age fifty-five. Your insistence on staying is totally unreasonable.

wǔ chǐ gāo de hàn zi 五尺高的汉子 (五尺高的漢子)

A six-foot tall man; a grown man (literally, five Chinese feet)

◆ 你哥一堂堂五尺高的汉子，一点办法也没有。

(From the TV series 大雪无痕)

> Your brother's a grown man. How come he can't find a way [to make a living]?

◆ **五尺高的汉子**败给了八岁的孩子！以后再也别吹你的篮球打得多好了。

> A grown man losing to an eight-year-old! I don't want to hear any more bragging about your basketball game.

wǔ mí sān dào 五迷三道

Clueless; muddle-headed; scatterbrained

◆ 你掉进富窝窝里，还**五迷三道**地转不过弯儿来。

(From the movie 红高粱)

> You hit the jackpot, but he is too clueless to see it.

◆ 没见过这么**五迷三道儿**的刑警，他总有一天惹出大祸来。

> I have never met such a scatterbrained detective. He's an accident waiting to happen.

...wǔr de ...伍儿的 (...伍兒的)

...and so on; or something like it

◆ 要不给你买点儿书**伍儿的**。

(From the TV series 今生是亲人)

> What if we buy you some books or something like that? [Asking what gift would be most appropriate.]

◆ 你要真想学个手艺，到街上找个训练班**伍儿的**。

(From the TV series 手心手背)

> If you really want to learn a trade, look for something like one of those training programs you can find on the street.

X

xī han 稀罕

"Rare"; value; treasure as a rare thing

◆ 钱我不**稀罕**，我跟他就不是钱的事儿。

(From the movie 有话好好说)

> I don't care about the money. Between him and me, it's not about money.

◆ 看样子你还挺**稀罕**这孩子。

(From the TV series 古船、女人和网)

Seems like you really think this kid is special.

xiā 瞎

"Blind"; in vain

◆ 您年年给他准备，年年**瞎**了。

Every year you prepare something for him, and every year it ends up being for nothing.

◆ 真倒霉，演员都找好了，**没承想**剧本没通过审查，咱们的计划又**瞎**了。

It's really a bummer! We already found the actors. Who knew the script wouldn't pass censorship! Once again our plans went to waste.

xiā bāi 瞎掰

"Break apart blindly"; talk nonsense; lie

◆ 谁说不让进？ **瞎掰**吧！

(From the TV series 一年又一年)

Who says we can't go in? I think that's bullshit! [The speaker was just told that only foreigners are allowed in posh hotels.]

◆ **瞎**他妈**掰**！赵向东也不是孙猴子，就凭这一张纸就当上总经理了？

(From the TV series 手心手背)

Stop talking fucking nonsense. Zhao Xiangdong is not Superman ["Monkey King"]. He made general manager based on just this piece of paper?

xiā cài 瞎菜

Beaten; failed; lost

◆ 后来，丫的也不知怎么抽上"白粉儿"了，这一抽，她在摇滚圈里更"**瞎菜**"了。

(From the novel 百年德性)

Afterwards that slut got started on heroin, God knows how. She was seen as even more of a total loser in the rock world.

◆ 你要是办不好这件事儿，在公司里你就彻底**瞎菜**了，趁早儿**走人**。

If you screw this up, you'll be finished in this company. You'd better get out of here while you still can.

xiā le nǐ de gǒu yǎn 瞎了你的狗眼

"Blinded your dog eyes"; Are you fucking blind?

◆ **瞎了你的狗眼**！

(From the TV series 康熙帝国)

You don't fucking know who you're talking to. [The addressee failed to recognize the speaker as one of the emperor's retainers.]

◆ **瞎了你的狗眼**了！ 要钱要到老子头上来了。

Are you fucking blind, trying to get money from me!

xiā māo pèng shang sǐ hào zi 瞎猫碰上死耗子 (瞎貓碰上死耗子)

"A blind cat ran into a dead mouse"; be unbelievably lucky; coincidental

◆ 你以为这是**瞎猫碰上死耗子**吗？人家是有备而来的。

(From the TV series 黑洞)

You think it was a coincidence? They came prepared!

♦ "能不能给我们讲讲你买卖股票的经验？怎么别人都赔了就你赚钱？""我哪儿有什么经验，**瞎猫碰上死耗子了**。"

"Can you tell us about your experience in the stock market? How come everyone else lost money but you made some?" "I have no experience to speak of. It was pure luck."

xiā v shénme 瞎V什么 (瞎V什麼)

"Do something blindly"; do something for no purpose

♦ 哎呀，好好躺着吧，又**瞎操什么心**！

(From the TV series 大宅门)
For heaven's sake, lie down! Why are you worrying yourself about nothing?

♦ "爸，妈，你们分居了？""小孩子家**瞎说什么**？"

(From the TV series 今生是亲人)
"Dad, mom, are you separating?" "Children shouldn't shoot their mouths off."

xiā zhā (zhà) hu 瞎咋呼

Talk excitedly and incoherently

♦ 这人不中用，整天就知道**瞎咋呼**。

(From the TV series 祥符春秋)
This guy is useless. All he knows how to do is shoot his mouth off all day.

♦ "听说你们家闺女和小张儿处上对象了？""**瞎咋呼什么**？人家小张儿已经结婚了。"

"I hear that your daughter and Xiao Zhang are an item now." "Shut up! Xiao Zhang is already married."

xià bèi zi 下辈子

Next life

♦ 吃大鱼大肉？等**下辈子**了。

(From the short story 粮食)
Eat big fish and big meat? Wait for the next life.

♦ "我也有出头的一天。""**下辈子**吧。"

"I'll have my day of glory." "Not in this life."

xià bu lái tán/xià de lái tán 下不来台/下得来台 (下不來台/下得來台)

"Can (or can't) come downstairs"; have (or not have) a face-saving exit

♦ 你总得让我**下得来台**吧？

(From the TV series 今生是亲人)
You've got to give me a graceful way out.

♦ 我给你解围，不求个谢字，可你也不能让我**下不来台**啊！

(From the TV series 手心手背)

I came to bail you out. I don't expect gratitude, but at least don't hang me out to dry.

xià dú/hēi shǒu 下毒/黑手

Lay murderous hands on; strike a vicious blow

◆   我饶你一条命，你他妈冲我下黑手！

(From the movie 红高粱)

I spare your life and you fucking want to stab me in the back!

◆   他总不能对我这个女婿下毒手吧？

(From the TV series 汽车城)

He wouldn't hurt me, would he? I'm his son-in-law!

xià sān làn 下三烂 (下三爛)

Rotten; low

◆   你以为我会做这种下三烂的事情吗？ 我是市长！ 不是黑帮的老大！

(From the TV series 欲罢不能)

You think I'd do something rotten like this? I'm the mayor, not a mafia boss!

◆   她给我留面子吗？ 非要干这下三烂的事儿，我打她她都不走。

(From the TV series 手心手背)

Reputation! Did she think about my reputation? She insists on acting like a two-bit whore, and even if I hit her she wouldn't leave that place. [He is speaking about a neighbor's teenage daughter, whom he found working in a dance hall, and who wouldn't leave even though he made a commotion. His employees are begging him to consider his reputation.]

xià zuò 下作

Obscene; low

◆   你想要钱就明说，干吗那么下作？

(From the TV series 特勤中队)

If you want money, just say so. Why did you have to stoop so low? [The speaker thinks that the man agreed to a sham marriage for money.]

◆   你这样做太下作了，你还有没有良心了？

What you did was really beneath contempt. Do you still have any conscience?

xiān bu qǐ duó dà fēng làng 掀不起多大风浪 (掀不起多大風浪)

"Can't do much to raise big wind or waves"; can't make much happen

◆   就凭他们几个人，掀不起多大风浪。

(From the TV series 红色康乃馨)

It's only a few people. They can't do much damage.

◆   区区几条小鱼儿啊，掀不起什么大浪来。不就是欠工人几个钱吗？ 回头补给他们就是了。

(From the TV series 问问你的心)

Little fish can't make waves. We just owe them some wages, right? We'll just make it up to them later. [Workers who didn't get their pay threaten to make trouble.]

xiān huā chā zài niú fèn shang 鲜花插在牛粪上 (鲜花插在牛糞上)

"Stick a fresh flower in a cowpie"; ruin a good thing through a gross mismatch

♦ 他们看不起汉生，他们认为小凤嫁给他是**鲜花插在牛粪上**。

(From the short story 过渡)

They look down on Hansheng and think that Xiaofeng's marrying him is pearls before swine.

♦ 他把她扶上车，听她抽抽嗒嗒地哭诉了几句，才知道这朵**鲜花又被牛粪糟蹋**了。

(From the novel 浮沈商海)

He helped her into the car. Only when she managed to sob out a few words did he realize that bastard had trampled her in the mud again. [An attractive and successful woman has been abused again by her violent husband.]

xiān máng qù le 先忙去了

Be excused (先 is used because one is leaving before others)

♦ 你们谈吧，我**先忙去了**。

(From the TV series 天骄)

Please continue the conversation. I'm afraid you'll have to excuse me.

♦ 要是没有别的事儿我**先忙去了**。

If there's nothing else, I'll be off.

xiān xiǎo rén hòu jūn zǐ 先小人后君子 (先小人後君子)

"Be a low life first and a gentleman later;" play hard ball first and soft ball later

♦ 我们**先小人后君子**，这玩艺算多少钱一块，太贵了我们也用不起。

(From the short story 围墙)

Let's ask the tough questions first. How much will these pretty things cost us? If they're too expensive we won't be able to afford them anyway. [Assessing an offer of glass bricks to repair a wall.]

♦ "等钱到了，怎么分你看着办吧！" "那可不行，咱们得定好了是平均分还是按股份多少分。这叫**先小人后君子**。"

"When the money gets here, split it any way you want." "No way. We have to decide if we're going to divide it equally or based on shares. Let's settle the tough questions first."

xián pai 显派 (顯派)

"Show style"; show off; showy

♦ 臭**显派**！ 结个婚把小半拉北京城都惊动了。

(From the TV series 北京女人)

Such rotten showing-off! Arranging a wedding that inconveniences half of Beijing! [Speaking of an ostentatious wedding procession.]

♦ 丈夫："你当是我跟你这儿**显派**呢？我是说这老外他**烧包**。" 妻子："别**得了便宜卖乖**了！"

(From the TV series 贫嘴张大民的幸福生活)

Husband: "You think I'm bragging? I'm just telling you what a showoff that foreigner was." Wife: "You should be thanking your lucky stars instead of boasting!" [A husband who works as a janitor at a luxury hotel tells his wife that a foreigner gave him a one-hundred-dollar tip.]

xián zhe yě shì xián zhe 闲着也是闲着 (閑著也是閑著)

One is not doing anything at the moment anyway; not have anything better to do

♦ 反正**闲着也是闲着**，打个分儿怕什么？

(From the movie 有话好好说)

I'm not doing anything right now. Why should I be afraid of rating them? I'll rate them, no big deal. [The workers are rating the women working at the club.]

♦ **闲着也是闲着**，赢了算你的，输了算我的，行吧？

(From the TV series 贫嘴张大民的幸福生活)

We've got nothing to do anyway. Win or lose, you get to keep the money. OK? [Trying to persuade the other person to play mahjong.]

xiàn shàng jiào xiàn zhā ěr duo yǎnr 现上轿现扎耳朵眼儿 (現上轎現紮耳朵眼兒)

"Pierce the bride's ears as she gets in the sedan chair"; do things at the last minute

♦ 恢复高考对于赵薇来说有些措手不及，突击了一个多月无异于**临时抱佛脚**。这种**现上轿现扎耳朵眼**的补救办法的结局，是她只能考进师范学院，就注定了她这辈子只得当一名孩子王。

(From the short story 留守女人)

The return of college entrance examinations caught Zhao Wei totally unprepared. She did a month's worth of last-ditch cramming, but the result of that eleventh-hour effort was only admission to a teachers' college. That meant she was doomed to the life of a grade school teacher.

♦ 早点动手准备，别净做**现上轿现扎耳朵眼儿**的事儿。

Start preparing early. Don't put everything off till the last minute.

xiàn zhǎng bú huàn 县长不换 (縣長不換)

"Wouldn't change places with a county magistrate"; I wouldn't change places with a king

♦ 这儿不愁吃不愁喝的，**给个县长也不换**。

(From the TV series 黑洞)

We're never short of food or drink here. I wouldn't trade it for the world. [A prisoner tries to console himself.]

♦ 多美个差事啊！**给个县长都不换**。

(From the TV series 一年又一年)

What a dream job! I wouldn't give it up for anything.

xiāng bō bo 香饽饽 (香餑餑)

"Sweet smelling steamed bun"; hotcakes; popular or highly desired

♦ "今儿怎么一下子冒出这么多人来？" "还不是因为这个工程是个**香饽饽**吗？"

(From the TV series 天堂鸟)

"Where did all these people come from?" "Well, everyone wants a piece of this construction project.

◆　过去知识分子是臭老九，现在又变成**香饽饽**了。

Used to be intellectuals were the scum of the earth. Now they're hot stuff again.

xiǎng qǐ yì chū shì yì chū 想起一出是一出

Come up with one crazy idea after another

◆　你看咱爹，想起一出是一出。

(From the TV series 古船、女人和网)

Look at our dad, he goes from one crazy affair to another. [Two daughters-in-law are discussing their widowed father-in-law's successive romances.]

◆　你现在是公司的经理，干什么事得有个计划，不能**想起一出是一出**。

You're the company manager now. You have to have a plan for everything. You can't do things by the seat of your pants!

xiǎng qīng fú 享清福 (享清福)

Enjoy ease and comfort

◆　我要是你，早就远走高飞到外面**享清福**去了。

(From the TV series 黑冰)

If I were you, I would have gone abroad to live it up long ago.

◆　您这把年纪，应该在家里抱孙子、**享清福**了。

At your age, you should be at home enjoying life with your grandchildren.

xiàng zhēn de yí yàng 象真的一样 (象真的一樣)

As if it were real; tell a good story

◆　我嘴上挺硬，心里已被他说得发虚：妈的，听上去有鼻子有眼，**像真的一样**。莫非我真撞见鬼了？

(From the novel 起伏人生路)

I talked tough, but inside I was scared: "Shit, it makes some sense, sounds as if it could be true. Did I really run into a ghost?" [The speaker and other four people got injured in a fire. Somebody just explained to him that the fire was set by the spirit of a lady who died innocently a few days earlier.]

◆　**象真的一样**，不就在外国人家当保姆吗！

(From TV series 涉外保姆)

She acts as if she's the real thing! She's nothing but a nanny for foreigners.

xiāo jiān nǎo dai wǎng...zuān 削尖脑袋往···钻 (削尖腦袋往···鑽)

"Sharpen one's head to burrow into"; do anything to...

◆　CNB〖公司〗每年有几千万的广告费投入。···因此，广告公司都**削尖了脑袋往CNB钻**。

(From the novel 浮沈商海)

CNB spends tens of millions on advertising every year, so all the ad agencies knock themselves out to get the CNB account.

♦ 前两年当兵**吃香**，年轻人都削尖脑袋往部队里钻。

A couple of years ago joining the army was very popular. Young men would do anything to get into the army.

xiāo tíng 消停

Letup; respite

♦ 就打那以后吧，我们俩再也没**消停**过。

(From the movie 洗澡)

Since then, we two haven't had a peaceful day. [打: from]

♦ 这些天怎么**消停**呢，越是这样我越觉乎着要出事儿。

(From the TV series 今生是亲人)

How come they've been so quiet these last few days? The more this goes on, the more I feel the axe is about to drop. [A couple who have been harassing the speaker and his wife with claims that their sons were switched at birth has suddenly become silent. In fact, the speaker is right and they are taking the matter to court.]

xiǎo 小

Almost; less than

♦ "这地方离这儿多远？" 〖出示纸条上的地址〗 "来回吧，得小两站地呢！"

(From the TV series 今生是亲人)

"How far is this place" [pointing to an address on paper]? "There and back, it's about the distance of three bus stops."

♦ 都小半年了，他一封信也没来。

It's been almost six months. He hasn't written once.

xiǎo bái liǎn 小白脸 (小白臉)

"Small white face"; pretty boy

♦ 好呀，拿我的钱去倒贴**小白脸**，难怪最近她老是向我要钱，帐户还凭空失踪了相当多钱，我还以为她拿去投资股票，结果却是投资这个小王八蛋。

(From the novel 堕落天使)

Great! She's been spending my money on her pretty boy. That's why she's always asking me for money lately and why so much money has disappeared from the account. I thought she was investing in stocks. Who knew? She was investing in that little son of a bitch.

♦ 现在的男演员越丑越粗就越**吃香**，**小白脸**儿根本**没戏**。

Nowadays it's the ugly, rough actors who sell tickets [the popularity of an actor is in direct proportion to how ugly and rough he looks]. Pretty boys don't have a chance.

xiǎo biē sān 小瘪三 (小癟三)

(Shanghai dialect) "a small beggar"; a nobody

♦ 这**小瘪三**算是成材了。

(From the TV series 汽车城)

That loser finally made something of himself. [His son became general manager of an automobile factory.]

♦   那个**小瘪**三绝对配不上您的千金，他是**癞蛤蟆想吃天鹅肉**。
    That loser is no match for your daughter. He's daydreaming.

xiǎo cài yì diér 小菜一碟儿 (小菜一碟兒)

"A small dish of food"; a piece of cake; small potatoes

♦   "这种新计算机你能修吗？""**小菜儿一碟儿**。"
    "Can you fix this new type of computer?" "Piece of cake."

♦   我这话**糙可**是**理不糙**。以你张大庆的本事，平安工程只是**一碟小菜儿**，你干点儿什么别的不行？
    (From the TV series 天堂鸟)
    My words may be clumsy, but the idea is not. Zhang Daqing, for someone of your ability, the Ping'an project is small potatoes. Why not take on something else? [Why must you compete with me?]

xiǎo dǎ xiǎo nàor 小打小闹儿 (小打小鬧兒)

A small matter; do something on a small scale

♦   我想这种联合起来的力量绝不是**小打小闹**了。
    (From the novel 盖世太保枪口下的中国女人)
    I think this kind of consolidated army will really be a force to contend with. [A Belgian guerrilla leader is talking about Allied Armies fighting the Nazis.]

♦   大家都知道**小打小闹儿**不行，做就要做大做强。
    (From the TV series 大赢家)
    Everyone knows small doesn't cut it. If you're going to do it at all, you have to go big. You have to get powerful. [A company must expand in order to succeed.]

xiǎo de liūr de 小的溜儿的 (小的溜兒的)

Small; insignificant

♦   "噢，这么说，你也算开拓型干部了。"晶晶欣赏地看着我。"**不敢当，小的溜的吧**。"
    (From the novel 浮出海面)
    "Oh, that means you're one of the leaders too, a trailblazer!" Jingjing looked at me with admiration. "Oh no, I'm only a minor player"

♦   咱不能跟头儿比。人家大把大把的拿钱，咱呢，**小的溜儿的**拿点儿就行了。
    We can't compare ourselves with the boss. He rakes in tons of money. Let's be happy with whatever scraps we can get."

xiǎo dù jī cháng 小肚鸡肠 (小肚雞腸)

"Small stomach, chicken intestines"; small-minded

♦   "我哪有那眼福啊？回头您那黄麻头〖蟋蟀品种〗我看在眼里拔不出来了。""你不想看**拉倒**啊！ 还**小肚鸡肠**，还记仇儿了。"
    (From the movie 洗澡)
    "Do my eyes deserve to see such a thing? Besides, what if I did get to see your Jutehead [species of cricket] and then coveted it?" "If you don't want to look, then forget it. I

didn't expect you to keep score and hold grudges like that." [The two older men had had an argument over some crickets the previous day.]

♦ 鲁鱼想没和那些泼妇骂街式的、飞言飞语式的、**小肚鸡肠**式的人住在一起，就算是自己走运了。

(From the novel 大学鲁鱼)

Lu Yu counted herself lucky that she didn't have to live with those bitchy, gossipy, small-minded people. [Speaking of college roommates.]

xiǎo ér kē 小儿科 (小兒科)

"Pediatric department"; child's play; childish

♦ "来我们公司干吧，我们也需要计算机人才。" "你们房地产公司的那点计算机业务都是**小儿科**。"

(From the TV series 超越情感)

"Come work for our company. It just so happens that we need computer talent." "You're a real estate company. Your computer work is child's play."

♦ 跟咱们刑警来这套，太**小儿科**了！

(From the TV series 黑洞)

We're the Crime Unit; don't play this kind of game with us. It's too infantile.

xiǎo hái zi jiā 小孩子家

Children

♦ "爸，妈，你们分居了？" "**小孩子家**瞎说什么？"

(From the TV series 今生是亲人)

"Dad, mom, are you separating?" "Children shouldn't shoot their mouths off."

♦ 这是大人的事儿，**小孩子家**别瞎打听。

This is a matter for grownups. You're just a kid. Keep your nose out of it.

xiǎo jiā zi qì 小家子气 (小家子氣)

"The air of a small family"; petty; ungenerous

♦ 冯大人这话**小家子气**了。

(From the TV series 康熙帝国)

Lord Feng, these terms are ungenerous. [An imperial convoy is negotiating the return of Taiwan with a representative of its government. Lord Feng is driving a hard bargain.]

♦ 他这个人做什么事都透着**小家子气**，成不了大气候。

He's petty in everything he does. He'll never amount to anything.

xiǎo jiě 小姐

"Miss"; euphemism for prostitutes

♦ 〖这个人是〗一个有点儿文化或者高级点儿的**小姐**都有可能。

(From the movie 一见钟情)

She may well be one of those cultured or high-class prostitutes. [He fell in love at first sight with a girl he met, and then she deceived him.]

♦   太不象话了，他不但公开向咱们索要礼物，还要让咱们付钱给他找小姐！

That's outrageous. He openly demands gifts from us, and he wants us to pay a prostitute for him!

xiǎo mì 小秘/蜜

"Small secretary/honey"; mistress

♦   我一开始还以为她是你在北京的那个什么，对，那个小秘呢！

(From the TV series 北京女人)

At first I thought she was your Beijing what do you call it—oh right, your sweetie.

♦   这年头，甭管有钱没钱，也甭管社会地位高低，婚外"傍"着一个"小蜜"，已然成了一种时尚。

(From the novel 百年德性)

These days it doesn't matter if you're rich or poor, upper-class or lower-class, having a mistress is the in thing.

xiǎo shì yì zhuāng 小事一桩 (小事一樁)

A small matter

♦   小事一桩，小事一桩，我知道你会开车，只是不会英文，才肯这么帮你。

(From the novel 我在新西兰当警官)

No big deal. I know you can drive. You just don't know English. That's why I'm willing to help you. [The speaker offers to help the other person cheat on a written driving test in New Zealand.]

♦   "您能不能请位名人给我们写个招牌？""小事一桩。"

"Can you find someone famous to do some calligraphy on our sign?" "No problem."

xiǎo tù zǎi zi 小兔崽子

"Small baby rabbit"; son of a bitch

♦   你说这小兔崽子，怎么跟爹说话的？

(From the TV series 今生是亲人)

You little brat, how dare you talk like that to your father?

♦   这个小兔崽子又来捣乱，我非得好好教训他一顿不可。

That bastard came to make trouble again. I'll have to teach him a lesson.

xiǎo xīn yǎnr 小心眼儿 (小心眼兒)

Narrow-minded

♦   你有的时候太小心眼儿。

(From the TV series 都市情感)

Sometimes you're too narrow-minded. [The speaker is complaining to her boyfriend, who wants her to avoid rich men.]

◆   你这个大老爷们儿怎么**心眼比针尖儿还小**？

How come a grown man like you has a mind as narrow as a pinpoint?

xiǎo yāo jng 小妖精

"Small evil spirit"; vamp; temptress

◆   他家也不着，孩子也不管，**敢情**都是你们这些**小妖精**勾搭的！

(From the TV series 手心手背)

He's never home, and he ignores his child. Turns out it's because you bimbos have seduced him! [A wife learns that her husband has been spending time at a nightclub.]

◆   你呀，一见你们办公室的**小妖精**就晕菜了。

You! The moment you see that bimbo from your office your head's in the clouds.

xiào diào dà yá 笑掉大牙

"Laugh till the big (front) teeth fall off"; laugh one's head off

◆   也不是因公殉职，得的是艾滋病，不怕人**笑掉大牙**！

(From the TV series 失乐园)

It's not as if it were a job-related death; it was AIDS. Aren't you afraid people will laugh their heads off? [Discussing a memorial service at the workplace, the speaker alludes to the stigma associated with AIDS.]

◆   把一个乡下姑娘领回来，左邻右舍都要**笑掉大牙**你知道不知道啊？

(From the TV series 走过花季)

You brought a peasant girl home. Don't you know the neighbors will die laughing? [A mother doesn't approve of her son going out with a migrant worker from the country.]

xiē cài 歇菜

Stop doing something (菜: a colloquial intensifier)

◆   "你要是不参加比赛，我就没竞争对手了。""**歇菜**吧你！"

(From the TV series 花样年华)

"If you don't enter the contest, I'll have no competition." "Come off it!" [A boy hopes that his female classmate will take part in a national writing contest.]

◆   "要是我坐进这间办公室〖局长办公室〗怎么样？""怕没有这一天了，等你进了这间办公室，哥早就退休**歇菜**了。"

(From the TV series 黑冰)

"What would you think if this becomes my office [office of the bureau director]?" "If that day ever comes, it'll be long after my retirement."

xié hu 邪虎/邪乎/邪忽

"Wicked"; way out there

◆   可你们玩的也**忒邪乎**了。我跟你一起这么多天，没见你有一点正经事。

(From the novel 浮出海面)

But you guys party way too much. I've been with you now for many days and I haven't seen you do anything serious.

◆   我又觉得这酒不光有假，而且假得挺**邪乎**，八成还有碍身体健康。

(From the novel 女性写真)

I think the wine is not only ersatz but it's way off, probably dangerous for your health.

xié ménr 邪门儿 (邪門兒)

"Wicked"; weird; out there

◆ 也真邪了门儿，"豁牙子"碰上老杜便拉稀了。他扛了没多大工夫，就秃噜了。

(From the novel 百年德性)

> It's really weird how Gaptooth got the runs when he saw Lao Du. He didn't hold out for long before he just caved in. [Lao Du is the police chief; previous investigators had gotten nothing out of Gaptooth.]

◆ 真是活见鬼了，门窗都好好的，被害人却死了，凶手也不见踪影，真他妈的邪门！

(From the novel 魔湖惊魂)

> Well, I'll be damned. The doors and windows are shut tight, but the victim is dead. There are no traces of the killer anywhere. This is fucking weird.

xié xing 邪性

Uncanny; hexed; weird

◆ 我也想不出来了，这孩子丢得真邪性。就出在那个带他看摔跤的人身上。

(From the TV series 大宅门)

> I don't remember anymore either. It's weird how that kid got lost. It was all the fault of that man who took him to the wrestling match.

◆ 这件事儿真有点儿邪性，他的大儿子刚让车撞死，二儿子又出了交通事故。

> This is really spooky. His oldest son was just run over by a car. His second son got into a traffic accident.

xiè mò shā lú 卸磨杀驴 (卸磨殺驢)

"Kill the donkey after unfastening it from the grindstone"; get rid of someone who is no longer useful

◆ 既然你爸爸卸磨杀驴要赶咱们走，咱也就不必再赖下去了。

(From the novel 空洞)

> Since your father used us and wants to throw us away, there's no point hanging around anymore. [A son-in-law worked as foreman on his father-in-law's construction project, but afterwards did not get the position he had hoped for. He urges his wife to leave her family.]

◆ 经理，我们辛辛苦苦把公司办起来，你又要把我们一脚踢开，这不是卸磨杀驴吗？

> Manager, it's our hard work that got the company started. Now you want to kick us out. Doesn't that amount to using people and then throwing them away?

xīn jí chī bù liǎo rè dòu fu 心急吃不了热豆腐 (心急吃不了熱豆腐)

(Proverb) "An impatient man can't eat hot tofu"; you can't accomplish anything if you're impatient

◆ 我比你还急，可心急吃不了热豆腐啊！

(From the TV series 祥符春秋)

I'm even more worried than you are. But worrying won't get us anywhere. [A theater troupe is running out of money and looking for a way to earn some.]

◆ **心急吃不得热豆腐**，海州毒品大案的背景很深，切忌处理案件简单粗放，操之过急只能导致**捡了芝麻丢了西瓜**。

(From the TV series 黑冰)

> Haste makes waste. There's more to that Haizhou drug case than meets the eye. The main thing is not to be superficial and careless. If we jump too fast we could miss the big prize.

xīn lǐ bú shì zī wèir 心里不是滋味儿 (心裏不是滋味兒)

"No flavor in the heart"; bad feeling

◆ 阿东看着眼前这情景，想着刚才看过的电视剧，**心里很不是滋味**，抱个枕头到沙发上去睡了。

(From the short story 太太的老板)

> A Dong considered the situation at hand and thought about the TV show he had just watched. It left a bad taste in his mouth, so he took a pillow and went to sleep on the sofa. [A Dong's wife is out with her boss entertaining clients. The TV show was about a woman landing a sugar daddy.]

◆ "我今天才懂得什么叫唇枪舌剑了，几句话就把这个肖静宜**挤兑**走了，你可真有一套。" "其实我看她流泪的样子，**心里挺不是滋味儿**的。"

(From the TV series 忠诚卫士)

> "Now I understand what a battle of words really is. You finished her off in just a few sentences. You're really something." "Actually, when I saw her cry, I kind of felt bad."

xīn lǐ yǒu shù 心里有数 (心裏有數)

"Have the numbers in one's heart"; have a plan; know in one's heart

◆ 放心吧，我**心里有数**。

(From the TV series 古船、女人和网)

> Relax, I've got it under control.

◆ 我对你怎么样，你**心里有数**，大家看得明白，你应该说句公平话。

(From the novel 我是你爸爸)

> You know in your heart how I treat you, and everyone sees it. Out of simple justice, you should say something.

xīn qìr tài gāo 心气儿太高 (心氣兒太高)

Too proud; too ambitious

◆ "挣那么多钱干什么啊？**熬着吃、炒着吃也咬不动**。" "我也这么想，可她**心气儿太高**。"

(From the TV series 贫嘴张大民的幸福生活)

"What's the point of making so much money? Stew it, stir fry it—you still can't bite into it." "That's the way I think, too, but she's too driven." [She is determined to open a second store.]

♦ 这孩子**心气儿**太高，没考上重点大学就觉得没脸见人了。

This kid set his sights too high. Since he didn't make it into a first-rank university, he feels he can't look people in the eye.

xīn shuō 心说 (心說)

Say to oneself; think

♦ 这小偷儿**心说**了，您横是不能光着屁股出来追我吧？

(From the movie 洗澡)

The thief thought to herself, "No way you'd go out buck naked to chase me down, would you?" [A thief stole someone's necklace in a public bath.]

♦ "接你的电话，我直胆儿小。我**心说**咱是守法公民，没犯事儿呀。怎么分局的人找我呢。" "别逗闷子了，跟你说点正事儿。"

(From the novel 百年德性)

"When you called, I was really scared. I said to myself, I'm a law-abiding citizen. I haven't done anything against the law. Why would the police want to talk to me?" "Stop fooling around. I have something serious to discuss with you."

xín si 寻思 (尋思)

"Search and think"; think; conclude

♦ 我**寻思**，这个人肯定不是这片儿的。

(From the TV series 今生是亲人)

I thought, this man is definitely not from around here. [A neighborhood crime watcher saw a suspicious-looking man waiting for someone.]

♦ 虽说你是把婚离了，可细**寻思**起来，街上能开车的女强人也不算多吧？

(From the TV series 北京女人)

Even though you're divorced and all that, when you think about it, how many superwomen are out there driving around on the streets? [A mother is consoling her divorced daughter: her marriage may have failed, but at least her career is successful. She has a company car at her disposal to show for it.]

xīng..., bù xīng 兴..., 不兴... (興..., 不興...)

OK for someone, but not OK for someone else

♦ **兴**你们告我们生产假冒伪劣，就**不兴**我们告你们渎职？

(From the TV series 蓝色马蹄莲)

It's OK for you to accuse us of making counterfeit or shoddy goods, but it's not OK for us to accuse you of dereliction of duty? [Speaking to a representative of the Industrial and Commercial Administration Bureau.]

♦ 怎么着？ 兴你包二奶就不兴我泡妞？

What? You can keep a mistress, but I can't chase girls?

xīng xǔ 兴许 (興許)

Perhaps; maybe

♦ "又是亮子的电话，不理他。" "回一个吧，**兴许**有什么要紧事儿呢。"

(From the TV series 一年又一年)

"It's Liangzi calling again. I'll just ignore him." "You better call him back. It could be something urgent."

♦ 你不说留给于大巴掌那老驴，我**兴许**还不要你的，你一说我偏要提走不可。

(From the short story 鱼市)

If you didn't tell me you were saving it for that ass Bighand Yu, I probably wouldn't ask you for it. Since you told me, I insist on taking it. [The speaker wants the best fish.]

xíng xing hǎo 行行好

Practice mercy; have mercy

♦ 我求求你**行行好**，帮我找间房子吧？

(From the TV drama 耷旯胡同)

I'm begging you, do me a favor. Help me find a room. [His house is leaking, and he is asking his boss for help.]

♦ 你**行行好**吧，我这孩子正发烧呢，您就别把他抓走了！

Please have mercy. This child of mine has a fever. Please don't take him away!

xióng yàng 熊样 (熊樣)

Origin unknown; pathetic

♦ 你瞧你那副**熊样子**！

(From the TV series 黑洞)

Look at you, you're pathetic! [Going around with a hangdog look after being wronged.]

♦ 瞧你这付**熊样子**！不就赔了二十万吗？**没什么大不了的。**

Stop whining! You just lost two hundred grand, that's all. What's the big deal?

xiū lǐ 修理

"Repair"; take care of

♦ 李掌柜，这事你不用怕，就凭那小子，还用得着马三爷出头？他敢来我们**修理**他，起码断他一条腿。

(From the novel 太监)

Steward Li, don't you worry about this. No need for Master Ma himself to take on such a loser. If he dares to show his face, we'll take care of him. At the very least we'll break one of his legs.

♦ 您这闺女，赶快抓空儿**修理**吧，这长大了，可不是一盏**省油儿的灯**啊！

(From the TV series 北京女人)

About this daughter of yours, you'd better hurry and nip the problem in the bud. When she grows up she's going to be a real handful. [The girl wants to start dating at the age of ten.]

xū tóu bā nǎo 虚头八脑 (虛頭八腦)

Incoherent; neither here nor there

♦ 你这一桶一桶地灌我们〖喝啤酒〗，说的又都是**虚头八脑**的话，我怎么有一种**遭你暗算**的感觉啊！

(From the movie 甲方乙方)

You keep offering us beer, and your remarks are neither here nor there. How come I can't help feeling you're trying to pull a fast one on me?

♦ 他总是说些**虚头八脑**的话，从来没见过他干点儿**实打实**的事儿。

He always speaks in woolly rhetoric. I've never seen him actually do anything concrete.

xuē bào 噱暴

(Taiwan expression) make a lot of money; make a bundle (噱＝赚钱, make money; 噱暴＝赚了很多钱)

♦ 文龙〖人名〗最近**噱暴**了。

(From the movie 台北爱情故事)

Wen Long made a killing recently?

♦ 他去上海**噱钱**，听说**噱暴**了。

He went to Shanghai to make money swindling people. I hear he made a fortune.

xuē tou/huā tou 噱头/花头 (噱頭/花頭)

(Shanghai dialect) trick; stunt; clever joke

♦ 你在鱼，汤二位面前最好少玩**噱头**。

(From the novel 魔手邪怪)

Don't try any funny business in front of Mr. Yu and Mr. Tang. [Yu, or 鱼得水,"Fish Attaining Water," and Tang are martial arts masters.]

♦ "什么作文比赛！就是你们学校**花头**多！"

(From the TV series 新七十二家房客)

"What writing contest? Trust your school to come up with one gimmick after another." [A son wants fifty yuan from his father to participate in a writing contest organized by the school.]

xué mo 趓摸

Look for

♦ 我说你这儿瞎**趓摸**什么呢？

(From the TV series 激情燃烧的岁月)

What are you rummaging around in here for?

♦ 你这烟袋锅不错，给我也**踅摸**一个？

Your smoke pipe is very nice. Can you find me one, too?

Y

yā 丫

(Vulgar) "Maiden"; born to an unmarried woman; bastard

♦ 后来，丫的也不知怎么抽上"**白粉儿**"了，这一抽，她在摇滚圈里更"**瞎菜**"了。

(From the novel 百年德性)

Afterwards that slut got started on heroin, God knows how. She was seen as even more of a total loser in the rock world.

♦ "刘哥，您能不能借给我两千块钱，我一发工资准还您。""你丫刚跟我借了一千五，才几天啊，怎么又来借啊，你当我是银行哪？"

"Brother Liu, could you loan me two grand? I'll pay you back as soon as I get my paycheck." "You bastard! You just borrowed fifteen hundred from me. How many days ago was that, andnow you're back to borrow more? What am I, your bank?"

yā 鸭 (鴨)

"Duck"; male prostitute [streetwalkers are called 鸡 (jī, chicken) —nearly homonymous with 妓 (jì, prostitute)—or 野鸡 (wild chicken), so male prostitutes are known as 鸭.]

♦ 大姐，这叫**各村有各村的**高招。仔细想想，女人挣钱没什么用。男人有权有钱，玩女人**泡妞**是个乐子，这钱也有个去处。女人就难了，有权有钱也**白搭**，这鸭店就是给有权有钱的女人开的。

(From the novel 都市危情)

Sister, this is called "different strokes for different folks." When you think about it, women have no use for the money they make. A man with money and power can have a good time womanizing, so he's got a use for his money. It's more of a problem for women. What can they do with their money and power? This male brothel was specially established for rich and powerful women.

♦ 我看那小白脸儿像是鸭，光那身打扮就看得出来。

That pretty boy seems like a male prostitute to me. You can tell just by the way he gets himself up.

yà gēnr 压根儿 (壓根兒)

"All the way from the root"; in the first place; (not) at all

♦ 把话**说白了**吧，我跟他压根儿就没什么交情。

(From the TV series 今生是亲人)

Let me level with you. He and I were not friends to begin with. [They were middle school classmates but not friends.]

♦ 其实，按我的本意，我是非常想介入侦破这个案子的。不是我**憋着**要立功，而是出于一种个人目的，这是埋在我心里有两年多的秘密，我压根儿没跟别人说过，包括我的师兄老杜。

(From the novel 百年德性)

Actually, what I really want is to get involved in this case and crack it. It's not that I'm dying to get points. I've got a personal reason, which I've kept secret for two years. I haven't told anyone at all, not even my partner Lao Du.

yā tou piàn zi 丫头片子 (丫頭片子)

"Maiden"; an inexperienced or immature young woman

◆ 钱，给这丫头片子交学费。

(From the TV series 今生是亲人)

Here, this is the money for the silly girl's tuition. [A brother hands over money he has earned to his father, to use toward his sister's education.]

◆ 雇几个小毛丫头片子，整天"经理不在"，"经理不在"的，糊弄谁呢你们？

(From the TV series 贫嘴张大民的幸福生活)

You hired a couple of schoolgirls to chant, "the manager isn't in," all day. Who do you think you're fooling? [The speaker is trying to collect a debt.]

yà mǎ lù 轧马路 (軋馬路)

"Level (roll) the road"; take a stroll (usually with a lover)

◆ 当然啦，既然是轧马路，当然要找那感觉。

(From the TV series 编辑部的故事)

When you're taking a walk with your sweetie, you naturally want to get into the right mood.

◆ 你找他啊？跟女朋友轧马路去了，你明儿再来吧。

You're looking for him? Well, he's taking a walk with his girlfriend. Why don't you come back tomorrow?

yán (yuán) shēngr 言声儿 (言聲兒)

"Make a sound"; say something; tell

◆ "你怎么不言声就进来了？""你们家又不是金銮殿，难道还得层层通报，扯着喉头叫破嗓门才行。"

(From the novel 日落紫禁城)

"How come you just walked in without asking permission?" "Your house isn't the imperial palace. Do you mean I can't get in without being announced from room to room, or yelling myself hoarse?"

◆ 昨天在公共汽车我检到一个钱包，我问了三遍是谁的，楞没一个人言声儿。我只好把钱包先揣起来了。

I found a wallet on the bus yesterday. I asked three times whose it was, but to my surprise no one said a word. All I could do was keep the wallet for the time being.

yǎn bā bā 眼巴巴

"Eyes (that show) eager anticipation"; eagerly; anxiously (巴巴: anticipation in the eye)

◆ 咱妈现在在家眼巴巴地等着你呢！

(From the TV series 手心手背)

Mother's holding her breath at home waiting for you to come back. [A brother is trying to persuade his runaway sister to go back home.]

♦ 你不知道吗？你父母眼巴巴等着你回电话，你怎么还在这儿跳舞啊？

Don't you know your parents are waiting anxiously for you to call them back? How come you're still dancing here?

yǎn bú jiàn, xīn bù fán 眼不见，心不烦 (眼不見，心不煩)

"If the eyes don't see, the heart doesn't care"; out of sight, out of mind

♦ "所以你干脆就到上海来避清闲？" "也不是，因为你也知道，最近你那公司可能有很大的变动，所以我怕金勇又找我麻烦，所以干脆就到这里来，**眼不见心不烦**。"

(From the TV drama script 风往南吹)

"So you just came to Shanghai to get away from it all?" "Not exactly. As you know, your company may go through some major changes soon. I'm afraid Jinyong will be on my case again, so I just came here. Out of sight, out of mind." [The speaker's ex-boyfriend, Jinyong, was caught taking kickbacks at his company. She is afraid he will think she was the one who turned him in.]

♦ "真没想到，好容易儿子考上了北京大学，还得为他操心。他非要学什么历史，我和他妈怎么劝他也不听。你儿子怎么样？" "现在的年轻人都一样。不过，他在上海上学，我在北京，我啊，是**眼不见，心不烦**。"

"I never dreamed that after my son managed somehow to pass the exams for Beijing University, I'd still have to worry about him. He insists on majoring in history and won't listen to his mother's advice or mine. How about your son?" "Young people are all the same these days. But he's studying in Shanghai and I'm in Beijing. So what I don't know doesn't hurt me."

yǎn chán 眼馋 (眼馋)

"Greedy-eyed"; green-eyed; envious; covet something

♦ 谁要看着**眼馋**就一块儿干，有我吃的就有他吃的，要是不敢来就算了，咱们不怕撑着，自己包啦！

(From the novel 亮剑)

If anyone's envious, join me and we'll work together. What I have, you'll have. But if you don't have the guts, then forget it. I'm not worried about having too much; I'm perfectly happy to keep it all for myself.

♦ 你要是看人家赚钱**眼馋**，你也自己开家饭馆儿嘛。

If you're envious of other people making good money, why not open a restaurant yourself?

yǎn dōu bú dài zhǎ de 眼都不带眨的 (眼都不帶眨的)

"The eyes don't blink"; not bat an eye

♦ 就你心眼好，人家退你稿儿可是**眼都不带眨的**。

(From the TV series 编辑部的故事)

You're the only one who's so nice. Those guys don't even bat an eye when they reject your manuscript.

♦ 梁宝心想，这老小子真是块当演员的好料子，撒谎扯皮，**眼都不带眨的**。

(From the novel 赝人)

Liang Bao thought to himself, this old bastard would make good acting material. He can lie or cheat without batting an eye.

yǎn dōu lù le/ lán le 眼儿都绿了/蓝了 (眼兒都綠了/藍了)

"Even the eyes turn green/blue"; so worried, angry, or jealous that one's eyes hurt; a strong emotional reaction caused by anger, anxiety, or jealousy

♦   你爸你妈急得眼儿都绿了！

(From the TV series 今生是亲人)

Your parents were so worried they were sweating blood! [Spoken to a child who ran away from home.]

♦   每当看到自己买不起的东西，别人却挤在那儿抢，我眼都蓝了。

(From the novel 我是你爸爸)

Whenever I see something I can't afford and everyone else is rushing out to buy it, I seethe inside.

yǎn hóng 眼红 (眼紅)

"Red-eyed"; jealous or furious

♦   最倒霉的就是我这样的人，看别人挣钱眼红，自己又不知道怎么办。

(From the TV series 一年又一年)

People like me are the most miserable of all. We go green with envy when we see other people get rich, but we haven't a clue how to go about it ourselves.

♦   我就巴不得他早点死，拿毒药毒死了他，陈家的财产不就让我一个人给占了，百万家产呀，我眼红着呢！

(From the novel 红檀板)

I can't wait for him to die. If we poison him, the Chen family fortune will be all mine. We're talking a million dollars worth of property. I'm dying to have it!

yǎn li jiànr/yǎn li jiàr 眼里见儿/眼力价儿 (眼裏見兒/眼力價兒)

"Eyes see things"; observant and sensible; be able to see a problem or understand a situation and then act appropriately

♦   就你烦人，没个眼力价，这会儿有你什么事？再嚷把你轰出去。

(From the novel 一点正经没有)

You're so annoying; you just don't have a clue. What's this got to do with you? One more word and you're out of here.

♦   我们家二小子一点儿眼里见儿都没有。我和他爹忙着刷房，累得差点儿吐血，他呢，就坐在那儿听音乐。

That second son of ours doesn't notice anything. His dad and I worked till we dropped painting the house. But he just sat there and listened to his music.

yǎn lǐ róng bù dé shā zi 眼里容不得沙/砂子 (眼裏容不得沙/砂子)

"Can't stand sand in the eye"; can't stand the sight of; intolerant of anything wrong or ugly

♦   娘娘眼里容不得沙子，把它吹掉不就得了吗？

(From the novel 大脚马皇后)

The empress won't put up with anything that offends her. Why not just eliminate the problem? ["The problem" is a new woman who won the emperor's heart.]

♦ 这赵三进省城不久傍上个老富婆，就把身子卖给人家了。刘山杏**眼里不揉沙子**，当然不会再和他来往。

    (From the novel 刘老根)

    Zhao San hadn't been in the provincial capital long when he dug up a rich old woman and sold her his body. Liu Shanxing is not someone to put up with that sort of thing. Naturally she broke off with him. [Liu was Zhao's girlfriend.]

yǎn pí dǐ xià 眼皮底下

    "Under one's eyelid"; under one's nose

♦ 我真马大哈，你爸这剃这头有好几年了，**谁承想**，在我**眼皮底**下闹出这么一出儿。

    (From the TV series 贫嘴张大民的幸福生活)

    Boy, was I blind. Your father's been going there for haircuts for quite a few years. Who thought he'd pull something like this right under my nose? [The speaker suspects her husband is having an affair with a hairdresser.]

♦ 我说你小子不要命了，敢到警察**眼皮底**下来卖毛片儿？

    You're one reckless bastard. Are you nuts, selling porn flicks right under the nose of the police?

yǎn xiàn 眼线 (眼線)

    Police informer; snitch

♦ 想让我当**眼线**，给你卧底？我怎么能干这个？

    (From the TV series 大雪无痕)

    You want me to turn informer and do undercover work for you? How could I do such a thing? [A reporter refuses her policeman boyfriend's request to collect information on a suspect.]

♦ 张董事长，根据我的了解，警方已经在咱们公司的高层安插了**眼线**，而且不止一个，您说话办事可千万要小心啊！

    Board Chairman Zhang, according to my information the police have already planted spies in our company's top management, and not just one either. You have to be really careful what you say and do.

yǎn yūn (yùn) 眼晕 (眼暈)

    "The eyes are dizzy"; dazzled; dizzy

♦ 自打一达回来以后，一年一个样，我看着都**眼晕**。

    (From the TV series 一年又一年)

Around the time Yida came back, it [Beijing] began to change completely every year. It makes my head swim.

♦ 这商店里里外外的摆设花里唬哨，让人眼晕。

This shop's interior and exterior displays are so garish they make people dizzy.

yǎn zhōng dīng ròu zhōng cì 眼中钉肉中刺 (眼中釘肉中刺)

"Nail in the eye and thorn in the flesh"; thorn in the flesh; sworn enemy

♦ 他平常也是把丁秃爪子看成**眼中钉肉中刺**的，恨不能一下子把他整出一中去。今天抓住这个事件怎能不抢先告他一状。

(From the novel 夜幕下的哈尔滨)

Besides, he always thought Baldy Claw Ding was a nuisance and a thorn in his flesh, and wished he could drive him out of Middle School No. 1. So how could he resist using today's incident and rushing to be the first to inform the authorities?

♦ 自从上次董事会上我对新项目提了不同意见以后，王总经理一直把我看成是**眼中钉**，处处跟我为难。

Ever since I raised some objections to the new project at the last board meeting, Manager Wang sees me as an adversary, and makes life difficult for me at every turn.

yàn bú xià zhè kǒu qì 咽不下这口气 (咽不下這口氣)

"Cannot swallow the anger"; find something hard to take; be unable to let something pass

♦ 娶不上媳妇还在其次，问题是回回都让人给蹬了，孩子**咽不下这口气**呀！

(From the movie 甲方乙方)

Not finding a wife is the least of it. The tough part is, he gets dumped every single time. That's hard for the kid to take.

♦ 他有什么？别说计算机，就是电灯他也不懂啊！不就仗着是校长的小舅子吗？动不动就来训我们这些干实事儿的科技人员，我真咽不下这口气。

What does he know? Forget computers, he can't even figure out a light bulb! He's just the college president's brother-in-law! And yet he's always lecturing us, the scientists who get things done around here. I really can't take it any more.

yáng máo chū zài yáng shēn shàng 羊毛出在羊身上
"Sheep wool comes from the sheep"; it all comes from the same place in the end; it's all the same.

♦ 我知道你的意思，这饭不是好吃的，先套住点儿感情，然后就要钱，这是羊毛出在羊身上，最后还不是得从我口袋里出。

I know what you mean. This dinner isn't for fun and games. First you get me involved emotionally, and then you ask for money. It all comes from the same place in the end—my pocket. [The supervisor of a construction project is complaining to a contractor who has invited him to dinner.]

♦ 羊毛出在羊身上，他们花了那么多钱作广告，到了儿还不是让我们这些买东西的出钱？

It all comes from the same place in the end. They spent so much money on advertising but when push comes to shove it's we, the consumers, who pay for it.

yāo é zi 幺讹子/妖蛾子 (麼訛子/妖蛾子)
Diabolical trick; elaborate, deceitful initiative; ploy

♦ 您说这些年啊，一会儿一个幺讹子，一会儿一个幺讹子。
(From the TV series 一年又一年)

I mean, for all these years it's been one diabolical invention after another. [Referring to new home appliances.]

♦ "张经理，我们这些搞软件的都喜欢在半夜工作，白天睡觉，您不如让大家回家去搞设计，只要到时候设计出来不就行了吗？" "少闹这妖蛾子！咱们是大公司，不是个体户，都给我老老实实在这儿坐着！"

"Manager Zhang, software writers like us prefer working at night and sleeping during the day. Why don't you just let us stay home and design our products, as long as we turn them in on time?" "Spare me your fancy ideas! We're a big company, not a mom and pop operation. Do me a favor and stay put!"

yǎo yá 咬牙
"Bite teeth"; bite the bullet; tough it out

♦ 梅生娘，你才三十几岁的人，可别说这丧气话，咬咬牙，把孩子拉扯大了，你就熬出头了。
(From the short story 粮食)

Meisheng's Mom, you're barely past thirty. Stop talking doom and gloom. Bite the bullet, bring the kid up, and you'll see light at the end of the tunnel. [Meisheng's mother doesn't have any food, and thinks it would best to die and put an end to her misery.]

♦ 现在我们**手头儿**是紧了一点儿，大家**咬咬牙**，等货款收到以后日子就好过了。

Things *are* a bit tight right now. But let's bite the bullet until we get the payment. Then we'll be all right.

yào shì...cái guài ne 要是...才怪呢

"It would be very strange if..."; it's inevitable that...; I would be surprised if it doesn't...

♦ 这块地**要是**批给咱们电视台**才怪呢**！

(From the TV series 大雪无痕)

I'd be amazed if this land were allocated to our television station.

♦ 你明明知道要跑长途，怎么还去酒吧？我**丑话说在头里**，你这样开车**要是**不出事故**才怪呢**！

You know you're going on a long drive, so why go to a bar? This isn't what you want to hear, but if you drive that way it'll be a miracle if you don't have an accident.

yào...méi yǒu, yào mìng yǒu yì tiáo 要...没有，要命有一条 (要...沒有，要命有一條)

"I don't have what you want, but if you want my life, take it"; over someone's dead body

♦ 他们让我写检查，我说，**要检查没有，要命有一条**。

(From the TV series 一年又一年)

They asked me to write a self-criticism. I told them, over my dead body.

♦ 赵明不肯交钱，说**要钱没有要命一条**，我去找他，他还想动手打人呢。

(From the novel 大厂)

Zhao Ming refused to hand over any money—said we'd have to kill him first. When I went to see him, he even tried to beat me up.

yào gē 要搁 (要擱)

If it were...

♦ **要搁**我啊，我上马路边儿上看下棋，也不看那玩意儿。

(From the TV series 一年又一年)

If it were me, I'd rather watch people play chess on the street than watch that kind of stuff. [Referring to a TV series.]

♦ 嘿！我说，你小子还真拿上硕士学位了！**要搁**过去是进士了吧？

Wow! What do you know, you bastard, you actually got yourself a master's degree! If it were the old days, you'd be a Jinshi, right? [进士: jìn shì, a successful candidate in the highest imperial examinations]

yē zhe cáng zhe 掖着藏着 (掖著藏著)

"Conceal and hide"; hide; evade

♦ 跟自己亲儿子还**掖着藏着**的？

(From the TV drama 昏阠胡同)

How come you'd keep it a secret from your own son? [Two elderly people are in love; one of them is afraid to tell his son.]

◆ "老张，有件事儿我早就想跟你说，可是又张不开口。" "有什么话你就直说吧，别**掖着藏着**的。"

    "Lao Zhang, there's something I've been wanting to tell you for a long time, but I don't know quite how to put it." "If you've got something to say, say it. Don't beat around the bush."

yě bú shì zénme le/yě bú zhī dào shì zénme le 也不是怎么了/也不知道是怎么了(也不是怎麽了/也不知道是怎麽了)

"Something that can't be named"; for no particular reason

◆ 也不是怎么了，我看见他就腻歪。

    (From the TV series 都市情感)

    For some reason the sight of him turns my stomach. [An artist is talking about a rich, uncultured businessman.]

◆ 也不知道是怎么了，自从我们那口子去海南出差以后，我一直心惊肉跳的，你说他在那儿会不会出事啊？

    I don't know why, but ever since my husband went to Hainan on business I've been jumpy. Do you think something might happen to him?

yě děi xìn ya/a 也得信呀/啊

"Have to believe"; You expect people to believe that? (rhetorical question); nobody would believe that

◆ 你说这象牙从狗嘴里吐出来，我**也得信呀**！

    (From the TV series 手心手背)

    You're telling me pigs have wings, and I'm supposed to believe you?

◆ 这一口京片子，你说你是在纽约来长大的，人家**也得信啊**！

    With that Beijing accent of yours, how do you expect people to believe it when you say you grew up in New York?

yě shuō 也说 (也說)

"(I must) say (this) too"; it must be said that…; but then

◆ **也说**小赵儿这闺女，嘴上不牢靠，一高了兴就给说出去了。

    (From the TV series 今生是亲人)

    But then, that Xiao Zhao girl is too much. She just runs off at the mouth. The moment she got excited she blurted it out. [She was asked to keep a secret.]

◆ **也说**大李那个不明事理的，女的不愿意说年龄，他还一个劲儿地问。

    You've got to admit that Big Li's really clueless. The woman didn't want to give her age, but he just kept on asking.

yě zhēn shì de 也真是的

"Really something"; he/she shouldn't have done this; this can't be happening; this is hard to believe!

◆ 妈**也真是的**，怎么能把咱家的地址随便告诉一个陌生人呢？

    (From the short story 让我怎么开口)

I don't know what to say about my mother. How could she just give our home address to some stranger?

◆ 张经理也**真是的**，我上班给我妈打个电话他也要我付电话费，还要扣我的奖金。

Manager Zhang is too much. I called my mother from work and he wants to charge me for it, plus he wants to cut my bonus.

yè yú huá qiáo 业余华侨 (業餘華僑)

"Amateur overseas Chinese"; overseas Chinese impersonator (sarcastic and humorous)

骂他们是**业余华侨**，可是他们根本就不理睬。

(From the novel 人生)

They were lambasted for posing as overseas Chinese, but they paid no attention.

◆ 我们科那个老李是有名的**业余华侨**，穿得挺港的不说，就连说话也学着广东腔儿，你说多叫人恶心！

That Lao Li guy from our department is famous for trying to pass as an overseas Chinese. Not only does he dress like someone from Hong Kong, he even tries to put on a Cantonese accent. Is that disgusting or what?

yí ge bí kǒng chū qì 一个鼻孔出气 (一個鼻孔出氣)

"Breathe through the same nostril"; talk and think in the same way; have the same idea; in agreement

◆ 哼，你们男人都是**一个鼻孔出气**！

(From the novel 我的情敌是幽灵)

Oh, you men are all the same.

◆ 我万万没想到，开董事会的时候，我的亲弟弟竟然和我的竞争对手**一个鼻孔出气**，非逼我把主席的职位交出来。

I never dreamed my own brother would be on the same page as my rivals at the board meeting, and force me to resign as chairman.

yí ge luó bo yí ge kēngr 一个萝卜一个坑儿 (一個蘿蔔一個坑兒)

"Each radish has its hole"; everyone has responsibility; no one can be absolved

◆ 我只准你１０天假，过了这期限可别怪我不客气，厂里都是一个萝卜一个坑，你自己拿主意吧。

(From the short story 请不要逼我)

I'm allowing you only ten days of vacation. If you go over, don't blame me if I'm hard on you. In this factory everyone has a job to do, so make up your mind.

◆   "李主任的孩子还没找到工作，你能不能给他在你公司安排一个职位？" "这可不行！我们公司是**一个萝卜一个坑儿**，要是安排他就得从现在的职工中找一个炒了。"

   "Director Li's kid hasn't landed a job yet. Can you create something for him in your company?" "No way! We're fully staffed. If we set up a job for him we'd have to let someone else go."

yí gè sài yí gè 一个赛一个 (一個賽一個)
Each one triumphs over the next; one is more…than the next

◆   你瞧咱请来这些人一个**赛**一个德行。

   (From the novel 一点儿正经没有)

   Take a look at the people we invited; one's more pretentious than the next!

◆   这几个家伙一个**赛**一个的抠门儿，一听到捐款就往回缩。

   With these guys, one's more stingy than the next. They back out the moment they hear the word "donation."

yí ge tóng bǎn bāi chéng liǎng bànr huā 一个铜板掰成两半儿花 (一個銅板掰成兩半兒花)
See 一分钱掰成两半儿花 yì fēn qián bāi chéng liǎng bànr huā

yí gùn zi dǎ sǐ 一棍子打死
Kill someone with one blow; surgically remove; deny someone a second chance

◆   朴一方够狠的啊，他是想给我**一棍子打死**。

   (From the TV series 问问你的心)

   Pu Yifang was ruthless. He wanted to polish me off with one blow. [He wanted to make the speaker's company go under.]

◆   "李秘书，请你通知老张，就说他已经被公司辞退了。" "经理，老张这次确实没有完成任务，给公司造成了损失，可把人**一棍子打死**也有点儿过。"

   "Secretary Li, please inform Lao Zhang that the company has fired him." "Manager, it's true Lao Zhang didn't fulfill his duties and the company suffered losses, but not giving him a second chance is going a bit far."

yí kuài duīr 一块堆儿 (一塊堆兒)
"In a lump"; all together; together

◆   你还有什么想问的，我**一块堆儿**告诉你。

   (From the novel 我是你爸爸)

What else do you want to know? I can give it to you all at once.

♦   我也想去看电影，咱们**块堆儿**去吧。
I'd like to see a movie too, so let's go together.

yí kuài xīn bìng 一块心病 (一塊心病)
"An illness of the heart"; secret worry; sore point

♦   有庆〖人名〗的事儿一直是我的**一块心病**。
(From the movie 活着)
I am always heartsick about that accident with Youqing. [He was driving the car that ran over and killed Youqing.]

♦   我确实挺想投资房地产的，看趋势这是千载难逢的好机会，但是又怕手里的旅游公司的业务受到不利影响，现在你要和我们一起投资，这可解了我的**一块心病**。
I'd really like to invest in real estate. It seems that opportunities like this come once in a blue moon. But on the other hand, I worry that it might have a bad effect on my travel business. Now that you're going to invest with us, that's a load off my mind.

yí shì 一势 (一勢)
"One direction"; birds of a feather

♦   他们是**一势**的，互相都勾着。
(From the novel 一点正经没有)
They're birds of a feather, in cahoots with each other.

♦   这两家店好象是在唱对台戏，但是其实是**一势**的，这据说是一种促销的招数。
The two stores may seem to be competing, but actually they're in collusion. This is supposed to be a promotion scheme.

yì bǎ nián jì 一把年纪 (一把年紀)
"A handful of years"; getting on in years; no longer young

♦   你当你是谁啊？**一把年纪**，罗锅弯腰，一点儿都不帅！
(From the TV series 大赢家)
Just who do you think you are? An old geezer, all hunched over, with no looks at all! [Spoken to a suitor.]

♦   您这**一把年纪**了，怎么专门去迪厅，酒吧这种年轻人去的地方？不怕人家笑话？
How come at your age you only hang out in discos and bars, young people's scenes? Aren't you afraid people will laugh at you?

yì bǎ shǐ yì bǎ niào 一把屎一把尿
"A handful of shit and a handful of piss"; the tedious and painstaking work of raising a child

♦   你妈**一把屎一把尿**的把你们拉扯大，容易吗？
(From the TV series 空镜子)
Your mother brought you all up, wiping your bottoms one by one. You think that was easy?

♦   我**一把屎一把尿**把孩子养这么大，您就把他还给我吧。
(From the TV series 黑洞)

I went to all that trouble to raise him, so would you kindly give him back? [Spoken to a child kidnapper.]

yì bí zi liǎ yǎn 一鼻子俩眼 (一鼻子俩眼)

"One nose with two eyes"; nothing extraordinary; same as everybody

♦ 德国人怎么样，不也是**一鼻子俩眼**吗？我就不信德国人办得到的咱们就办不到。

(From the TV series 汽车城)

So what about the Germans? They've got a nose and two eyes, right? If they can do it, I refuse to believe we can't.

♦ "咱们不能跟人家小朱比，他学了一个月的英文就能和老外聊天儿了，这是天才！" "我看你还是功夫下得不够。他姓朱的难道不是一**鼻子俩眼**？"

"We can't compare ourselves to Xiao Zhu. He studied English for one month, and he could carry on a conversation with foreigners. That takes a genius!" "I think you just didn't work hard enough. This Zhu guy has a nose and two eyes, just like everyone else."

yì bǐ hú tu zhàng 一笔胡涂账 (一筆糊塗賬)

A messy account; a messy record

♦ 尤其是那帮头头儿，请吃请喝，请桑拿，请旅游，请这请那，都是一**笔笔的胡涂账**。

(From the TV series 红色康乃馨)

Especially those bosses, they invite people to restaurants, bars, saunas, and sightseeing trips. It's always either this or that, and every entry in the account book is messy.

♦ "他的账有没有问题？" "我查了，他记的是**一笔胡涂账**，就连一共卖了多少东西都看不出来。"

"Any problems with his accounts?" "I checked. He kept such messy records I can't even tell how much merchandise was sold."

yì chuí zi mǎi mài 一锤子买卖 (一錘子買賣)

"Sold with one hit of the gavel"; one-shot deal; one-shot chance

♦ 本世纪能不能冲出亚洲，就这**一锤子买卖**。

(From the TV series 一年又一年)

The team has just one chance to make it out of Asia in this century. [If the Chinese soccer team wins this game, it will play in the World Cup.]

♦ "经理，天太热，冰镇啤酒都快卖光了，咱们兑点儿水吧？" "不能做这种**一锤子买卖**，要不然就不会有回头客了。"

"Boss, it's a scorcher today. The iced beer is selling out fast. Why don't we just mix in a little water?" "If we do one-shot deals like that, forget about getting return business." [回头客: returning customers]

yì fēn qián bāi chéng liǎng bànr huā 一分钱掰成两半儿花 (一分錢掰成兩半兒花)

"Split pennies in two"; scrimp

♦ 我啊，苦日子过惯了，**一分钱掰成两半儿花**。

(From the TV series 一年又一年)

Me? I'm used to a hard life and pinching pennies.

◆ 现在这个年月，一分钱掰成两半儿花不行了，你非得大手大脚地往外
砸钱，才能发大财，赚大钱。

These days mend and make do doesn't cut it anymore. If you don't throw your money around there's no way you can earn big and get rich.

yì gēn shéng shàng de mà zha 一根绳上的蚂蚱 (一根繩上的螞蚱)

"Locusts on the same string"; in the same unfortunate situation; in the same boat

◆ 咱们俩是一根绳儿上的蚂蚱，要死都得死。

(From the TV series 康熙帝国)

We two are in the same boat. If one of us drowns, so will the other.

◆ "你们两个牛奶公司原来竞争得你死我活，怎么现在要联合行动
了？" "现在和过去不一样了，三四个跨国乳业集团很快就要进来
了，过去的对手成了一根绳儿上的蚂蚱，不联合只有死路一条。"

"Your two dairies used to be in mortal competition. How come you're working together now?" "It's not like the old days. Three or four international dairy groups are about to enter the market, so old enemies are now in the same camp. If we don't hang together, we'll hang separately."

yì hú cù/liǎng hú cù 一壶醋/两壶醋 (一壺醋/兩壺醋)

"A bottle of vinegar"; small change; chickenfeed

◆ 你刚进矿才多长时间，挣不了一壶醋钱，骑这么好的车子干啥？卖给
我吧？

(From the novel 空洞)

How long have you been a miner? You couldn't have earned much money. What's the point of riding a fancy bike like this? Why not sell it to me?

◆ "你怎么会把千金嫁给小梁了？他家虽然有点儿底子可是跟你根本不
在一个档次上啊！" "我是看小梁有出息，要说家业，他们梁家的那
点儿钱还不够我买两壶醋的呢！"

"Why did you marry your precious daughter to Xiao Liang? His family has some property, but they're not in your league." "I think Xiao Liang has promise. As for the Liang family property, it's not enough to pay for my taxi fares."

yì huí shēng èr huí shú 一回生二回熟

"Strangers the first time, friends the second time"; a friendship can be established quickly; a little familiarity (or practice) goes a long way

◆ 咱们一回生二回熟，下次我还坐你的车。

(From the TV series 至爱亲朋)

Now we're not strangers anymore. I'll ride in your car next time too. [Spoken to a taxi driver.]

♦ 演戏看起来很难，但一回生两回熟，演几次你就忘了自己是在演戏了。

Acting may seem hard at first, but a little practice goes a long way. Once you've acted a few times, you'll forget you're on stage.

yì jiā huo 一家伙 (一傢夥)

"In one strike"; at one sitting; nonstop

♦ 在狱里我就想，一出来碰上卖羊肉串儿的，**一家伙**就吃它十串！

(From the TV series 天堂鸟)

This is what I thought about in jail: the moment I get out and see a lamb kebob stand, I'll eat ten skewers at one sitting.

♦ 原先我看人家下得挺好，可我这一跟他们真下，还就赢了。**一家伙**就下了一晚上，饭也没吃。

(From the novel 棋王)

At first, I thought they were really good chess players. But as soon as I actually played them, what do you know, I won! All at once I was playing the whole night through and didn't even take a bite of food.

yì jīng yí zhà 一惊一乍 (一驚一乍)

"Surprised one moment and shocked the next"; easily startled; jumpy

♦ "别**一惊一乍**的。" 我厉声喝道，推开她伸过来的双手，"我好好的，什么事也没有。"

(From the novel 永失我爱)

"Stop being so panicky, will you?" I said in a stern voice, pushing away her outstretched hands. "I'm perfectly all right. Nothing happened to me."

♦ "快跑吧，听这炮声日本兵很快就要过来了。" "你别总是**一惊一乍**的，日本人离咱们这儿还远着呢。"

"Run for your life. You can tell from the artillery noise, the Japanese soldiers will be here any minute." "Why are you always so jumpy! The Japanese are still a long way from here."

yì kē shù shàng diào sǐ 一棵树上吊死 (一棵樹上吊死)

"Hang on one tree till you die"; stuck in a dead end; waiting helplessly in a bad situation, even though other options exist

♦ 此处不留爷，自有留爷处。天地大着呢，干吗非在**一棵树上吊死**？

(From the TV series 大赢家)

If they don't want you here, go somewhere else. It's a big world out there. Why stick around in the same rut? [A marketing director was suspended. The owner of another company is persuading him to leave his old job.]

♦   老李，你别太想不开，人不能在一棵树上吊死，炒股失败了咱们还可以干别的，开个饭馆，跑跑运输，能赚钱的事情多了！
> "Lao Li, don't take this too much to heart. You can't get stuck in a rut. We lost money in the stock market, but there are plenty of other things we can do. Open a restaurant or a transportation service; there are lots of ways to make money!"

yì kǒu chī ge pàng zi 一口吃个胖子 (一口吃個胖子)
"Eat a fat person in one bite"; push something too fast; seek instant gratification

♦   "这饭总得一口一口吃。""不，我就要一口吃个胖子！"
(From the TV series 大赢家)
> "Not so fast, eat your food one mouthful at a time." "Not me. I mean to gulp it all down!" [Referring to risking everything on one investment.]

♦   孩子刚五岁，你就让他学高中的数学？想一口吃个大胖子啊？你这样会把孩子害了！
> The kid is only five and you want him to study high school math? Are you trying to force-feed him? You'll ruin the kid!

yì mǎ guī yì mǎ 一码归一码 (一碼歸一碼)
"Let one issue be one issue"; don't mix apples and oranges; A is one thing and B is another

♦   他是他，他哥是他哥，一码归一码。
(From the TV series 手心手背)
> He's himself and his brother is his brother. Don't confuse the two. [The listener is angry at one brother, and wants to take it out on the other.]

♦   卖粮食的钱和卖地的钱得分开了算，一码归一码。
(From the movie 顽主)
> Keep the money from grain sales and the money from land sales separate. Don't mix the two together.

yì mǎ shìr 一码事儿 (一碼事兒)
"one thing"; the same thing

♦   爱情和婚姻不是一码事
(From the movie 顽主)
> Love and marriage are not the same thing.

♦   "你说安排我儿子来公司上班的事儿，我是找张头儿好还是找李头儿好呢？""一码事儿。依我看，这事儿根本没戏。"
> "Tell me, should I talk to Boss Zhang or Boss Li about getting my son a job in the company?" "Doesn't matter. I don't think it's going to happen."

yì mén xīn sī xiǎng 一门心思想 (一門心思想)
"Desire with a single mind"; crave single-mindedly; driven

♦   孟局长的女儿，一门心思想当演员，可考了两年电影学院都没考上。
(From the TV series 都市情感)

Director Meng's daughter has her heart set on acting, but she flunked the film academy exams two years in a row.

♦ 他是一门心思想赚钱，整天往上海和广东跑，连春节都是在外边过的。

He thinks of nothing but making money. He goes to Shanghai and Guangdong all the time. Even during the New Year holidays he's away from home.

yì mǔ sān fēn dìr 一亩三分地儿 (一畝三分地兒)

A small piece of land (亩 and 分 are land measurements. 十分 makes 一亩, which is 0.1644 acre.)

♦ 在这一亩三分地儿，我大小也算个人物。

(From the TV series 黑冰)

In this neck of the woods, they think I'm somebody.

♦ 我就是要在这一亩三分地儿上跟他争个高低。

It's right in this little arena that I'd like to take him on.

yì nǎo mén zi guān si 一脑门子官司 (一腦門子官司)

"Lawsuits written all over one's forehead"; look worried

♦ 刘总，轻松点儿，别老一脑门子官司，那样会老得快！

(From the TV series 大赢家)

Manager Liu, relax. Don't look so worried all the time. It'll make you get old fast!

♦ 赵海大叫："姐，出什么事了？你怎么一脑门子官司呀？"

(From the novel 经典爱情)

Zhao Hai shouted, "Sister, what happened? Why do you look so upset?"

yì...qì jiù bù dǎ yí chù lái 一...气就不打一处来 (一...氣就不打一處來)

"As soon as (something happens) anger comes from all directions"; find something intolerable

♦ 我一看他系着个领带，背着个空皮包，到处吆喝，气就不打一处来。

The moment I see him making his pitch everywhere with that tie around his neck and that empty bag on his back, I just flip out.

♦ 我一听郭小鹏的名字，气就不打一处来。

(From the TV series 黑冰)

When I hear the name Guo Xiaopeng I see red.

yì rén chī bǎo quán jiā bú è 一人吃饱全家不饿 (一人吃飽全家不餓)

"One person is full and the family feels no hunger"; a one-person family; having no dependents

♦ 你敢情一人吃饱了全家都不饿，我可是有老婆有孩子的主儿！

(From the TV series 黑冰)

Of course, you've only got yourself to care for. But I've got a wife and kid! [An older policeman is complaining to his younger boss about a dangerous mission.]

◆ 你别替我担心，我是一人吃饱全家不饿。

   You don't have to worry about me. I don't have a family to take care of.

yì shuǐ 一水

"Of the same water"; completely; uniformly

◆ "这次您放心，不但有（舞会），还是一水的'的士高'。"

   (From the movie 顽主)

   Don't worry this time. Not only will there be a dance, but it's going to be straight disco.

◆ 咱跟人家比不了，人家是一水的德国设备。

   We can't compare ourselves to them. All of their equipment is German made.

yì tiáo dàor zǒu/bǎo dào hēi 一条道儿走/跑到黑 (一條道兒走/跑到黑)

"Walk/run on the same road until dark"; keep doing the same thing until you hit a dead end

◆ "好啦好啦，汽车跑一程子还停一停呢，你是不是也该到站了？" "你要这么说，我就永远不到站." "一条道跑到黑？"

   (From the novel 永失我爱)

   "OK, all right. Even buses stop once in a while. Haven't you reached your stop?" "Since you bring it up, I'm never going to reach a stop." "You mean until you run into the wall?"

◆ 要是花店开不下去了，你可以想想别的办法啊，不能一条道儿走到黑啊。

   If the flower shop isn't working out, you can think of something else. You can't just keep going until you hit a dead end.

yì tuī liù èr wǔ 一推六二五

"Push everything aside"; wash one's hands of; shirk; pass the buck

◆ 家里的事儿，你别一推六二五的。

   (From the TV series 今生是亲人)

   You can't just wash your hands of family obligations.

◆ 他自称"姜太公"，就因为他办什么事儿都放在明面儿上，不玩儿阴的，也就是"愿者上钩"的意思。不信，明天一早你去找他试试，准保他不会一推六二五的。

   (From the novel 九死还魂草)

   He calls himself "Jiang Taigong" because he lays everything on the table and doesn't play dirty tricks. You take the bait willingly. If you don't believe me, give it a shot tomorrow morning. I guarantee he won't brush you off. [Jiang Taigong is a legendary character who fishes without a hook, waiting for the fish to come to him willingly.]

yì wǎn shuǐ duān píng 一碗水端平

"Hold a bowl of water level"; impartial; fair

◆ "你们处长怎么来了？" "这是临时决定的。你放心，他来不来我都会一碗水端平的。"

   (From the TV series 问问你的心)

"How come your director is here?" "It was a last-minute decision. But don't worry, I'll be impartial whether he's here or not."

♦ 姐，累点我不怕，我就怕**一碗水没端平**，老百姓骂我呀。

(From the novel 希望的田野)

Sister, I'm not afraid of hard work. My only fear is of not handling things fairly and arousing people's anger.

yì zhǔnr 一准儿 (一準兒)

Surely; definitely; most certainly

♦ 甭问，那**一准儿**是当官儿的给儿孙要的房。

(From the TV drama 耷儿胡同)

Don't even ask. That apartment is definitely set aside for an official to give to his children or grandchildren.

♦ 我要是您啊，**一准儿**给自己梦一大高楼！

(From the TV series 贫嘴张大民的幸福生活)

If I were you, I'd surely dream up a big building for myself!

yīn gōu fān chuán 阴沟翻船 (陰溝翻船)

"Shipwreck in a sewer"; a small, usually unexpected failure

♦ 大江大河都过来了，个把**阴沟翻了船**也该含笑爬起来。

(From the TV series 编辑部的故事)

I've sailed in many big rivers, so if I run aground in a little stream I can climb out and laugh about it.

♦ 李局长一路升迁，大家都以为他迟早会做到个省长什么的。没想到两个二奶因争风吃醋闹得不可开交，把他的作风问题捅到了市政府。结果是**阴沟里翻了船**，仕途上再也站不起来了。

Director Li was promoted over and over again, so everyone thought sooner or later he'd become provincial governor or something like that. Who knew, two of his mistresses had a jealous rivalry that got out of hand, and brought his sexual indiscretions to the attention of the municipal government. Because of this peccadillo he'll never have a political career again. [作风问题: zuò fēng wèn tí, a euphemism for sexual indiscretion]

yǐng dōu méi jiàn 影都没见 (影都沒見)

"See not even a shadow"; not find a trace of someone

♦ 前两天县里来了几个人，查了三天，连个**影儿都没见**。

(From the movie 红高粱)

A few guys came down from the county government a couple of days ago. They searched for three days and couldn't even find a trace.

♦ 他刚一回国就跑到深圳去了，我连**影儿都没见**着。

He went to Shenzhen as soon as he returned to China, so I didn't even get a glimpse of him.

yīng xióng jiù měi 英雄救美

"Hero rescuing a beauty"; ride to the rescue; knight in shining armor aiding a damsel in distress

♦ 俗话说**英雄救美**，你倒好，美女救英雄啊！

(From the TV series 手心手背)

Talk about a hero rescuing a damsel in distress! You let the damsel rescue you.

◆ "电影好看吗？" "不咋地，还是**英雄救美**的老一套。"
"Was the movie good?" "Not really, it was the old knight in shining armor and the damsel in distress bit."

yìng pèng yìng 硬碰硬 (硬碰硬)

"Hard strikes hard"; eyeball to eyeball; solid

◆ 这钱可是**硬碰硬**的东西，如果没有，我敢在你的面前说有吗？
(From the TV series 问问你的心)
Money is cold, hard stuff. If I didn't have it, would I dare to say to your face that I do?

◆ 赵刚虽然参加过不少次战斗，但这种**硬碰硬**的白刃战还是第一次碰上。
(From the novel 亮剑)
Zhao Gang was in many a battle before, but this was the first time he met hand-to-hand combat like this.

yóu bu de 由不得

Not be in control; not have freedom of choice

◆ 逼到这一步，也就**由不得**我了。
(From the TV series 今生是亲人)
I've been forced into this position and I have no choice.

◆ 虽说姓王的手里有几个破钱，但是这一亩三分地儿上的事儿也**由不得**他来作主。
This Wang guy may have a few lousy pennies to his name, but it's not up to him how things are run in this corner of the world.

yóu píng zi dǎo le dōu bú dài fú de 油瓶子倒了都不带扶的

"Not pick up a bottle of oil that's been knocked over"; not lift a finger; not do the simplest thing

◆ 人们说，这家伙一看就是个**油瓶子倒了**也不知道扶的公子哥儿。
(From the novel 寻找无双)
They all say this guy is a spoiled brat who doesn't lift a finger around the house.

◆ "我是宁可不吃，也不做饭。" "没错，饿死事小，失节事大，不能**跌这个份儿**，我们家**油瓶常倒，我从来不扶**。"
(From the TV series 编辑部的故事)
"I'd rather starve than cook." "That's right. Dying of starvation is nothing compared to losing your dignity. You just can't let yourself look bad like that. I, for one, never lift a finger around my house."

yóu zhe xìng zi lái 由着性子来 (由著性子來)

"Follow the dictates of one's temperament"; do as one pleases

◆ 这可不是小事儿，你不能让他**由着性子来**。
(From the TV series 今生是亲人)

This isn't a trivial matter; you can't just let him do as he wants.

◆ 生意场上的事儿你得能屈能伸，不能**由着性子来**。

> In business, you've got to be flexible. You can't just do what you feel like doing.

yǒu bìng 有病

"Be sick"; mentally ill; crazy

◆ "你**有病**啊！""你才**有病**呢！"

(From the movie 有话好好说)

> "Are you crazy?" "You're the one who's crazy!"

◆ 我都明〖人名〗也是生在新社会，长在红旗下，**挖国家墙角**、拆社会主义大厦的事儿我能干吗？再说咱们**退一万步讲**，我都明就这么傻啊？明知道违法乱纪的事儿还要以身试法，我**有病**啊？

(From the TV series 大赢家)

> I, Duming, was born in the new society too and raised under the red flag. How could I undermine the foundation of the country and shatter the socialist structure? Besides, I would never be that stupid. Do you think I'd plunge into something I know very well is illegal? You think I'm crazy?

yǒu bí zi yǒu yǎn jing 有鼻子有眼睛

"Have a nose and eyes"; have the necessary details; convincing

◆ 她说得**有鼻子有眼睛**的，你让我到底相信谁？

(From the TV series 田教授的二十八个保姆)

> She's supplied convincing details. Who am I supposed to believe? [Her nanny claims she had an affair with the speaker's husband. The husband denies it.]

◆ 行啊，杰哥，你撒谎水平不低啊！说的**有鼻子有眼**，我要不是亲眼所见，都能给你感动的流泪。

(From the short story 没人知道我们有多坏)

> Bravo, Brother Jie, you really tell first-class lies! Your story sounded so true to life that if I hadn't seen what happened with my own eyes, I would have been moved to tears.

yǒu de shì 有的是

Have plenty of; in abundance

◆ 规模大小无所谓，但要隆重，奖品丰厚，租最豪华的剧场，请些知名度高的人。我**有的是**钱。

(From the movie 顽主)

> It doesn't have to be large scale, but it does have to be high class, with lavish prizes. Rent the most luxurious theater and invite high-profile celebrities. Don't worry about the money; I've got plenty.

◆ 街上大款**有的是**，你干吗找我这个要什么没有的**穷光蛋**呢？

(From the TV series 手心手背)

Millionaires are a dime a dozen everywhere you look. Why bother with someone like me, who has no money and nothing to offer? [A man is speaking to a young woman with a romantic interest in him.]

yǒu jù huà bù zhǐ dāng jiǎng bù dāng jiǎng 有句话不知当讲不当讲 (有句話不知當講不當講)

There are some words I'm not sure I should say; I don't know if I should say this or not

◆ "有句话不知当讲不当讲。" "说吧，没关系。"

(From the TV series 大雪无痕)

"I don't know if I should say this." "Go ahead. It's all right."

◆ "有句话不知该讲不该讲。" "你怎么也吞吞吐吐起来了？"

(From the TV series 大赢家)

"I don't know if I should say this." "When did you start beating around the bush too?"

yǒu lǐ bú zài shēng gāo 有理不在声高 (有理不在聲高)

"Shouting doesn't make you right"

◆ **有理不在声高**，你敢动刀，我让你吃不了兜着走。

(From the TV drama 旮旯胡同)

Raising your voice won't get you anywhere. If you dare to use your knife, I'll make sure you regret it.

◆ 你别激动，慢慢讲，俗话说**有理不在声高**嘛。

Don't get all worked up. Slow down. As they say, you can't win an argument just by raising your voice.

yǒu lǐ zǒu biàn tiān xià 有理走遍天下

With justice on your side you can go anywhere; justice prevails in the end

◆ 我就相信这个理儿，**有理走遍天下**。

(From the movie 有话好好说)

This is what I believe: if you have justice on your side, you will prevail anywhere in the world.

◆ **有理走遍天下**，我就不信告不倒他姓孙的。市里不行我告到省里，省里不行我告到北京去！

Justice prevails in the end. I just don't believe that Sun guy can't be brought down. If the municipal government doesn't respond, I'll take it to the provincial level; and if that doesn't work I'll appeal it to Beijing!

yǒu liǎn 有脸

"Have face"; have no shame; have the nerve; shame on you; Have you no shame? (rhetorical question)

◆ 上次咱们的账还没清呢，你还**有脸**又来找我借钱？

(From the TV series 问问你的心)

We haven't settled accounts from last time, and you have the nerve to ask for another loan?

♦ 你考试考成这个样子，还有脸来跟我要钱去旅游？

You got a grade like that on the exam, and you have the nerve to ask me to pay for a vacation trip?

yǒu liǎng xià zi 有两下子 (有兩下子)

"Have two moves"; be on the ball; know a thing or two

♦ "嗯？你哪儿来的牌？" "你们打架的时候我偷的。" "你有**两下子**，快回家！"

(From the TV series 大宅门)

"Hey, where'd you get that card?" "I stole it while you were fighting." "You're really something. Go home right away."

♦ 你三年就拿了两个博士学位，看来你真**有两下子**。

In just three years you earned two PhDs. You've really got the right stuff.

yǒu ménr 有门儿 (有門兒)

"Have a door"; hopeful; possible

♦ 我看**有门**。雨季水往上冒，旱天水往下沉，咱就揭开地皮看看，**兴许**能打出泉水来？

(From the novel 好爹好娘)

I think there's hope. The water level rises in the rainy season and falls in the dry season. So let's poke around ["let's peel the earth off and take a look"]. Who knows, we might strike a spring.

♦ 听媒人的话咱们闺女这婚事儿**有门儿**了。

From what the matchmaker says, the outlook is good for our daughter's marriage.

yǒu nǎi jiù/biàn shì niáng 有奶就/便是娘

"If it has milk, it's the mother"; compromise principles for expediency's sake; go where the money is

♦ 这年头**有奶就是娘**，有钱就是爹，俺扑通一声跪在了他的面前，给他磕了一个响头，唱戏一样地喊：儿媳叩见公爹！

These days, whoever has milk is your mother and whoever has money is your father. So I dropped to my knees, banged my head on the ground, and shouted like a Beijing opera singer, "Your daughter-in-law salutes her father-in-law!" [Her husband's long-lost father has shown up. Although she is skeptical of his identity, she hears he's rich, so she kowtows to him.]

♦ "王总裁待咱们不错，你说咱们扔下他去投奔美国公司，这么做合适吗？" "嗨，**有奶便是娘**。"

"President Wang was really nice to us. Do you think ditching him for an American company is the right thing to do?" "Hey, you have to go where the money is."

yǒu nǐ hǎo kàn de 有你好看的

"There is something pretty ahead for you"; (ironic); you just wait

♦ 你跟他们说了我们这么多坏话，**有你好看的**！

(From the novel 布衣青天杨剑昌)

You've badmouthed us to them so often. Just wait; you'll get what's coming to you.

♦   我要是给你说出去，你就出了大名，**有你好看的！**

(From the TV series 田教授的二十八个保姆)

If I spill the beans about you, you'll be famous all right. You'll have a nice surprise coming. [A warning to a son who mistreats his mother.]

yǒu nǐ/nín zhè jù huà 有你/您这句话 (有你/您這句話)

"With those words from you (as a promise or compliment)"; your word on it; your seal of approval

♦   **有您这句话**，比赏我什么都强。

(From the TV series 手心手背)

Such words from you mean more to me than any prize.

♦   只要**有你这句话**，我这趟北京就没白来。

(From the TV series 天堂鸟)

My whole trip to Beijing was worth it just because of those few words from you.

yǒu pài 有派

"Have style"; have class; with style

♦   生气归生气，窝火归窝火，人家服了软儿，递过了话儿，你就得见好就收，那才透着自己**有"派"**。

(From the novel 耍叉)

So you were furious, seething with anger. But they have apologized and sent word that they want to reconcile. Now you'd better accept it. That would show you really have class.

♦   看你穿得挺**有派**的，怎么一张嘴就是脏字儿啊？

The way you dress is classy, but how come every time you open your mouth it's nothing but gutter talk?

yǒu pàn tóur 有盼头儿 (有盼頭兒)

"Have something to look forward to"; have good prospects; have hope; see light at the end of the tunnel

♦   对于追他的人来说，一点儿**盼头儿都没有**。

(From the TV series 手心手背)

As for those women who are chasing him, they stand no chance.

♦   你现在连参赛的资格都没有了，我活着还有什么**盼头儿**啊？

(From the TV series 失乐园)

Now that you haven't even qualified for the competition, what do I have to look forward to in life? [She has striven for over ten years to make her daughter a star athlete.]

yǒu qián néng shǐ guǐ tuī mò 有钱能使鬼推磨 (有錢能使鬼推磨)

"With money you can make a devil turn the millstone"; money can do anything; money can move mountains

♦   我疏通了一下，罚了一些款，就没事儿了。真是**有钱能使鬼推磨**！

(From the TV series 一年又一年)

I pulled some strings, so they let me off with a fine. Money can move mountains. [The speaker broke the law with the way he was doing business.]

◆ 谁又敢去惹这四位凶神恶煞呢？**有钱能使鬼推磨**，很多事情，靠银子便能不了了之了。

> Who has the guts to take on these four ruthless villains? When money talks, everyone listens. It's often like that. If you have money, the impossible becomes possible. [Four hoodlums always manage to bribe the officials and avoid punishment.]

yǒu rì zi 有日子

"It's been days"; awhile

◆ 我们有日子没联系了。

(From the movie 有话好好说)

> We've been out of touch for awhile.

◆ 老孙，你可有日子没来了，去哪儿发财了？

> Lao Sun, you haven't been here for awhile. Did you strike it rich somewhere?

yǒu tóu yǒu liǎnr 有头有脸儿 (有頭有臉兒)

"Have head and face"; people with prestige and power

◆ 你这回改这条线你得触犯多少人的利益呀？**平头百姓**，没多大能耐，触犯也就触犯了。可那些**有头有脸**的，你不能不考虑。

(From the novel 希望的田野)

> This plan of yours to change the route will harm the interests of many people. If you step on the toes of ordinary people, well, that's life, but you'd better give some thought to the big shots you're inconveniencing. [Discussing a highway construction project.]

◆ 昨一电影明星过生日，政府里**有头有脸儿**的来了不少。

> A movie star had a birthday party yesterday. Quite a few top brass from the government showed up.

yǒu wán méi wán 有完没完

"Is there an end or not?"; Will you ever stop?

◆ 方雨林，你还**有完没完**？

(From the TV series 大雪无痕)

> Fang Yuling, will you ever stop?

◆ 你**有完没完**？就这么点儿鸡毛蒜皮的事儿说了八百六十遍了。

> "Are you done? Such a piddling matter, and you've brought it up eight hundred times!

yǒu xì 有戏 (有戲)

"There is a play"; there is hope for; have a chance

◆ 兄弟，咱们明白人面前不做暗事，这平安工程到底**有戏没戏**，你给我句痛快话。

(From the TV series 天堂鸟)

Brother, honest folks like us don't mince words. Please give it to me straight. Does this Ping'an Project have a chance, or not?

♦   这事王局长点头儿了，我看有戏。
    Director Wang gave us the nod on this, so I think it'll work out.

yǒu yǎn bù shí tài shān 有眼不识泰山 (有眼不識泰山)
"One has eyes but cannot see Mount Tai"; too ignorant or stupid to recognize greatness

♦   晚辈有眼不识泰山，冒犯了前辈。

(From the TV series 铁齿铜牙纪晓岚)
   I was too ignorant to recognize you and thus I offended Your Honor. [晚辈: wǎn bèi, of a later generation; 前辈: qián bèi, of an earlier generation. Both are expressions of humility and honor.]

♦   都怪我有眼不识泰山，原来你就是大名鼎鼎的孙中山先生！别说没
    钱，就是倒找钱我也愿意啊！

(From the TV series 孙中山)
   Blame it all on my ignorance. So you're the famous Mr. Sun Yat-sen! Doesn't matter if you don't have money to pay me. I'd be happy to pay you! [The words of a ferryman taking Sun Yat-Sen across a river.]

yǒu yì dā wú/méi yì dā 有一搭无/没一搭 (有一搭無/沒一搭)
"Sometimes with a purpose, sometimes without"; say something just to keep a conversation going; do something without paying full attention

♦   你将车兜来兜去。我们俩有一搭无一搭地说了些前后毫不连贯的话。
(From the novel 习惯死亡)
   You drove the car around in circles and the two of us just talked to fill the time, so what we said had nothing to do with anything.

♦   她那么吃不香睡不稳、干什么都有一搭无一搭的，好象受了多大委屈
    一样。
(From the novel 绝对隐私)
   She can't enjoy her food and she doesn't sleep well. She can't concentrate on anything. It seems as if she feels very wronged.

yǒu yí ge suàn yí ge 有一个算一个 (有一個算一個)
"Count every one of them"; each and every one; all of them

♦   你那些朋友没有好东西，有一个算一个。
(From the novel 蝴蝶公主)
   None of your friends are any good. Not one.

♦   市里那些领导干部，有一个算一个，全都是贪官。
   All the officials in the municipal government, and I mean all of them, are corrupt.

yǒu yì shǒu/yǒu yì jiǎo/yǒu yì tuǐ 有一手/有一脚/有一腿 (有一手/有一脚/有一腿)
"Have a hand/foot/leg"; have a secret sexual relationship

♦   你是不是跟她有一手啊？
(From the TV series 祥符春秋)

Are you having an affair with her?

♦   你可别小看这个女人，听说她跟咱们的顶头上司有一脚。
     Don't underestimate this woman. They say she's sleeping with our boss.

yǒu yí yàngr 有一样儿 (有一樣兒)

"There is one thing"; there is this one thing; but then…

♦   怎么说随你，你这张嘴不是挺能白唬的吗？但有一样儿，别暴露我的
     身份。
     (From the novel 百年德性)
     I'll let you do the talking. You're a smooth talker. But just one thing: don't reveal my
     identity. [A policeman wants to work undercover at a nightclub, so he asks a friend to
     arrange a job for him there.]

♦   哪些人该下岗，由你来定。但是有一样儿，老模范、老党员都得给我
     留下来。
     You decide who gets laid off. Just one thing, though. You have to keep all the old model
     workers and veteran party members, got that?

yǒu zháo luò 有着落 (有著落)

"Have a place to land"; yield results; settled or fixed

♦   你住院的费用肯定有着落，我们公司不是给每个人买了份保险吗？你
     叫张秘去找出你的那份来，找找保险公司那边。
     (From the short story 秉烛夜谈)
     Your hospital costs will definitely be covered. Didn't our company buy insurance for
     everyone? Why don't you ask Secretary Zhang to find a copy of your insurance policy
     and take it to the insurance company?

♦   太巧了，金华公司的老板是你的同班同学，我看这下儿你的工作有着
     落了。
     What a coincidence! The owner of Jinhua Company was your classmate. Seems to me
     your job is in the bag this time.

yǒu zhǒng 有种 (有種)

"Have seeds"; have balls; have guts

♦   行，算你有种，你有本事呆在里头一辈子都别出来。
     (From the movie 洗澡)

All right, you're tough. If you're so tough, let's see if you're going to stay in there forever. [A wife is speaking to her husband who's hiding in a bathhouse after a fight with her.]

♦   "我就是饿死也不把画儿卖给他胡三，这画儿挂他们家纯粹是糟蹋了。" "行，你有种儿。不过我劝你还是好好想想，现在能买得起这种画儿的除了胡爷恐怕没有几个了。"

"I'd rather starve than sell this painting to that Hu San. This painting would be wasted hanging in their house." "OK. You've got balls. But I'd advise you to think it over. Except for Master Hu I'm afraid there aren't many people who can afford paintings like this now."

yǒu zhǔr 有主儿 (有主兒)

"Has a master"; (a woman who is) unavailable

♦   我要是还能走得动，就回青县咱老家看看，也不知当年你爹给你说下的那个媳妇儿小兰有主儿了没有。

(From the TV series 小站稻传奇)

If I could still walk, I'd go back to our old home in Qing County for a visit. I wonder if the bride your father arranged for you back then, Xiao Lan, is still unmarried.

♦   你少打小徐的主意，人家早就有主儿了，是局长的公子，你呀，死了这条心吧！

Don't get any ideas about Xiao Xu. She's already taken, by the son of the bureau chief, so you might as well forget about it!

yòu yào mǎ ér hǎo/páo yòu yào mǎ ér bù chī cǎo 又要马儿好/跑又要马儿不吃草 (又叫馬兒跑又叫馬兒不吃草)

"Order the horse to run, but order it not to eat"; have it both ways; have your cake and eat it too

♦   又要马儿好，又要马儿不吃草；又想当婊子，又想立牌坊。世界上的好事就只让你一个人全占了？

(From the novel 抉择)

You want to have it both ways. You want to be both a whore and a virgin. You want everything life has to offer, all for yourself.

♦   王厂长，你让马儿跑，你也得给马儿吃点儿草啊！我不是轮休呢吗？

(From the TV series 大赢家)

Director Wang, if you want a horse to run, you've got to feed it. I'm in the middle of a vacation, remember? [The director had asked the speaker to attend a business meeting.]

yú sǐ wǎng pò 鱼死网破 (魚死網破)

"The fish dies, the net gets torn"; 1. it's do or die; life for one and death for the other 2. mutual destruction; a no-win situation

♦   反正我也是没有退路了，我就跟他谢小同拼个鱼死网破。

(From the TV series 闽南名流世家)

I have no retreat in any case. I am resolved on a life and death struggle with Xie Xiaotong.

♦ 要是你不愿意看到**鱼死网破**的结局，咱们就各让一步。
Unless you want us to go down together, we've both got to compromise a bit.

yú yǒu yú lù, xiā yǒu xiā lù 鱼有鱼路，虾有虾路 (魚有魚路，蝦有蝦路)

"The fish has the ways of a fish, and the shrimp has the ways of a shrimp"; everyone has their own way of solving a problem; everyone has some connections

♦ 汉明单位里也有人遇到拆迁的麻烦，他们骂骂咧咧的烦躁了几天，最后就安静了，最后他们都找到了过渡的房子。汉明很羡慕他们的社会关系，都说**鱼有鱼路，虾有虾路**，汉明也算个干部，就是没有路。
(From the short story 过渡)
> Other people in Hanming's work unit had the same problem finding new housing because of demolition. They griped and fretted for a few days, and in the end they all found temporary housing. Hanming envied their connections. As they say, everyone knows someone. But even though he's an official, Hanming couldn't find a way out. [拆迁: demolition and relocation, a government program of forced relocation when housing is to be demolished for government or business projects.]

♦ "现在申请私车牌照这么难，他们怎么没几天都拿到了？" "嗨，**鱼有鱼路，虾有虾路**。"
> "These days it's hard to get registration plates for private cars. How come they all got them in just a few days?" "Well, everyone has some connections."

yuān dà tóu 冤大头 (冤大頭)

"Big-headed (rich) sucker"; a fool parted from his money

♦ 住上大楼头晕的土包子别到咱们这儿来呀！嫌钞票扎手的**冤大头**别到咱们这儿来呀！
(From the novel 萧尔布拉克)
> Peasants who feel dizzy in high-rise buildings, and suckers who don't like the feel of money, need not apply! [Someone is shouting on the street to recruit workers.]

♦ "你看这花瓶挺漂亮的，只卖四百块一个，咱们一人来一个好不好？" "这贵得**离谱**了！要买你买吧，我可不愿意当这**冤大头**。"
> "Look at these beautiful vases, only four hundred yuan each. Why don't we each get one?" "That price is way out of line. Buy it if you want, but I'm not going to be ripped off like that."

yuán chǎng 圆场 (圓場)

(From Beijing opera) "Smooth out a performance"; take the edge off an awkward situation; mediate; smooth things over

♦ 这不是你那特情提供的情况吗，你就再替他**圆圆场**吧，就说有人举报你们走私文物。你该道歉的就别顾面子了，人家**弄不好**还告咱们呢。
(From the novel 永不瞑目)
> Wasn't it your special intelligence guy who provided the information? Why don't you smooth things over for him? Just say someone informed you that they were smuggling cultural relics. If you need to apologize, don't stand on your dignity. If things go badly they could even bring a lawsuit against us. [Police had been wrongly informed that a company was selling drugs, but actually the company was selling a new, manufactured

Buddha statue. To avoid trouble, the speaker recommends the police claim the mistaken tip was that the statue was an antique that could not be legally sold.]

♦ 骁哥，你无论如何不能走，起码要把今天这个**场子给圆**过去。

(From the TV series 北京女人)

Brother Xiao, there's no way you can leave, at least not before doing something to iron things out today. [The bridegroom has had a sudden change of heart and wants to call off the wedding.]

yuǎn lái de hé shàng huì niàn jīng 远来的和尚会念经 (遠來的和尚會念經)

"Monks from afar chant the sutra better"; outsiders know best

♦ 也不知道郭健是咋想的？咱们自己内部就找不着合适的人呀？客房部和营销部经理我都能干，郭健就是不让我干。他就相信**远来的和尚会念经**。

(From the novel 红尘世界)

I don't know what's going through Guo Jian's mind. Can't we just find a suitable internal candidate? I could manage room service or sales, but Guo Jian just won't let me. He always thinks someone from outside is better.

♦ "咱们这儿不是有不少会计算机儿的吗？头儿干吗非从外边儿请人来修理呢？""这你就不懂了，**远来的和尚会念经**啊！"

"Don't we have plenty of people here who know computers? Why did the boss have to get someone from outside to fix the problem?" "You don't get it; outsiders always know best!"

yūn cài 晕菜

"Pass out like a vegetable"; lose one's cool; become dysfunctional

♦ 蓝姐这么能干，可一看陈建国就**晕菜**了。你现在是不是也**晕菜**了？

(From the TV series 都市情感)

Sister Lan is so capable, but she loses her cool the moment she sees Chen Jianguo. Aren't you acting just like her now?

♦ "快干！别**泡蘑菇**！""主任，我们这不正**玩儿命**呢吗？都快**晕菜**了！"

"Faster! Stop goofing off!" "Director, don't you see we're busting our guts? We're all about to pass out!"

yún lǐ wù lǐ 云里雾里 (雲裏霧裏)

"In the clouds and the mist"; confused; confusing; without the foggiest idea

♦ 你娘舅说话总是这么**云里雾里**的。

(From the TV series 天下第一情)

Your uncle always talks in riddles like this. [The uncle is opening a restaurant with only one table and says he has his own ways of making money.]

♦ 我的画家朋友拍了一部号称是先锋艺术的电影。我连看了三遍，还是**云里雾里**的，不知他想说个啥。

A painter friend of mine made what he claims is an avant-garde film. I watched it three times in a row and still don't have the foggiest idea what he's trying to say.

Z

zá guō mài tiě 砸锅卖铁 (砸鍋賣鐵)

"Break the pot and sell the scrap"; to exhaust all of one's resources; to do whatever it takes

♦ 就是**砸锅卖铁**我们也要把工程进行下去。

(From the TV series 天堂鸟)

We'll keep the project going even if it means giving up everything we have. [A serious shortage of funds is jeopardizing a project.]

♦ 现在大学的学费要六七千块钱，我这个下岗工人就是**砸锅卖铁**也供不起孩子上学啊！

College tuition is six or seven thousand yuan these days. I'm a laid-off worker; I just couldn't afford to send a child to college even if I sold everything I have.

ză zhěng 咋整

(Northeastern dialect) "how did it happen"; what happened?

♦ 枣花姐，**咋整**的？ 咋这么乱啊？

(From the TV series 古船、女人和网)

Sister Zaohua, what happened? What's with this mess? [Zaohua and her husband just had a big fight.]

♦ **咋整**的，新买的电视看了两天就坏了？

How could that be? Only two days, and the new TV set is already broken?

zāi 栽

"Fall"; to tumble; to go down; down

♦ 我就奇了怪了，像咱们老老实实的人，都混得挺**栽**的。

(From the TV series 其实男人最辛苦)

It's beyond me. Good, honest guys like us are all down and out.

♦ "听说没有？对面商店的张经理被警察抓走了！""我能不知道吗？他把公司的钱都花在那个叫莉莉的**小蜜**身上了，我早说过，早晚有一天他要**栽**在那个女人手里。"

> "Did you hear? Manager Zhang from the store across the street was taken away by the police." "How could I miss it! He spent all the company's money on his bimbo Lili. I told you before: someday that woman would ruin him."

zǎi rén 宰人

"Butcher people"; to overcharge; to rip off

♦ 太贵了，这有点儿**宰人**吧？

(From the movie 一见钟情)

> Too expensive! Wouldn't you say that's kind of a rip-off? [A haircut costs 150 kuai.]

♦ 这家商店真够**宰人**的，别人卖八十的皮鞋他们敢卖八百。

> This shop really knows how to fleece customers. Shoes that sell for eighty elsewhere cost eight hundred here.

zài háng 在行

"In the business"; know the business; good at

♦ 你还挺**在行**，这方面。

(From the movie 有话好好说)

> You're pretty good at this [knowing how to retaliate violently without getting punished].

♦ 看你在这儿站了半天了，也没开张。卖东西怎么能不吆喝呢？ 你要是不会我教你，吆喝我可比你**在行**。

> You've been standing here for a long time without a sale. How can you sell anything without making a pitch? If you don't know how, I can teach you. I'm an expert at hawking goods.

zán men shéi gēn/hé (hàn) shéi a 咱们谁跟/和谁啊 (咱們誰跟/和誰啊)

"You and I, what's our relationship?" We're not strangers, are we? We're friends!

♦ "你这一早上得少拉多少活啊？""**咱们谁和谁啊**，不兴论这事儿。"

(From the TV series 今生是亲人)

> "You must have lost quite a bit of business this morning." "How long have we been friends? We shouldn't even be discussing this. [A cabby is helping a sick friend gratis.]

♦ "这计算机真是美国进口的吗？听说现在有很多东西都是假的。""我能骗你吗？**咱俩谁跟谁**啊！"

> "Is this computer really imported from America? I hear there are a lot of fakes around these days." "Would I cheat you? We're friends, aren't we?"

zāo àn suàn 遭暗算

"Fall victim to a hidden attack"; be the victim of a conspiracy or plot

♦ 你这一桶一桶地灌我们〖喝啤酒〗，说的又都是**虚头八脑**的话，我怎么有一种**遭**你**暗算**的感觉啊！

(From the movie 甲方乙方)

You keep offering us beer, and your remarks are neither here nor there. How come I can't help feeling you're trying to pull a fast one on me?

♦ "我的官司打赢了，警察把他们的公司查封了。" "别太得意了，小心遭暗算。他们破产了，狗急跳墙，什么坏事都干得出来。"

"I won the lawsuit and the police sealed off their office." "Don't get excited too soon. Watch out for undercover attacks. They went under, but when they're cornered and desperate they might not stop at anything."

zāo lǎo tóu zi 糟老头子 (糟老頭子)

"Sloppy old man"; old timer; old codger

♦ 二位在百忙之中还来给我这个糟老头子过生日，谢谢啊！

(From the TV series 黑洞)

With your busy schedules, you two found a moment to help this old coot celebrate his birthday. Thanks! [A sarcastic comment on the belated arrival of two guests.]

♦ 介绍人说这个人是大公司的经理，还有美国的学位，照片看上去也还精神。谁知道和真人一见面儿，天哪！原来是个糟老头子！

The matchmaker said the guy was the general manager of a big company, and he had an American degree too. Besides, his photo looked pretty good. But who knew, when I saw him in person, my God, he was nothing but an old geezer!

zào 造

To spend; abuse; squander

♦ 看见了吧？你就是累吐血了也不够她们造的呀！

(From the TV drama script 老宋和他的女儿)

Did you see that? You can work till you spit blood but you still can't make enough for them to fritter away. [Commenting on the spendthrift ways of modern young women.]

♦ 我知道你要说什么，什么也别说！咱俩之间根本不是钱的事。废话我不讲了，这钱你就使劲儿造，回头我再给你送来。

(From the novel 其实不想走)

I know what you're going to say. Don't say it! Money is not the basis of our relationship. I'm not going to waste my breath. Just take the money and spend it any way you please. I'll get you more lately.

zào niè/zuò niè 造孽/作孽

"To commit a crime or sin"; do evil; evil; sin against the principles of heaven

♦ 我今生作了什么孽啊？

(From the TV series 田教授的二十八个保姆)

What did I do wrong? [The speaker's son is a scoundrel who not only asks her for money but also scolds her.]

♦ 我儿子和儿媳结婚还不到一年，就把这么好的家具都扔了，又买了一套新的，真是**造孽**啊！

My son and his wife haven't been married a year, and they throw away their good furniture and buy another set. It's a sin!

zào xing 造性

(Vulgar) "Conduct or behavior"; inappropriate or disgusting conduct or behavior

♦ 他怎么这**造性**？爷爷病了也不回来看看？

(From the TV series 今生是亲人)

What kind of behavior is this? His grandfather's sick and he doesn't even come home to see him?

♦ 街上拉皮条的都一个**造性**，坑完小姐坑客人。

Street corner pimps are all the fucking same. They exploit both the prostitutes and the Johns.

zéi 贼 (賊)

"Thief"; awfully (an intensifier)

♦ 这四个小时逛商场，什么都没买，还累得**贼**死，你图个什么啊？

(From the TV series 大赢家)

Four hours in the mall and you buy nothing, and exhaust yourself in the process. What's the point of it all?

♦ 最近不知道怎么了，蔬菜的价格**贼**贵，黄瓜楞要十块钱一斤！

I don't know what's up, but suddenly vegetables are wicked expensive. They charge you ten yuan for just one jin of cucumbers!

zěn me chár 怎么茬儿 (怎麽茬兒)

"How's that a problem?"; What's the problem?

♦ "**怎么茬儿**？有话好好说，别挡道，妨碍交通。"

(From the novel 耍叉)

"What's your problem? Whatever it is, we can talk it over. Just don't stand there blocking traffic." [A bicyclist is blocking the way of a car.]

♦ **怎么茬儿**啊？我们又没卖违法的商品，你们凭什么封我的商店？

What's the problem? We're not selling anything illegal. On what basis are you closing down my shop?

zhá biǎn tou 轧扁头 (軋扁頭)

(Shanghai dialect) "Crush and flatten one's head"; very crowded

♦ 修建站**轧扁头**的情况你也不是不了解，怎么能做这样的保证呢？

(From the novel 围墙)

You know very well how backed up our construction team is. How could you make such a promise? [A worker is speaking to his boss, who had promised his own superior a construction project would be finished in three days.]

♦ 圆圆住在外婆家里的时候，跟芳芳好得**轧扁头**，天天在一起玩。

(From the short story 家庭风景二十章)

When Yuanyuan lived with her grandma, she and Fangfang were joined at the hip; they hung out every day.

zhà miào 炸庙 (炸廟)

"Blow up the temple"; explode; fly off the handle

◆   说起来，我有点对不住他。老杜，我的头儿，也是我的大哥，我会跟他打马虎眼？想起来，让我睡觉都不踏实。可是话又说回来，我真把这层窗户纸给捅了，他肯定得炸了庙，敢跟我动拳头。

(From the novel 百年德性)

I think I'm not really dealing straight with him. My boss Lao Du is like a big brother to me. Could I keep him in the dark? When I think about it I can't sleep. But on the other hand, if I tell him the truth he'll blow up for sure and might even get violent. [He is afraid to tell Lao Du that he's dating a girl who is a nightclub singer and drug abuser.]

◆   我担心这下岗名单一公布，厂子里立马儿就会炸庙。

I'm afraid that as soon as the list of laid-off workers is out, there'll be a riot in the factory.

zhān biānr 沾边儿 (沾邊兒)

"Touch the border or margin of"; border on; have something to do with

◆   李忠祥呢，当过杠夫，拉过洋车，跑过堂儿，事儿倒干过不少，可没有一件是和唱戏沾边儿的，退休前倒在剧团当门房来着，可那是话剧团。

(From the novel 找乐)

This Li Zhongxiang guy, he's been a porter, a rickshaw driver and a waiter. He did a lot of things, but nothing with any connection to opera. Before he retired he was gatekeeper for a theatrical troupe, but that was spoken theater, not opera.

◆   我一听你就是外行，说了半天没有一句沾边儿的。告诉你吧，这狗生病完全是食物不对造成的，跟室温没有任何关系。

I can tell right away you're an amateur. You said a lot, but none of it is relevant. Let me tell you, this dog got sick because it ate something bad. It has nothing to do with the room temperature.

zhǎn yì dāo 斩一刀 (斬一刀)

(Shanghai dialect) "Cut a slice with a knife"; fleece; rip off

◆   这么晚了有什么好玩的吗？女人晚上很晚睡觉可是会衰老得很快的哟，再说到哪里玩不会被人家当巴子斩一刀啊？

(From the novel 我要你的爱)

Is there anything that's fun to do this late at night? Staying up late makes women age faster, you know. Besides, I don't know if there's any fun place where they won't think we're suckers and try to rip us off.

◆ "二百块？太贵了！" "咱们是亲戚，我还能**斩你一刀**吗？这进货价就是二百，我一分钱没赚你的。"

　　"Two hundred yuan? That's way too expensive!" "We're family. You think I would rip you off? Two hundred is the wholesale price; I'm not making a cent off you.

zhàn zhe máo kēng bù lā shǐ 占着茅坑不拉屎 (占著茅坑不拉屎)
"Sit on the toilet without shitting"; take up a position but not fulfill its duties

◆ 听外面又是车又是马的，许是府上来了个有钱的公子爷，你可别**占着茅坑不拉屎**，你揣给我的那两吊半的银子儿，还不够我涂脂抹粉的呢！

(From the novel 宫廷情猎)

　　I hear a horse and carriage outside; I can tell it's a rich customer arriving. Shit or get off the pot. That two and half taels of silver you gave me isn't even enough to buy makeup. [A prostitute is turning away one customer so she can entertain a richer one.]

◆ 你要是觉得没有把握让这个工厂扭亏为盈，最好别**占着茅坑不拉屎**，现在的汽车市场这么火，咱们这个汽车零件厂不发起来实在说不过去。

　　If you're not sure you can turn this factory around ["turn losses into profits"], you'd better make way for someone who can. The auto market is so hot right now, it's unacceptable that our parts factory can't make it big.

zhàn zhe shuō huà bù yāo téng 站着说话不腰疼 (站著說話不腰疼)
"People who can talk standing up don't get sore backs"; It's easy to talk if you're not in the same situation; easy for you to say

◆ "中国人考试怕过谁？关键是多练，你天天开，不出两星期准能考过。" 曹嘉文觉得假如苏南不是故意逗他开心，就是盲目乐观。"**站着说话不腰疼**！" 他负气地说，"小姐啊！练车要有四年驾龄的人陪我，要车没有，要人也没有。呵呵，你说我怎么练？"

(From the novel 没有影子的行走)

　　"Chinese are the best at taking tests, right? The key is practice. Drive every day, and you'll pass the test for sure in two weeks." Cao Jiawen thought Su Nan was either teasing him or just blindly optimistic. "It's easy for you to talk!" he said huffily. "Missy, you're not allowed to practice unless someone with four years of driving experience is in the car. I have neither the car nor the person. Now you tell me how I'm going to practice!"

◆ "那个女的怎么天天哭啊？有病治病不就完了吗？" "你别**站着说话不嫌腰疼**，她得的是癌症，而且已经到了晚期了。"

　　"How come that woman is crying all the time? If she's sick, she should go get treatment. Isn't it as simple as that?" "Easy for you to say! She's got cancer, and it's already advanced."

zhāngr 张儿 (張兒)
"A sheet"; slang for a ten-yuan bill; ten years

◆ 你呢，都三**张儿**半了，也是眼太高。

(From the TV series 一年又一年)

You're already thirty-five. Your standards are too high. [Referring to the listener's bachelor status.]

♦ 你说的这些道理我也明白，可大姐我都四**张儿**多了，还能有男人要吗？

(From the TV series 北京女人)

I understand your reasoning, but this big sister of yours is over forty. Would any man want me? [Her younger sister is trying to persuade her to get divorced and find another man.]

zhāng jiā cháng, lǐ jiā duǎn 张家长，李家短 (張家長，李家短)

"The longs of the Zhang family and the shorts of the Li family"; gossip

♦ 司机的家属有好些不上班，妇女们来回串门子，少不了说**张家长，李家短**。

(From the novel 萧尔布拉克)

Many of the chauffeurs' wives don't work, so they visit with each other all the time. And inevitably they gossip.

♦ 你一个大老爷们儿，总是扯这些**张家长李家短**的事儿，烦不烦啊？

You're a man but you're always gossiping. Doesn't it get stale?

zhāng luo 张罗 (張羅)

"Arrange"; make arrangements; take care of business; attend to

♦ 凡事，还得你多**张罗**。

(From the movie 红高粱)

Whatever comes up, I count on you to handle it. [A new female owner is speaking to the head clerk.]

♦ 老二也不小了，你这个当大哥的得费点儿心，帮他**张罗**个对象。

My second son's not so young any more. You're his big brother; you should make an effort to help him find a girlfriend.

zhǎng liǎn 长脸 (長臉)

"Make somebody's face grow bigger"; make somebody proud; do credit to somebody

♦ "瞧我干什么？嫌你爸爸给你丢人了？" "没有，您给我**长脸**了，这下谁都知道我有个底气十足的爸爸了。"

(From the movie 顽主)

"What's that look supposed to mean? Did I (your father) do something to embarrass you?" "No, you did me proud. Now everyone knows my dad's a real loudmouth. [The father went to school and made a scene.]

♦ 乡亲们都以为你们俩是到北京去做生意了，谁知道你们是去那儿捡垃圾的！你们可真给咱们老李家**长脸**啊！

All the villagers thought you two went to Beijing to do business. Who knew, you were trash-picking! You really did our Li family credit!

zhǎng xīn yǎnr 长心眼儿 (長心眼兒)

"Grow in mind's eye"; grow mentally; become sophisticated; grow alert

♦ 最近她老在外边漂着，没犯老毛病吧？你啊，还是**长点儿心眼好**。

(From the TV series 贫嘴张大民的幸福生活)

She's been out on the town a lot lately. I hope she isn't back to her old ways. I'm telling you, you keep an eye out. [Talking about the listener's wife, who had an affair in the past.]

♦ 这孩子个儿没怎么长，**心眼倒长了不少**，学会说瞎话了！

This kid hasn't gotten much bigger, but he's gotten a lot smarter. Now he knows how to lie.

zhǎng háng shi 涨行市 (漲行市)

"Market price goes up"; one's market value goes up; a rise in status

♦ 你这两天又**涨行市**了，是不是？不服啊？

(From the TV series 古城童话)

You think your market value went up in just two days? You're not taking orders anymore? [The leader of a gang of young beggars is angry that a new recruit didn't hand over a stolen sweet potato to him.]

♦ "有什么事你就跟我说吧，我现在是办公室主任。""呵！**涨行市**了！告诉你吧，除非你们老板亲自出马，要不然什么也不用谈。"

"Whatever it is, you can discuss it with me. I'm now the office chief of staff." "Wow! You're moving up in the world! OK, let me give it to you straight. Unless your boss shows up in person, nothing gets discussed."

zhāo shéi rě shéi 招谁惹谁 (招誰惹誰)

"Whom did I offend?" What did I do wrong?

♦ 你凭什么跟我急啊？我**招谁惹谁**了。

(From the TV series 问问你的心)

Why did you get mad at me? What did I do wrong?

♦ 我没**招谁没惹谁**，糊里胡涂地就让他们打了一顿，这叫什么事儿啊？

I didn't offend anybody. They beat me up and I don't have a clue why. Is this crazy or what?

...zháo le ...着了 (...著了)

"Hit the spot"; got it right (usually by accident)

♦ 您问我还真问**着**了。这大院儿里的人我都认识。

(From the TV series 今生是亲人)

You came to the right person. I know everyone living in this courtyard.

♦ 让你**说着**了，他们两个真的分手了。

You got that right. The couple did split up.

zháo (or zhāo) jí shàng huǒ 着急上火 (著急上火)

"Anxious and overheated"; anxious; worried sick (上火: suffer from excessive internal heat)";

♦ 你现在**着急上火**，当时干什么来着？

(From the TV series 大雪无痕)

Now you're worried! What were you doing then? [Spoken to someone under investigation for taking bribes.]

♦ 我们几个着急上火帮你找孩子，你自己倒有闲心去唱卡拉OK，你脑子进水了？

We're all tearing our hair out to help you find your kid. But you yourself relax and go sing karaoke. Have you totally lost it?

zhǎo bu zháo běi 找不着北 (找不著北)

"Cannot find the north"; get disoriented; lost

♦ 我刚出来那时候，也**找不着北**。

(From the TV series 黑洞)

When I first got out [of jail], I was lost too.

♦ 中国这一入世，跨国公司立马就要进来，原来那些靠垄断市场，得意洋洋赚大钱的中国公司就有点儿**找不着北**了。

Now that China's entering the WTO, multinational companies will immediately rush in. Those self-satisfied Chinese companies who depended on monopolies to earn big bucks won't know what hit them.

zhǎo bú zì zai 找不自在

"Ask for discomfort"; look for trouble

♦ "你小声点儿。又发牢骚，让别人听见又去告你，到头来还得乖乖地作检讨。你这是何苦呢？"郑克信领情地看他一眼，声音小了些："我是**死猪不怕开水烫**了。"周为民："那也不能老给自己**找不自在**呀。"

(From the novel 誓言无声)

"Lower your voice. You're complaining again. If someone hears and informs on you, you'll end up writing a self-criticism like a good little boy. Why put yourself through it?" Zheng Kexing gave him an appreciative look and spoke a bit more softly: "I have nothing more to lose." Zhou Weiming replied, "Well, that's no reason to go looking for trouble all the time."

♦ 千万别去提什么意见，除非你想**找不自在**！头儿这两天烦得厉害，正想找人撒气呢。

No matter what, don't raise any objections unless you're into pain. The chief is in a pretty bad mood lately and is just looking for someone to take it out on.

zhǎo chár 找茬儿 (找茬兒)

"Look for problems"; find fault; find an excuse to start a fight

♦ 你要是成心跟我**找茬儿**我舍命奉陪。

(From the TV series 手心手背)

If you want to pick a fight with me, bring it on.

◆ 这电视机我们给你换了六台了，可你还是不满意，一会儿说图像不清
楚，一会儿说声音不好。我看你根本不是来买东西的，你是来**找茬儿**
的。

We've exchanged that TV set for you six times already and you're still not satisfied.
Either the picture's not sharp, or the sound is poor. Seems to me you're not here to
shop—you're here to make trouble.

zhǎo ge dì fèngr zuān jìn qu 找个地缝儿钻进去 (找個地縫兒鑽進去)

"Find a crack in the ground to crawl into"; be so ashamed that one wants to hide

◆ 那一吆喝，身边肯定能围上密密层层的人。可那一吆喝他也得**找个地
缝儿钻进去**。
(From the novel 耍叉)

If he makes a pitch, he'll certainly draw huge crowds of people. But the problem is, once
he starts hawking his wares, he'll feel so embarrassed he'll look for a hole to crawl into.
[Spoken about a first-time peddler.]

◆ 倒数第二！你还以为我不知道呢！丢人不丢人呀！我要是你我就**找个
地缝钻进去**！
(From the TV script 朗朗星空)

Next to last! You thought I wouldn't find out? What an embarrassment! If I were you, I'd
crawl into a hole in the ground! [A father is scolding his son for bad grades.]

zhào 照

"By the standard of"; to the extent of; to the point of

◆ 当你特别爱一个人的时候，他有点不识抬举，你可以**照死了**揍他。
(From the novel 看上去很美)

If you love someone so much and he doesn't appreciate it, you should beat the living
daylights out of him.

◆ 我当领导的时候是批评过你，但是并没**照死了**害你。现在我下台了，
你当了领导了，就组织人调查我的什么经济问题、作风问题，你这是
照死了害我啊！

When I was your superior, I criticized you but I never tried to destroy you. Now that I've
stepped down and you're the boss, you've assigned people to investigate my so-called
financial crimes and sexual indiscretions. You're trying to destroy me! [作风问题: zuò
fēng wèn tí, a euphemism for sexual indiscretion]

zhào hú lu huà piáo 照葫芦画瓢 (照葫蘆畫瓢)

"Draw a gourd ladle using a gourd as a model"; copy; imitate; follow somebody's example

◆ 他用英文问我，我翻译成中文，他便用他的文字注上音，**照葫芦画瓢**
地念。
(From the short story 外国鬼子记)

He asked me questions in English and I translated them into Chinese. He took notes, added phonetic notations, and read them back like a parrot.

♦ 你看人家老李开了个西餐馆儿赚了不少钱，咱们也可以**照葫芦画瓢**开它一个。

> Look at Lao Li. He opened a Western-style restaurant and made a lot of dough. We should follow his example and open one too.

zhào v bú wù 照V不误 (照V不誤)

"Act without fail in accordance with the rules"; execute a task without fail

♦ 别看你现在是公司上上下下的大**红人儿**，并且在陈老总那儿也挂了名儿，你要是用了那个戏子，给我**捅出漏子**来，我**照炒**你**不误**。

(From the TV series 北京女人)

> Even though you're the company's golden boy at the moment, and you've gotten a reputation with General Manager Chen, don't think I won't fire you if you hire that two-bit actor and get us into trouble!

♦ 你是局长的小舅子？告诉你，就是局长自己违章我也**照罚不误**！

> So what if you're the director's brother-in-law? Let me tell you something: if it were the director himself who violated the rules, I would fine him for sure!

zhào mén 罩门 (罩門)

"Vulnerable spot"; Achilles' heel (A martial arts term referring to a gap in a magical protective shield.)

♦ 走私是他的致命处，是他的**罩门**。像丁吾法这种人，不可能靠正常方式搞企业做生意，……只要抓住他的致命点，在**罩门**重拳一击，崩溃起来，比他兴起还快。

(From the novel 走私档案)

> Smuggling is his fatal flaw, his Achilles' heel. A man like Ding Wufa couldn't possibly start a normal enterprise or run a normal business....If we find his fatal flaw, strike at his Achilles' heel, and he'll fall even faster than he rose.

♦ "他那么凶，徐姐一位女同志对付得了吗？" "你不知道，徐姐是他的**罩门**。"

> "He's so tough. Could a woman like Sister Xu handle him?" "You don't realize it, but Sister Xu is his weak spot."

zhè bú 这不 (這不)

"Now, see this?" Look at this (and then you'll know why)"; this is why...

♦ "他病了。" "真的？" "不是真的还是假的？**这不**，我刚给他送碗绿豆稀饭不才回来吗？"

(From the TV series 古船、女人和网)

> "He's sick." "Really?" "Would I lie to you? Look, I just got back from taking him a bowl of mung bean porridge."

♦ "可是钢铁公司亏了三亿七千万！" "我知道了。**这不**，我就来了。"

(From the TV series 红色康乃馨)

"But the steel company lost 370 million!" "I know. That's why I came right away."

zhè kuài liàor 这块料儿 (這塊料兒)

"This piece of material"; quality of goods; (have) the right stuff; be cut out for

◆ 我他妈的瞎眼了，找了他妈的**这么一块料儿**！

(From the TV drama 爷儿胡同)
I was fucking blind when I got myself this piece of junk! [Talking about his wife.]

◆ 考不上大学就算了，你不是**这快料儿**，就是考上了也受罪啊。

It's OK if you don't pass the university exam. You're not cut out for it. You'll have a hard time even if you do get in.

zhè shān wàng zhe nà shān gāo 这山望着那山高 (這山望著那山高)

"The other hill seems taller than this one"; the grass is always greener on the other side; never satisfied with what one has

◆ 明白了，就是说放弃人生的追求了，不再**这山望着那山高**了。**爱谁谁了**。

(From the TV series 编辑部的故事)
Now I get it. You're giving up your life's dreams; you're not going to look for greener grass anymore. What happens, happens. [Spoken to someone who formerly had lofty goals in life, but now only wants to find a mate and settle down.]

◆ 我看不惯你们现在这些年轻人，总是**这山望着那山高**，一年换六七个工作，我在这个工厂一干就是四十年。

I hate it when I see you young people these days, always thinking the grass is greener on the other side. You change jobs six or seven times a year. I took a job at this factory forty years ago and I'm still here.

zhè shēn pí 这身皮 (這身皮)

"The skin on this body"; uniform

◆ 干脆把**这身皮**脱了，公司里还给你留着位子呢。

(From the TV series 黑洞)
Just get out of that uniform. The company is saving a position for you. [Trying to persuade a policeman to quit his job and go into business.]

◆ 咱们消防队员也是人，也知道水火无情的道理，可是既然穿上了**这身皮**，你就得硬着头皮往上冲。

We firefighters are human beings too, and we know very well that floods and fires have no mercy on anyone. But since we wear this uniform, we have no choice but to meet disasters head on.

zhè shì zěn me huàr shuō de/zhè shì zǎ shuō de 这是怎么话儿说的/这是咋说的 (這是怎麼話兒說的/這是咋說的)

"What kind of talk is this?" How can this be? How can this be explained?

◆ "不愿意去也不要紧，等着这事儿的人多着呢！" "**这是怎么话儿说的**，她哪能不愿意呢？"

(From the TV series 大宅门)

"If she's not interested, no problem. Plenty of people will jump at the opportunity."
"What are you talking about? How could she possibly not be interested?" [A brother is trying to secure a servant's job for his sister, who is hesitating to accept it.]

♦ 这是怎么话儿说的，昨下午他还好好的呢，今就不行了。

How can this be? Yesterday afternoon he's perfectly fine, and now he's about to die?

zhè suàn shì nǎ yì chū 这算是哪一出 (這算是哪一出)

"Which aria is this?" What the heck is this? Isn't this weird? (一出戏：yì chū xì, a segment or episode in an opera)

♦ 我越想越好笑：这算是哪一出？这究竟算是我们的洞房花烛呢，还是偶然的"醉入花丛"，算是我人生经历中颇具回味的一夜呢？

(From the novel 二劳改和女人们)

The more I think about it, the funnier it gets. I mean, what is this about? Is this our wedding night, or is it "a drunkard stumbling into a flower bed," something to remember for the rest of my life? [A housing shortage forces the bride's two sisters to share the wedding couple's bed. Here flowers are a metaphor for women.]

♦ 我刚把一大群记者请来，校长就来电话说，他有事不能主持这个新闻发布会，让我这个小秘书替他回答记者的问题，这算是哪一出儿啊？

I'd just collected a big crowd of reporters when the school head phoned in and said he was busy and couldn't host the press conference. I'm just a secretary, but he asked me to answer the reporters' questions for him. Is this crazy or what?

zhè xiàr hǎo le 这下儿好了 (這下兒好了)

"Now this is just wonderful (sarcastic)"; now look what happened (when good advice was not heeded); now what?

♦ 我早就跟你说了，不要在那个公司干，这下儿好了！

(From the TV series 黑洞)

I told you long ago you should quit that company. Now look what happened! [The company is in serious trouble for economic crimes.]

♦ 我跟他说了多少次了，开车的时候不能喝酒。这下好了，撞了一辆崭新的大奔，我看他怎么赔！

I told him a million times he shouldn't drink and drive. Now see what happened. He hit a brand new Mercedes. I'd like to see how he's going to pay for it!

zhēn jiānr dà de kū long dǒu dà de fēng 针尖儿大的窟隆斗大的风 (針尖兒大的窟隆鬥大的風)

"A pinprick becomes a wind as big as a basket"; blow something way out of proportion (斗: a container for grains used as a metaphor for something big)

♦ 省上有批示的，就是要保护典型。你们没有看见么，先前药厂只要有针尖大个事，报纸电视台就要吹出斗大的风，如今出了这么大的事，你们见到记者的人影了么？下了死命令的：不准曝光！

(From the novel 将军镇)

The provincial government has decreed that model work units must be protected. Didn't you guys notice? Before, if there was even a minor event at the pharmaceutical plant, it really got blown up in the newspapers and on TV. But now there's a major crisis, and did you see any shadow of a report? Now there are strict orders: nothing gets leaked.

◆　咱们几个当头儿的把这笔钱偷偷分了，下边的工人能不知道吗？俗话说的好，**针尖儿大的窟隆斗大的风**。

If we bosses divide up that money in secret, what makes you think the workers won't find out? As they say, a molehill can look like a mountain.

zhēn yǒu nǐ de 真有你的

"You're really something"; you're incredible

◆　**真有你的**，你都和人家说了些什么，那么快就搭上了？

(From the movie 顽主)

You're awesome. What did you say that made the two of you click so soon? [The speaker is curious how the addressee managed to set up a date for him with a girl they just met on the road.]

◆　**真有你的**，积压了两年的东西十天就卖出去了。

You're amazing! In ten days you sold out two years' worth of overstocks.

zhēn zhao 真着 (真著)

"Real contact"; hitting the mark solidly; real and solid

◆　前面看的**真着**。

(From the TV series 编辑部的故事)

If you sit up front [in the cinema] it's much more real.

◆　这是法院的判决书，你看**真着**了！上边说了，你必须在十天内把拖欠的房租和水电费都交清！

This is the court ruling. Take a real good look at it! It says you have just ten days to pay the overdue rent, plus the water and electricity bills!

zhěn biān fēng 枕边风 (枕邊風)

"Pillow breeze/buzz"; pillow talk; bedroom talk

◆　在这种情况下，我依靠天时地利，就跟王副局长的老婆、我们科的会计郑小娜拉关系，希望她能吹吹**枕边风**，最终使王副局长替我美言几句……

(From the short story 痰)

Under the circumstances, I took advantage of being in the right place at the right time, and got friendly with Deputy Director Wang's wife. She's Zheng Xiaona, the accountant in our department. I'm hoping pillow talk will work, and that eventually she can get Deputy Director Wang to put in a word for me.

◆ 他现在是答应了，可是到晚上他老婆**枕边风**一吹说不定就变卦了。

He says yes now, but when his wife gets to him at night, who knows, he may change his mind.

zhēng yì zhī yǎn, bì yì zhī yǎn 睁一只眼，闭一只眼 (睜一隻眼，閉一隻眼)

"To keep one eye open and one eye closed"; to cut someone slack; to turn a blind eye; to be flexible

◆ 这些年我之所以对你**睁一只眼闭一只眼**，我就是觉得你大龙够朋友，万一哪天我真是**栽**了的话，你能帮我。

(From the TV series 问问你的心)

I've been turning a blind eye all these years because I felt you [Dalong] were a friend and that if I really got in trouble some day you'd help me. [He let Dalong get away with stealing money, and now it's payback time.]

◆ 对这些从农村来的小保姆你不能要求太严，**睁一只眼闭一只眼**就行了。

You can't be too strict with those young nannies from the countryside. You've just got to turn a blind eye sometimes.

zhěng 整

To do; to get

◆ 小玲，我的"地图"喂了没有？别给我饿着，**赶明个我也整**两条"银龙"，省得那**老不死**的金大头总在我面前**臭显**。

(From the novel 东北一家人)

Xiao Ling, did you feed the Map? Don't let it starve. Soon I'll get a couple of Silver Dragons just so that damned old Big Head Jin will stop showing off in front of me. [Map (Oscar cichlid) and Silver Dragons (Asian Arowana) are different varieties of tropical fish.]

◆ "村长，这是一点儿小意思，您就同意我们在这儿盖房吧！等将来房子盖好了，我一定请您过来喝酒。""少**整**这事儿，把你这钱拿回去！你给的钱再多我也不能同意违章建房。"

"Chief, this is a small token of our appreciation. Give us permission to build a house here. When it's built, I won't fail to invite you over for a drink." "Don't do this sort of thing. Take back your money. No matter how much you offer, I won't allow you to build anything that goes against regulations.

zhèng gér 正格儿 (正格兒)

"Formal and serious"; for real; serious

◆ 你都三十大几的人了，来点儿**正格儿**的好不好？

(From the TV series 今生是亲人)

You're well past thirty. Could you please get your act together?

♦ "我觉得朱莉对你挺有意思的。""开什么玩笑？人家一个美国大学生怎么会看上我这个中国工人。""我这可不是跟你开玩笑，我是说正格儿的，她昨天还跟我打听你结没结婚呢！"

   "I think Julie's interested in you." "Are you kidding? Why would an American college student be interested in a Chinese worker?" "I'm not kidding, I'm serious. Just yesterday she asked me if you were married."

zhí qǐ jī pí gē da 直起鸡皮疙瘩 (直起雞皮疙瘩)

"Get chicken skin"; to give someone goose bumps; to give someone the creeps

♦ 你妹妹整天哼哼叽叽的，听得我直起鸡皮疙瘩。
   (From the TV series 一年又一年)
   Your sister hums and croons all day long. It really gives me the creeps. [Singing pop songs.]

♦ 听她嗲声嗲气地说话我直起鸡皮疙瘩。
   Her affected way of talking makes my flesh crawl.

zhǐ bú dìng 指不定

"There's no telling"; possibly; probably

♦ 人家都以为我们家出了大款，指不定多趁钱呢！
   (From the TV series 一年又一年)
   Everybody thinks we now have a millionaire in our family. They probably think we're loaded. [Actually, they are a very poor family.]

♦ 你说咱们这整天忙忙活活的忙活什么呢？指不定哪天睡下去就醒不过来了。
   (From the TV series 贫嘴张大民的幸福生活)
   Tell me, what point is there to our busy, hustling lives? Probably a day will come when we'll go to sleep and never wake up again.

zhǐ bú shàng 指不上

Cannot count on

♦ 刘震汉我是指不上了。
   (From the TV series 黑洞)
   I can't count on Liu Zhenhan anymore. [The speaker thought his good friend Liu Zhenhan wouldn't seriously investigate his wrongdoing, but he was mistaken.]

♦ "我真羡慕你啊，两个儿子都住在附近。""养儿子有什么用啊，什么事都指不上。还是女儿靠得住。"
   I really envy you having two sons living nearby." "What's the point of raising sons when you can't count on them for anything? Daughters are more dependable."

zhǐ lǐ bāo bú zhù huǒ 纸里包不住火 (紙裏包不住火)

"You can't wrap fire in paper"; the truth cannot be concealed; the truth will out

♦ 吴总，我不想隐瞒什么。我知道，纸里包不住火。
   (From the TV series 手心手背)

General Manager Wu, I don't want to hide anything because I know the truth will out. [He committed manslaughter in the past.]

♦ **纸里包不住火**！你想和他保持这种关系，为他生下这个孩子，又不让别人知道，可你这个没结婚的人肚子一天天大起来了，大家能不猜到他的头上吗？

> The truth will out. You want to maintain the relationship and give birth to his child, but you don't want anyone else to know. But you're not married and as your belly gets bigger every day, how can people not suspect him?

zhì qì 掷气/治气 (擲氣/治氣)

"To get angry"; to act willfully; to allow pride and anger to take over

♦ 你得跟他好好谈谈，这可不是**掷气**的事儿。

> (From the TV series 今生是亲人)
> You've got to talk it out with him. This isn't a matter to be settled in a fit of anger. [Referring to the issue of divorce.]

♦ "我真恨我自己，太没本事，人家都有汽车了，我连摩托都买不起。""别跟自己**治气**，骑车还能锻炼身体呢！"

> "I really hate myself. I'm such a loser. Everyone else has a car and I can't even afford a motorcycle." "Don't be so hard on yourself. Riding a bike is good exercise, right?"

zhì yu (yū) ma 至于吗 (至於嗎)

"(Is it worth it to) go to that extent?" Is it worth it? Has it come to this?

♦ 年轻人，**至于吗**？不就是为了个叫安红的女孩儿吗？

> (From the movie 有话好好说)
> Young man, is this worth it? Just because of that girl An Hong? [The young man intends to commit a violent act for An Hong's sake.]

♦ "我要是有大哥这样的好福气，死了都值。""**至于吗**？"

> (From the TV series 都市情感)
> "I'd die to have your good fortune!" "Isn't that going a bit far?" [A nanny is admiring her employer's lavish lifestyle.]

zhòng mó 中魔

"Hit by the devil/demon"; bewitched; possessed

♦ 我们俩都像**中**了**魔**。从此，我们的生活发生了改变。

> (From the movie 爱情麻辣烫)
> We two were bewitched. Our lives changed from that moment on. [Two adults fell in love with children's toys.]

♦ 你**中**什么**魔**了，这两天见天儿在报纸上画来画去的？

> What got into you? For two days now you've been drawing on the newspaper nonstop.

zhú lán dǎ shuǐ yì chǎng kōng 竹篮打水一场空 (竹籃打水一場空)

"Fetch water in a bamboo basket and end up with nothing"; all the effort goes to waste; all in vain

♦ 你怎么能告诉她呢？万一她说出去，这几个月你想保住得艾滋病的秘密，就成了**竹篮打水一场空**了。

> (From the TV series 失乐园)

How could you tell her? If she talks, all that effort you spent keeping your AIDS a secret for the last few months will go down the drain.

♦ 我原来想这回分房一定有我一套，装修公司都订好了，没想到最后是竹篮打水一场空！

I thought that when they assigned housing this time around I'd get an apartment for sure. I even lined up decorators. Turned out it was all for nothing.

zhú tǒng dào dòu zi 竹筒倒豆子

"Like beans spilling out of a bamboo canister"; talk or speak fast, freely and without reservation

♦ 对组织可要忠诚老实啊。你这孩子本质不坏，要竹筒倒豆子，痛痛快快，不要像挤牙膏一样，挤一点说一点。

(From the novel 血色黄昏)
You have to be loyal and honest with the organization. You're a good kid, so you have to tell everything like it is, freely and voluntarily. Don't hold anything back. Don't make them squeeze it out of you like toothpaste from a tube.

♦ 三天之内，我要让他竹筒倒豆子。

(From the TV series 黑洞)
Within three days, I'll get him to spill the beans. [Interrogating a prisoner.]

zhǔ shú (shóu) de yā zi fēi le/páo le 煮熟的鸭子飞了/跑了 (煮熟的鴨子飛了/跑了)

"The cooked duck flew away/ran away"; let a sure thing get away

♦ 小心点儿，别让煮熟的鸭子飞了！

(From the TV series 欲罢不能)
You'd better be careful. Don't lose what's almost within your grasp. [The speaker is urging someone recommended for promotion to conduct himself carefully.]

♦ 他等了这么多年，现在煮熟的鸭子跑了，他能不着急吗？

(From the TV series 天堂鸟)
He had waited so many years and now the bird, already in his hand, just flew away. How could he not be upset? [Just before their wedding, his fiancée changed her mind.]

zhǔr 主儿 (主兒)

"Host"; the type of guy that...

♦ 你以后少招惹他。他是个不要命的主儿。

(From the TV drama 爷兒胡同)
Don't stir him up. He's the type who doesn't know when to stop.

♦ 别看他平时没话，却是个沾酒便来话的主儿。

(From the novel 找乐)
He may seem quiet most of the time, but he's the type whose words start flowing once he has a drink.

zhuā xiā 抓瞎

"Grasp and miss (like a blind person)"; to have nothing to hold on to; to find oneself at a loss

♦ 我们今天约好的嘉宾，到现在愣没来！今晚上就要播的节目，你说这不是抓瞎吗！

(From the TV drama script 朗朗星空)

The guests we invited for today still haven't showed up! And the program is supposed to be broadcast tonight! Talk about being left high and dry!

♦ "老李现在可**抓瞎**了。""怎么了？他不是开了个英语学校吗？"
"是啊，老师都已经从英国请来了，本想着一定能招上五六百学员，赚上一笔，结果只有十几个人报名，连房租都不够交的。"

> "Now Lao Li's up Shit Creek without a paddle." "What happened? Didn't he open an English language school?" "Yes, he did, and the teachers are already here from England. He thought he would get five or six hundred students for sure and make a bundle. Turned out only a dozen people registered. The money's not even enough to pay the rent."

zhuā zhù xiǎo biàn zi 抓住小辫子 (抓住小辫子)

"Grab someone's little queue"; find small but incriminating evidence; catch the hand in the cookie jar

♦ "你是等着检举呢还是自己交待？"〖把材料扔到对方办公桌上〗
"这回让你**抓住小辫子**了。"
(From the TV series 手心手背)

> "Would you rather wait for others to expose you, or would you rather confess?" [Throws a file onto the desk.] "I'm afraid you caught my hand in the cookie jar this time."

♦ 我也不是那种不讲理的女人，再说现在什么朝代了，我也不会**揪住你那点小辫子**不放，关健是态度问题，你明白吗。
(From the short story 我们身边的爱情)

> I'm not an unreasonable woman. Besides, times have changed. I'm not going to hold this piece of evidence against you. But the key question is your attitude, you understand? [She has found a piece of woman's hair on her boyfriend's bed.]

zhuǎi/zhuǎn 拽/转 (拽/轉)

"Churn out"; talk in a stupid and showy matter; flaunt one's knowledge in speech

♦ 还郁郁寡欢，少跟我臭**转**你会的那几个词！留神一下用光了！
(From the novel 我是你爸爸)

> "Melancholy!" Stop trotting out the few fancy words you know. Watch out, you might run out of them pretty quick.

♦ 你肚子那点儿墨水儿，跟我**拽拽**"子曰"、"莎翁"的还差不多，别跟人大学教授**拽**啊！你那不是等着**露怯**呢吗？

> Doesn't matter if you trot out a few "Confucius says," or something from the few nuggets of Shakespeare you know when you're talking to me. But parading them in front of a college professor? Isn't that revealing your ignorance instead?

zhuàn yāo zi 转腰子 (轉腰子)

"Twist the waist"; pace back and forth in agitation; toss and turn

♦ 这小子吃人饭不拉人屎，**转着腰子**算计刘大海那没过门的媳妇。
(From the novel 天桥演义)

This bastard eats human food but he doesn't produce human shit. He walks the floor all night laying plots to get Liu Dahai's fiancée.

◆ 你别跟这儿**转腰子**了，你再转两天三夜赌输了的钱也回不来啊！

Stop pacing around in here. You can pace for two days and three nights, and you still won't get back any of the money you lost gambling.

zhuāng dà gèr 装大个儿 (裝大個兒)

"Pretend to be a big guy"; pretend to be tough or rich; pretend to be what one is not

◆ 谁他妈也别想跟我这儿**装大个**的枣我是流氓我怕谁呀！

(From the novel 一点正经没有)

Don't anyone fucking think you can act like a tough guy with me. I'm a rotten egg myself, and I'm not afraid of anyone.

◆ "老刘，我今儿有钱，请你喝酒。" "别**装大个儿**了，我知道你这钱是卖血得来的。"

"Lao Liu, today I have money, so let me offer you a drink." "Stop talking big; I know you got that money selling your blood."

zhuāng suàn 装蒜

To feign ignorance; act innocent; to play a fool

◆ "哎，用不用滴两滴口水在纸上？" "这么严肃的事，你别这么嘻嘻哈哈地开玩笑。" "你别**装蒜**了！"

(From the novel 我是你爸爸)

"Well, should I drool on the paper a little?" "This is a serious matter. Stop cracking silly jokes." "Give me a break!" [The first speaker wants to put some saliva on a self-criticism paper to look like tears of regret.]

◆ "老王，对你的处境我非常同情。" "**装什么蒜**啊？我知道你看我倒霉心里高兴着呢。"

"Lao Wang, I really feel for you in this situation." "Cut the crap, will you? I know you're only too happy to see me in trouble."

zhuāng sūn zi 装孙子 (裝孫子)

"To act like a grandson (to invite sympathy)"; to make oneself look pitiable; to be a pathetic liar

◆ 不瞒大哥说，我还真不认识抽那玩艺儿的，您要说我不认识几个"三陪"小姐，那是我**装孙子**。

(From the novel 百年德性)

Brother, I wouldn't lie to you. I really don't know anyone who smokes that kind of stuff [drugs]. But of course if I told you I didn't know any "escort girls," you'd know I was lying.

♦ "你们经理呢？让他出来。" "对不起，经理去上海出差了。有什么事儿您跟我说，等他回来我一定转告。" "少给我这儿**装孙子**，我刚才眼看着他进了这个门儿！"

> "Where's your manager? Get him out." "Sorry, the manager is in Shanghai on business. You can tell me what you want and I'll be sure to inform him when he gets back." "Cut the bullshit. I just saw him walk in this door."

zhuàng dǎn 壮胆 (壯膽)

"To strengthen the gallbladder"; to embolden; to boost one's courage

♦ 酒壮俗人胆，我放了一通炮，可我说的可不是醉话。

(From the TV drama 眷儿胡同)

> Liquor gives ordinary people a shot of courage, but when I fired off a round it wasn't the alcohol talking.

♦ "刘主任，您饶了我吧，别看我平常能瞎侃一气，我哪儿敢给一千多人作报告啊？" "别害怕，该说什么就说什么。到时候我坐在旁边给你**壮胆儿**。"

> "Director Liu, can you let me off the hook please? OK, so I'm usually talkative, but I don't have the guts to give a speech in front of over a thousand people!" "Don't be afraid. Just say whatever you're supposed to say. I'll sit next to you for moral support."

zhuàng le ge zhèng zháor 撞了个正着儿 (撞了個正著兒)

"To bump right into"; to bump into; to run into

♦ 他热血沸腾，在厨房拿上菜刀，奔小娟家来了。也活该那老东西倒霉，也正从家里出来，和可东**撞了个正着**。

(From the novel 永远的情人)

> His blood was boiling. He grabbed a knife from the kitchen and ran to Xiaojuan's house. That old lecher had the bad luck he deserved; he was walking out of the house just then, right into Kedong's grasp. [Kedong is Xiaojuan's boyfriend. He came to avenge her death on the old man, Xiaojuan's great-uncle, who raped her and caused her suicide.]

♦ 那俩小偷刚想把东西搬走，让我**撞了个正着儿**。

> Those two thieves were just moving the stuff out when I bumped right into them.

zhuàng nán qiáng 撞南墙 (撞南牆)

"To hit the south wall (the ultimate obstacle)"; to hit a snap; to run up against a wall

♦ 你**两眼一摸黑**，一脚踩进去，想拔出来就难了。我是关照你一声，怕你**撞到南墙**上。

(From the novel 都市危情)

If you plunge ahead blindly and get in too deep, you won't be able to get out. I'm just trying to warn you. I don't want you to bang your head against the wall. [Advising someone not to investigate a case.]

♦ "我大哥也真是的，现在的饭馆儿这么多，他还要开饭馆儿，这不是等于白白扔钱吗？" "你大哥的脾气我知道，永远是不**撞南墙**不回头。"

"I don't know what to say about my older brother. Now there are so many restaurants around, and he wants to open one more. Isn't that just throwing money away?" "I know your brother's disposition. He's always banging his head against the wall."

zhuàng qiāng kǒu shang 撞枪口上 (撞槍口上)

"To hit the mouth/barrel of a gun"; to stumble into the line of fire

♦ 现在正查这个呢，这回咱们是**撞枪**口上了。

(From the TV series 一年又一年)

They're cracking down on this right now. We're walking right into the line of fire this time. [They have been selling banned imported used clothes.]

♦ 那小子今儿又闯红灯，结果整**撞警察枪**口上了。

That bastard ran a red light again today, but he was caught in the act by a cop.

zī máor 滋毛儿 (滋毛兒)

"Grow hair"; to kick up some dust; to make trouble

♦ 所长，没事，丫**挺**的有前科，不敢**滋毛**。

(From the novel 前科)

It's all right, Chief. That son of a bitch has a criminal record. He won't dare kick up a fuss. [After a night of interrogation, the police discovered they had the wrong man. The chief is embarrassed, but his subordinate thinks it doesn't matter.]

♦ "这些从农村招来的民工开始的时候挺听话，干活也踏实，可是过了五六个月就开始**滋毛儿**了，什么工作时间太长啊，劳动保护不够啊，真麻烦。" "能赖人家吗？我看是你们这些老板的心太黑了。"

"These workers we hire from the villages are pretty docile and hardworking at first. But give them five or six months, and they start to make trouble. The work hours are too long, there are not enough safety measures, and so on. What a headache." "Can you blame them? I think it's because you bosses are too greedy."

zí dàng 只当 (只當)

"Only take (it as)"; just take it as; just treat it as though

♦ 今儿的事儿，就只当师傅对不起你了。

(From the TV series 贫嘴张大民的幸福生活)

Please regard what happened today as my failing you. I'm sorry. [An apprentice was laid off and his master tried in vain to prevent it.]

♦ "我两年前从他们公司跳槽去了一家日本公司，结果一直不景气，现在只好又回原来的公司应聘，你说面谈的时候多尴尬？" "怕什么，凭本事吃饭，你也用不着求他们。你就只当根本不认识他们。"

　　"I left their company two years ago for a Japanese firm that hasn't been doing so well. Now I have to ask my old company to hire me again. You can imagine how awkward the interview will be." "Don't worry, it's your ability that gets you a job. You don't need to beg them—just pretend you never met them before."

zǐr 子儿 (子兒)

"Coin"; nickel and dime; pittance

♦ 省这么一根木头能省几个子儿啊？

(From the TV series 今生是亲人)

　　How many pennies can you save by using one less timber? [Referring to room remodeling.]

♦ 为俩臭子儿，给人家当儿子，也不怕给祖宗八代丢脸？

(From the TV series 其实男人最辛苦)

　　You agree to be her son for a couple of stinking coins. Aren't you afraid of shaming your ancestors? [He is making money by taking care of an old woman as her adopted son.]

zì gěr 自个儿 (自個兒)

"Self"; oneself

♦ 你别说外头了，我自个儿都觉着丢份。

(From the TV drama 昏晃胡同)

　　Never mind the outsiders. I'm embarrassed for myself.

♦ 这菜是不好吃，可这是我自个儿挣来的。

(From the TV series 古城童话)

　　It's true the food isn't good, but I paid for it with the money I earned.

zǒu bèi zìr 走背字儿 (走背字兒)

"Walk the path of bad luck"; to have bad luck; to go through a difficult time; in distress
(variation: 走背运)

♦ 盘那个皮鞋店是我一个人的主意，走背字儿也是从那儿开始的，以后有什么事儿我和大军顶着。

(From the TV series 贫嘴张大民的幸福生活)

　　Taking over that shoe store was my idea, and that's when our bad luck began. But if there are any problems, Dajun and I will take full responsibility. [Dajun's wife is talking to her husband's brothers and sisters, promising that she won't let the store be a financial liability for them.]

♦ 你说这米汝成，早不犯皇法，晚不犯皇法，非等咱哥儿俩走背字儿的时候犯皇法。

(From the TV series 天下粮仓)

Look at this Mi Rucheng. He never broke the law before, but the moment we've had a run of bad luck he has to violate it. [The speaker thought he and his friends could count on the help of Mi Rucheng, a powerful official. But Mi Rucheng has just been jailed.]

zǒu guāng 走光

"To be exposed to light"; be exposed; be seen

◆ "小姐，你走光了。"羽容好心提醒她。从她坐的位置来看，那女孩低胸洋装内的风光可是一览无遗。

(From the novel 复制灵魂)

"Miss, your dress must have slipped down a bit," Yurong kindly informed her. From Yurong's seat, the low cut of the girl's Western dress left nothing to the imagination. [Yurong and the other girl are both being interviewed for a modeling job.]

◆ 这衣服我能穿吗？会不会走光？

Can I get away with wearing this? Or is it too revealing?

zǒu mài chéng 走麦城 (走麥城)

"Flee Maicheng"; to be defeated; to experience humiliation

◆ 自然，当着晚辈儿，他会没结没完地跟你抖落肚子里那些"过五关斩六将"的事儿，生怕没人拿他当关云长。可是"走麦城"的事儿，他就跟你打马虎眼了。

(From the novel 百年德性)

In front of the young people, naturally, he would just spin out all the stories of his victories, fearing that people might not recognize him as a Napoleon. But when it came to his Waterloos, he would just hem and haw. [The reference is to the victories and defeats of the general Guan Yunchang, from the *Romance of the Three Kingdoms*. He was famous for his victories, killing six generals at Five Passes (过五关斩六将) and for his humiliating defeat at Maicheng (麦城).]

◆ 你总提你过五关的事儿，**走麦城**的事儿怎么从来不说啊？

How come you always keep talking about your achievements, but you never say a word about your failures?

zǒu rén 走人

"Walk off"; walk away; take one's leave

◆ 你呀，把工作服交了，打铺盖卷儿，**走人**！

(From the TV series 其实男人最辛苦)

You! Hand over your uniform, roll up your bedding and get the hell out of here! [Being fired.]

◆ 我把丑话说在头里，每人每月拉一个客户，拉不到就**走人**。

(From the TV series 其实男人最辛苦)

I'm laying it on the line for you right at the start. Everyone has to land one customer a month. If you can't do that, you'll have to leave. [The manager of an advertising company is lecturing his salesmen.]

zǒu xué 走穴

"To travel around"; to go on a performing tour for money like an itinerant or homeless artist of the old times; to barnstorm

◆ 那她为什么不走呢？回去如果**走穴**，说不定能赚大钱呢！

(From the novel 寂寞的太太们)

Why doesn't she leave? If she goes back to China and takes her show on the road, who knows, she might make it bigtime! [She now lives in poverty abroad.]

♦ 现在不但演员**走穴**，当大夫的也有**走穴**的。

These days, it's not only performing artists who take to the road for money, but doctors do it too.

zǒu zhe qiáo 走着瞧 (走著瞧)

See 等着瞧 děng zhe qilo

zòu 揍

"Beaten"; made of; born out of; (the clay one is) made of

♦ "何雷，你这人怎么就能红一阵儿白一阵儿，说狠就狠，**翻脸不认人**，什么**揍**的？" "变色龙**揍**的。"

(From the novel 永失我爱)

"He Lei, how can you blow hot and cold like that? Suddenly you're a mad dog, turning on people. What kind of creature are you?" "A chameleon, that's the kind of creature I am."

♦ 这小兔崽子是怎么**揍**的？话总是捡难听的说。

You little bastard, what sort of crap are you made of? Why do you always have to say the nastiest things?

zuān niú jiǎo jiānr 钻牛角尖儿 (鑽牛角尖兒)

"Reach the tip of the cow's horn" 1. too obsessed with one option to see the rest; drive oneself to a dead end 2. split hairs

♦ 爸爸，冷静点儿，你这么**钻牛角尖**地想下去会把自己弄疯的。

(From the novel 我是你爸爸)

Dad, calm down, OK? If you keep obsessing about this you'll drive yourself nuts.

♦ 我不跟你这样的人争，你太爱**钻牛角尖**了。

I don't want to argue with people like you because you're too fond of splitting hairs.

zuān sǐ hú tòngr 钻死胡同儿 (鑽死胡同兒)

"Hit a dead end"; get stuck; stubborn

♦ 依我看啊，你是**钻进死胡同儿**里去了。

(From the TV series 今生是亲人)

I think you're too hung up on this. [Trying to console someone who learned that his parents were not his biological parents.]

♦ 在这生意场上不能**钻死胡同儿**，买卖不赚钱了就得另想辙。

You can't afford to be inflexible in business. When your business stops earning money, you've got to explore different courses of action.

zuàn shí wáng lǎo wǔ 钻石王老五 (鑽石王老五)

"Diamond bachelor"; ideal candidate for a husband; the most eligible bachelor

♦ 他有权有势，有才有貌，是标准的**钻石王老五**，众家妹妹眼中的抢手货。

(From the novel 浪子情深)

He's got power and clout, talent and looks. He's the perfect catch, the hottest goods out there in the eyes of many a young lady.

♦   超级钻石王老五，还怕没女孩子喜欢？

(From the novel 蜜糖儿)

He's the super eligible bachelor. How could he be afraid the girls won't like him?

zuǐ lǐ v ge bǎ ménr de 嘴里V个把门儿的 (嘴裏V個把門兒的)

"(Set) a doorkeeper at the mouth"; need something to control one's tongue

♦   我知道，到这儿嘴里得添个把门儿的。

(From the TV series 手心手背)

I know you have to watch what you say around here. [Working in a big corporation.]

♦   这小子的**嘴上就是没个把门儿的**，专门造谣、听谣、传谣。

(From the TV series 大赢家)

This bastard runs off at the mouth. His specialty is creating, enjoying, and spreading rumors.

zuǐ méi zhǔn tou 嘴没准头 (嘴沒準頭)

"Mouth that shoots and misses"; talk irresponsibly or inaccurately

♦   行了行了，别乱说了，你那**嘴整天没个准头**。

(From the novel 大厂)

OK, enough already. Stop talking nonsense. You just run off at the mouth all day.

♦   "他说咱们头儿要把公司卖给德国人，这样一来咱们恐怕都要下岗了！" "别听他的！他的**嘴没有准头儿**。"

"He said our boss was going to sell the company to some Germans. If that's true we'll all get laid off." "Pay no attention to him! He's talking through his hat."

zuǐ shàng méi máo, bàn shì bù láo 嘴上没毛，办事不牢 (嘴上沒毛，辦事不牢)

"Someone with no beard around his mouth can't do a good job"; you can't count on a person who's too young

♦   其实我倒还真信不过你，**嘴上没毛，办事不牢**，问题是我们刚子信你，我也没有办法。

(From the TV series 编辑部的故事)

As a matter of fact, I really don't have much confidence in you. I wouldn't hire a boy to do a man's job. But the problem is, our Gangzi trusts you and I can't do anything about that. [Gangzi's mother is speaking to someone who offered to find Gangzi a girlfriend.]

♦ 我跟你说过多少回了，**嘴上没毛，办事不牢**，可你偏偏把这么重要的事儿交给这么年轻的人来做，现在后悔了吧？

How many times did I tell you, don't hire a boy to do a man's job? But you left this important matter in the hands of such a young man anyway. Now you're sorry, right?

zuǐ yìng 嘴硬

"Tough mouth"; talk tough

♦ "徐科长，反正事情犯了，您就看着处理吧，该怎么着就怎么着." 徐科长一把揪住小个子的脖领子，狠狠打了一个耳光："你他妈的还**嘴硬**！"

(From the novel 大厂)

"Chief Xu, the crime's been committed. You go ahead and do what you have to do. " With one hand Chief Xu grabbed the short guy by the collar and with the other slapped him hard on the face. "That's for talking tough, you asshole!" [A thief was caught.]

♦ "前天你把小梅气哭了，也该去向人家承认错误了。""天下的好姑娘有的是，我干吗非得去给她赔不是？""得了，别**嘴硬**了，我知道你心里早就后悔了。"

"You made Xiaomei cry the day before yesterday. It's time you apologized to her." "There are plenty of nice girls in the world. Why do I have to go tell her I'm sorry?" "OK, no more tough talk. I know deep down you really regret it."

zuō biě zi 㞗瘪子 (㞗瘪子)

Be forced to do the impossible and feel caught; get stuck; be put on the spot

♦ 什么事，他宁愿自己抱屈，也不让手下的弟兄**㞗瘪子**。

(From the novel 百年德性)

Whatever happens, he'd rather take the blame himself than let his subordinates be put on the spot.

♦ "你别说了，收购华光公司的决定我绝对不改！""你要是这么不听劝，就等着**㞗瘪子**吧！"

"That's enough. There's no way I'm going to change my decision on purchasing the Guanghua Company." "If you won't listen to advice, get ready to find yourself in a tough spot."

zuǒ ěr duo jìn qu yòu ěr duo chū lai 左耳朵进去右耳朵出来 (左耳朵進去右耳朵出來)

"Enter the left ear and go out the right ear"; in one ear and out the other; turn a deaf ear; pay no attention

♦ Jack后来的话我记不太清了，好象是从我**左耳朵进去右耳朵出来**一样。

(From the short story 寂寞假日)

I can't really remember what Jack said after that. His words went in one ear and out the other.

◆ 他这个人啊，你跟他说什么他都不往心里去，总是**左耳朵进去右耳朵出来**。

That guy, you tell him something and he never takes it to heart. It's just in one ear and out the other.

zuò 做

(Gangster/mafia jargon) "do"; to kill; to finish off; to waste

◆ "哥，要不然把他们给做了？""不行，已经出了**几条人命**了，不能再干了。"

(From the TV series 黑洞)

"Brother, maybe we should finish them off?" "No. We've already polished off a few. Can't do it anymore."

◆ "我昨天看到老王去公安局了，他是不是要揭发咱们走私汽车的问题呢？""看来现在咱们没有别的选择了，只能把这个**吃里爬外**的家伙做掉。"

"Yesterday I saw Lao Wang going into the security bureau. You think he's going to rat on our car smuggling business?" "Looks like we've got no choice; we have to finish off this stool pigeon."

zuò là 坐蜡 (坐蠟)

"Sit (on) wax"; in a quandary; caught in the middle

◆ 庆春也知道这事是非常**坐蜡**了，但她还是压着懊恼问了一句。

(From the novel 永不瞑目)

Qingchun also realized she had been put on the hotseat, but she suppressed her anger and managed a question. [Qingchun is a police officer on a drug bust, but she had been wrongly informed and the suspects were legitimate business people.]

◆ 为了帮助你度过资金短缺的难关，我把几家银行和信用社的头儿头儿都请来了，可你这个总经理连见也不见人家一面的，这不是让我**坐蜡**吗？

To help you through your cash shortage, I invited the heads of several banks and credit unions over here. But you, the general manager, wouldn't even meet with them. Isn't that hanging me out to dry?

zuò nán 作难 (作難)

"Make difficult"; make or find something difficult, put someone on the spot

◆ 你要是**不作难**的话，娶凤霞的时候多叫点儿人热闹热闹。

(From the movie 活着)

If it's not too difficult for you, inviting a few more people to your wedding with Fengxia will make things livelier. [Fengxia's parents talking to their future son-in-law.]

◆   我觉得这次交通事故的赔款你应该自己扛着，别让你爹妈**作难**。他们的钱都是一分一分省下来的。

zuò (or zuō) sǐ 作死

"Do to die"; have a death wish; court trouble

◆   **作死**的小七，偷看人洗澡呀！

(From the short story 好一片春雨)

Little Seven, you troublemaker, are you spying on those girls taking a bath? [Little Seven, a teenaged boy, hid in a tree to watch two girls bathing in a pond.]

◆   文化局的人就在隔壁检查，你倒好，盗版碟照卖，这不是**作死**吗？

People from the Cultural Bureau are right next door conducting a search. But you're selling your pirated DVDs as though nothing's happening. Do you have a death wish or something?

Cheng & Tsui Publications of Related Interest

Masterworks *Compiled by Qin-Hong Anderson*

An introduction to the best possible teachers of Chinese prose: the most acclaimed and imitated writers in the Chinese language. Designed for heritage learners, but equally effective for advanced non-native students.

Across the Straits: 22 Miniscripts for Developing Advanced Listening Skills *By Jianhua Bai, Juyu Sung, and Hesheng Zhang*

Recordings of unscripted conversations offer a dynamic way to improve language skills; designed to facilitate discussions.

The Cheng & Tsui Chinese-Pinyin-English Dictionary for Learners *Edited by Wang Huan*

A best-selling compendium of 30,000 richly detailed entries, including pinyin pronunciation, grammar notes, and numerous sample sentences.

Open for Business: Lessons in Chinese Commerce for the New Millennium *By Jane C. M. Kuo*

An in-depth perspective on contemporary Chinese business communications, designed for students in their third or fourth year of Chinese at the undergraduate or graduate level.

The Cheng & Tsui English-Chinese Lexicon of Business Terms with Pinyin *Compiled by Andrew C. Chang*

A practical, clear, and easy-to-use lexicon with over 9,000 entries. The first specifically designed to serve the needs of English speakers doing business in and with China and other Chinese-speaking areas.

Cheng & Tsui titles are available through your bookstore,
or directly from the publisher.

Cheng & Tsui Company
25 West St., Boston, MA 02111-1213 USA
Toll free orders: 1-800-554-1963
Fax: (617) 426-3669
orders@cheng-tsui.com
www.cheng-tsui.com